Bibliographical Series
of Supplements to 'British Book News'
on Writers and Their Work

GENERAL EDITOR
Geoffrey Bullough

JOHN GAY

from an engraving after a portrait by W. AIKMAN

JOHN GAY

by

OLIVER WARNER

Life is a jest, and all things show it:
I thought so once, and now I know it.

Lines on Gay's Monument.

PUBLISHED FOR
THE BRITISH COUNCIL
AND THE NATIONAL BOOK LEAGUE
BY LONGMANS, GREEN & CO.

LONGMANS, GREEN & CO. LTD.
48 Grosvenor Street, London, W.1

*Associated companies, branches and
representatives throughout the world*

First published 1964
© Oliver Warner 1964

*Printed in Great Britain by
F. Mildner & Sons, London, E.C.1*

CONTENTS

¶ .JOHN GAY was baptized on 16 September 1685 at Barnstaple, Devon. He died on 4 December 1732 in London, and was buried in Westminster Abbey.

JOHN GAY

I

GAY lives mainly through the continued attraction of his most successful work, *The Beggar's Opera*, though it is not his only claim to remembrance. He was the friend of Steele, Pope and Swift; he wrote the libretto for Handel's *Acis and Galatea;* and one of his earlier biographers was Samuel Johnson. Reprints of his poems, complete or in selection, have proliferated from his own day to the present. His monument by Rysbrack stands in Westminster Abbey, and carries an epitaph by Pope as well as the flippant couplet, composed by Gay himself, which appears on the title-page of this essay. 'I have always observed', wrote Washington Irving,

that the visitors to the Abbey remain longest about the simple memorials in the Poets' Corner. A kinder and fonder feeling takes the place of that cold curiosity or vague admiration with which they gaze on the splendid monuments of the great and the heroic. They linger about there as about the tombs of friends and companions. (*Sketch Book*)

Irving, a kindly American visitor, wrote early in the nineteenth century, but there is still much in what he says:[1] certainly, with Gay, the mood in which he is read derives from affection, not duty. If we enjoy him, it is for himself, and not with any idea of illustrious example.

An amusing illustration of this occurs in one of the more celebrated scenes in Boswell's *Johnson*. The year was 1775 and Johnson, in company with Boswell, Reynolds and others, was looking over the books of a certain Mr. Cambridge. It was the evening when Boswell remarked to Reynolds that, in argument, Johnson had 'no formal preparation, no flourishing with his sword; he is through

[1] Since Irving's time Gay has been elevated to the triforium.

7

your body in an instant'. The talk turned to Gay, Johnson asserting that no man was ever made a rogue by being present at *The Beggar's Opera*. Then, said Boswell, reconsidering the matter, and 'collecting himself, as it were, to give a heavy stroke', he added: 'There is in it such a *labefaction* of all principles, as may be injurious to morality.' While he 'pronounced this response', said Boswell, 'we sat in a comical sort of restraint, covering a laugh, which we were afraid might burst out'.

Had Gay been present, it is unlikely that he would have been so self-controlled.

II

Gay was a Devonian, born at Barnstaple in the reign of Charles II, of a respectable family long settled there. By the age of ten he was an orphan, but an uncle seems to have taken good care of him, and he was so well taught at the local grammar school that he kept a love for the classics all his life. The translations which he made from Ovid's *Metamorphoses* are creditable to his skill, and there survives a copy of Horace, in the Forster Collection, with annotations in his beautiful script.

London was the obvious place for a young man with a taste for learning and with literary ambitions, but the employment which his uncle found for him as apprentice to a mercer was uncongenial. Gay's reaction was positive: he sought the acquaintance of authors, began to write, and at the age of twenty-three published anonymously his first poem, which was in praise of wine. By the year 1712 he had found his first patron. He became secretary or domestic steward to the Duchess of Monmouth, widow of the ill-starred rebel who had been beheaded in the year that Gay was born. The Duchess, who later married Lord Cornwallis, had many more years to live, but Gay did not stay with her long, for in 1714 Swift helped to get him employment in the .

household of Lord Clarendon, with whom he went to Hanover, where the Elector was about to succeed to the throne of Britain as King George I. In the same year Gay published his *Shepherd's Week*, mocking the older pastoral style, and two years later *Trivia: or, the Art of Walking the Streets of London*.

In an unpretentious way the author had now made something of a name for himself, and his reputation steadily grew. He could generally rely on some form of salaried service in a noble household, or even government employment, and his character and amiability were such that to the end of his life he was never without an attentive patron.

In 1717 Gay was at Aix with the Earl of Bath; a little later he was 'rambling from place to place' on the Continent, and making so many useful friends that when, in 1720, his *Poems* appeared in two quarto volumes, with a frontispiece by the architect William Kent, Lord Burlington and Lord Chandos subscribed for fifty copies each, and Lords Bathurst and Warwick for ten. The profits, which were at least £1,000, were invested in the South Sea Company, and when that most famous of all speculations burst in the famous Bubble, Gay, who had been urged to sell out, but who unwisely held on, was said to have lost £20,000. It was, therefore, somewhat ironical that his next employment, which lasted almost until the end of his life, should have been in the official post of Lottery Commissioner, to which a salary of £120 a year was attached.

Gay, who never married, now depended for society almost entirely on his aristocratic benefactors. Lord Burlington was his frequent host, but his closest friends were the Duke and Duchess of Queensberry, and he grew attached to their Wiltshire home, Amesbury Abbey. He was also given lodgings in Whitehall, and there he afforded hospitality to Swift.

Some years before his visit to Gay, Swift had written to Pope giving it as his view that 'the Pastoral ridicule is not exhausted', and that 'a porter, footman or chairman's

pastoral might do well, or what think you of a Newgate ✳
pastoral among the whores and thieves there?' The matter
was to be put to the test, for by 1727 Gay's *Beggar's Opera*
was completed, and although it was refused at Drury Lane,
John Rich, the manager at Lincolns Inn Fields, being of the
same mind as the Duke of Queensberry that it would either
be a huge success or an utter flop, took a chance on it, and
found his courage triumphantly justified. The first performance was on Valentine's Day, 1728, and by the end of the
year the printed version had run through two editions.

The current joke was that the piece made Gay rich and
Rich gay: in fact, Gay netted £693 13s. 6d. out of four
'author's nights', but Rich made thousands, and continued to
reap profits, for *The Beggar's Opera*, after a run of over sixty
performances, which was sensational for the time, was soon
transported to Dublin and elsewhere, playing to entranced
audiences.

Gay was quick with a sequel, *Polly*, but the piece was
forbidden the stage by the Lord Chamberlain, from whom
there was no appeal. This caused Queensberry to withdraw
from Court, and might have been a blow for the author had
he not done well from the sale of the text, for to ban *Polly*
from the stage was to help it in the bookshops. Over ten
thousand copies were printed within a few months, and
Gay received £1,200 as his profits. It was almost his last
sustained work. His health was giving increasing concern to
his friends, and after writing some additional Fables to a
series begun in 1727, a classical opera *Achilles*, and seeing
Acis and Galatea, which he had written many years earlier,
produced at the Haymarket in 1732, he died suddenly in
London the same year, leaving the not inconsiderable sum of
£6,000.

The Queensberrys had proved Samaritans. Not only had
they taken Gay's part over *Polly*, but they had carefully
husbanded his resources, allowing no further Bubble
speculations. Had he lived longer, it is likely that he would
have continued to prosper, for he was only forty seven, at

the height of his fame and success, and his work was so
much to the taste of his day that he continued to be reprinted. Gay aimed to please, and his wish was granted.

III

Gay's first serious attempt to win recognition as a poet of
more than occasional flights was made in 1714, when he
published *The Shepherd's Week*. This work was in the
tradition of which Pope had written:

A pastoral is an imitation of the action of a shepherd, or one considered
under that character. The form of this imitation is dramatic, or narrative,
or mixed of both; the fable is simple, the manners not too polite nor too
rustic: the thoughts are plain, yet admit a little quickness and passion,
but that short and flowing: the expression humble, yet as pure as the
language will afford; neat, but not florid; easy, and yet lively. In short,
the fable, manners, thoughts, and expressions, are full of the greatest
simplicity in nature. (*A Discourse on Pastoral Poetry*, 1704.)

The exemplar in the pastoral mode was Theocritus of
Syracuse, who wrote in the 3rd century B.C. His *Idylls* were
imitated later by Virgil and by poets of every country to
which the tradition descended. By the reign of Elizabeth I
the taste was beginning to spread to England. Shakespeare's
As You Like It and Fletcher's *The Faithful Shepherdess* were
within a sphere which was developed by Milton in *Comus*,
and which enjoyed a considerable vogue in the later 17th
and early 18th centuries, particularly in the hands of Pope.
    The six pastorals contained in *The Shepherd's Week*—one
for each week-day—were partly designed to make fun of
Ambrose Philips, a Shropshire versifier now forgotten,
whose work, though feeble enough, excited the jealousy and
enmity of Pope, and of Richard Blackmore, a writer buried
still deeper in oblivion.

In a mannered Proem or foreword, Gay explained:

That principally, courteous reader, whereof I would have thee to be
advised, (seeing I depart from the vulgar usage) is touching the language
of my shepherds; which is, soothly to say, such as is neither spoken by
the country maiden nor the courtly dame; nay, not only such as in the
present times is not uttered, but was never uttered in times past; and, if I
judge aright, will never be uttered in times future . . . Granted also it is,
that in this my language, I seem unto my self, as a *London* mason, who
calculateth his work for a term of years, when he buildeth with old
materials upon a ground-rent that is not his own, which soon turneth to
rubbish and ruins . . .

This argues no very high claim for the work, which would
indeed have been foreign to Gay's nature; yet his rustics do
in fact have a rough correspondence with reality; his
shepherdesses actually milk cows, and clean out pigsties.
The straight descriptions, though inviting mirth and even
ridicule, bear the impress of direct knowledge of country
pursuits, and an individual poetic quality. The opening of
'Tuesday, or the Ditty' is a fair enough example:

> Young *Colin Clout*, a lad of peerless meed,
> Full well could dance, and deftly tune the reed;
> In ev'ry wood his carrols sweet were known,
> At ev'ry wake his nimble feats were shown.
> When in the ring the rustick routs he threw,
> The damsels pleasures with his conquests grew;
> Or when aslant the cudgel threats his head,
> His danger smites the breast of ev'ry maid,
> But chief of *Marian*. *Marian* lov'd the swain,
> The Parson's maid, and neatest of the plain.
> *Marian*, that soft could stroke the udder'd cow,
> Or lessen with her sieve the barley mow;
> Marbled with sage the hardn'ing cheese she press'd,
> And yellow butter *Marian's* skill confess'd;
> But *Marian* now devoid of country cares,
> Nor yellow butter nor sage cheese prepares.
> For yearning love the witless maid employs,

And *Love*, say swains, *all busie heed destroys*.
Colin makes mock at all her piteous smart,
A lass, who *Cic'ly* hight, had won his heart,
Cic'ly the western lass who tends the kee,[1]
The rival of the Parson's maid was she.
In dreary shade now *Marian* lyes along,
And mixt with sighs thus wails in plaining song.
 Ah woful day! ah woful noon and morn!
When first by thee my younglings white were shorn,
Then first, I ween, I cast a lover's eye,
My sheep were silly, but more silly I.
Beneath the shears they felt no lasting smart,
They lost but fleeces while I lost a heart.

The burlesque attitude to rustic life is explained in the titles: Monday, or The Squabble; Tuesday, or The Ditty; Wednesday, or The Dumps; Thursday, or The Spell; Friday, or The Dirge; Saturday, or The Flights. 'An Alphabetical Catalogue of Names, Plants, Flowers, Fruits, Birds, Beasts, Insects, and other material things mentioned in these Pastorals' suggests just how seriously the matter is to be taken.

As a Londoner by necessity, if not by birth or perhaps by inclination, Gay has much to say in *Trivia: or, the Art of Walking the Streets of London* (1716), which is exactly what it states, a practical, light-hearted guide to the negotiation of the capital in early Georgian days. There is none of Johnson's power and splendour in his poem on the same subject of twenty years or so later:[2]

Here malice, rapine, accident, conspire,
And now a rabble rages, now a fire;
Their ambush here relentless ruffians lay,
And here the fell attorney prowls for prey:
Here falling houses thunder on your head,
And here a female atheist talks you dead.

Instead:

[1] cows   [2] 'London'

> Through winter streets to steer your course aright,
> How to walk clean by day, and safe by night,
> How jostling crouds, with prudence to decline,
> When to assert the wall, and when resign.

Shoulder-notes are briefly descriptive: Of Shoes; Of Coats; Of Canes; Of the Weather; Implements proper for female Walkers; What Trades prejudicial to Walkers; To whom to give the Wall; To whom to refuse the Wall; Of whom to enquire the Way; Of narrow Streets; The Pleasure of walking through an Alley; Inconveniences that attend those who are unacquainted with the Town; Remarks on the Crys of the Town; Of avoiding Paint; How to know a Whore; Of Watchmen; Of Rakes. And if a present day pedestrian, patiently awaiting his signal to cross a traffic-lane, or, taking his life in his hands, essaying an independent dash, should be tempted to think nostalgically of the easier times of his ancestors, Gay for one had an eye wide open to the different perils of his more leisurely age:

Of Crossing   If wheels bar up the road, where streets are crost,
the Street: With gentle words the coachman's ear accost:
> He ne'er the threat, or harsh command obeys,
> But with contempt the spatter'd shoe surveys.
> Now man with utmost fortitude thy soul,
> To cross the way where carts and coaches roll;
> Yet do not in thy hardy skill confide,
> Nor rashly risque the kennel's spacious stride;
> Stay till afar the distant wheel you hear,
> Like dying thunder in the breaking air;
> Thy foot will slide upon the miry stone,
> And passing coaches crush thy tortur'd bone,
> Or wheels enclose the road; on either hand
> Pent round with perils, in the midst you stand,
> And call for aid in vain; the coachman swears,
> And car-men drive, unmindful of thy prayers.
> Where wilt thou turn? ah! whither wilt thou fly?
> On ev'ry side the pressing spokes are nigh.
> So sailors, while *Carybdis'* gulph they shun,
> Amaz'd, on *Scylla's* craggy dangers run.

One of the liveliest descriptions concerns a fire, and at a time when the Great Fire of London was a mere half century in the past, and therefore well within living memory, it is interesting to note the equipment of the fire-fighter and the acceptance of the practice of demolition by gunpowder to prevent a conflagration spreading:

> But hark! distress with screaming voice draws nigh'r,
> And wakes the slumb'ring street with cries of fire.
> At first a glowing red enwraps the skies,
> And born by winds the scatt'ring sparks arise;
> From beam to beam the fierce contagion spreads;
> The spiry flames now lift aloft their heads,
> Through the burst sash a blazing deluge pours,
> And splitting tiles descend in rattling show'rs.
> Now with thick crowd th'enlighten'd pavement swarms,
> The fire-man sweats beneath his crooked arms,
> A leathern casque his vent'rous head defends,
> Boldly he climbs where thickest smoak ascends;
> Mov'd by the mother's streaming eyes and pray'rs,
> The helpless infant through the flame he bears . . .
> See forceful engines spout their levell'd streams,
> To quench the blaze that runs along the beams;
> The grappling hook plucks rafters from the walls,
> And heaps on heaps the smoaky ruine falls . . .
> Hark! the drum thunders! far, ye crouds, retire:
> Behold! the ready match is tipt with fire,
> The nitrous store is laid, the smutty train
> With running blaze awakes the barrell'd grain;
> Flames sudden wrap the walls; with sullen sound
> The shatter'd pile sinks on the smoaky ground.

Gay sums up his scope and purpose in *Trivia* in a few modest lines, and it is tolerably certain that students of urban life and customs of the past will continue to find pleasure in his observation:

> Consider, reader, what fatigues I've known,
> The toils, the perils of the wintry town;

What riots seen, what bustling crouds I bor'd,
How oft' I cross'd where carts and coaches roar'd;
Yet shall I bless my labours, if mankind
Their future safety from my dangers find.

IV

Gay's occasional verse is often pleasing, and in song he is
generally at his best, as in the ballad 'Sweet William's
Farewell to Black-ey'd Susan' (1720), with its spirited
opening, the vitality of which is sustained through eight
stanzas:

All in the *Downs* the fleet was moor'd,
    The streamers waving in the wind,
When black-ey'd *Susan* came aboard.
    Oh! where shall I my true love find!
Tell me, ye jovial sailors, tell me true,
If my sweet *William* sails among the crew.

William, who high upon the yard,
    Rock'd with the billow to and fro,
Soon as her well-known voice he heard,
    He sigh'd and cast his eyes below:
The cord slides swiftly through his glowing hands,
And, (quick as lightning,) on the deck he stands.

So the sweet lark, high pois'd in air,
    Shuts close his pinions to his breast,
(If, chance, his mate's shrill call he hear)
    And drops at once into her nest.
The noblest Captain in the *British* fleet,
Might envy *William's* lip those kisses sweet.

O, *Susan*, *Susan*, lovely dear,
    My vows shall ever true remain;
Let me kiss off that falling tear,
    We only part to meet again.
Change as ye list, ye winds; my heart shall be
The faithful compass that still points to thee.

More often chosen for anthologies is 'To a Lady on her Passion for old China', with its conclusion, so approved by lyric poets:

> Love, *Laura*, love, while youth is warm,
> For each new winter breaks a charm;
> And woman's not like *China* sold,
> But cheaper grows in growing old;
> Then quickly chuse the prudent part,
> Or else you break a faithful heart.

One 'occasional' poem, 'The Birth of the Squire' (1720), has so much more sting than most works of its kind that perhaps Gay had a particular case in mind: certainly, whatever his feelings as to the nobility, his patrons, he never seems to have had much tenderness for the lesser gentry who then controlled so much of England, as one of his plays *The What d'ye Call it*, which will claim attention in its place, bears witness.

Rural characters conspire, at his birth, to bring the future squire pleasure:

> Ye sylvan Muses, loftier strains recite,
> Not all in shades, and humble cotts delight.
> Hark! the bells ring; along the distant grounds
> The driving gales convey the swelling sounds;
> Th'attentive swain, forgetful of his work,
> With gaping wonder, leans upon his fork.
> What sudden news alarms the waking morn?
> To the glad Squire a hopeful heir is born.
> Mourn, mourn, ye stags; and all ye beasts of chase,
> This hour destruction brings on all your race:
> See the pleas'd tenants duteous off'rings bear,
> Turkeys and geese and grocer's sweetest ware;
> With the new health the pond'rous tankard flows,
> And old *October* reddens ev'ry nose.

His hero's career does not belie the promise. Nimrod is his aint, and when the time comes for education:

How shall his spirit brook the rigid rules,
And the long tyranny of grammar schools?
Let younger brothers o'er dull authors plod,
Lash'd into *Latin* by the tingling rod;
No, let him never feel that smart disgrace:
Why should he wiser prove than all his race?

Amours follow:

The milk-maid (thoughtless of her future shame)
With smacking lip shall raise his guilty flame.

Later there is Parliament, where he 'snores debates away',
and the magistrates' bench, where he becomes the terror of
the poaching breed. All the while, he drinks, and in a final
vision Gay delivers his creation back to his Maker:

Methinks I see him in his hall appear,
Where the long table floats in clammy beer,
'Midst mugs and glasses shatter'd o'er the floor,
Dead-drunk his servile crew supinely snore;
Triumphant, o'er the prostrate brutes he stands,
The mighty bumper trembles in his hands;
Boldly he drinks, and like his glorious Sires,
In copious gulps of potent ale expires.

Gay's *Fables* obey the conventions of a *genre* which has
been popular since man first began to savour the pleasures of
formal literature, and possibly long before that time.
Strictly speaking, the Fable is a short story in either prose or
verse whose characters are generally, though not necessarily,
animals, insects, fish or birds, which points a moral, sometimes ironically.

The earliest extant collection of fables is in Sanskrit, the
ancient and sacred language of India, and in western literature the best-known examples derive from Aesop, who is
believed to have lived in the 6th century B.C. and whose
work was preserved and developed by later writers including

Phaedrus, a Thracian in the service of the Emperor Augustus, and by Maximus Planudes, a Byzantine monk. The mode was used by Marie de France in the 12th century, and was brought to perfection by Jean la Fontaine (1621-1695).

In English literature the fable form had been exploited by many earlier writers including Chaucer, Lydgate and Henryson, and it experienced a revival in the 17th and 18th centuries, a notable practitioner being Matthew Prior (1664-1721), whose work preceded Gay's.

Gay's examples, some fifty of which were published in 1727 and a further sixteen posthumously in 1738, are on the whole of a piece with the bulk of his verse, pleasing, yet without the passion with which, at his best, he can infuse his lines, and the Morals are often as arguable as in more classical examples. One of the shortest, 'The Wild Boar and the Ram', which contains an original idea, is representative of the rest:

> Against an elm a sheep was ty'd,
> The butcher's knife in blood was dy'd;
> The patient flock, in silent fright,
> From far beheld the horrid sight;
> A savage Boar, who near them stood,
> Thus mock'd to scorn the fleecy brood.
> All cowards should be serv'd like you.
> See, see, your murd'rer is in view;
> With purple hands and reeking knife
> He strips the skin yet warm with life:
> Your quarter'd sires, your bleeding dams,
> The dying bleat of harmless lambs
> Call for revenge. O stupid race!
> The heart that wants revenge is base.
> I grant, an ancient Ram replys,
> We bear no terror in our eyes,
> Yet think us not of soul so tame,
> Which no repeated wrongs inflame;
> Insensible of ev'ry ill,
> Because we want thy tusks to kill.
> Know, Those who violence pursue

Give to themselves the vengeance due,
For in these massacres they find
The two chief plagues that waste mankind.
Our skin supplys the wrangling bar,
It wakes their slumbring sons to war,
And well revenge may rest contented,
Since drums and parchment were invented.

An Advertisement prefaced to the extended edition of
1738 states:

These FABLES were finished by Mr. GAY, and intended for the Press, a
short time before his Death; when they were left, with his other Papers,
to the care of his noble Friend and Patron, the DUKE OF QUEENSBERRY:
His Grace has accordingly permitted them to the Press, and they are here
printed from the Originals in the Author's own Hand-writing. We hope
they will please equally with his former Fables, though mostly on
Subjects of a graver and more political Turn: they will certainly shew
Him to have been (what he esteemed the best Character) a Man of a
truly honest Heart, and a sincere Lover of his Country.

The later Fables are in general longer, but not noticeably
graver than the original series. 'The Pack-Horse and the
Carrier', a fair example, is dedicated to a young nobleman
and it enjoins him not to rely on any virtue in his ancestors.
Noblesse oblige: it is necessary to re-mint the phrase in every
generation:

Superior worth your rank requires,
For that mankind reveres your sires:
If you degen'rate from your race,
Their merits heighten your disgrace.

The Moral is pointed by the complaint of a pack-horse,
through his own demerits reduced to that status, who is
snorting in his loose-box at the viler breeding of his companions. How can he tolerate their propinquity?

Vain-glorious fool, (the Carrier cry'd,)
Respect was never paid to pride.

Know 'twas thy giddy, wilful heart
Reduc'd thee to this slavish part.
Did not thy headstrong youth disdain
To learn the conduct of the rein? . . .
Ask all the carriers on the road,
They'll say thy keeping's ill-bestow'd.
Then vaunt no more thy noble race,
That neither mends thy strength or pace.
What profits me thy boast of blood?
An ass hath more intrinsick good.
By outward show let's not be cheated:
An ass should like an ass be treated.

V

Gay had made various earlier attempts at writing for the stage before he turned his attention to a 'Newgate pastoral'. They met with small success, though they gave him experience of what was appropriate for the theatre. *The Mohocks*, a 'Tragi-Comical Farce' on the subject of the well-born bullies who, calling themselves by the name of a fierce Red Indian tribe, roved the town by night and terrorized the watch, attacking quiet citizens and insulting women, was printed in 1712 but never produced. It contains one song in Act I, Scene I, prophetic of those which were to appear in later works:

Come fill up the Glass,
Round, round, let it pass,
'Till our Reason be lost in our Wine:
Leave Conscience's Rules
To Women and Fools,
This only can make us divine.

Chorus.   Then a *Mohock*, a *Mohock* I'll be,
No Laws shall restrain
Our Libertine Reign,
We'll riot, drink on, and be free.

We will scower the Town,
Knock the Constable down,
Put the Watch and the Beadle to flight:
We'll force all we meet
To kneel down at our Feet,
And own this great Prince of the Night.

Chorus.   Then a *Mohock*, a *Mohock*, etc.

The Grand Seignior shall own
His Seraglio outdone,
For all Womankind is our booty;
No Condition we spare
Be they Brown, Black or Fair
We make them fall down, and do Duty.

Chorus.   Then a *Mohock*, a *Mohock*, etc. . . .

Not much can be said for the pastiche, *The Wife of Bath*, which was actually staged in 1713, for the surviving fragments are such doggerel as to make Chaucer positively twirl in his grave—and the next venture was little better. This was a Tragi-Comi-Pastoral-Farce, called *The What d'ye Call it*. It made a brief appearance in 1715, and it was followed, two years later, by a comedy, *Three Hours after Marriage*, which was produced at the Theatre Royal, Gay acknowledging help from Pope and from their mutual friend Dr. John Arbuthnot.

Only the Prologue, Epilogue and fragments of *Three Hours after Marriage* are printed in the standard edition of Gay's work, and they are unremarkable. *The What d'ye call it*, though fully preserved, gives no indication of the qualities which would blossom in *The Beggar's Opera*. There is pace and vivacity, but it is clear that the author was attempting too much, and the text reads more like a charade than a piece worthy of professional actors.

Using the frame-work of a play within a play, Gay takes off rustic characters, and above all country justices, not in the spirit of Shakespeare in *Henry IV*, but in that of a more degenerate age. A squire has got a girl into trouble, and his intention is to cause an innocent man, enamoured of another, to make an honest woman of her, or go to the wars. The victim refuses, and is duly drafted as a soldier, in which capacity he is soon due to go before a firing squad for running away. Ghosts of those they have punished or otherwise injured haunt the justices, and it is soon made plain that the methods of the press gang were as obnoxious in the Hanoverian army as in the navy. After a number of extravagant twists of fortune, the condemned is reprieved, lovers are joined together in more or less holy matrimony, and all ends in a dance.

Most of the play is written in decasyllabic rhymed verse, the rest in prose, and there is one ballad, ' 'Twas when the seas were roaring', which shows Gay's felicity in composing lines to be sung, but there is little to prepare the reader for the triumph one day to come.

Finally, there is Gay's only tragedy, *The Captives*. He read this aloud to one of the royal princesses: it was published in 1724, and it was acted at Drury Lane. It would have been natural to expect that this blank-verse play, in which the prosody is slip-shod, and in which there is not a single memorable passage, would prove insufferable to modern taste, yet, however flat the lines, the plot carries them along.

Phraortes, King of Media, has beaten the Persians in battle and has taken prisoner Sophernes, a prince whom he treats with great consideration. Hydarnes and other Persians plot against Phraortes's life, but Sophernes takes no part in this. His sorrows are concentrated on his captive state, and on the loss of Cylene his wife, who has supposedly been carried off to slavery, or been slain in battle.

Phraortes's queen, Astarbe, secretly detests her husband, though she wields most of the royal power. Her affections centre upon Sophernes, to whom she offers freedom if he will fly with her. The wretched man refuses, and Astarbe's revenge is to have him condemned for plotting against the King. At this stage, Cylene returns to the Median capital, disguised, and she tells a tale of such piteous wrongs done to her through Sophernes that the King agrees that she should be his executioner. When the time comes for her to visit Sophernes in his dungeon, she reveals her true identity, and begs her husband to fly: she will pay the forfeit. Sophernes, though he reluctantly obeys, secretly returns to the palace in time to save the King's life from the real conspirator. The Queen's misfeasances are exposed, and she stabs herself. Sophernes and Cylene are happily re-united.

The final lines, which should be moving, give a fair indication of the quality of the whole.

> *Sophernes.* What I did was due.
>   I've only paid a debt of gratitude;
>   What would your bounty more?—you've giv'n me all.
>   For in these arms I ev'ry wish possess.
> *Phraortes.* Life is a voyage, and we with pain and labour
>   Must weather many a storm to reach the port.
> *Sophernes.* Since 'tis not giv'n to mortals to discern
>   Their real good and ill; let men learn patience:
>   Let us the toils of adverse fate sustain,
>   For through that rugged road our hopes we gain.

It is sad that so respectable a plot should be so very feebly clothed, line after line reading like a botched translation of one of the Greek masters, and it is with some amusement that the reader discovers a passage in the fulsome and well-turned letter to the princess who had to endure the author's declamation: 'If it had the good fortune to gain Your ROYAL HIGHNESS's approbation', wrote Gay,

I have been often reflecting to what to impute it, and I think, it must have been the Catastrophe of the fable, the rewarding virtue, and the relieving the distressed: For that could not fail to give you some pleasure in fiction, which, it is plain, gives you the greatest in reality; or else Your ROYAL HIGHNESS would not (as you always have done) make it your daily practice.

VI

In the four years which separate the last of
theatrical attempts and the composition of his m
he made an immense advance in technical skill. *The*
Opera is assured throughout: there is no faltering
redundancy. Even the prose rises consistently above an
thing which Gay had been able to sustain in his earlier work.
From the Beggar's opening line: 'If Poverty be a title to
Poetry, I am sure no-body can dispute mine', to Macheath's
final song: 'Thus I stand like a Turk, with his doxies
around' there is no doubt that the author has full control
of his material, and that the audience, if the players and
singers do their part, will be held captive.

The reasons are manifold. To begin with—surprise: and
the start which Gay afforded his own age must be imagined
to be far greater than anything we are now likely to experience, when the theatre has been the subject of experiment, some of it outrageous, for generations. Setting and
characters were truly novel. This was a piece where rogues
were rogues, and if they came to grief it was because they
were betrayed for money by their accomplices, not because
they were overtaken by justice. An analogy with current
politics was perceived, and was intended. As the Beggar
says: 'Through the whole piece you may observe such a
similitude of manners in high and low life, that it is
difficult to determine whether (in the fashionable vices) the
fine gentlemen imitate the gentlemen of the road, or the
gentlemen of the road the fine gentlemen.'

What in fact helped to spark off *The Beggar's Opera* was
the career of Jonathan Wild, the course of which had
opened people's minds to the ramifications of crime in
London. Wild's life was brief but sensational. He had
originally worked as a buckle-maker but found thieving so
profitable that he not only turned himself into the leader
and brains of a large corporation of thieves and pick-pockets,
but actually opened offices in various parts of London for the

recovery and restoration of property stolen by his dependents.

Such ingenuity was worthy of a better cause. Wild, having enjoyed considerable success, since he found the authorities very bribable, was at last charged and convicted. He was hanged at Tyburn in 1725. Daniel Defoe, ever quick to seize upon a character or an event which would enable him to turn a penny or so by means of the printing press, published an account of Wild's 'Life and Actions' shortly after his execution. Gay revived the excitement while it was still fairly fresh, and some years later, in 1743, Fielding made Wild the peg for a study of 'greatness' (as distinct from 'goodness') in a satirical romance.

As with the less, so with the greater. *The Beggar's Opera* was written and produced during the long régime of Sir Robert Walpole as Prime Minister to the early Hanoverians; Walpole, who openly bought the votes of Members of Parliament, rewarded his supporters with sinecures, and had no use for enthusiasm. The opera is, in fact, the capital city in miniature, leaving out those decent, unobtrusive folk who in every age have somehow contrived to keep moral standards from disappearing altogether.

With the sole exception of Polly Peachum, the characters, men and women alike, are something more positive than amoral. The men send their fellows to the gallows at a nod, and are always liable to be betrayed themselves. Peachum, a central figure, calculates matters of life and death without a trace of sentiment or compunction, the scales balanced on his ledger; and an edge is given to his remarks by the knowledge that the Newgate of Gay's time was much as in the play, and that men, women and even children could be and were hanged, or at best sent to work in the slave-plantations of the West Indies, for what would now be termed petty theft. If the characters work against Society, they also work against one another: they hang together only until they hang separately.

In contrast to this realistic spice is the absurdly romantic

constancy of Polly in her love for the highwayman
Macheath, and the engagingly innocent airs to which Gay
set his songs, most of them traditional. The public had grown
sick of the fashionable Italian opera, sung by often un-
attractive people in the language the groundlings could not
understand. Refreshingly, Gay's English was as clear as a
stream, and although he employed a German, Dr. Pepusch,
to write bases, the tunes were familiar and beloved.
Finally, and here again the opera was happily different
from the mode then in fashion, Gay knew when to leave off.
The moment must be before, not after, listeners had had
enough. Like Oliver Twist, they must ask for more.

Congreve, an old and brilliant stage hand who had long
given up writing plays, predicted, so Pope said, that *The
Beggar's Opera* would 'either take greatly, or be damned
confoundedly', the view taken by Rich and Queensberry.
Even before the end of the first act, Pope and other friends
of Gay had heard the Duke of Argyle, sitting in the next box
exclaim: 'it will do—it must do—I see it in the eyes of them.'
The duke was a sound judge, and he was not deceived.

The Beggar and the Player having ended their prelimin-
aries, the scene opens upon Peachum, sitting at a table before
his accounts. He sings:

> Through all the employments of life
>> Each neighbour abuses his brother;
> Whore and Rogue they call Husband and Wife:
>> All professions be-rogue one another.
> The Priest calls the Lawyer a Cheat,
>> The Lawyer be-knaves the Divine;
> And the Statesman, because he's so great,
>> Thinks his trade as honest as mine.

The tone is set, and when Filch enters, the audience is fully
prepared for the review of the pick-pocketing gang—
Crook-finger'd Jack; Wat Dreary, alias Brown Will;
Harry Padington; Slippery Sam; Mat of the Mint; Tom
Tipple; Robin of Bagshot, alias Gordon, alias Bluff Bob,

alias Carbuncle, alias Bob Booty—whose fingers swell the store of Peachum's stolen goods.

Booty, who has been put down on Peachum's black list, inspires a defence from the woman who is Mrs Peachum by courtesy, not by the marriage lines, and she adds a note of sentiment which—though it will not be sustained in her own case—finds an echo in a younger bosom:

Mrs Peachum. You know, my dear, I never meddle in matters of Death; I always leave those affairs to you. Women indeed are bitter bad judges in these cases, for they are so partial to the brave that they think every man handsome who is going to the Camp or the Gallows.

Presently, the highwayman Macheath comes under consideration. He is of altogether different metal from the rest, and Polly Peachum's mother is already aware that her daughter's affections are engaged. Peachum will have none of it. As he says: 'My daughter to me should be like a court-lady to a minister of state, a key to the whole gang.'

Polly's first song, delivered when her father approaches her to learn how far matters have gone, 'Virgins are like the fair flower in its lustre', is as fine as anything Gay composed for the part: it is quickly answered by her mother, who has found out the truth from Filch: the girl is actually married. 'Can you support the expence of a husband, hussy, in gaming, drinking and whoring', she asks:

have you money enough to carry on the daily quarrels of man and wife about who shall squander most? There are not many husbands and wives, who can bear the charges of plaguing one another in a handsome way. If you must be married, could you introduce no-body into our family, but a highwayman! Why, thou foolish jade, thou wilt be as ill us'd, and as much neglected, as if thou hadst married a Lord!

Song succeeds song in reproach and animation:

O *Polly*, you might have toy'd and kist.
By keeping men off, you keep them on.

Polly: But he so teaz'd me,
And he so pleas'd me,
What I did, you must have done.

'Well, *Polly*', says Mrs Peachum, 'as far as one woman can forgive another, I forgive thee.—your father is too fond of you, hussy.' 'Then', says Polly, 'all my sorrows are at an end.' 'A mighty likely speech in troth', replies her mother, 'for a wench who is just married!'

Indeed, Mrs Peachum is right, for in family conclave Peachum enunciates what he holds to be the proper advantage of marriage—that it may lead to widowhood:

The comfortable estate of widowhood, is the only hope that keeps up a wife's spirits. Where is the woman who would scruple to be a wife, if she had it in her power to be a widow whenever she pleas'd? If you have any views of this sort, *Polly*, I shall think the match not so very unreasonable.

Even Mrs Peachum is forced to agree that 'to have Macheath peach'd is the only thing could ever make me forgive her'— a very lively qualification of her earlier gesture to her daughter.

It was at this stage that Polly, with her song

O ponder well! be not severe;
So save a wretched wife!
For on the rope that hangs my dear
Depends poor *Polly's* life.

first brought the house down. The original singer was Lavinia Fenton, an actress of such beauty and talent that she won the love of the Duke of Bolton, who in due time made her his duchess.

The First Act ends with the entrance of Macheath, who swears eternal constancy to Polly, their duet being one of the prettiest in the opera:

Macheath: Were I laid on *Greenland's* coast,
And in my arms embrac'd my lass;
Warm amidst eternal frost,
Too soon the half year's night would pass.

Polly: Were I sold on *Indian* soil,
Soon as the burning Day was clos'd,
I could mock the sultry toil,
When on my charmer's breast repos'd.

Macheath: And I would love you all the day,
Polly: Every night would kiss and play,
Macheath: If with me you'd fondly stray
Polly: Over the Hills and far away.

VII

The critic was perceptive who thought 'Over the Hills and far away' to be one of the most evocative lines in poetry, but the next scene is indoors, and heavy with the fumes of wine and the smoke from tobacco: it is a tavern near Newgate where Peachum's gang are drinking. The ruffians include some not already noted in Peachum's ledger—for instance, there is Jemmy Twitcher, whose name was to be bestowed, with opprobium, on the fourth Earl of Sandwich, an unpopular First Lord of the Admiralty later in the century. There is Nimming Ned and Ben Budge. 'Fill ev'ry glass', they sing, 'for wine inspires us, And fires us With courage, love and joy.' They await Macheath, preparatory to an adventure on the Western Road, but when the highwayman enters it is to report a difference with Peachum, and to give orders that the others must act on their own. No sooner is he by himself than he sings 'If the heart of a man is deprest with cares'—and then calls for women.

There enter Mrs Coaxer, Dolly Trull, Mrs Vixen, Betty Doxy, Jenny Diver, Mrs Slammerkin, Suky Tawdry and Molly Brazen, the Ladies of the Town, and in an instant the music of a cotillion, and the song 'Youth's the season made

for joys', show that Macheath's troubles are not very taxing
and that, free as ever with his money, his pleasures will be
much the same as before.

Alas, Jenny Diver for one is in Peachum's pay, and she
betrays her red-coated customer. Peachum himself enters
with constables, and Macheath is taken off to prison.
He sings:

> At the Tree I shall suffer with pleasure,
> At the Tree I shall suffer with pleasure,
>   Let me go where I will,
>   In all kinds of ill,
> I shall find no such Furies as these are.

The audience echo him, but Newgate under Lockit and his
turnkeys is as venal as the rest of London, and the victim is
soon bargaining for a lighter set of fetters. Lucy Lockit is
another matter. Macheath has got her into trouble and now,
it seems, he is in her power. She demands marriage. She will
save him—provided there is no truth in the rumour of his
affair with Polly!

Peachum and Lockit are meanwhile in conference, and
their discussion is such as to make the song appropriate:

> When you censure the age,
> Be cautious and sage,
> Lest the Courtiers offended should be:
>   If you mention vice or bribe,
>   'Tis so pat to all the tribe;
> Each cries—That was levell'd at me.

The pair soon quarrel, until Peachum, with his 'Brother,
brother—we are both in the wrong—we shall both be
losers in the dispute—for you know we have it in our
power to hang each other . . .' calls a halt, and they make it
up.

Macheath is quickly at work with plans for squaring
Lockit, saying to Lucy: 'If I could raise a small sum—

Would not twenty guineas, think you, move him?—Of all the arguments in the way of business, the perquisite is the most prevailing—Your father's perquisites for the escape of prisoners must amount to a considerable sum in the year. Money well tim'd, and properly apply'd, will do anything.'

Matters become complicated when Polly appears. She and Lucy inevitably squabble, and Macheath sings his famous lament:

> How happy could I be with either,
>   Were t'other dear charmer away!
> But while you thus teaze me together,
>   To neither a word will I say.

The scene ends with Lucy relenting, and Macheath once more free. Not for long, however, for the third and last Act unfolds the hero's second betrayal, this time on the information of Diana Trapes. Lucy later tries, without success, to poison Polly with a glass of cordial, while Macheath suffers re-incarceration from which there is this time no escape. Not only so, but all his women and their offspring come to see his fate.

When the curtain falls, the following dialogue ensues:

Player: But honest friend, I hope you don't intend that *Macheath* shall be really executed.

Beggar: Most certainly, Sir.—To make the piece perfect, I was for doing strict poetical Justice.—*Macheath* is to be hang'd; and for the other personages in the Drama, the Audience must have suppos'd they were all either hang'd or transported.

Player: Why, then, friend, this is a down-right deep Tragedy. The catastrophe is manifestly wrong, for an Opera must end happily.

Beggar: Your objection, Sir, is very just; and is easily remov'd. For you must allow, that in this kind of Drama, 'tis no matter how absurdly things are brought about—So—you rabble there—run and cry a Reprieve—let the prisoner be brought back to his wives in triumph.

Even this is not quite good enough, for what about poor
Polly? Macheath on his brief return—before transportation,
for he cannot be wholly excused punishment—says: 'Ladies,
I hope you will give me leave to present a Partner to each of
you'—sweeping his hand towards the Rabble. 'And (if I may
without offence) for this time, I take *Polly* for mine.—And
for life, you Slut,—for we were really marry'd.—As for
the rest.—But at present keep your own secret.'

The way is open for a sequel.

VIII

Gay has generally been referred to as an indolent man, but
the last years of his life show a burst of creative activity and
achievement: for *The Beggar's Opera*, however delectably it
reads and stages, is an affair involving thought and crafts-
manship, and there is invention and character-drawing
calling for sustained energy.

Gay meant to exploit every bit of the fame he had won
from his hit. Ballad-opera in his manner had taken on, and
moreover it would last, for it was particularly suited to the
English taste, a fact which Gilbert and Sullivan were to re-
discover in a later century. As for Polly, she had stolen more
hearts than that of his Grace of Bolton. She must have an
opera of her own, and so it was.

By 1729 the text was at the printers, but before that
bureaucracy had intervened. No doubt, far too many shafts
in *The Beggar's Opera* had struck home. Gay wrote in his
Preface:

'Twas on SATURDAY morning DECEMBER 7TH, 1728, that I waited upon
the Lord Chamberlain; I desir'd to have the honour of reading the Opera
to his Grace, but he order'd me to leave it with hi⌐
expectation of having it return'd on the Monday
it not 'till THURSDAY DECEMBER 12TH, when I receiv
with this answer; that it was not allow'd to be acted

be supprest. This was told me in general without any reasons assign'd, or any charge against me of my having given any particular offence.

It was rumoured that the new King, George II, though not much inclined to what he described as 'Boetry and Bainting', had given the Lord Chamberlain direct orders on the subject of Mr Gay: but even he could not interdict the printing of a piece which, in Gay's words 'was to lash in general the reigning and fashionable vices, and to recommend and set virtue in as amiable a light as I could; to justify and vindicate my own character, I thought my-self obliged to print the Opera without delay in the manner I have done'.

The Poet and Player who occupy the stage at the opening speak a few lines of plain truth:

Poet: A SEQUEL to a Play is like more last words. 'Tis a kind of absurdity; and really, Sir, you have prevail'd upon me to pursue this subject against my judgment.

1st Player: Be the success as it will, you are sure of what you have contracted for; and upon the inducement of gain no body can blame you for undertaking it.

The principal characters are Polly, Ducat, a West Indian planter, and a much disguised Macheath. Polly has followed her husband in his exile, but Macheath, with his usual agility, has run away from the plantation to which he has been condemned, and is thought dead, though he is in fact disguised as Morano, chief of the local pirates. Mrs Trapes, another character from the earlier success who now exercises the calling of procuress, tries to sell Polly to the amorous Ducat, and Polly is saved from dishonour partly by an attack by the pirates on the settlement. Disguised as a man she joins the loyal Caribs, helps to beat off the attack, takes Morano prisoner, but learns his identity too late to save him from execution. In the end, she marries an Indian prince, a conclusion about as unsatisfactory as could be imagined. It is scarcely surprising that those who have attempted to revive *Polly* have sometimes taken liberties with the original:

it almost asks for it, though it is by no means without merit
on its own account, and more than one of the songs are in
Gay's best style. If the milieu were such as to give the
author reasonable scope, instead of being mere 'theatre', it
could have become worthy of its predecessor, though
sequels are too often, as the poet describes them, 'a sort of
absurdity'.

In point of fact, Gay was trying the Establishment rather
hard. For instance, Act I is no further advanced than the
fourth scene when Mrs Trapes, of all people, is made to sing
as follows:

> In pimps and politicians
>   The genius is the same;
> Both raise their own conditions
>   On others guilt and shame:
> With a tongue well-tipt with lyes
> Each the want of parts supplies,
> And with a heart that's all disguise
>   Keeps his schemes unknown.
> Seducing as the devil,
>   They play the tempter's part,
> And have, when most they're civil,
>   Most mischief in their heart.
> Each a secret commerce drives,
> First corrupts and then connives,
> And by his neighbours vices thrives,
>   For they are all his own.

There is, moreover, shrewd truth in the verses:

> When kings by their huffing
> Have blown up a squabble,
> All the charge and cuffing
> Light upon the rabble.
> Thus when Man and Wife
> By their mutual snubbing,
> Kindle civil strife,
> Servants get the drubbing.

Gay's worldly sense is well shown in Jenny Diver's song:

> When gold is in hand,
> It gives us command;
> It makes us lov'd and respected.
> 'Tis now, as of yore,
> Wit and sense, when poor,
> Are scorn'd, o'erlook'd and neglected.
> Tho' peevish and old
> If women have gold,
> They have youth, good-humour and beauty:
> Among all mankind
> Without it we find
> Nor love, nor favour nor duty.

Again, not many politicians would read with much pleasure Polly's own contribution in Act II:

> The sportsmen keep hawks, and their quarry they gain;
> Thus the woodcock, the partridge, the pheasant is slain.
> What care and expence for their hounds are employ'd!
> Thus the fox, and the hare, and the stag are destroy'd.
> The spaniel they cherish, whose flattering way
> Can as well as their masters cringe, fawn and betray.
> Thus staunch politicians, look all the world round,
> Love the men who can serve as hawk, spaniel or hound.

Considering how little such interpolations have to do with the ostensible plot of the opera, it is easy enough to understand the reason for the Lord Chamberlain's decision not to allow it on the stage, and its success in printed form is not surprising. If the ban was unjust, it was all too natural: the victim, or one of them, was confirming the satirist's diagnosis by his own behaviour.

If attempts have been made to make something of *Polly* on the stage, such neglect has befallen *Achilles*, the opera which was published shortly after Gay's death, that although it was performed at the Theatre Royal, Covent Garden, it is impossible that it should be revived. The theme is Achilles in petticoats. His mother Thetis clothes him thus, in order to save him from the perils of the Siege of Troy. His adventures are ludicrous—sought after by Lycomedes, whom he spurns, and loved by Deidamia, of whom he takes advantage, Achilles, it is almost needless to say, in the end goes off to the wars, having, in his own phrase, heard his mother's advice, and followed his own.

The scenes, though sometimes well enough, are not the equal even of the best of *Polly*. The songs, the line in which Gay was usually so assured, are as a whole lack-lustre, for he was clearly tired. There is one, however, which deserves such small preservation as may be afforded by a current tribute:

> Think of Dress in ev'ry Light;
>   'Tis Woman's chiefest Duty;
> Neglecting that, our selves we slight
>   And undervalue Beauty.
> That allures the Lover's Eye,
>   And graces ev'ry Action;
> Besides, when not a Creature's by,
>   'Tis inward Satisfaction.

IX

Among the varied works accomplished by the late Sir Geoffrey Faber was the standard edition of Gay. This was published in 1926, when the version of *The Beggar's Opera* staged by Nigel Playfair at the Lyric Theatre, Hammersmith, was fresh in public memory. It is fitting that he should be quoted in judgement on an author to whose text he applied such scrupulous attention. 'Like all men of his age', wrote Faber, Gay 'likes to feel his feet on the firm earth; and if at times the irresistible breath of song lifts him off it, he is not carried far. No counterfeit Olympus for him; the lower slopes of a friendly Parnassus, where his playful ironic fancy breathes a congenial air—these are his spiritual home.'

Gay had tried verse, and had done well enough; he had

tried moralizing, and found favour; then, gathering his strength, he had combined his gifts in a flawless ballad-opera, and every generation has thanked him for it.

JOHN GAY

A Select Bibliography

(Place of publication London, unless stated otherwise)

Collected Works:

POEMS ON SEVERAL OCCASIONS, 2 Vols. (1720)
—revised text, 1731, supervised by Gay.

PLAYS (1760).

THE WORKS, 4 Vols. Dublin (1770).

POEMS AND FABLES, 2 Vols. Aberdeen (1772).

THE WORKS, 4 Vols. (1773).

THE POETICAL WORKS, 3 Vols. (1777).

THE POETICAL DRAMATIC AND MISCELLANEOUS WORKS, 6 Vols. (1795)
—includes a reprint of Johnson's account of Gay, first published in
The Lives of the English Poets, 1779.

THE POETICAL WORKS, 2 Vols. Boston (1854).

THE POETICAL WORKS, ed. J. Underhill. 2 Vols. (1893)
—in the Muses Library.

THE PLAYS, 2 Vols. (1923).

THE POETICAL WORKS, ed. G. C. Faber. Oxford (1926)
—the standard text, including plays and fragments, with a bibliography.

SELECTED POEMS, ed. A. Ross (1950).

Separate Works:

WINE. A Poem (1708). *Verse*
—published anonymously.

THE MOHOCKS (1712). *Drama*

RURAL SPORTS (1713). *Verse*

THE WIFE OF BATH (1713). *Drama*

THE FAN (1713). *Verse*

THE SHEPHERD'S WEEK (1714). *Verse*

THE WHAT D'YE CALL IT (1715). *Drama*

TRIVIA: OR THE ART OF WALKING THE STREETS OF LONDON (1716). *Verse*

THREE HOURS AFTER MARRIAGE (1717). *Drama*

THE CAPTIVES (1724). *Drama*

TO A LADY ON HER PASSION FOR OLD CHINA (1725). *Verse*

FABLES (1727). *Verse*
—additional Fables were published in the sixth edition, 1738.

THE BEGGAR'S OPERA (1727). *Ballad Opera*
—an edition containing the music first appeared in 1728.

POLLY (1729). *Ballad Opera*

ACIS AND GALATEA (1732). *Opera*

ACHILLES (1733). *Opera*

Some Biographical and Critical Studies:

LECTURES ON THE ENGLISH POETS, by W. Hazlitt (1818)
—includes an account of Gay.

ENGLISH HUMOURISTS OF THE EIGHTEENTH CENTURY, by W. M. Thackeray (1853).

LIFE AND LETTERS OF JOHN GAY, by L. Melville (1921).

THE BEGGAR'S OPERA, ITS PREDECESSORS AND SUCCESSORS, by F. Kidson (1922).

ENGLISH COMIC DRAMA, 1700-1750 by F. W. Bateson (1929).

SOME VERSIONS OF PASTORAL, by W. Empson (1936).

JOHN GAY, by P. Fenwick Gaye (1938).

POPE AND HIS CONTEMPORARIES, ESSAYS PRESENTED TO GEORGE SHERBURN, ed. J. L. Clifford and L. A. Landa (1949)
—includes a study of Gay by J. R. Sutherland.

JOHN GAY, SOCIAL CRITIC, by S. M. Armens. Stanford U.P., New York (1954).

Bibliographical Series
of Supplements to 'British Book News'
on Writers and their Work

GENERAL EDITOR
Geoffrey Bullough

¶ WILLIAM COLLINS was born in Chichester in 1721 where he died in 1759. A monument by Flaxman to the poet's memory (see frontispiece) was erected in 1795 in Chichester Cathedral. The *Gentleman's Magazine* for December 1824 thus describes it: 'In the nave a neat tablet by Flaxman to the unfortunate poet Collins, who was born and died in this city. He is represented as just recovering from one of those fits of phrenzy to which he was subject, and in a calm and reclining posture, seeking refuge from his misfortunes in the Gospel, while his lyre and one of his first poems lie neglected on the ground. Above are the figures of Love and Pity entwined in each other's arms.'

THIS MONVMENT WAS ERECTED BY A VOLVNTARY SVBSCRIPTION,
IN HONOR OF WILLIAM COLLINS,
WHO WAS BORN IN THIS CITY, MDCCXXI,
AND DIED IN A HOVSE ADIOINING TO THE CLOISTERS
OF THIS CHVRCH. MDCCLIX.

WILLIAM COLLINS

*A detail from the monument by JOHN FLAXMAN (1755-1826)
in Chichester Cathedral*

WILLIAM COLLINS

by

OSWALD DOUGHTY

PUBLISHED FOR
THE BRITISH COUNCIL
AND THE NATIONAL BOOK LEAGUE
BY LONGMANS, GREEN & CO.

LONGMANS, GREEN AND CO. LTD.
48 Grosvenor Street, London, W.1

*Associated companies, branches and representatives
throughout the world*

First published 1964
© Oswald Doughty 1964

*Printed in Great Britain by
F. Mildner & Sons, London, E.C.1*

WILLIAM COLLINS

I

WILLIAM COLLINS, biographically, is unsatisfactory. We know too little about him to permit a convincing portrait. So slender is the material: two biographically disappointing letters, the few pages of his poetry, a brief memoir published four years after his death with some of his poems in an anthology, and two years later an edition of his poems with a biographical preface. Dr. Johnson's account of him in his *Lives of the Poets* appeared thirty years after his friendship with Collins, and for the rest we have but one or two allusions to him in contemporary letters by acquaintances and friends, with one or two short reminiscences of him by them long afterwards. To this scanty gleaning may be added the few allusions to him in post-contemporary magazines and the very little of value produced by considerable modern research.

★　　★　　★　　★

William Collins, Mayor of Chichester, a somewhat pompous hatter who boasted a friend of the great Mr. Pope among his customers, was a man of forty-seven when on Christmas Day, 1721, his wife, seven years his junior, gave birth to the poet at the family home and shop, 21 East Street. The only other members of the family were two sisters, Elizabeth and Ann, respectively 17 and 16 years old when William, the final addition to the family, arrived. Collins's mother, Elizabeth Martin, who came from a neighbouring village, had a brother Edmund—a Lieutenant-Colonel—and a clerical nephew, Dr. William Payne, a Fellow of Magdalen College, Oxford. Both the brother and nephew were destined to play a part in the little we know of Collins's life.

The parents, ambitious for their son, early intended him

for the church; and on 19 January, 1733, Collins entered Winchester College as a 'scholar', to remain there for the next seven years. Joseph Warton, destined to be a minor poet and headmaster of Winchester, was his schoolmate. Literary enthusiasm permeated the school, and before leaving Collins composed four 'Persian Eclogues'.

On 21 March, 1740, he entered Queen's College, Oxford, and in July 1741, was elected a demy of Magdalen. He disliked university life, feeling, as Gilbert White, an undergraduate friend, declared, 'a sovereign contempt for all academic studies and discipline', and complained of 'the dulness of a college life'. His father had died before Collins left Winchester, and his affectionate uncle, the Lieutenant-Colonel, supported him throughout his university career.

At Oxford Collins was soon noted for cleverness and indolence, but also as a scholarly and cultured man, with, said White, 'fine abilities, which properly improved must have raised him to the top of any profession'. Johnson, later, praised him as 'a man of extensive literature, and of vigorous faculties, acquainted not only with the learned tongues, but with the Italian, French and Spanish languages', and also as 'a man of uncommon learning and abilities'.

At Oxford he continued to write poetry, published anonymously his 'Persian Eclogues' in 1742, and the following year graduated B.A. A month later he published, also anonymously, but 'By a Gentleman of Oxford', his 'Verses to Sir Thomas Hanmer', a contemporary editor of Shakespeare's works. By this time, restlessness and instability, as well as solitary and visionary tendencies, were appearing as deeply integrated elements in his nature. The 'dulness' of academic life became intolerable; the attractions of the outer world, its amusements and excitements, irresistible; and Oxford debts were an anxiety. He would fly the university and 'see life' in London.

There were other anxieties too. He had vexed Dr. Payne by overspending his uncle's allowance, which Payne distributed, and had also appeared before the clerical doctor and Fellow of Magdalen, 'gaily dressed, and with a feather in his hat'. And when the outraged Payne told him 'his appearance was by no means that of a young man who had not a single guinea he could call his own', Collins, not daring to answer the man who held the purse strings, spoke of him afterwards as 'a damned dull fellow'. After this, his failure to obtain a Magdalen Fellowship may not have surprised, but it certainly disgusted him, and increased his intention to leave Oxford. But above all other reasons, his friends declared, was his longing to 'partake of the dissipation and gaiety' of London.

'The Manners', the most autobiographical of his poems, which he was now writing, not only corroborates the evidence of his friends, but also clearly illuminates his general mental and emotional state at this time:

> Farewell, for clearer Ken design'd,
> The dim-discover'd Tracts of Mind:
> Truths which, from Action's Paths retir'd,
> My silent Search in vain requir'd!
> No more my Sail that Deep explores,
> No more I search those magic Shores,
> What regions part the World of Soul,
> Or whence thy Streams, *Opinion*, roll:
> If e'er I round such Fairy Field,
> Some Pow'r impart the Spear and Shield,
> At which the Wizzard *Passions* fly,
> By which the Giant *Follies* die!

On 6 July, 1744, his mother died, leaving him a share of her fortune. Now an orphan with means, at this critical moment able to choose his way of life, he left Oxford for London, 'to partake of the dissipation and gaiety', but also secretly spurred by literary ambitions.

★ ★ ★ ★

The fog which descends at frequent intervals and for long periods upon Collins's life, is all the more exasperating to the

biographer because of the few intriguing glimpses we gain
whenever it lifts for a moment. Thus, shortly after arrival
in London, Collins is worried about a friend, 'Captn.
Hargrave', who 'was quite abandoned' and 'frequented
night cellars'. Three months later, Collins's old school
friend, John Mulso, his next door neighbour in Soho,
breakfasted with him, while 'Captn. Hargrave played on
the harpsichord; which', Mulso told Gilbert White, 'he has
not forgotten quite so much as he has himself'. Whether
the 'Captn.' was that 'certain gentlewoman, properly called
Nell Burnet but whose *nom de guerre* was "Captn. Har-
graves", in an officer's habit', thus described two years later
by the Cambridge don and poet Gray, when a Pembroke
College student, her cavalier, hid her in a cupboard, and
the proctors and their men searched for her, is an unanswerable question.

But we know that, as 'a man about Town', Collins haunted
such pleasure resorts as Ranelagh and Vauxhall, theatres and
coffee-houses, anxious to meet writers and actors, believing,
said White, that 'his superior abilities would draw the
attention of the great world, by means of whom he was to
make his fortune'. Collins's geniality in such company soon
won for him distinguished friends, including Garrick, Quin
and Foote, who are said to be 'among the gentlemen who
loved him for a genius', and often asked his opinion upon
plays before accepting them. Habitually indolent, though
eager for pleasure and excitement, he idled his time away,
but surely it was more than indolence that led him to lounge
at the famous bookshop of the actor, Tom Davies, where,
long after poor Collins's death, Johnson was for the first
time to meet Boswell. 'Passionately fond of music, good-
natured and affable, warm in his friendships, and visionary
in his pursuits; very temperate in his eating and drinking';
so White described him at this time. But we also learn of
his keen, satiric observation of the men and manners he
encountered, and of the amusement he provided for his
intimate friends by his witty descriptions and comments.

His way of life was now evidently such as he had anticipated in 'The Manners'; the rejection of mere study for the keen observation of real life. For the poem shows us Collins the man of the world, for whom even Fancy turns but a cynical eye upon the crowd around him:

> Youth of the quick uncheated Sight,
> Thy Walks, *Observance*, more invite!
> O Thou, who lov'st that ampler Range,
> Where Life's wide Prospects round thee change,
> And with her mingling Sons ally'd,
> Throw'st the prattling Page aside:
> To me in Converse sweet impart,
> To read in Man the native Heart,
> To learn, where Science sure is found,
> From Nature as she lives around:
> And gazing oft her Mirror true,
> By turns each shifting Image view!
> Till meddling *Art's* officious Lore,
> Reverse the Lessons taught before,
> Alluring him from a safer Rule,
> To dream in her enchanted School . . .
>
> O Nature boon, from whom proceed
> Each forceful Thought, each prompted Deed;
> If but from Thee I hope to feel,
> On all my Heart imprint thy Seal!
> Let some retreating Cynic find,
> Those oft-turn'd Scrolls I leave behind,
> The *Sports* and I this Hour agree,
> To rove thy Scene-full World with Thee!

With which intention the poem ends.[1]

Literary ambitions still held him. He planned works to make him famous, works but seldom begun and never finished. Occasionally he would write an ode and read it to applauding friends; then, dissatisfied, and despite their protests, he would destroy it. His means dwindled, and

[1] The Notes are on pp. 40–1.

poverty began to haunt him. 'Entirely an author, and hardly speaks out of rule', the satiric Mulso described him in July, 1744. 'A literary adventurer, with many projects in his head and very little money in his pocket', wrote Johnson, now his friend. Another friend, John Ragsdale, similarly describing him at this time, added a significant comment: 'In this manner he lived, with and upon his friends.' Then for the next fourteen months the mists close in again on Collins.

★   ★   ★   ★

His next appearance—September, 1745—is surprising; in London, seeking a bishop to make him a curate. He had visited his uncle, then fighting the French in Flanders, and the Colonel, disappointed by his nephew's indifference to everything but intellectual interests, had sent him home to be a parson, as 'too indolent even for the army'. Mulso, meeting Collins as potential curate, informed White: 'Don't laugh, . . . This will be the second acquaintance of mine who becomes the thing he most derides.' But unlike Joseph Warton, 'the second acquaintance' referred to, Collins was quickly persuaded by a London tobacconist to drop the plan. Shortly afterwards, he appeared at Guildford Races with Joseph Warton, both 'in very high spirits', planning a joint volume of odes, for his share in which Collins would demand at least ten pounds from the publisher. Perhaps because of this exorbitant demand, when Warton's and Collins's odes appeared in December 1746 they were in separate volumes by different publishers.

Throughout the preceding spring and summer, Collins was floundering in debts, demoralization and illness. 'The wandering Knight', one acquaintance sardonically named him, and a month later another saw him 'in good clothes and a wretched carcass at all the gay places'. Shortly before, he had been arrested for bilking his landlady, and it was probably about this time that Johnson saved him from a 'prowling bailiff', by raising money from publishers on

Collins's promise to translate Aristotle's *Poetics* for them, a promise quickly evaded when he could repay the loan. On 7 June, his 'Ode to a Lady on the Death of Colonel Ross' appeared in *Dodsley's Museum*. The lady involved is said to have previously rejected Collins as a suitor. Pursuing creditors probably explain the poet's absence abroad again as August opened. From Antwerp he sent Mulso a 'rapturous' letter (Mulso), about his journey through Holland, and was 'in high spirits though near the French', as he made for the army, meeting 'many wounded and sick countrymen as he travelled'.

*　　*　　*　　*

Some compensation for the general neglect of his 'Odes', Collins found in close friendship with James Thomson, the poet, famous for his 'Seasons' and now writing his charming 'Castle of Indolence', of which several stanzas were said (though not without question) to describe Collins. To be near a friend so akin to himself in temperament, Collins removed to Richmond, where he became a happy member of Thomson's distinguished circle. But the year in which 'The Castle of Indolence' was published, 1748, was also that of Thomson's death. Collins then wrote his lovely 'Ode to Thomson's Memory' (published the following year), and left Richmond for ever.

In April, 1749, Colonel Martin, who had been nursed for the last two years by Collins's sisters, died of war wounds. To the poet he left some two thousand pounds, 'which', wrote Johnson, 'Collins could scarcely think exhaustible, and which he did not live to exhaust'. Thus rescued from poverty, Collins returned to Chichester, and collected a distinguished library, including old and rare works. Angered by the neglect of his *Odes*, he now bought all unsold copies and burned them with his own hands. In October, the *Gentleman's Magazine* published his charming 'Dirge in Cymbeline', and before the year closed he wrote his last known poem, 'Ode on the Popular Superstitions of the Highlands of Scotland', addressed to John Home, the dramatist, with whom as a fellow guest he then spent two or three weeks in a friend's house at Winchester.

On 2 July, 1750, a musical performance of his ode, 'The Passions. An Ode for Music', was given in the Oxford theatre. In November, Collins, who had only just heard of this performance, wrote one of his two surviving letters, offering the Professor of Music, who had composed the accompaniment, another ode: 'On The Music of the Grecian Theatre'—'a nobler subject'; which, if it ever existed, is lost. Thus in the mid-year of the century, Collins seemed about to enter upon a happy and poetically productive future, of greater promise than the past.

*   *   *   *

But the future was only 'smiling to betray'. 'Man', wrote Johnson, 'is not born for happiness. Collins, who, while he studied to live, felt no evil but poverty, no sooner lived to study than his life was assailed by more dreadful calamities, disease and insanity.' These last eight years of Collins's life, from 1751 to the end, present a darkening scene, in which at long intervals we gain a few harrowing glimpses of him as he deteriorates into melancholia and intermittent, sometimes violent, insanity. Visits to France and to Bath failed to arrest the disease. In 1754 he was removed from a London asylum to the care of his sister Ann, at Chichester. There, in September, Joseph and Thomas Warton found him 'in high spirits at intervals' on the first day of their visit, but unable to see them on the second.

It was then that he showed them his ode, 'Popular Superstitions of the Highlands' (not published until 1788), and another poem, now lost, 'The Bell of Arragon', based on the Spanish legend that whenever a King of Spain was dying, the great bell of the Cathedral of Saragossa spontaneously tolled. The only lines which Thomas Warton remembered and quoted are depressingly prophetic of Scott's romantic verse:

> The bell of Arragon, they say,
> Spontaneous speaks the fatal day ...
> Whatever dark aërial power
> Commissioned, haunts the gloomy tower ...

The poem ended, we are told, with 'a moral transition to his own death and knell, which he called "some simpler bell" '.

Near the close of this year, he spent a month at Oxford, where Thomas Warton saw much of him, but found him too 'weak and low' for conversation, and once saw him attempt a short walk, 'supported by a servant'. White 'saw him under Merton wall, in a very affecting situation, struggling, and conveyed by force, in the arms of two or three men, towards the parish of St. Clement, in which was a house that took in such unhappy objects'. That is the last glimpse we have of Collins. Johnson, who felt a sincere affection for the poet, followed his decline with a concern that was partly personal. 'Poor dear Collins!' he wrote to Tom Warton on Christmas Eve, that same year, 'Let me know if you think it would give him pleasure if I should write to him. I have often been near his *state*, and therefore have it in great commiseration.'

For five more years of living death the poet lingered on, in the care of his difficult, eccentric and miserly sister, Ann, married to a Lieutenant of Marines. According to Johnson and others he turned much to the Bible now for consolation, though Johnson also tells us he found other sources of consolation as well, 'eagerly snatching that temporary relief with which the table and the bottle flatter and seduce'. He died on 12 June, 1759, aged 37. After his death, his sister, who had been angered by his habit during these last years of giving money to the cathedral choirboys in the cloisters, followed her brother's example (and unconsciously suggested that they had similar, hereditary temperaments),

by burning whatever she could find of his poetic manuscripts.

The uncertainty which pervades so much of Collins's
history, and even led his friends to misdate his death by
several years, is equally obvious in the records of his physical
appearance. 'Decent', Johnson described it, probably
meaning 'comely'. Another remembered or misremembered
him as a 'pockfretted man with keen black eyes', who
'associated very little'; another as 'in stature somewhat above
the middle size, of a brown [= dark] complexion, keen
expressive eyes, and a fixed, sedate aspect, which from
continual thinking had contracted an habitual frown'.
Gilbert White, however, remembered him as 'of a moderate
stature, of a light and clear complexion, with grey eyes, so
very weak at times as hardly to bear a candle in the room'.

The only estimate of Collins's character that we have,
Johnson's, suffers from an atmosphere of benevolent
ambiguity:

His morals were pure, and his opinions pious: in a long continuance of
poverty, and long habits of dissipation, it cannot be expected that any
character should be exactly uniform ... That this man, wise and virtuous
as he was, passed always unentangled through the snares of life, it would
be prejudice and temerity to affirm; but it may be said that at least he
preserved the source of action unpolluted, that his principles were never
shaken, that his distinctions of right and wrong were never confounded,
and that his faults had nothing of malignity or design, but proceeded
from some unexpected pressure or casual temptation.

Doubtless all true enough; but the realist must regret that
Miss Bundy, the Soho landlady whom he bilked, has left
us no account of him.

Collins was buried in St. Andrew's Church, Chichester,
where there is a memorial tablet to him and to other members of his family. In 1795 a monument by Flaxman, with
memorial verses by the poetaster Hayley, was erected in
Chichester Cathedral. It shows the poet seated, with his

Bible open before him. Instead of Hayley's verbose epitaph, a better one would have been Collins's own fatalistic lines in his 'Ode to Pity', asking whether

> CHANCE OR HARD INVOLVING FATE
> O'ER MORTAL BLISS PREVAIL.

II

It is not surprising that Collins's four 'Persian Eclogues', written when he was seventeen and published when he was twenty, have little merit as poetry. Their heroic couplets, weakly imitative of Pope's 'Pastorals', are generally flat and monotonous. In one line only do they attain the verbal distinction which can turn verse into poetry, the description in the 'First Eclogue', of Chastity: 'Cold is her breast, like Flow'rs that drink the Dew . . .' Nevertheless there are occasional passages of felicitous expression in these poems.

In the first eclogue the Persian poet, Selim, preaches 'virtue' to the shepherds and shepherdesses: ''Tis Virtue makes the Bliss, where'er we dwell.'

In the second, Hassan, the camel driver, crossing the desert on a trade journey, and almost dead through hunger, thirst and fear of wild animals, remembers, conveniently, the loving, weeping and anxious Zara in 'Schiraz', feels (equally conveniently) a moral revulsion against the sacrifice of love and happiness to mere gold, and returns to Zara:

> Curst be the Gold and Silver which persuade
> Weak Men to follow far-fatiguing Trade.
> The Lily Peace outshines the silver Store,
> And Life is dearer than the golden Ore . . .
> Thrice happy they, the wise contented Poor,
> From Lust of Wealth, and Dread of Death secure;
> They tempt no Desarts, and no Griefs they find;
> Peace rules the Day, where Reason rules the Mind.

The last line reminds us of the age in which Collins was born; the 'Age of Reason', by which he was influenced, but which he unconsciously assisted in its gradual transition towards romance. And in doing so he inevitably adapted 'an Augustan style to an eighteenth-century sensibility', as T. S. Eliot has said.

The third eclogue is a love romance in which the King of Persia, 'Royal Abbas', out hunting, falls in love, and marries the shepherdess Abra. Although happy, and a Queen, Abra so regrets absence from her former simple pastoral life and friends that every spring she rejoins them for a time, and even 'Royal Abbas', when able to escape from the cares of State, comes too. The description of Abra rises above the general level of the verse:

> From early Dawn the live-long Hours she told,
> 'Till late at silent Eve she penn'd the Fold.
> Deep in the Grove beneath the secret Shade,
> A various Wreath of od'rous Flow'rs she made:
> Gay-motley'd Pinks and sweet Junquils she chose,
> The Violet blue, that on the Moss-bank grows;
> All-sweet to Sense, the flaunting Rose was there;
> The finish'd Chaplet well adorn'd her Hair . . .
> Yet midst the Blaze of Courts she fix'd her Love,
> On the cool Fountain, or the shady Grove;
> Still with the Shepherd's Innocence her Mind
> To the sweet Vale and flow'ry Mead inclin'd,
> And oft as Spring renew'd the Plains with Flow'rs,
> Breath'd his soft Gales, and led the fragrant Hours,
> With sure Return she sought the sylvan Scene,
> The breezy Mountains, and the Forests green.
> Her Maids around her mov'd, a duteous Band!
> Each bore a Crook all-rural in her Hand:
> Some simple Lay, of Flocks and Herds they sung,
> With Joy the Mountain and the Forest rung . . .

Near the close of the eclogue, a couplet states its democratic moral—already implied in the two preceding poems—the moral equality, if not indeed superiority, of the poor, simple pastoral community, to the highest in the land:

> What if in Wealth the noble Maid excel;
> The simple Shepherd Girl can love as well.

The fourth eclogue, the last, attempts the dramatic, as in a less degree the second had already done. In that, fear and horror were caused by Nature; but in this, their cause is Man. The effect is intensified here by the contrast of human misery with the peace, dignity and indifference of the natural environment presented:

> At that still Hour, when awful Midnight reigns,
> And none but Wretches haunt the twilight Plains;
> What Time the Moon had hung her Lamp on high,
> And past in Radiance thro' the cloudless Sky: ...

two brothers, shepherds, fly from the marauding Tartars. For

> ... none so cruel as the *Tartar* Foe,
> To Death inur'd, and nurst in Scenes of Woe:
> He said; when loud along the Vale was heard
> A shriller Shriek, and nearer Fires appear'd:
> Th' affrighted Shepherds thro' the Dews of Night,
> Wide o'er the Moon-light Hills, renew'd their Flight.

Such was the close of this last eclogue.

Even in these earliest poems, Collins's romantic tendency is revealed in several aspects; in his attitude to 'Nature', to love, to human drama, human emotion, however faintly expressed. But when we come to Collins's later verse, so generally destitute of normal 'human feeling', it is well to remember that in these earliest poems he expressed horror and fear of wild life in Nature, and a greater horror and fear of wild life in Man. Scorned, even beyond their deserts, by most critics, the 'Eclogues' were equally overrated by Goldsmith, but were also found 'admirable' 'in parts', by no less a critic than Hazlitt, who generally knew what he was talking about.

In 1743, the year following the publication of the
'Eclogues', Collins published only a single poem. It was
addressed to Sir Thomas Hanmer, whose sumptuous but
badly edited Shakespeare was then appearing. Apart from
some fatuous compliments to Hanmer, the poem is an
expression of Collins's love and reverence for Shakespeare's
works, and therefore illuminates Collins's own personality.
The poem thus has a value independent of its eighty plod-
ding heroic couplets, many of them below the 'Eclogues' in
poetic quality. Collins reveals his ardent admiration for the
poetic imagination of 'th'unletter'd Bard', as he calls
Shakespeare, and his own sense of poetic inadequacy,
particularly of inadequate human feeling. His consciousness
of this preyed upon him, as his later poems show. So now
he praises Shakespeare above all his Elizabethan contemporaries:

> But stronger *Shakespeare* felt for Man alone:
> Drawn by his Pen, our ruder Passions stand
> Th' unrivalled Picture of his early Hand.

Like the 'Eclogues', these verses to Hanmer attained a
second edition in Collins's life-time. This, when a little later
his exquisite Odes found no appreciation, was but an
additional irritation to him.

Collins's next publication, the most important of his
poetical works, 'Odes on Several Descriptive and Allegorical
Subjects', appeared in December 1746, but dated 1747. It
consisted of only twelve short poems: odes to 'Pity', 'Fear',
'Simplicity', 'The Poetical Character', 'Mercy', 'Liberty',
'Evening', 'Peace', 'The Manners', 'The Passions',—ten
abstract subjects—and two human ones: 'How sleep the
Brave', and 'To a Lady on the Death of Colonel Ross in
the Action of Fontenoy'.

Like 'The Manners', though less explicitly, 'Fear' and
'The Poetical Character' reveal much of Collins's temperament. The intensity of a deeply personal experience,

whether 'real' or imaginative, vitalizes 'Fear', almost in the manner of Blake, who was doubtless indebted to the poem, as to others by Collins:

> Thou, to whom the World unknown
> With all its shadowy Shapes is shown;
> Who see'st appall'd th' unreal Scene,
> While Fancy lifts the Veil between:
>> Ah *Fear*! Ah frantic *Fear*!
>> I see, I see Thee near.
> I know thy hurried Step, thy haggard Eye!
> Like Thee I start, like Thee disorder'd fly.
> For lo! what *Monsters* in thy Train appear!
> Danger! whose Limbs of Giant Mold
> What mortal Eye can fix'd behold?
> Who stalks his Round, an hideous Form
> Howling amidst the Midnight Storm,
> Or throws him on the ridgy Steep
> Of some loose hanging Rock to sleep:
> And with him thousand Phantoms join'd,
> Who prompt to Deeds accurs'd the Mind:
> And those, the Fiends, who near allied,
> O'er Nature's wounds, and Wrecks preside;
> While *Vengeance*, in the lurid Air,
> Lifts her red Arm, expos'd and bare:
> On whom the rav'ning Brood of Fate,
> Who lap the Blood of Sorrow, wait;
> Who, *Fear*, this ghastly Train can see,
> And look not madly wild, like Thee? . . .
> O *Fear*, I know Thee by my throbbing Heart,
>> Thy with'ring Pow'r inspir'd each mournful Line,
> Tho' gentle *Pity* claim her mingled Part,
>> Yet all the Thunders of the Scene are thine!

This is not the only passage in Collins's verse that unwittingly almost suggests his later insanity, due to 'Fear'—*anxiety*. His illness began as melancholia, and the following passage from 'The Passions' probably owes something already to personal experience, as well as to Milton's 'Il Penseroso':

With Eyes up-rais'd as one inspir'd,
Pale *Melancholy* sate retir'd,
And from her wild sequester'd Seat,
In Notes by Distance made more sweet,
Pour'd thro' the mellow *Horn* her pensive Soul:
    And dashing soft from Rocks around,
    Bubbling Runnels join'd the Sound;
Thro' Glades and Glooms the mingled Measure stole,
Or o'er some haunted Stream with fond Delay,
    Round an holy Calm diffusing,
    Love of Peace, and lonely Musing,
In hollow Murmurs died away.

From the imaginative intensity of the opening of 'Fear',
Collins soon turns with relief to playing with fancies on
the theme:

Thou who such weary Lengths hast past,
Where wilt thou rest, mad Nymph, at last?
Say, wilt thou shroud in haunted Cell,
Where gloomy *Rape* and *Murder* dwell?
Or, in some hollow'd Seat,
'Gainst which the big Waves beat,
Hear drowning Sea-men's Cries in Tempests brought!
Dark Pow'r, with shudd'ring meek submitted Thought
Be mine, to read the Visions old,
Which thy awak'ning Bards have told:
And lest thou meet my blasted View,
Hold each strange Tale devoutly true;
Ne'er be I found, by Thee o'eraw'd,
In that thrice-hallow'd Eve abroad,
When Ghosts, as Cottage-Maids believe,
Their pebbled Beds permitted leave,
And *Gobblins* haunt from Fire, or Fen,
Or Mine, or Flood, the Walks of Men!
    O Thou whose Spirit most possest
The sacred Seat of *Shakespear's* Breast!
By all that from thy Prophet broke,
In thy Divine Emotions spoke:
Hither again thy Fury deal,

Teach me but once like Him to feel:
His *Cypress Wreath* my Meed decree,
And I, O *Fear*, will dwell with Thee!

The transition to Shakespeare, whose *Tempest* inspired the allusion to 'drowning seamen', and whose *Midsummer-Night's Dream* helped Milton's 'L'Allegro' to inspire the folk-lore passage, is therefore less irrelevant than it first appears.[2]

The poet's belief that poetic inspiration is a divine gift, conferred on few, he expressed in his 'Ode on the Poetical Character', choosing as symbol, Spenser's tale of Florimel's girdle, which refused to fasten when unchaste women tried to wear it. Then the poet continues:

> Young *Fancy* thus, to me Divinest Name,
>   To whom, prepar'd and bath'd in Heav'n,
>   The Cest of amplest Pow'r is giv'n:
>   To few the God-like Gift assigns,
>   To gird their blest prophetic Loins,
> And gaze her Visions wild, and feel unmix'd her Flame!

> The Band, as Fairy Legends say,
> Was wove on that creating Day,
> When He, who call'd with Thought to Birth
> Yon tented Sky, this laughing Earth,
> And drest with Springs, and Forests tall,
> And pour'd the Main engirting all,
> Long by the lov'd *Enthusiast* woo'd,
> Himself in some Diviner Mood,
> Retiring, sate with her alone,
> And plac'd her on his Saphire Throne,
> The whiles, the vaulted Shrine around,
> Seraphic Wires were heard to sound,
> Now sublimest Triumph swelling,
> Now on Love and Mercy dwelling;
> And she, from out the veiling Cloud,
> Breath'd her magic Notes aloud: . . .

Thus Collins describes his fantasy of the birth of a poet; the offspring of Fancy (the 'lov'd Enthusiast') and of Creative Power—'God'.

The next, the final section of this ode, expressing the poet's devotion to Milton, alludes to his favourite oak (in 'Il Penseroso'), and to Collins's rejection of the poet Waller (1606–1687), then still remembered for his smooth couplets and love verses. The conclusion laments the decline of poetry since Milton. As in the earlier parts of the poem, which include some of Collins's best verse of the semi-academic kind, there is occasional clumsiness of phrase and consequent obscurity. But this section begins with one of the best of the poet's romanticized landscapes:

> High on some Cliff, to Heav'n up-pil'd,
> Of rude Access, of Prospect wild,
> Where, tangled round the jealous Steep,
> Strange Shades o'erbrow the Valleys deep,
> And holy *Genii* guard the Rock,
> Its Gloomes embrown, its Springs unlock,
> While on its rich ambitious Head,
> An *Eden*, like his own, lies spread,
> I view that Oak, the fancied Glades among,
> By which as *Milton* lay, His Ev'ning Ear,
> From many a Cloud that dropp'd Ethereal Dew,
> Nigh spher'd in Heav'n its native strains could hear . . .
> With many a Vow from Hope's aspiring Tongue,
> My trembling Feet his guiding Steps pursue;
>   In vain—Such Bliss to One alone,
>   Of all the Sons of Soul was known,
>   And Heav'n and *Fancy*, kindred Pow'rs,
>   Have now o'erturn'd th'inspiring Bow'rs,
> Or curtain'd close such Scene from ev'ry future View.

So the poem ends, upon a pastoral note inspired by Milton.

This little volume of odes appeared at a critical moment in English history. One of the eighteenth century's interminable wars was in progress (or rather regress, from the English

point of view), for on 11 May, 1745, England and her
Continental allies had been defeated by the French at
Fontenoy, and two months later the Jacobite Scots began
an invasion of England which ended only with their defeat
at Culloden in April, 1746. Several of the odes reflect these
events more or less clearly, and so have been called the
'patriotic' odes. Although patriotic, they are not jingoistic
outbursts, but deeply humane utterances, clearly revealing
the poet's pain at the miseries of war, and his hatred of
violence, as well as his admiration for those who make
sacrifices in a noble cause such as Freedom.

Unfortunately Collins adopted in these odes the clangor-
ous style of Dryden in his 'Alexander's Feast', generally
considered at that time to be the finest of all English lyrics.
This extravert *bravura* of Dryden was so contrary to Collins's
essentially introvert nature, given to 'Love of Peace and
lonely Musing', that reading these odes we are reminded of
Johnson's rebuke to Gray for a similar reason: 'He has a
kind of strutting dignity, and is tall by walking on tiptoe.'
It was this that led Collins to describe in 'The Passions'—
echoing Dryden—how

> *Revenge* impatient rose,
> He threw his blood-stain'd Sword in Thunder down,
> And with a with'ring Look,
> The War-denouncing Trumpet took,
> And blew a Blast so loud and dread,
> Were ne'er Prophetic Sounds so full of Woe,
> And ever and anon he beat
> The doubling Drum with furious Heat;
> And tho' sometimes each dreary Pause between,
> Dejected *Pity* at his side,
> Her Soul-subduing Voice applied,
> Yet still He kept his wild unalter'd Mien,
> While each strain'd Ball of Sight seem'd bursting from his
> Head.

Thus it is with all these 'patriotic' odes: Mercy, Pity,
Peace, are ever at the side of the war gods, pleading,

restraining, sorrowing, a complete contrast to their noisy, bellicose associates. In this way these odes proceed:

> Now sublimest Triumph swelling,
> Now on Love and Mercy dwelling,

as he wrote in the 'Ode on the Poetical Character'. It is the same in his 'Ode to Mercy', inspired by the Scottish revolt. There too Mercy overpowers the 'Fiend of Nature'—evil influences over Man—which has caused the conflict:

> When he whom ev'n our Joys provoke,
>   The *Fiend of Nature* join'd his Yoke,
> And rush'd in Wrath to make our Isle his Prey;
>   Thy Form, from out thy sweet Abode,
>   O'ertook Him on his blasted Road,
> And stop'd his Wheels, and look'd his Rage away.
>
> I see recoil his sable Steeds,
>   That bore Him swift to Salvage Deeds,
> Thy tender melting Eyes they own;
> O Maid, for all thy Love to *Britain* shown,
>   Where *Justice* bars her Iron Tow'r,
>   To Thee we build a roseate Bow'r,
> Thou, Thou shalt rule, our Queen, and share our Monarch's Throne!

Liberty inspires Collins with warlike enthusiasm, and his ode to it begins and concludes its opening strophe with true Drydenian uproar, as it proceeds to trace the vicissitudes of Liberty through history: 'Who shall awake the Spartan Fife?' he begins, and after concluding the section with 'many a barb'rous Yell', cries in the epode 'Strike, louder strike th'ennobling Strings', for Freedom. Yet even here too, he looks forward, anxiously, to 'Concord' at last:

> *Concord*, whose Myrtle Wand can steep
> Ev'n *Anger's* blood-shot Eyes in Sleep:
> Before whose breathing Bosom's Balm,
> *Rage* drops his Steel, and Storms grow calm.

But it is in 'Peace' (technically the worst of the odes), that Collins most fully voices his detestation of war, and invokes Peace and reassures her that war will be destroyed:

> Tir'd of his rude tyrannic Sway,
> Our Youth shall fix some festive Day,
>   His sullen Shrines to burn:
> But Thou who hear'st the turning Spheres,
> What Sounds may charm thy partial Ears,
>   And gain thy blest Return!
>
> O *Peace*, thy injur'd Robes up-bind,
> O rise, and leave not one behind
>   Of all thy beamy Train . . .

When from these generalizing patriotic odes in which what I may call the 'official' manner prevails, Collins turns to a personal situation, the consoling of a friend bereaved by war, and praise of the soldier dead, the 'official' mood alternates with the personal; Dryden with Collins, as in the 'Ode to a Lady on the Death of Colonel Ross':

> While, lost to all his former Mirth,
> *Britannia's* Genius bends to Earth,
>   And mourns the fatal Day:
> While stain'd with Blood he strives to tear
> Unseemly from his Sea-green Hair
>   The Wreaths of chearful *May* . . .
>
> The Thoughts which musing Pity pays,
> And fond Remembrance loves to raise,
>   Your faithful Hours attend:
> Still Fancy to Herself unkind,
> Awakes to Grief the soften'd Mind,
>   And points the bleeding Friend.

In the next two stanzas of the poem, Collins characteristically and skilfully (but somewhat incongruously, as the 'Village Hind' is Dutch, and the river Scheldt slow), brings

Shakespearian pastoralism and fairies into this lament for a soldier's death:

> By rapid Scheld's descending Wave
> His Country's Vows shall bless the Grave,
>   Where'er the Youth is laid:
> That sacred Spot the Village Hind
> With ev'ry sweetest Turf shall bind,
>   And Peace protect the Shade.
>
> Blest Youth, regardful of thy Doom,
> Aërial Hands shall build thy Tomb,
>   With shadowy Trophies crown'd:
> Whilst *Honor* bath'd in Tears shall rove,
> To sigh thy Name thro' ev'ry Grove,
>   And call his Heros round.

The remainder of the poem consists of two 'official' stanzas calling on 'The warlike Dead of every Age', to welcome the dead Colonel to their company, while 'Freedom' lies on the ground in dishevelled garments, weeping until Victory comes. There are also two more stanzas, addressed to the lady, more impersonal and less emotional than the one, already quoted, to the 'Blest youth', the dead soldier.

The poem, then, is far from being a masterpiece; but from those last two stanzas just quoted there sprang, when genuine inspiration came to the poet shortly afterwards, not only one of Collins's two finest poems, but a poem which has rightly taken its place among the finest lyrics of English poetry:

ODE

Written in the beginning of the Year 1746

> How sleep the Brave, who sink to Rest,
> By all their Country's Wishes blest!
> When *Spring*, with dewy Fingers cold,
> Returns to deck their hallow'd Mold,
> She there shall dress a sweeter Sod,
> Than *Fancy's* Feet have ever trod.

By Fairy Hands their Knell is rung,
By Forms unseen their Dirge is sung;
There *Honour* comes, a Pilgrim grey,
To bless the Turf that wraps their Clay,
And *Freedom* shall a-while repair,
To dwell a weeping Hermit there!

That is as near perfection as any lyrist may ever hope to attain. The miracle appears the more miraculous when we note that at least *ostensibly* the ode is general, 'official'—though in fact it is inspired by an exquisitely delicate sentimentality and a personal feeling, like Wordsworth's, 'too deep for tears'. More remarkable still, it is made up of the eighteenth century's stock poetic images (e.g. the Pilgrim and the Hermit), stock personifications (Fancy, Honour, Freedom, Spring), and of Collins's Shakespearian pastoralism and fairies. But the miraculous moment brought a complete fusion of all elements; of Collins's classicism and romanticism; one bringing a cold generality of statement and dignity of phrase and rhythm; the other, personal emotion, all the more effective for classical restraint in expression. And below all, deep in the unconscious of the poet, was the lyric power of the Shakespeare that he had assimilated. It was no accident that Shakespeare admittedly inspired his 'A Song from Cymbeline' ('Sung by Guiderius and Arviragus over Fidele, supposed to be dead'), the lyric closest to this of all Collins's poems, and with much of its charm, published two years before:

To fair Fidele's grassy Tomb
  Soft Maids, and Village Hinds shall bring
Each op'ning Sweet, of earliest Bloom,
  And rifle all the breathing Spring.

No wailing Ghost shall dare appear
  To vex with Shrieks this quiet Grove:
But Shepherd Lads assemble here,
  And melting Virgins own their Love.

No wither'd Witch shall here be seen,
  No Goblins lead their nightly Crew;
The Female Fays shall haunt the Green,
  And dress thy Grave with pearly Dew!

The Red-breast oft at Ev'ning Hours
  Shall kindly lend his little Aid:
With hoary Moss, and gather'd Flow'rs,
  To deck the Ground where thou art laid.

When howling Winds, and beating Rain,
  In tempests shake the sylvan Cell,
Or 'midst the Chace on ev'ry plain,
  The tender Thought on thee shall dwell.

Each lonely Scene shall thee restore,
  For thee the Tear be duly shed:
Belov'd, till Life could charm no more,
  And mourn'd, till Pity's self be dead.

Collins's writing of that played its part too in the miracle. To another lyric of Shakespeare's, Ophelia's, in *Hamlet*:

He is dead and gone, lady,
  He is dead and gone;
At his head a grass-green turf,
  At his heels a stone,

we owe Collins's 'Song':

Young Damon of the vale is dead,
  Ye lowly hamlets, moan;
A dewy turf lies o'er his head,
  And at his feet a stone . . .

The lovely dirge is an excellent and typical example of Collins's assimilation of 'influences', and their conversion into essential Collins, by his own rhythms and verbal music, and sometimes, as here, by the introduction of his favoured pastoral note.

One other threnody he wrote, a poem of ten stanzas on the death of Thomson, published in 1749. It is one of his best poems, though uneven. Space allows only a short quotation, enough however to show the poet's usual imagery for these dirges, his skill also in transmitting emotion to his personifications:

> In yonder Grove a Druid lies[3]
>   Where slowly winds the stealing Wave!
> The *Year's* best Sweets shall duteous rise
>   To deck *its* Poet's sylvan Grave! . . .
>
> Remembrance oft shall haunt the Shore
>   When Thames in Summer Wreaths is drest,
> And oft suspend the dashing Oar
>   To bid his gentle Spirit rest!
>
> And oft as Ease and Health retire
>   To breezy Lawn, or Forest deep,
> The Friend shall view yon whitening Spire,
>   And 'mid the varied Landscape weep.
>
> But Thou, who own'st that Earthy bed,
>   Ah! what will every Dirge avail?
> Or Tears, which Love and Pity shed,
>   That mourn beneath the gliding Sail? . . .
>
> And see the Fairy Valleys fade,
>   Dun *Night* has veil'd the solemn View!
> Yet once again, Dear parted Shade,
>   Meek Nature's Child, again adieu . . .

That 'Fancy', imagination, was of supreme importance to him, Collins showed, as we have seen, in his 'Ode on the Poetical Character'. In his verses to Hanmer he describes Fancy as the creator of phantasies:

> Where'er we turn, by Fancy charm'd, we find
> Some sweet Illusion of the cheated Mind.
> Oft, wild of Wing, she calls the Soul to rove
> With humbler Nature, in the rural Grove;

> Where Swains contented own the quiet Scene,
> And twilight Fairies tread the circled Green:
> Drest by her Hand, the Woods and Vallies smile,
> And Spring diffusive decks th' *enchanted Isle.*

(Again Shakespeare's *Tempest.*) In 'The Manners' he speaks of Fancy's 'potent spell', and this 'spell' was, as the word suggests, romantic. Dr. Johnson, indeed, gives us a valuable insight into this aspect of the poet's nature, revealing his romanticism as more fantastic than his poetry suggests. But Johnson percipiently added: 'This was, however, the character rather of his inclination than of his genius.' He continued:

He had employed his mind chiefly upon works of fiction and subjects of fancy; and, by indulging some peculiar habits of thought, was eminently delighted with those flights of imagination which pass the bounds of nature, and to which the mind is reconciled only by a passive acquiescence in popular traditions. He loved fairies, genii, giants and monsters; he delighted to rove through the meanders of inchantment, to gaze on the magnificence of golden palaces, to repose by the waterfalls of Elysian gardens.

But Fancy's visions were not only pleasant. Fancy raises the veil that in 'Fear' had hidden from him the terror-stricken world of anxieties and fears. And at times Fancy passes from mere fantasy into the deeper level of creative imagination. It is thus with Collins's two finest poems; 'Fancy' appears but once by name, in each casually, but though invisible, it dominates, as poetic imagination.

Fancy at the lower level, fantasy, achieves its finest effects in the 'Ode on the Popular Superstitions of the Highlands of Scotland', his last poem. Home's tales of Highland folk-lore had appealed to the poet's love of the strange and fantastic, a taste recently developed by acquaintance with Tasso, whom in this same poem he praises:

> How have I trembled, when, at Tancred's stroke,
> Its gushing blood the gaping cypress pour'd;

> When each live plant with mortal accents spoke,
> And the wild blast up-heaved the vanish'd sword!

This appeal to the lower 'romantic' taste for the merely marvellous (which Johnson had recognized in him, but as not of his 'genius') had free play in this poem, and accounts for one's feeling of disappointment with it as a whole, despite fine passages.

Thomson, in a notable stanza of 'The Castle of Indolence', had touched upon this same theme of Scottish folklore:

> As when a shepherd of the Hebrid Isles,
> Placed far amid the melancholy main,
> (Whether it be lone fancy him beguiles,
> Or that aerial beings sometimes deign
> To stand embodied to our senses plain)
> Sees on the naked hill or valley low,
> The whilst in ocean Phoebus dips his wain,
> A vast assembly moving to and fro;
> Then all at once in air dissolves the wondrous show.

It was in this mood of Thomson that Collins wrote his Scottish ode, delighting in his freedom to relapse from the romanticism of his adult mind into the merely fanciful romance of childhood, creating supernatural agencies which range from the merely mischievous to the intimidating and murderous!

> 'Tis Fancy's land to which thou sett'st thy feet;
> Where still, 'tis said, the fairy people meet
>   Beneath each birken shade on mead or hill.
> There each trim lass that skims the milky store,
>   To the swart tribes their creamy bowl allots;
> By night they sip it round the cottage-door,
>   While airy minstrels warble jocund notes.
> There every herd, by sad experience knows,
>   How, wing'd with fate, their elf-shot arrows fly;
> When the sick ewe her summer food foregoes,
>   Or, stretch'd on earth, the heart-smit heifers lie.

But his attempts at the dramatic, at horror-history or fantasy, are highly wrought: overwrought indeed, and his wild, ancient Scots, whose 'sturdy clans pour'd forth their bony swarms', amidst 'wat'ry strath' and 'quaggy moss' along with a 'kelpie' (a kind of 'Loch Ness Monster' that drowns people), are all very Hollywood. Yet just before drawing a lurid picture of the Kelpie's victim's ghost visiting his wife, *poetry* suddenly reappears. Here, as often, literature is more inspiring to Collins than life or death or superstitions; for the passage is inspired by a description in Lucretius, which Collins adapts to portray the dead man's wife and family, ignorant of his death, anxiously awaiting him:

> For him, in vain, his anxious wife shall wait,
>   Or wander forth to meet him on his way;
> For him, in vain, at to-fall of the day,
>   His babes shall linger at th' unclosing gate!

Occasionally too, mere Fancy takes fire, and raises the verse to a definitely imaginative level, as in the following lines, the best in this kind in Collins's verse, evidently influenced also by the passage quoted from 'The Castle of Indolence'. For Collins's Muse can now

> extend her skirting wing,
> Round the moist marge of each cold Hebrid isle,
> To that hoar pile which still its ruins shows:
> In whose small vaults a pigmy-folk is found,
> Whose bones the delver with his spade upthrows,
>   And culls them, wond'ring, from the hallow'd ground!
> Or thither where beneath the show'ry west
>   The mighty kings of three fair realms are laid;
> Once foes, perhaps, together now they rest.
>   No slaves revere them, and no wars invade:
> Yet frequent now, at midnight's solemn hour,
>   The rifted mounds their yawning cells unfold,
> And forth the monarchs stalk with sov'reign pow'r
>   In pageant robes, and wreath'd with sheeny gold,
> And on their twilight tombs aerial council hold.

It is very good, and for such passages some have overpraised the poem. But good as they are, they are a *tour de force*, not the essential Collins.

'Nature' in Collins's verse means reality; and as such includes both good and evil, just as 'Fancy' does. 'The Fiend of Nature' incites strife; creates bad psychological and moral influences and impulses; such as the

> thousand Phantoms join'd
> Who prompt to Deeds accurs'd the Mind,

and

> the Fiends who near allied,
> O'er Nature's Wounds and Wrecks preside . . .

In these and similar lines Collins shows his awareness of then obscure psychological realities, of 'All the shad'wy Tribes of Mind', the wicked elements, which join their 'murmurs' with 'Heav'n's ambrosial Flow'rs', the good influences.

Collins had also a conception, unusual in his day, of vast geological changes in the earth; if not indeed some vague fore-shadowing of evolution.[4] The grandeur of these conceptions, his imaginative realization of the magnitude of stupendous changes over vast periods of time, aroused the romantic wonder which inspires the following fine passage in 'Liberty', referring to a belief that at one time Britain was a part of the Continent:

> Beyond the Measure vast of Thought,
> The Works the Wizzard *Time* has wrought!
>   The *Gaul*, 'tis held of antique Story,
> Saw *Britain* link'd to his now adverse Strand,
>   No Sea between, nor Cliff sublime and hoary,
> He pass'd with unwet Feet through all our Land.
>   To the Blown *Baltic* then, they say,
>   The wild Waves found another way,

Where *Orcas* howls, his wolfish Mountains rounding;
    Till all the banded West at once 'gan rise,
A wide wild Storm ev'n Nature's self confounding,
    With'ring her Giant Sons with strange uncouth Surprise.
        This pillar'd Earth so firm and wide,
            By Winds and inward Labors torn,
        In Thunders dread was push'd aside,
            And down the should'ring Billows born.

Here Fancy, stimulated by Collins's sense of primaeval power and mystery, successfully employs a *bravura* that is in complete harmony with the vastness of the theme.

Nevertheless, it is an almost entirely contrary aspect of Nature—contrary but for the presence of awe and wonder here also—that inspires Collins's only other poem comparable with 'How sleep the Brave', if not, indeed, as some think, superior to it. The peace, the beauty and mystery of evening as it descends amidst country solitude, moves the poet to an exquisite and entirely personal utterance, permeated though it is in both form and diction by the influence of Milton. For 'Evening' expresses the deepest harmonies of his own nature, now for a moment finding satisfaction in those of the external world:

ODE TO EVENING

If ought of Oaten Stop, or Pastoral Song,
    May hope, O pensive *Eve*, to soothe thine Ear,
        Like thy own brawling Springs,
        Thy Springs, and dying Gales,
O *Nymph* reserv'd, while now the bright-hair'd Sun
Sits in yon western Tent, whose cloudy Skirts,
        With Brede ethereal wove,
        O'erhang his wavy Bed:
Now Air is hush'd, save where the weak-ey'd Bat,
With short shrill Shriek flits by on leathern Wing,
        Or where the Beetle winds
        His small but sullen Horn,

As oft he rises 'midst the twilight Path,
Against the Pilgrim born in heedless Hum:
      Now teach me, *Maid* compos'd,
      To breathe some soften'd Strain,
Whose Numbers stealing thro' thy darkning Vale,
May not unseemly with its Stillness suit,
      As musing slow, I hail
      Thy genial lov'd Return!
For when thy folding Star arising shews
His paly Circlet, at his warning Lamp
      The fragrant *Hours*, and *Elves*
      Who slept in Buds the Day,
And many a *Nymph* who wreaths her Brows with Sedge,
And sheds the fresh'ning Dew, and lovelier still,
      The *Pensive Pleasures* sweet
      Prepare thy shadowy Car.
Then let me rove some wild and heathy Scene,
Or find some Ruin 'midst its dreary Dells,
      Whose Walls more awful nod
      By thy religious Gleams.
Or if chill blust'ring Winds, or driving Rain,
Prevent my willing Feet, be mine the Hut,
      That from the Mountain's Side,
      Views Wilds, and swelling Floods,
And Hamlets brown, and dim-discover'd Spires,
And hears their simple Bell, and marks o'er all
      Thy Dewy Fingers draw
      The gradual dusky Veil.
While *Spring* shall pour his Show'rs, as oft he wont,
And bathe thy breathing Tresses, meekest *Eve*!
      While *Summer* loves to sport,
      Beneath thy ling'ring Light:
While sallow *Autumn* fills thy Lap with Leaves,
Or *Winter* yelling thro' the troublous Air,
      Affrights thy shrinking Train,
      And rudely rends thy Robes.
So long regardful of thy quiet Rule,
Shall *Fancy*, *Friendship*, *Science*, smiling *Peace*,
      Thy gentlest Influence own,
      And love thy fav'rite Name!

So the poem ends: suddenly; as after the waxing and waning of a fitful sunset, Night descends. It is a perfect transposition of natural beauty into an exquisite correspondence of both abstract and imitative imagery, verbal, metrical and rhythmical harmonies, akin to the art of the musician.

Space, unfortunately, allows but a fleeting glimpse of Collins's rise to posthumous fame. It is not surprising that one usually so remote in his verse from normal human interests and emotions, and so soon silenced by disease and death, attracted little interest among his contemporaries, and even less appreciation. Gray said that despite many faults he 'deserved to last some years but would not'. Johnson, despite his affection for the man, harshly condemned his verse after his death. Goldsmith, his only appreciative contemporary of note, highly praised the 'Eclogues' and 'Evening', and denounced the neglect of the poet and his works.

Although Cowper, a quarter of a century after Collins's death, first heard of him through reading Johnson's *Lives of the Poets*, and showed no appreciation of his poetry, the years of neglect were already yielding to recognition in periodicals, anthologies and such, while 'echoes' of his verse gradually permeated the poetry of both major and minor poets as the romantic movement grew. Burns praised, Blake assimilated his influence, and romantic poetesses and women horror-novelists took him to their sentimental and maternal hearts, chiefly because of 'Fear', and of 'neglect'.

Coleridge, in 1796, felt 'inspired and whirled along with greater agitations of enthusiasm than the most impassioned scene in Schiller or Shakespeare' by part of 'The Poet's Character'. Two years later, Wordsworth's well-known verses to Collins's memory appeared in *Lyrical Ballads*. Southey praised; Byron, like Johnson, was interested in his illness on personal grounds; Shelley thought him 'a cold, artificial writer', and Keats's only mention of him in his letters is a casual remark in February, 1818, that he is attending Hazlitt's lectures, and that the last one included

Collins and Gray. At that lecture Keats must have heard Hazlitt's enthusiastic and detailed appreciation of the poet, in which he praised him for 'that genuine inspiration, which alone can give birth to the highest efforts of poetry', and described him as 'the only one of the minor poets of whom, if he had lived, it cannot be said that he might not have done the greatest things'.

At the very time of Hazlitt's lecture, Keats was revising his 'Endymion'; and a comparison of a famous passage there, by Keats at his best in the style, with one in the same style by Collins, is interesting. The first, from 'The Passions', is typically Collins, almost colourless, intellectual, unsensuous, marmoreal—nevertheless, *living* marble:

> . . . *Chearfulness*, a Nymph of healthiest Hue,
> Her Bow across her Shoulder flung,
> Her Buskins gem'd with Morning Dew,
> Blew an inspiring Air, that Dale and Thicket rung,
> The Hunter's Call to *Faun* and *Dryad* known!
> The Oak-crown'd *Sisters*, and their chast-eyed *Queen*,
> Satyrs and sylvan Boys were seen,
> Peeping from forth their Alleys green:
> Brown *Exercise* rejoic'd to hear,
> And *Sport* leapt up, and seiz'd his Beechen Spear.

Whether consciously influenced by Collins or not cannot be said, but Keats continues the spirit of the preceding passage, with the addition of colour and detail from Titian's famous painting, *Bacchus and Ariadne*. This Collins too would have appreciated, being attracted, as Keats was, by the romanticized classicism of the Renaissance. Indeed I doubt, if the following extract from Keats were printed immediately after the preceding quotation from Collins, whether many persons would suspect that it was from a different poem by a poet writing more than half a century after Collins's death. But the fact shows how the poetic manner of Collins was already permeating English poetry. Nor was Keats's resemblance to Collins limited to this vital, processional form. In the marmoreal, coldly classical 'Ode on a Grecian Urn', Keats comes, in spirit, close to the poet of 'Evening', and of 'How sleep the Brave'.

But we must return to 'Endymion':

> Within his car, aloft, young Bacchus stood,
> Trifling his ivy-dart, in dancing mood,
> With sidelong laughing;
> And little rills of crimson wine imbrued
> His plump white arms, and shoulders, enough white,
> For Venus' pearly bite:
> And near him rode Silenus on his ass,
> Pelted with flowers as he on did pass
> Tipsily quaffing.

In these last years of the eighteenth century and the first years of the next, Collins's popularity continued to increase. Lamb, Campbell, Keble and Clare, amongst many, praised, or imitated, or did both, while the poet became a fixed star in the poetic firmament as the Victorian Age arrived. But as his influence merged more and more completely in the poetic stream, it lost identity and recognition, even by poets such as Arnold, who mentions Collins but once—with a respectful reference—in his essay on 'Gray', and not at all in that on the 'Study of Poetry'. Yet Arnold's own verse is permeated with obvious resemblances to various aspects of Collins, both as man and as poet. Swinburne praised Collins in characteristically hysterical terms, taking him, without reason, for an exponent of Tyrannicide because of his 'Ode to Liberty'! But there is not room here to follow Collins among the Victorians. Certain poetic developments then, militated against appreciation of him, particularly the passing of the love of Abstractions and Personifications, which like such 'Gothic' terms as *Pilgrim, Druid, Hermit*, held for the eighteenth century poetic magic.

With the Victorians the arts, following political and social conditions, turned bourgeois, and poetry suffered bourgeois limitations. The great moral forces, such as Pity,

Mercy, Sorrow and Fear, the abstract contemplation of which moved Collins to such emotion as the mathematical Neoplatonists of Alexandria felt when contemplating the intellectual beauties of the circle, meant nothing to the average Victorian reader, unless apprehended through personal, individual and preferably sentimental manifestations, as in Tennyson's 'May Queen'. In this present age of abstract art and of scientific abstractions which are also often tremendous and sometimes terrifying realities, we should be better able to appreciate the contrast between Tennyson's poem and Collins's 'Evening' and 'How sleep the brave'. The contrast brings home to us that, in the hands of such a poet as Collins, the eighteenth century's typical poetic attitude of emotional restraint, generalization, and personification, is not necessarily inimical to the finest poetry.

Such was the poetry of Collins; the poet of an age of transition; of declining classicism and dawning romance, which, reflected in his verse, reminds us of his own design for the temple to Liberty:

> In *Gothic* Pride it seems to rise,
> Yet Graecia's graceful Orders join,
> Majestic thro' the mix'd Design.

Notes

[1] *Page 9.* If, as I suspect, the following passage from 'The Manners' is a satire on Dr. Payne, lecturing in his ecclesiastical and academic garments at Magdalen, it is the only example we have of Collins's satirical wit (to which his friends testify):

> Farewell the Porch, whose Roof is seen,
> Arch'd with th'enlivening Olive's Green:
> Where *Science*, prank'd in tissued Vest,
> By *Reason*, *Pride*, and *Fancy* drest,
> Comes like a Bride so trim array'd,
> To wed with *Doubt* in *Plato's* Shade!

[2] *Page 21.* Literary 'influences' in the verse of Collins are so frequent that individual indication of them would require a large volume. Pope, the first, dominated the early 'Eclogues' and 'Verses to Hanmer', and occasionally appears in the later poems, though by then the heroic couplets of Pope were discarded, and only occasional 'echoes' remain.

About the time of Pope's death, 1744, two years before Collins's Odes appeared, he turned from Pope to the poetic ideal of his own, emerging generation, Milton. One might almost say that everything he wrote from this time to the end, was Milton; and yet not Milton but essentially Collins. As a cow converts grass into cow—to take a crude but convenient illustration—so Collins assimilated Milton (as he did other sources after Pope). Milton's pastoral, folk-lore, remote, antiquarian and classical interests, his verse forms and diction, all were appropriated and absorbed. The literary detective has listed 744 echoes and imitations from Milton in the small corpus of Collins's poetry, but the Miltonic influence is much greater and more important than that. (cf. Miltonic *denouncing* = prophesying, in 'The War-denouncing Trumpet'. See, p. 23.)

Shakespeare's fairy lore, plays and lyrics and diction were similarly but much less frequently employed, and are less obvious but not less important in general effect. The influence of Spenser is comparatively small. Only twice is he mentioned in the poems, but echoes and, more important, a general romantic quality of his can be detected, though seldom obvious.

[3] *Page 29.* I read *grove grave;* is the usual text, taken from the 1749 edition of the poem. But in Fawkes & Woty's *Poetical Calendar* (1763)— which Garrod rightly regards as the first edition of the Collected Works, and in Pearch's *Collection of Poems* (1775) the word is *grove.* My reasons for preferring *grove* are (1) *grave* occurs again three short lines below, which repetition Collins could not have tolerated. (2) That second grave is 'sylvan' i.e. in a wood. (3) *Grove* suits *Druid,* for we are told 'groves of oak and circles of stone were their places of worship'. (4) *Grove* better fits the winding, 'stealing wave' in the next line of the poem. The result of this change of text is a complete change and improvement in the poetical imagery that is the background of the whole poem; a change from an ordinary churchyard to the solitude and silence of a woodland grave. Whether in fact it was so, would not affect Collins. Cf. *grove,* in 'A Song from Cymbeline'.

Druid: then a poetically 'magic word', 'Gothic', romantic. For Collins, the literary order called Bards was chiefly in his mind, men who sang their poems to the harp, and gave poetry a priestly and mystical association. 'I have frequently wondered that our modern writers have made so little use of the Druidical times, and the traditions of the old bards, which afford fruitful subjects of the most genuine poetry, with respect to both imagery and sentiment.' Joseph Warton, *Essay on the Genius and Writings of Pope* (1756-82), I., p. 355.

[4] *Page 33.* Collins's note on this is interesting: 'This tradition is mentioned by several of our old Historians. Some Naturalists too have endeavoured to support the probability of the Fact, by Arguments drawn from the correspondent Disposition of the two opposite Coasts.' The note suggests an interest in scientific subjects, and that when Collins uses the word *Science,* he may sometimes mean not merely *knowledge,* as was usual, but also *science* in the modern sense. Despite Spenser's allusion to this belief (*Faerie Queene,* II, x, 5), Collins adds: 'I don't remember that any Poetical Use has been hitherto made of it.' Stranger still, as Collins's 'Liberty' is derived from Thomson's 'Liberty', is Collins's apparent ignorance of Thomson's allusion to this same belief about Britain and France in 'Liberty' IV. 460-463.

A Select Bibliography
(place of publication London, unless stated otherwise)

Bibliography:

THE POEMS OF WILLIAM COLLINS, W. C. Bronson. (Boston 1898)
—bibliography, pp. lxxix-lxxxv.
SEVEN EIGHTEENTH-CENTURY BIBLIOGRAPHIES, by I. A. Williams (1924)
—1st editions only.
THE CAMBRIDGE BIBLIOGRAPHY OF ENGLISH LITERATURE, ed. F. W.
    Bateson. 4 vols. Cambridge (1940)
—Vol. 2, pp. 335-338.
FROM DRYDEN TO JOHNSON, ed. B. Ford (1957)
—Pelican Guide to English Literature, Vol. 4.

Collected Poems:

THE POETICAL CALENDAR, ed. F. Fawkes and W. Woty. Vols. 11, 12
    (1763)
—incomplete, and includes in error, as Collins's, 'To Miss Aurelia
    C-R'. Also includes a *Life* by Hampton and a *Character* by Dr.
    Johnson.
THE POETICAL WORKS, ed. J. Langhorne (1765)
—contents same as in *The Poetical Calendar* but excludes 'To Miss
    Aurelia C-R'. Includes Langhorne's *Memoirs* of Collins and his
    Observations on his Genius and Writings. Reprinted 1771, 1776, 1781.
THE WORKS OF THE ENGLISH POETS, ed. S. Johnson, vol. xlix (1779)
—includes Johnson's *Life* of Collins.
POETICAL WORKS. Glasgow (1787)
—Foulis Press folio edition, with preface and notes.
THE POETICAL WORKS, ed. A. Dyce (1827)
—includes Johnson's *Life*, Langhorne's *Observations*, and biographical
    and critical notes by Dyce.
THE POETICAL WORKS, ed. Sir S. E. Brydges (1830; reprinted 1853)
—the Aldine edition. Includes Sir Harris Nicolas's *Memoir* of
    Collins, and Brydges' Essay on the genius and poems of Collins.
POETICAL WORKS, ed. M. Thomas (1858, 1866, 1894, 1901)
—the Aldine edition. Excellent biographical preface.
POEMS, ed. C. Stone (1907).

THE POETICAL WORKS [With Gray], ed. C. Stone and A. L. Poole. Oxford (1917, 1926)

—in the Oxford Standard Authors' Revised editions, 1937, 1961.

THE POEMS, ed. with an Introductory Study by E. Blunden (1929).

GRAY, COLLINS, AND THEIR CIRCLE, ed. W. T. Williams and G. H. Vallins [1937].

Separate Works:

PERSIAN ECLOGUES (1742) [Anon.]

—renamed and republished as *Oriental Eclogues*, 1757.

VERSES HUMBLY ADDRESS'D TO SIR THOMAS HANMER (1743) [Anon.]

—republished and revised as *An Epistle*: *Addrest to Sir Thomas Hanmer*. 'The Second Edition', 1744, with the addition of Collins's 'A Song from Cymbeline' ('To fair Fidele's grassy tomb').

ODES ON SEVERAL DESCRIPTIVE AND ALLEGORICAL SUBJECTS (1747)

—1,000 copies published December 1746. Facsimile edition [The Noel Douglas Replicas], 1926.

ODE OCCASION'D BY THE DEATH OF MR. THOMSON (1749)

—facsimile edition, Oxford, 1927.

THE PASSIONS, AN ODE [1750]. Set to Musick by Dr. Hayes. Performed at the Theatre in Oxford, 2 July, 1750

—originally published in *Odes*, 1747, this is the first separate edition. A variant, also undated, is recorded with a Winchester N.D. [1750] imprint. Both the Oxford and Winchester editions have the last twenty-four lines rewritten (and spoiled) by the Earl of Lichfield, Vice-Chancellor of the University of Oxford.

'An Ode on the Popular Superstitions of the Highlands of Scotland, considered as the Subject of Poetry', in the *Transactions of the Royal Society of Edinburgh*, Vol. I, pp. 67-75, Edinburgh, 1788.

DRAFTS AND FRAGMENTS OF VERSE, ed. J. C. Cunningham. Oxford (1956).

Letters:

MS. LETTER OF COLLINS TO JOHN GILBERT COOPER [author of 'Letters Concerning Taste', 1755]. Dated London, 10 November, 1747 (B.M. Add. 41178.I.)

—this letter is printed in full by H. O. White in his 'Letters of William Collins', *Review of English Studies*, January 1927, Vol. iii, No. 9, pp. 12-21.

A LETTER OF COLLINS TO DR. WILLIAM HAYES [Professor of Music in the University of Oxford]. Dated Chichester, Sussex, 8 November, 1750
—the original has disappeared. It was first printed in W. Seward's 'Supplement to Anecdotes of Some Distinguished Persons', 1797, p. 123. Moy Thomas reprints it in his Preface to the *Poems*, 1901.

Some Biographical and Critical Studies:

CENSURA LITERARIA, by S. E. Brydges. 2nd edn., 10 vols. (1815)
—Vol. 7.
MISCELLANIES, by A. C. Swinburne (1886)
—also in *The English Poets*, ed. T. H. Ward, Vol. 3, 1880.
HEURES DE LECTURE D'UN CRITIQUE, par E. Montegut. Paris (1891).
THE LIVES OF THE POETS, by S. Johnson. Ed. G. Birkbeck Hill, 3 vols. Oxford (1905)
—vol. 3.
POET'S COUNTRY, ed. A. Lang (1907)
—two good articles by J. C. Collins.
GREEK INFLUENCE ON ENGLISH POETRY, by J. C. Collins (1910).
THE PEACE OF THE AUGUSTANS, by G. Saintsbury (1916).
ENGLISH LYRIC IN THE AGE OF REASON, by O. Doughty (1922).
'Collins and the English Lyric', by J. W. Mackail. [In *Trans. of the Royal Society of Literature*, 1921. Also in *Studies of English Poets*, by J. W. Mackail, 1926.]
THE INFLUENCE OF MILTON ON ENGLISH POETRY, by R. D. Havens. Cambridge, Mass. (1922).
COUNTRIES OF THE MIND, by J. M. Murry (1922).
'The Poetry of Collins', by H. W. Garrod. British Academy Lecture, 1928.
COLLINS, by H. W. Garrod. Oxford (1928).
'Collins and the Creative Imagination', by A. S. P. Woodhouse. [In *Studies in English*, ed. M. W. Walker, Toronto, 1931.]
POOR COLLINS: HIS LIFE, HIS ART, AND HIS INFLUENCE, by E. G. Ainsworth. New York (1937).

Bibliographical Series
of Supplements to 'British Book News'
on Writers and Their Work

GENERAL EDITOR
Geoffrey Bullough

DOROTHY WORDSWORTH

THREE WOMEN DIARISTS

CELIA FIENNES · DOROTHY WORDSWORTH
KATHERINE MANSFIELD

by

MARGARET WILLY

PUBLISHED FOR
THE BRITISH COUNCIL
AND THE NATIONAL BOOK LEAGUE
BY LONGMANS, GREEN & CO.

LONGMANS, GREEN & CO. LTD.
48 Grosvenor Street, London, W.1

*Associated companies, branches and
representatives throughout the world*

First published 1964
© Margaret Willy 1964

*Printed in Great Britain by
F. Mildner & Sons, London, E.C.1*

CONTENTS

¶ Thanks are due to the Society of Authors, as the literary representatives of the Estate of the late Katherine Mansfield, for permission
to quote from the author's work.

¶ Celia Fiennes was born in 1662 at Newton Toney, near Salisbury. She died in London in 1741.

¶ Dorothy Wordsworth was born on 25 December, 1771 at Cockermouth in Cumberland. She died on 25 January, 1855.

¶ Katherine Mansfield was born at Wellington, New Zealand on 14 October, 1888. She died on 9 January, 1923 near Fontainebleau.

THREE WOMEN DIARISTS

I

INTRODUCTION

THE keeping of diaries, as demonstrated by men from Pepys and Evelyn onwards, is by no means a mainly feminine province. Nevertheless there is something in the activity which strongly appeals to female instinct and inclination. The figure of the young girl writing up her private journal in her room late at night is a familiar one in fiction. And in fact, although we might hesitate to go as far as the writer who suggested 'that women make more refreshing, more effective diarists than men', the art of the English diary has been enriched by a good many notable contributions on the distaff side.

Feminine chroniclers of court life have included Mary, Countess Cowper, wife of a Lord Chancellor of the day, recording in the first two decades of the eighteenth century the scandals and intrigues at the court of the Princess of Wales; and a little later, the far more famous Fanny Burney (1752-1840). Her lively diaries, begun at the age of sixteen for 'the pleasure of popping my thoughts down on paper', and originally addressed to 'a certain Miss Nobody', span a period of over seventy years. For only five of these she was a Mistress of the Robes to Queen Charlotte. Unhappy as she often felt during the drudging monotony of her duties as a royal lady's maid, after the freedom of her musician father's home,[1] she proves an acute and amusing commentator on life at the court of George III. She had already made her impact on the literary world with *Evelina*, published anonymously in 1778; and Fanny Burney's gifts as a novelist are well displayed in her diaries. She was a spontaneous and accomplished *raconteuse*, handling narrative with verve and

[1] A fuller account of the life and work of Fanny Burney will appear as a later essay in this series.

7

skill, possessing a keen ear for dialogue and a shrewdly observing eye for character and situation. Even more interesting than her court gossip are her many vivid glimpses of the great. Although plain and shy, she had a warmth, vivacity and quick intelligence which endeared her to some of the most brilliant personalities of her time: the statesman Burke, the dramatist Sheridan, the painter Reynolds—and, of course, Dr. Johnson. His 'little Burney' is probably best known for her portrait of him, and of the ruling Royal Family: in both she emerges at her zestful and humorous best.

Somewhat earlier another woman diarist, Elizabeth Byrom (daughter of the hymn-writer John Byrom), offers a brief sight of a very different royal personage. During the Jacobite Rebellion of 1745 she was an eye-witness of the entry into Manchester of Prince Charles Edward, the Young Pretender—'dressed in a Scotch plaid, a blue silk waistcoat with silver lace, and a Scotch bonnet with J.R. on it'.

Turning from historical to domestic, we have Nancy Woodforde, one of a Norfolk family of inveterate diarists who, between them, provide a detailed panorama of the English leisured class at home during the latter part of the eighteenth century. Less favoured by circumstances was a lady named Ellen Weeton, who committed her vicissitudes as a poor governess, and rebel against the tyranny of the male, to the pages of the diaries she kept between 1807 and 1825. Sharp-tongued and independent, this embattled feminist depicts with vigour the small-town life of her day in the north of England. The intellectual Caroline Fox was more fortunate in background and education. Daughter of a prominent Quaker family, she, like Fanny Burney, began to keep her diary when she was sixteen; and she, too, was the friend of distinguished men. The great Victorians who appear in her anecdotal pages, which cover the years from 1835 almost up to the time of her death in 1871, include the Carlyles, John Stuart Mill, Florence Nightingale and

Tennyson. No survey of women diarists is complete without mention of the Laureate's sovereign. Throughout her long life Queen Victoria was an industrious chronicler of her doings. Her journals have much historical interest, in their revelation of the private emotions of a formidable public personality. Especially memorable and moving are the passages mourning the death of her beloved Albert, or, years earlier, the nineteen-year-old girl's account of the most solemn occasion of her life, her coronation day.

Space forbids any closer exploration of these writers, who have added a rewarding variety to the diary form. This essay will confine itself to considering three of the most interesting women who kept journals. The first is a contemporary of Pepys and Evelyn: an enterprising and intrepid traveller who put on record the findings of her horseback journeys through England, Scotland and Wales at the end of the seventeenth century.

II

CELIA FIENNES

Although writing between about 1685 and 1703 (as she mentions only one date in the course of her journeys, their times have to be deduced from internal evidence), Celia Fiennes did not make her literary début before 1812. In that year Southey published a miscellany in which he included two anonymous extracts 'from the manuscript journal of a lady'. It was not until 1888 that a descendant of the author came into possession of that small octavo volume, and published it under the title of *Through England on a Side Saddle in the time of William and Mary*.

Little is known biographically about Celia Fiennes. She was born in 1662 in her father's manor house at Newton Toney, near Salisbury, and died in London in 1741. She came of strongly Puritan stock. Her paternal grandfather, the first Viscount Saye and Sele, had been one of the bitterest and most powerful parliamentary opponents of Charles I's government, and a leading influence in pre-cipitating the Civil War (he had, declared Clarendon, the 'deepest hande in the originall contrivance of all the calami-tyes which befel that unhappy kingdome'). His son was a member of the Council of State and Keeper of the Great Seal under Cromwell. This background explains Celia Fiennes's frequent references to the number of Dissenters in the towns she visited, as well as the occasional scathing or complacent comment on the delusions and 'ignorant blind zeale' of Papists, 'to be pity'd by us that have the advantage of knowing better'.

During the course of her travels Celia Fiennes endured many vicissitudes with little feminine fuss and survived them without apparent harm. Sometimes, on her expeditions in all weathers, 'haile and raine . . . drove fiercely on me but the wind soone dry'd my dust coate', and at others she was soaked to the skin. Her physical stamina and resilience clearly equalled the toughness of nerve which will later be observed. Thus it is amusing to learn from her Foreword to the *Journeys* that they were initially undertaken for the sake of her health. Seriously as she regarded the ritual of visiting the spas to take the waters, this could have been with her little more than the fashionable hypochondria. Far more pro-bably was it the excuse of an unconventional spirit, in an age when the English gentlewoman was still so restricted in mobility, to satisfy a restless itch for action and her lively impulses of curiosity in everything going on around her. In this Celia Fiennes was completely a child of her time. With Pepys and Evelyn she shared the eager enquiry of the seventeenth-century mind: both its taste for 'wonders' and its appetite for collecting facts and their meticulous docu-mentation. These she set down, so she affirmed, for the bene-fit of her relatives or anyone who might question her about her travels. Although she disclaimed any intention of publishing her journal, various remarks addressed to her readers—especially in the Foreword she wrote for the volume—suggest that she probably had a wider public in view. The keeping and publication of diaries and travel journals were then becoming increasingly fashionable.

This was an era when topographers, antiquaries and men like Thomas Fuller, with his portraits of native 'worthies', were going more and more in search of England rather than the hitherto modish novelties of foreign parts. Celia Fiennes likewise stresses the 'improving' aspects of staying at home to explore appreciatively the beauties and achievements of one's own country. Such activity, she briskly informs her readers, would be 'a souveraign remedy to cure or preserve from these epidemick diseases of vapours, should I add Laziness?' Certainly that is the last vice of which *she* could have been accused. Indefatigable in pursuit of the England of her day, and avid for fact and detail, she succeeds in creating a picture which G. M. Trevelyan regarded as 'a valuable source of economic and social history, in the same class as Defoe's Tour of a few years later'; and, one might add, as Cobbett's still later *Rural Rides*.

Like Evelyn, Celia Fiennes appears to have made detailed notes at the time of her travels, but not to have written them up until some time afterwards. A number of allusions suggest that her main account was set down about 1702, when she was recording her impressions of London. The first thing that strikes any present-day reader of her *Journeys* —the earliest in the south, the northern journey and tour of Kent in 1697, and her 'Great Journey to Newcastle and to Cornwall' in the following year—is this woman's extraordinary energy and initiative. Apart from a handful of servants, Celia Fiennes travelled mostly alone, and on horseback, along roads so bad that few wheeled vehicles could pass (in the Lake District there could be 'noe carriages but very narrow ones like little wheelbarrows'). Their stony steepness in many districts made 'the strange horses slip and uneasye to go' and have constantly to be re-shod, and most were impassable after the winter rains. In the fen country

Celia's horse nearly fell into a deep dyke beside the flooded causeway, and was often 'quite down on his nose' on the rain-logged clay of Cornwall or the slippery chalk of the Home Counties: once near Winchester his rider was 'shott off his neck upon the bank, but noe harm I bless God'. A mere nine miles of the precipitous Derbyshire ways needed six hours to negotiate, and on another occasion it took 'near 11 hours going but 25 mile'. Signposts were only just coming into use; and travellers losing their way received scant help from the natives, who—perhaps not surprisingly —knew 'scarce 3 mile from their home'. These were the conditions implicit in such a laconic statement as 'It was in all above 1551 miles and many of them long miles'. When the diarist records that 'This yeare makes about 1045 miles of which I did not go above a hundred in the Coach', her pride is entirely pardonable.

Execrable roads were not the only hazards of travel in those days. Sometimes Celia Fiennes stayed with relations or friends in the neighbourhood, or was fortunate in chance hospitality; but more often she braved the risks and discomforts of the local inns. These were noisy and 'sometymes . . . so crowded that three must lye in a bed', and frequently 'very dear to strangers that they can impose on'. Celia complains of a 'young giddy Landlady' near Carlisle, 'that could only dress fine and entertain the soldiers', who ran her up 'the largest reckoning for allmost nothing'. In Scotland she was smoked out of one of the primitive houses with no chimneys, and in Cornwall by the people's pet habit of an evening pipe round the fire, 'which was not delightfull to me when I went down to talke with my Landlady'. There was, however, still worse to be contended with than these things, 'dirty blanckets', or losing her nightclothes en route. In the muddy city of Ely a tired traveller found 'froggs and slow-worms and snailes in my roome'—an experience calculated to discourage many a more squeamish female from further excursions.

Celia Fiennes's nerves were indeed robust. Serenely

surveying the shipping on the Thames from Shooter's Hill, she casually observes that this 'is esteemed as a noted Robbing place'. Later, in Cheshire, she was actually waylaid and dogged by highwaymen: '2 fellows . . . truss'd up with great coates and as it were bundles about them which I believe was pistolls'. Happily her 'speciall providence', which was responsible for many another 'remarkable deliverance' and for which Celia repeatedly offered up pious thanks, decreed her escape once again. Cheerfully undismayed by these dangers and near-disasters, she continued her dauntless explorations: clambering over the rocks at Land's End 'as farre as safety permitted me'; scrambling underground, forced to 'stoop very low even upon [her] breast and creep in', through the caves of Derbyshire; and venturing recklessly into Scotland, then a country known to need a guide for physical protection (Macaulay recorded that no one went there without making his will), and among the 'barefoote . . . nasty sort of people' of Wales.

Looking alertly about her, Miss Fiennes was intensely 'contemporary' in her approvals and dislikes. She preferred 'new building of the new fashion, and sash windows'; the 'lofty and large' buildings and 'broad and handsome streets' of, for example, Nottingham ('the neatest town I have seen') or in the 'noble town' of Newcastle, to the 'old and indifferent' or 'old rambling ones' in places like Chester or the 'meane appearance' of York. For her, unashamedly a modern, the 'old fashion'd form . . . and mode' existed merely for that renovation ('capable of being made very fine') which was going on now all over England in a prosperous merchant society.

She had, too, what seems a somewhat unfeminine interest in the different trades and industries of the places she visited. Not content merely to catalogue these, she went whenever she could to watch the work in progress, and set down with painstaking exactitude details of manufacturing processes. We hear of glove-making in Derby and stocking-weaving in Nottingham, and the cloth trade of Colchester, Norwich and Leeds; of shipbuilding in the dockyards at Rochester; of the hopfields and cherry-orchards of Kent, the cultivation of liquorice in Pontefract, and cider-making in Somerset and Herefordshire. Fuller accounts are given of the manufacture of products, from salt in Cheshire to serge in Exeter; of the silk-weaving and paper-making activity at Canterbury, of the drainage system in the fens, and above all of mining —marble, copper, tin and lead, and coal (of which she favourably compares the price in the midlands with what she has to pay in London).

A housewifely thrift informs all Celia Fiennes's comments on the abundance, quality and price of food in the provinces. An assiduous visitor to the markets, she noted in Ripon, for example, the cheapness and excellence of beef, veal and lamb, and in Chesterfield bought herself two fat white pullets 'for 6 pence both'. At Beverley she

was offered a large Codfish for a shilling and good Pearch very cheape' we had Crabbs bigger than my two hands, pence apiece, which would have cost 6 pence if not a shilling in London, and they were very sweete.

Her appetite was as frank and healthy—if not perhaps so monumentally hearty—as Pepys's own. In Yorkshire she dined off 'a very large Salmon . . . very fresh and good and above 3 quarters of a yard long', and 'paid dear' in Colchester to gratify her weakness for oysters. At Woburn Abbey she enjoyed 'a great quantety of the Red Coralina goosberry', and writes with relish of the West Country tart she had in Cornwall, 'the most acceptable entertainment that could be made me'. On the rival merits of beer in different parts of the country she was a sternly exacting expert, constantly recording such verdicts as 'not too stale very clear good Beer well brew'd'. She was also partial to an 'exceeding good Clarret . . . the best and truest French wine I have dranck this seven year', such as materialized, somewhat unexpectedly, at one Scottish inn.

Ale and wine were not the only drinks upon which Celia

Fiennes pronounced with decision. Her journal is tersely authoritative about the quality of the waters available at the popular spas of England, from Bath ('very hot and tastes like the water that boyles eggs') to Buxton ('not so warme as milke from a cow'). Judicious in comment on the soil and mineral content of the springs, on which waters were 'a quick purger' or good for rheumatism, she seems to have known them all. She had, she said, 'dranke many years with great advantage' at Tunbridge Wells, and visited St. Mungo's Well in Yorkshire for '7 severall seasons and 7 tymes every season and would have gone in oftener could we have staid longer'. Her description of the ceremonial ritual of immersion at Bath is especially detailed, and at times unintentionally amusing; as in the prim propriety of the allusion to the ladies' bathing costumes, made so that 'your shape is not seen, it does not cling close'. Unconventional as she was in the masculine freedom of her wanderings, Celia Fiennes appears from time to time in a pose of ladylike rectitude through which her Puritan ancestry shines plain. On a visit to Burghley House she was shocked at 'the immodesty of the pictures, especially in my Lords appartment . . . all without Garments or very little'; while Hinchingbrooke, the seat of Pepys's cousin Lord Sandwich, was also guilty of a Venus 'fine . . . were it not too much uncloth'd'.

Looking at the landscape of her day, Celia Fiennes proves as informative as in describing the activities of her fellow-countrymen at work and leisure. Characteristically it is the practical aspects of the rural scene—enclosures, crops, soil fertility—rather than the picturesque which chiefly engage her attention. She noticed that in Oxfordshire, for example, the earth was 'rich red mould and deepe so as they are forced to plough their ground 2 or 3 tymes for wheate and cannot use wheeles to their ploughs'. Coming from Derbyshire into Staffordshire she saw 'quite a different Soyle, sand and gravell and some clay and very pretty sort of pebbles in the ground, some of a bright green like an emerald, others veined, some clear like christall'.

Her architectural observations are as detailed as her rural, and the many portraits in her journal of towns and cities at that time are interesting to compare with their present-day appearance. Of London in particular—its streets, parks and buildings, procedure in the courts of justice and Houses of Parliament, and ceremonial pomp of the Lord Mayor's Show and royal funerals and coronations in Westminster Abbey—she includes a close and faithful account. She is also an enthusiastically loquacious guide to the interiors of cathedrals and the homes of the aristocracy. Conscientious as any contemporary house-agent, she itemizes the carved ceilings, furniture, tapestries, paintings, and costly curiosities, with a sharp feminine eye for the colour, texture and embroidery of materials, as in her description of the sumptuous hangings in the State Rooms at Windsor Castle. Then she conducts her reader out into the ornamental gardens to admire their arbours, groves and grottoes, statues and fountains. Amid all this—it must be admitted, rather exhausting—volubility, we are from time to time disarmed by some small touch which reveals the diarist herself as clearly as the sight she records. She is full of naïve wonder at the fountain-figures at Wilton House 'that can weep water on the beholders', and at the water which 'makes the melody of Nightingerlls and all sorts of birds'. Visiting Chatsworth, she marvels at the brass willow-tree which 'raines from each leafe and from the branches like a shower', and at the Earl of Chesterfield's house is enchanted by the water-clock which plays 'Lilibolaro on the Chymes'.

It is this artless freshness of response which is perhaps the most engaging feature of the *Journeys* of Celia Fiennes. She was, like Pepys, eager as a child for the novel and curious, and to try everything for herself. In the printing room of the Sheldonian Theatre at Oxford 'I printed my name severall tymes', and visiting York Minster she saw them at work in the mint there 'and stamp'd one halfe crown my self'. The great bell in Lincoln Cathedral was 'rarely ever rung but only by ringing the Clapper to each side—which we did'.

She went aboard a 'man of warre' at Hull, and on ' a pretty turbulent Sea . . . in a little boate' in Scarborough Harbour. After watching a man spinning glass in Nottingham 'I spunn some of the glass and saw him make a Swan presently'. Unafraid of being the compleat tourist, she bore home 'for Curiosity sake' many trophies of her travels: a fragment of moss turned by a Yorkshire spring into 'crisp'd and perfect stone'; a piece 'as long as halfe my finger' of the stone 'clear as Christal which is called Cornish Diamonds'; Derbyshire marble, ore from the nearby tin and lead mines 'which looks full of silver its so bright', and copper given her by the manager of a Staffordshire mine.

Mines and caves seem to have held a special fascination for Celia Fiennes. She gives long and vividly visual impressions of Wookey Hole in Somerset and of the Derbyshire caves which were among the 'Wonders of the Peak': of stalactites and stalagmites worn into grotesque similitudes from a crowned lion to a cathedral organ, a salted flitch of bacon to a chair of state 'all glistring like diamonds or starrs'. Inevitably she 'had some broken off, which looks like the insides of oystershells or mother of pearle, some looks like alabaster'.

Modestly in her Foreword the diarist excuses 'the freedom and easyness I speak and write [with] as well as my deffect in all', hoping that her readers 'will not expect exactness or politeness in this book, tho' such embellishments might have adorned the descriptions and suited the nicer taste'. Certainly she tends to prattle on about all she sees and does so with a fine disregard for spelling and punctuation and a tumbling breathlessness reminiscent, as one critic has remarked, of Jane Austen's Miss Bates. Yet this in itself is part of her appeal, communicating far better than any more polished narrative the eagerness of her exploration. Sometimes her resources of vocabulary—its approbatory adjectives seldom extending beyond the oft-repeated 'neate', 'fine', or 'genteele'—seem pitifully limited. Then suddenly some flat, informative passage will be redeemed by an image arresting in its aptness.

There is Salisbury spire, 'sharpe as a Dagger yet is in the compass on the top as bigg as a carte wheele'; or the country church in Kent 'all built with flints headed so curiously that it looks like glass and shines with the suns reflection'. Derbyshire is 'a world of peaked hills which from some of the highest you discover the rest like steeples'. In the flooded fens the swans 'on little hillocks of earth in the wett ground ...look as if swimming with their nests'; while the River Trent

rann and turn'd its silver streame forward and backward into Ss which looked very pleasant circleing about the fine meadows in their flourishing tyme, bedecked with hay almost ripe and flowers.

Such glimpses do much to enliven a prose pre-eminently practical in its depiction of the seventeenth-century landscape with figures, from the great embellishing their stately homes, and the prosperous bourgeoisie in the modish pursuit of health, down to the poor meagrely scraping an existence in their 'sad little hutts . . . and hovels . . . like barnes'. The vigorous directness of her style in describing people and places is well illustrated by Celia Fiennes's somewhat caustic impressions of life in the Border Country:

All here about which are called Borderers seem to be very poor people which I impute to their sloth; Scotland this part of it is a low marshy ground where they cutt turff and peate for the fewell [fuel], tho' I should apprehend the sea might convey coales to them; I see little that they are employ'd besides fishing which makes provision plentiful, or else their cutting and carving turff and peate which the women and great girles bare legg'd does lead a horse which draws a sort of carriage the wheeles like a dung-pott and hold about 4 wheele barrows; these people tho' with naked leggs are yet wrapp'd up in plodds [plaids] a piece of woollen like a blanket or else rideing hoods, and this when they are in their houses; I tooke them for people which were sick seeing 2 or 3 great wenches as tall and bigg as any women sat hovering between their bed and chimney corner all idle doing nothing, or at least was not settled to any work, tho' it was nine of the clock when I came thither, haveing gone 7 long miles that morning. . .

Then I went up to their Church which looks rather like some little house built of stone and bricke such as our ordinary people in a village

live in: the doores were open and the seates and pulpit was in so dis-
regarded a manner that one would have thought there was no use of it,
but there is a parson which lives just by whose house is the best in the
place and they are all fine folks in their Sundays cloathes.

In its own, very individual way, this indomitable
gentlewoman's record of her journeys forms a social picture
quite as absorbing as any drawn by her more famous
contemporaries.

III

DOROTHY WORDSWORTH

Visiting Hull in 1697, Celia Fiennes wrote that 'the
buildings . . . are very neate, good streets, its a good tradeing
town'. Dorothy Wordsworth, surveying it over a century
later, found it 'a frightful, dirty, *brick-housey*, tradesmanlike,
rich, vulgar place'. Their respective reactions illustrate the
most important difference between the attitudes of these two
women diarists. While Celia Fiennes invariably admired all
signs of thriving trade and artificial 'improvements' on
nature, Dorothy Wordsworth was 'pained' to see—as at
Windermere—'the pleasantest of earthly spots deformed by
man'. She could enjoy a landscape only when she could
'juggle away the fine houses', and observed with satisfaction:
'Happily we cannot shape the huge hills, or carve out the
valleys according to our fancy.' A true 'Child of Nature', as
Wordsworth called her, Dorothy was, like him, attuned to
its moods with a contemplative, even mystical raptness.
Often the trees would seem to her 'more bright than earthly
trees', and 'Earth and sky . . . so lovely that they . . . made
my heart almost feel like a vision to me'.

Possibly no major English poet ever owed more, both as a
writer and a man, to any woman than did Wordsworth to
his sister Dorothy. She was born in 1771, eighteen months
after him, in Cockermouth in Cumberland. The early loss

of their parents split up the young family, and Dorothy was separated from her three brothers and brought up by different relatives. But she and William, with whom she was closest in affinity and affection, had long planned to live together; and in 1795 their cherished dream was realized —first in Dorset, then in the Quantock Hills in Somerset, and finally, for many years, in the Lake District. In later life a housebound invalid, Dorothy died in 1855, outliving Wordsworth by five years.

It was at Alfoxden, in Somerset, where their friend Coleridge was their neighbour, that Dorothy began in 1798 to write those journals which ministered so richly to her brother's creative activity. Her main purpose in chronicling the small events of their daily life together was, she said, to 'give William pleasure by it'. How much he did in fact draw upon her diary jottings may be seen from a close comparison of many poems of his with passages from Dorothy's prose. One May day in 1800, for example, she records how

a very tall woman, tall much beyond the measure of tall women, called at the door. She had on a very long brown cloak and a very white cap, without Bonnet; her face was excessively brown . . . She led a little bare-footed child about 2 years old by the hand, and said her husband, who was a tinker, was gone before with the other children. I gave her a piece of Bread. Afterwards on my road to Ambleside . . . I saw two boys before me, one about 10, the other about 8 years old, at play chasing a butterfly. They were wild figures, not very ragged, but without shoes and stockings; the hat of the elder was wreathed round with yellow flowers, the younger whose hat was only a rimless crown, had stuck it round with laurel leaves. They continued at play till I drew very near, and then they addressed me with the Beggars' cant and the whining voice of sorrow. I said 'I served your mother this morning'. (The Boys were so like the woman who had called at the door that I could not be mistaken.) 'O!' says the elder, 'you could not serve my mother for she's dead.'. . . I persisted in my assertion, and that I would give them nothing. Says the elder, 'Come, let's away', and away they flew like lightning.

As Wordsworth was elsewhere at the time, it was not his

own recollection of the episode but Dorothy's Journal version which furnished, two years later, the material for his poem 'Beggars':

> She had a tall Man's height, or more;
> No bonnet screen'd her from the heat;
> A long drab-colour'd Cloak she wore,
> A Mantle reaching to her feet:
> What other dress she had I could not know;
> Only she wore a Cap that was as white as snow.

>   .   .   .   .   .

> I left her, and pursued my way;
> And soon before me did espy
> A pair of little Boys at play,
> Chasing a crimson butterfly;
> The Taller follow'd with his hat in hand,
> Wreath'd round with yellow flow'rs, the gayest of the land.

> The Other wore a rimless crown,
> With leaves of laurel stuck about:
> And they both follow'd up and down,
> Each whooping with a merry shout;
> Two Brothers seem'd they, eight and ten years old
> And like that Woman's face as gold is like to gold.

> They bolted on me thus, and lo!
> Each ready with a plaintive whine;
> Said I, 'Not half an hour ago
> Your Mother has had alms of mine.'
> 'That cannot be', one answer'd—'She is dead.'
> 'Nay but I gave her pence, and she will buy you bread.'

> 'She has been dead, Sir, many a day.'
> 'Sweet Boys, you're telling me a lie;
> 'It was your Mother, as I say—'
> And in the twinkling of an eye,
> 'Come come!' cried one; and, without more ado,
> Off to some other play they both together flew.

Again, Dorothy describes a lakeside walk on 15 April, 1802:

When we were in the woods beyond Gowbarrow park we saw a few daffodils close to the water-side . . . as we went along there were more and yet more; and at last, under the boughs of the trees, we saw that there was a long belt of them along the shore, about the breadth of a country turn-pike road. I never saw daffodils so beautiful. They grew among the mossy stones about and about them; some rested their heads upon these stones as on a pillow for weariness; and the rest tossed and reeled and danced, and seemed as if they verily laughed with the wind, that blew upon them over the lake; they looked so gay, ever glancing, ever changing.

The lyrical simplicity of that passage, which Wordsworth asked its writer to read out to him to revive his memory of the incident, makes an impact as immediate as the poem he then wrote, 'I wandered lonely as a Cloud'. Constantly the notes in the sister's journal fed the brother's genius: her description of the old leech-gatherer whom he portrayed in 'Resolution and Independence'; of the child Alice Fell crying for her torn cloak 'as if her heart would burst' (William uses Dorothy's phrase in his poem); or of the view from Westminster Bridge seen one summer morning on their way through London to France. Coleridge, too, owed much to Dorothy Wordsworth's observing eye. A number of the images in 'Christabel' directly echo what she had noted in her journal. In March 1798 she recorded:

One only leaf upon the top of a tree—the sole remaining leaf—danced round and round like a rag blown by the wind;

which became, in Coleridge's poem,

> The one red leaf, the last of its clan,
> That dances as often as dance it can,
> Hanging so light, and hanging so high,
> On the topmost twig that looks up at the sky.

Dorothy undoubtedly did 'please William' by her activity as a diarist. Moreover she left posterity a rare portrait of the home life of a poet, and of an intimate and moving fraternal relationship. Wordsworth would have been, quite simply, lost without the loyal devotion of this 'dear Companion' which he celebrates in various poems. Dorothy acted both as amanuensis and attentive listener to his latest work, as she sat at home mending stockings, or out of doors on their wanderings. Through her solicitous eyes we see Wordsworth agonizing in the throes of unsuccessful composition until she too is 'oppressed and sick at heart'. Because she participated in his creative struggles with such generous, ungrudging self-identification, he tapped her energy as relentlessly as his own ('William wore himself and me out with labour' . . . 'We walked backwards and forwards . . . till I was tired. William kindled, and began to write the poem . . . I was tired to death'). There are amusing glimpses of the absent-mindedness of poetic absorption: lost gloves on a walk and a jacket left behind on a bank, or an unexpected visitation by the muse at breakfast:

With his Basin of Broth before him untouched, and a little plate of Bread and butter he wrote the Poem to a Butterfly! He ate not a morsel, nor put on his stockings, but sate with his shirt neck unbuttoned, and his waistcoat open while he did it.   *14 March, 1802*

To Dorothy Wordsworth, who never married (a number of references in her journal strongly suggest that she may have been in love with Coleridge), her brother was the object of all the affection her ardent nature might have lavished on a husband and children. Maternally concerned for his health, she recorded every small indisposition, petted and read him to sleep when he was tired or despondent, and would lie awake cold all night 'for fear of waking William' by fetching herself extra bedclothes. His occasional short absences were invariably spent in longing for letters and listening for the return of her 'Beloved':

I *will* be busy [she resolves], I *will* look well, and be well when he comes back to me. O the Darling! Here is one of his bitten apples. I can hardly find it in my heart to throw it into the fire . . . I was full of thoughts about my darling . . . Blessings on that Brother of mine!

4-5 March, 1802

Many are the glimpses of their blissful domestic harmony:

We sate in deep silence at the window—I on a chair and William with his hand on my shoulder. We were deep in Silence and Love, a blessed hour.   *2 June, 1802*

Riding in a shower on the outside of a coach, they

buttoned ourselves up both together in the Guard's coat, and we liked the hills and the Rain the better for bringing us so close to one another—I never rode more snugly.   *8 July, 1802*

Whatever her private and sorrowing sense of having been supplanted in her brother's affection, it was typical of Dorothy that she should have given so generous a welcome to her new 'Sister', as she called Mary Hutchinson on the day of her marriage to Wordsworth in October 1802. Once, looking ahead to the future, Dorothy wrote: 'I shall be beloved—I want no more.' And indeed that—the need to give and receive love—was the mainspring of her existence. Her passionate protectiveness encircled the unlucky Coleridge, whose 'sad melancholy' or 'heartrending' letters she awaited with such a mingling of hope and trepidation, agonizing and losing sleep over the financial and marital troubles that plagued him, the failing health and constitutional melancholy which so constantly hampered his endeavours:

Every sight and every sound reminded me of him—dear, dear fellow of his many walks to us by day and by night, of all dear things. I was melancholy, and could not talk, but at last I eased my heart by weeping —nervous blubbering, says William. It is not so. O! how many, many reasons have I to be anxious for him.   *10 November, 1801*

Its writer's gentleness and warmth of heart are everywhere in evidence in her journals. She weeps 'very much' at the funeral of a poor, unknown woman, and compassionately contemplates the hard, uncomplaining labour of the postman ('our patient bow-bent Friend, with his little wooden box at his Back'), or the lot of others less fortunate than themselves as beggars come in a steady stream to their door. Her grief at the fall of a swallows' nest in the garden ('Poor little creatures, they could not themselves be more distressed than I was') is characteristic of the woman who, as a child, used to chase butterflies but did not catch them because she 'was afraid of brushing the dust off their wings'.

In his 1897 edition of Dorothy Wordsworth's Journals William Knight remarks that they 'contain numerous trivial details . . . but there is no need to record all the cases in which the sister wrote "To-day I mended William's shirts", or "William gathered sticks", or "I went in search of eggs", etc.' Quoting this editorial comment in *her* journal, Katherine Mansfield adds the tart retort: 'There is! Fool!!' Her impatience is understandable; for it is through these very simplicities that we catch the authentic feel and flavour of life in the Wordsworth *ménage*. Her many glimpses of herself as housekeeper show Dorothy so full of domestic activity that it is small wonder how often she has to record being 'tired with making beds, cooking, etc.', or 'so weary I could not walk'. In addition to making 'a nice piece of cookery for William's supper' and all his other meals—baking bread, tarts and pies, preserving fruit—she did all the household washing, ironing and mending; sometimes, for diversion, making dresses for one of Coleridge's children, a mattress, or shoes for herself. 'It is natural to me', she confessed, 'to do everything as quick as I can, and at the same time.' Busily she whitewashed ceilings and swept chimneys, helped William put a new window in the cottage and papered his room in his absence. Dorothy was also a keen gardener. We see her in the kitchen-garden putting in kidney-beans and spinach, transplanting radishes and sticking peas; planting foxgloves and honeysuckle round the yew, and gathering roots of wild thyme, columbine and orchis on their walks. A doughty walker, complimented on it by local people, she sometimes found that her companions 'walked too slow for me'. Her journals abound in descriptions of wanderings with William in all weathers (which gave her the 'Gipsy Tan' remarked by De Quincey): gathering mosses in the woods, visiting the baker, blacksmith and shoemaker, waylaying the postman for letters, or paying a social call on neighbours to drink tea. Sometimes they went sailing and fishing on the lake, at others sat quietly at home reading. Dorothy was constantly absorbed in the plays of Shakespeare as well as in Chaucer and the old ballads, and read with pleasure Ben Jonson, Spenser and Milton, and Fielding.

An entry for 17 March, 1802, records the brother and sister walking in the orchard before dinner: 'He read me his poem. I broiled Beefsteaks.' One of the chief joys of Dorothy's journals is this engaging blend of prosaic with poetic: details of the domestic trivia which occupied so much of her time faithfully chronicled in the same breath as the poetry which pervaded both their lives, quickening her responses to the changing moods and seasons of the earth around her. The 'many exquisite feelings' which she owns in the presence of natural beauty indeed 'made [her] more than half a poet'. If she was unable to translate these perceptions into rhyme and metre, Dorothy nevertheless possessed a poet's sensibility and the power to express it in her prose. 'Watchful in minutest observation of nature', as Coleridge said of her, she could capture the essence of scene or atmosphere with the utmost delicacy and precision. From almost every page of her journal springs some felicity which—in one of her own most memorable phrases—'calls home the heart to quietness'. In winter the snow looks 'soft as a down cushion. A young Foxglove, like a star, in the centre.' After the dark days, 'the country seems more populous. It peoples itself in the sunbeams'. She sees 'Mount-ains dappled like a sky', or in moonlight 'white and bright, as if they were covered with hoar frost'; 'locks of wool still spangled with the dewdrops . . . the sheep glittering in the

sunshine . . . the waving of the spiders' threads'; and on a
March morning,

> The shapes of the mist, slowly moving along, exquisitely beautiful;
> passing over the sheep they almost seemed to have more of life than those
> quiet creatures. The unseen birds singing in the mist.   *1 March, 1798*

No less alertly did she listen—to 'the half dead sound of the
near sheep-bell', to the 'sound of waters . . . the voice of the
air', to 'the hum of insects, that noiseless noise which lives
in the summer air'. And with what telling economy does
she evoke the stirrings of a summer-like February morning:

> The young lasses seen on the hill-tops, in the villages and roads, in
> their summer holiday clothes—pink petticoats and blue. Mothers with
> their children in arms, and the little ones that could just walk, tottering
> by their side. Midges or small flies spinning in the sunshine; the songs
> of the lark and redbreast; daisies upon the turf; the hazels in blossom;
> honeysuckles budding. I saw one solitary strawberry flower under a
> hedge. The furze gay with blossom.   *4 February, 1798*

Dorothy Wordsworth's ear was as sensitive to the sounds
of words as to those of nature. The cadences of her prose
have an ease and naturalness 'as inevitable in its movement',
said Helen Darbishire, 'as a mountain stream, its language as
transparently clear'. Some of her most striking images occur
in describing the effects of light and wind on water: on the
sea in Somerset, or on her beloved lakes. Over Grasmere by
night the moon shines 'like herrings in the water', and by day
the breezes, 'brushing along the surface of the water . . .
spread out like a peacock's tail'. Rydal Water at twilight has
'spear-shaped streaks of polished steel', and one winter day,
'a curious yellow reflection . . . as of corn fields'. Colour,
too, in all its subtleties, glows from these descriptions.
On a January day 'there was an unusual softness in the prospects as we went, a rich yellow upon the fields, and a soft
grave purple on the waters'. The diarist sees 'the springing
wheat like a shade of green over the brown earth', the 'lively
rough green' of a turnip field, a summer valley 'greener than
green'. In autumn 'the Fern of the mountains now spreads

yellow veins among the trees', and the distant birches resemble 'large golden Flowers'.

Of all the trees noticed in her Journal, Dorothy's favourite was the birch—and one in particular, growing down by the lake: in May 'all over green in *small* leaf, more light and elegant than when it is full out'; in November,

> yielding to the gusty wind with all its tender twigs, the sun shone upon it, and it glanced in the wind like a flying sunshiny shower. It was a tree in shape, with stem and branches, but it was like a Spirit of water. The sun went in, and it resumed its purplish appearance.

Flowers are observed with the same attentive accuracy: the January snowdrops in her Somerset garden, the roadside speedwell 'the colour of the blue-stone or glass used in jewellery'; columbine growing among the rocks ('a graceful slender creature, a female seeking retirement'), the wild strawberry which she 'uprooted rashly' but 'felt as if I had committed an outrage, so I planted it again', and the early primroses she was tempted but forebore to pick and left 'to live out their day'.

That is typical of the tenderness Dorothy Wordsworth shows towards all living things that inhabit the landscape she loves: from the lambs with 'thick legs, large heads, black staring eyes', which run 'races together by the half-dozen, in the round field near us', to the birds whose songs and habits she so delightfully describes. She rejoices in 'the slender notes of a redbreast', and the voice of their 'own dear thrush . . . shouting with an impatient shout' before cockcrow in the orchard. Swallows building in her garden hang against the window-panes 'with their white Bellies and their forked tails, looking like fish . . . They swim round and round and again they come'. There is an enchanting glimpse of 'the little birds busy making love, and pecking the blossoms and bits of moss off the trees'; and of how 'young Bullfinches, in their party-coloured Raiment, bustle about among the Blossoms, and poize themselves like Wire-dancers or tumblers, shaking the twigs and dashing

off the Blossoms'. On their walks she observes the play of
stonechats, a heron swimming; a bird circling the crags
which 'looked in thinness and transparency, shape and
motion like a moth', and crows becoming 'white as silver
as they flew in the sunshine, and when they went still further,
they looked like shapes of water passing over the green fields'.
The raven she heard call so that 'the Dome of the sky seemed
to echo . . . and the mountains gave back the sound, seeming
as if from their center; a musical bell-like answering to the
bird's hoarse voice', appears in Book IV of 'The Excursion'
(ll.1178-87):

> One voice—the solitary raven, flying
> Athwart the concave of the dark blue dome,
> Unseen, perchance above all power of sight—
> An iron knell! with echoes from afar
> Faint—and still fainter—as the cry, with which
> The wanderer accompanies her flight
> Through the calm region, fades upon the ear,
> Diminishing by distance till it seemed
> To expire; yet from the abyss is caught again,
> And yet again recovered!

Essentially Dorothy Wordsworth was a solitary ('I want
not society', she said, 'by a moonlight lake'). Nevertheless
she took a keen delight in her fellow-beings: 'interesting
groups of human creatures, the young frisking and dancing
in the sun, the elder quietly drinking in the life and soul of
the sun and air.' Her many thumb-nail portraits of people
show an almost Chaucerian relish for the detail of appearance—for a beard 'like grey plush' or a 'coat of scarlet in a
thousand patches'. She enjoys the vitality of a young girl
driving a cow or of lads dancing round a bonfire ('a sight
I dearly love') as much as that of the drunken soldiers 'very
merry and very civil' who 'fought with the mountains
with their sticks'. Such humours are savoured with quiet
amusement—the woman who was 'an affecting picture of
patient disappointment, suffering under no particular

affliction', or the inquisitive landlady at an inn trying in vain
to ferret his business out of a secretive traveller. Best and most
detailed of all are Dorothy's pictures of pedlars and beggars,
that motley crew of derelict humanity met on the roads and
at her door asking for money or bread. Pitying, yet with a
shrewdly noticing eye, she shows us the solitary women
with their tales of woe, the hungry, ragged children turned
out of doors; and the ex-soldier and -sailor casualties of the
Napoleonic wars, like the old man described in her entry
for 22 December, 1801, who after fifty-seven years at sea
was pensionless and destitute.

Dorothy Wordsworth kept journals other than those
chronicling her life with William in Somerset and at
Grasmere. Later in the year (1803) that the Grasmere
Journal ends, she set down her impressions of a six-week
tour with William and Coleridge in Scotland. The country's
wildness afforded ample scope for her descriptive powers,
and its inhabitants she found mostly as friendly ('everyone
had a smile for us') as to Celia Fiennes they had seemed
churlish, dirty and lazy. And there is an account of a continental tour made seventeen years later with William and
his wife Mary, in which an older diarist surveys foreign
wonders with an eye as fresh and eager as for the earlier
sights of home. But it is to the Alfoxden and the Grasmere
Journals that we go in search of the essential Dorothy, and
find best embodied the quality of 'Wordsworth's exquisite
sister', as Coleridge called her. William himself warmly
acknowledged his debt to this 'dearest Friend' in two of his
greatest poems, 'Tintern Abbey' and 'The Prelude':

> She, in the midst of all, preserved me still
> A Poet, made me seek beneath that name,
> And that alone, my office upon earth.
>
> ('The Prelude', Book XI)

No higher tribute could have been paid to the intuitive
sympathy and selfless love of one who, subordinating her

literary gifts to her brother's genius, still remains a word-artist in her own right.

IV

KATHERINE MANSFIELD

Twice in her Journal Katherine Mansfield appreciatively quotes Dorothy Wordsworth (although in the first instance gently mocking, in a verse parody, her worship of William). Dorothy's 'calm, irresistible well-being—almost mystic in character', and her 'thoughts that are fed by the sun', strongly appeal to one as sensitive in her response to nature—if far more apt to see it as a reflection of her own moods.

Katherine Mansfield is certainly the most self-conscious of the women diarists. From her Journal, spanning the years between 1904 to within a few months of her death of tuberculosis at the beginning of 1923, she planned to write up 'a kind of *minute notebook*, to be published some day'. It seems clear that she did not envisage the publication of the entries as we have them ('I don't mean that any eye but mine should read this', she wrote in July 1921, 'This is—*really private*'). The Journal is a random assortment of unposted letters to friends, and comments on or passages copied from her reading; of poems, glimpses of characters and settings or scraps of scene and dialogue, for her stories; fragmentary diaries of her doings, and introspective agonizings over her problems as a woman and as a writer.

Mainly, in fact, Katherine Mansfield used her 'huge, complaining diaries', as she called the earlier ones which she destroyed, both as a sounding-board for her creative ideas and a confessional for the unburdening of her doubts and difficulties. 'Nothing', she once admitted, 'affords me the same relief.' Thus her Journal is prodigal in self-revelation: of a woman passionate, petulant over grievances real or imagined, given much to self-pity and extravagant self-dramatization. Early on we see an eager hedonist, feverish in pursuit of experience at all costs: in love with the idea of love and inflating every casual encounter into an amorous conquest ('We exchanged a long look and his glance inflamed me like the scent of a gardenia'). Voluptuously the ardent apostle of freedom savoured her role of lonely rebel against parental authority and society alike, exulting in *'ma douleur'*, as she calls it. The oft-repeated plaint 'I am very unhappy', whatever her surroundings, from the prosperous philistinism of New Zealand to the bohemian poverty of England,[1] ceases in time to have much significance. It is a relief when occasionally the writer abandons her pose: as in that refreshingly ingenuous admission of the discrepancy between how she would like to appear in society —'slightly condescending, very much *du grand monde* . . . the centre of interest'—and the disconcerting shyness which makes her 'conscious of [her] hands, and slightly inclined to blush'. The hectic, querulous intensity of the adolescent, hungry 'to find the limit of [her]self', remained with Katherine Mansfield all her life, exacerbated by the growth of her disease. Perpetually and perversely, too, she craved to be where she was not: in London ('the thunder of the traffic —the call of life') when in New Zealand or France; nostalgically yearning for her native countryside, for Paris, or the south of France when living in London. 'Oh, to be in New York!' is a characteristic cry, on her way to Bavaria. 'Hear me! I can't rest.'

Yet the reason why this diarist was 'so carried away *and* borne under' by her experience, for ever see-sawing between rapture and despair, was that very hyper-sensitivity to every impression which gave her so avid an appetite for living, and made her the kind of writer she was. The very first entry of the fifteen-year-old in her journal, for 1 January, 1904, celebrates 'What a wonderful and what a lovely world this

[1]For fuller details of Katherine Mansfield's life see 'Writers and their Work' No. 49: *Katherine Mansfield*, by Ian A. Gordon.

is! I thank God to-night that I *am*.' A quivering receptivity to the joy as well as the pain of existence informs all her later pages:

The sky is filled with the sun, and the sun is like music. The sky is full of music. Music comes streaming down these great beams . . . The shape of every flower is like a sound . . . Praise Him! Praise Him!

Illness only intensified her sense of the richness and the miracle of living. Very near the end she was still consumed by desire for 'warm, eager, living life—to be rooted in life'.

But the interest of Katherine Mansfield's Journal lies less in its personal self-portrait than in the extraordinarily detailed and searching insights it affords into the creative process. Here is a brilliantly illuminating picture of the making of a writer and of her attitude towards her craft. Even that self-dramatizing element which is often, humanly speaking, so tiresome, is after all no more than an instinctive and essential part of every author. Compulsively impelled to probe his motives and take his emotional pulse at frequent intervals, in order to record the response, he is not only a participant in but a spectator of his own reactions in all circumstances. No experience is too trivial or ignominious to be put to good use. Of her lumbago Katherine Mansfield noted, 'I must remember it when I write about an old man', and of sciatica, 'What a pain it is. Remember to give it to someone in a story one day.' She would, she surmised, be 'so interested in the process' of her own death that she would 'lie there thinking: this is very valuable to know; I *must* make a note of this'. The occupational characteristic of the creative writer is also apparent in her habit of some-times—as in her account of nerving herself for a rebellious encounter with her father—slipping into the third person to scrutinize her feelings as if they belonged to some fictional heroine. It was only natural that any young woman who had decided that 'I must be an authoress' should also find that 'I am colossally interesting to myself'.

Her absorption in human nature was not, of course,

confined to the individual she knew best. Katherine Mansfield's Journal shows her endlessly fascinated by those small, everyday incidents, humorous, pathetic or bizarre, which constitute the writer's raw material and the springboard for his imagination. 'The amount of minute and delicate joy I get out of watching people and things when I am alone', she wrote, 'is simply enormous ... it's enormously valuable ... the detail of life, the *life* of life.' Everywhere she found it: in the theatre, where she jotted down scraps of inconsequential conversation among the audience; in cafés and restaurants—the gusto of a French family at table in Paris, a glimpse of a rabbity little woman crouched writing a letter ('the foxy waiter had his eye on her'); or in children at play in the Luxembourg Gardens. She amusedly depicts, in a few swift strokes, a middle-aged English couple on a continental train with their Dundee cake and thermos flask of tea; or gypsies seen on a London bus, with their quick, darting eyes, babies, and baskets of flowers. At home, she watched from her window the people down in the street —the lovers, gossiping charwomen, workmen eating their lunch, or the dumb charade of some humble private tragedy:

A little procession wending its way up the Gray's Inn Road. In front, a man between the shafts of a hand-barrow that creaks under the weight of a piano-organ and two bundles. The man is small and greenish brown, head lolling forward, face covered with sweat. The piano-organ is bright red, with a blue and gold 'dancing picture' on either side. The bundle is a woman. You see only a black mackintosh topped with a sailor hat; the little bundle she holds has chalkwhite legs and yellow boots dangling from the loose ends of the shawl. Followed by two small boys, who walk with short steps, staring intensely at the ground, as though afraid of stumbling over their feet.

No word is spoken; they never raise their eyes. And this silence and preoccupation gives to their progress a strange dignity.

They are like pilgrims straining forward to Nowhere ...

That is observed with beautiful precision and restraint. So, too, are her descriptions of nature, quickened by that minute observation and delicacy of touch which abound in

Dorothy Wordsworth. Even amid her early emotional extravagances, Katherine Mansfield seldom succumbed to the temptation of over-writing in her evocations of her native landscape:

Across the blue sea a boat is floating with an orange sail. Now the Maori fishermen are sailing in—their white sail bellying in the wind. On the beach a group of them—with blue jerseys, thick trousers rolled to their knees. The sun shines on their thick crisp hair, and shines on their faces so that their skins are the colour of hot amber. It shines on their bare legs, and firm brown arms. They are drawing in a little boat called *Te Kooti*, the wet rope running through their fingers and falling in a mystic pattern on the foam-blown sand.

There, and elsewhere, she succeeds most vividly in achieving her wish to 'make our undiscovered country leap into the eyes of the Old World'. For all her youthful revolt against the restrictions of New Zealand, its natural beauties bred in Katherine Mansfield that sensuous delight which was with her everywhere. We see it in her description of trees in the London squares in spring, 'with their butterfly leaves just ready to fly'; or of the Paris *quais* where 'white clouds lay upon the sky like sheets spread out to dry', and children sat 'stolid and content, their hair glistening in the sun'. An evening sky shines 'like the inside of a wet sea-shell', and September in Switzerland has 'always that taste of a berry rather than scent of a flower in the air'. Travelling south, she sketches the scene from the train:

Everywhere the light quivered green-gold. The white soft road unrolled, with plane-trees casting a trembling shade. There were piles of pumpkins and gourds: outside the house the tomatoes were spread in the sun. Blue flowers and red flowers and tufts of deep purple flared in the road-side hedges. A young boy, carrying a branch, stumbled across a yellow field, followed by a brown high-stepping little goat. We bought figs for breakfast, immense thin-skinned ones. They broke in one's fingers and tasted of wine and honey.

In the atmospheric exactitude of that, as in the best of her stories, Katherine Mansfield is a worthy disciple of her idolized master, Tchehov. Quotations from his stories and letters, more than from the work of any other writer, and invocations of his genius, recur throughout the pages of her Journal. 'I am the English Anton T.', she once claimed in a flippant quatrain, adding: 'God forgive me, Tchehov, for my impertinence.' This was the 'precious friend' who could make her laugh when she was depressed and ill; with whom she felt so close an affinity that she mourned: 'Tchehov! why are you dead? Why can't I talk to you . . .?' Katherine Mansfield's reading, as recorded in her comments on books and authors, ranged from Shakespeare and Dr. Johnson, Dickens and Dostoevsky, Coleridge and Keats's letters, to the French writer Colette and Joyce's *Ulysses*. It provides an interesting index not only to her literary tastes but to different phases in her emotional development. Those mutinous early pages, for example, are crammed with quotations from the hero of the moment who represented the polestar of her philosophy and determined all her youthful attitudes. Oscar Wilde was, she declared in October 1907, 'so absolutely the essence of *savoir faire*'.

Many of the passages describing people and scenes in Katherine Mansfield's Journal were intended as notes for projected work: ideas to be lived with and brooded over, polished and refined, until their emergence in the form now familiar to readers of her stories. It is interesting to identify here the genesis of a number of these in her own experience; to watch her transmuting fact into fiction, and to compare embryo idea or rough draft with the finished tale. The detailed recollections of their New Zealand childhood, which she began to set down after her beloved brother's death in the First World War, are recognizably work-notes for 'The Aloe' and 'At the Bay'. Sometimes an isolated passage is drafted, as for the story 'Second Violin', or a character, like the woman with 'pink roses in her belt and hollow lovely eyes and battered hair', who probably served as the original of Miss Moss in 'Pictures'. There are snippets of description for 'Je ne Parle Pas Français'—a story which enshrined

Katherine Mansfield's own feeling, frequently expressed in the Journal, of being alone and abandoned in a foreign country. The story 'An Indiscreet Journey' clearly grew out of the episode described in her entries for February 1915, when the author made a trip to Paris for a rendezvous with a former lover.

Katherine Mansfield's verdicts on her work were quite uncompromising. Her Journal reveals her as her own severest critic: 'not altogether pleased' with 'Mr. and Mrs. Dove'; feeling that in 'An Ideal Family' she 'didn't get the deepest truth out of the idea, even once'; and finding 'The Garden Party' only 'moderately successful', although better than 'At the Bay' ('flat, dull, and not a success at all'). Her ruthlessness about her failures to achieve her intention, and her shrewd awareness of such faults as 'a pretty bad habit of spreading myself at times—of over-writing and under-stating', made her repeatedly wish to destroy all 'false starts' and begin afresh. Single-minded in dedication to her art, she aspired not towards success or fame but to 'write better, more deeply, more *largely*'. In the relentless honesty of her self-criticism and self-communings about her difficulties and disappointments, Katherine Mansfield probes to the very heart of her chosen vocation as 'a *writer*, a real writer given up to it and to it alone'.

At the age of nineteen she had decided for authorship rather than a career as a musician; and she ought, she considered with the naïvely airy confidence of youth, to make a good author. 'I certainly have the ambition . . . the brain and also the inventive faculty. What else is needed?' She was soon to discover, through the long, exacting struggle for mastery of her medium which lasted until the time of her death. Passionate aspiration, she was forced before long to recognize, was far from synonymous with the power to realize it. 'I have a perfectly frantic desire to write something really fine', she grieved, 'and an inability to do so which is infinitely distressing' . . . 'In my head, I can think and act and write wonders—wonders; but the moment I really try to put them down I fail miserably' . . . 'I long and long to write, and the words just won't come.' No author ever communicated better the frustration of these barren patches:

If I could write with my old fluency for *one day*, the spell would be broken. It's the continual effort—the slow building-up of my idea and then, before my eyes and out of my power, its slow dissolving.

And this poses the delicate and perennial problem: 'Now who is to decide between "Let it be" and "Force it"?'

Another enemy to be wrestled with was that sloth known to every artist which makes him shrink from, and perpetually put off, the initial effort of creation. Again and again we find Katherine Mansfield owning guilt for her 'immense idleness—hateful and disgraceful', her procrastination and lack of will-power in 'invent[ing] excuses for not working', although instinctively knowing that 'once fairly alight— how I'd blaze and burn!' What was it, she complained, which made 'the moment of delivery so difficult' for her? Often the stories were sufficiently shaped in her mind to be ready 'to write themselves . . . And don't I want to write them? Lord! Lord! it's my only desire—my one *happy issue*.' Yet

there the work is, there the stories wait for me, *grow tired*, wilt, fade, because I will not come. And I hear and *acknowledge* them, and still I go on sitting at the window, playing with the ball of wool. What is to be done?

Part temperamental, part physical as illness tightened its grip on her, this lassitude seems to have been one of Katherine Mansfield's most formidable obstacles to achievement. The lament of 'not working as I should be working—wasting time', or simply 'Wasted! Wasted!' echoes with peculiar poignancy through the later pages of the Journal. Its writer felt 'pursued by time' because, like Keats, she was 'haunted every single day of [her] life by the nearness of death and its inevitability'; and by the fear accompanying that premonition, of being overtaken and silenced before she had said her say. 'How unbearable it would be to die—leave "scraps", "bits" . . . nothing real finished', she mourned. 'I really only ask for time to write it all. Then I don't mind dying. I live to write.' Unconsciously, no doubt, this echoed exactly the sentiment in Keats's sonnet 'When I have fears that I may cease to be'. Again Katherine Mansfield sounded a very Keatsian note when she declared:

All that I write—all that I am—is on the border of the sea. It's a kind of playing. I want to put *all* my force behind it, but somehow, I *cannot*!

Yet if the familiar agonies of the writer are here—from being plagued by mundane interruptions, on the one hand, to finding, on the other, 'the driving necessity' to write paradoxically mocked by the stubbornness of words and will to co-operate—then so, too, are the exaltations. There was no feeling, Katherine Mansfield affirmed, 'to be compared with the joy of having written and finished a story . . . There it was, *new* and complete'. This satisfaction of giving birth is matched, throughout her Journal, by an intensely religious sense of vocation. For her, as for Rilke, creative activity was analogous to prayer. Thus, when she had done no work, she found herself unable to pray: 'I was not in an active state of grace.' Her writing, she confessed, took 'the place of religion—it *is* my religion—of people—I create my people: of "life"—it *is* Life'.

No more than Keats or Rilke was this tormented and completely dedicated woman an orthodox Christian. Yet it was in a Christian invocation that she most memorably epitomized her life's aim and the patient humility of her endeavour:

Lord, make me crystal clear for thy light to shine through!

THREE WOMEN DIARISTS

A Select Bibliography

(Place of publication London, unless stated otherwise)

CELIA FIENNES

THROUGH ENGLAND ON A SIDE SADDLE IN THE TIME OF WILLIAM AND MARY, ed. E. Griffiths (1888)
—the first edition of her diaries (privately printed), incompletely and inaccurately transcribed by a descendant.

THE JOURNEYS OF CELIA FIENNES, ed. C. Morris (1947)
—a complete transcription of the text from the original manuscript in the possession of Lord Saye and Sele, with a very full and illuminating introduction and useful historical notes.

DOROTHY WORDSWORTH

Note: The Journals comprise the following separate works: The Alfoxden Journal (1798); the Journal of a Visit to Hamburgh and of A Journey from Hamburgh to Goslar (1798); the Grasmere Journal (1800-1803); Recollections of a Tour made in Scotland (1803); Journal of a Mountain Ramble by Dorothy and William Wordsworth (1805); Journal of a Tour on the Continent (1820); A Tour in Scotland (1822); a Tour in the Isle of Man (1828).

JOURNALS OF DOROTHY WORDSWORTH, ed. W. Knight, 2 vols. (1897)
—several subsequent reprints.

THE COMPLETE JOURNALS OF DOROTHY WORDSWORTH, ed. E. de Selincourt, 2 vols. (1941)
—the definitive edition, published from the original manuscripts. Reprinted in 1952.

JOURNALS OF DOROTHY WORDSWORTH, ed. H. Darbishire (1958)
—an edition of the Alfoxden and Grasmere Journals, by a leading Wordsworthian scholar, in the World's Classics series. Especially useful is the appendix of Wordsworth's shorter poems written during the period and referred to by his sister in the Journals.

KATHERINE MANSFIELD

For a Select Bibliography of KatherineMansfield's novels and stories, and of some critical and biographical studies of her, see KATHERINE MANSFIELD by I. A. Gordon (*Writers and Their Work*: No. 49).

THE JOURNAL OF KATHERINE MANSFIELD, ed. J. Middleton Murry (1927) —the definitive edition, which included additional material, was published in 1954.

LETTERS, ed. J. Middleton Murry, 2 vols. (1928).

THE SCRAPBOOK OF KATHERINE MANSFIELD, ed. J. Middleton Murry (1939).

LETTERS TO JOHN MIDDLETON MURRY, 1913-1922, ed. J. Middleton Murry (1951) —containing the full text of letters published only in extracts in the earlier edition.

SOME OTHER WOMEN DIARISTS

MARY, COUNTESS COWPER (1685-1724)

THE DIARY (1714-20), ed. S. Cowper (1864) —Court diary of a lady-in-waiting to the Princess of Wales.

ELIZABETH PERCY (1716-76)

DIARY ILLUSTRATIVE OF THE TIMES OF GEORGE IV: EXTRACTS FROM THE DIARIES OF THE FIRST DUCHESS OF NORTHUMBERLAND, ed. J. Greig (1926).

ELIZABETH BYROM (1722-1801)

THE JOURNAL, ed. R. Parkinson (1857) —diary of affairs during the Jacobite Rebellion, covering the months between August 1745 and January 1746. Included in the Chetham Society Publications XLIV.

FANNY BURNEY (1752-1840)

THE DIARY AND LETTERS, ed. C. F. Barrett, 7 vols. (1842-6) —published under the author's married name of Madame D'Arblay.
THE EARLY DIARIES OF FRANCES BURNEY, ed. E. R. Ellis, 2 vols. (1889).
THE DIARY AND LETTERS OF FRANCES BURNEY, ed. A. Dobson, 2 vols. (1904).

FANNY BURNEY'S DIARY, ed. J. Wain (1961)
—Folio Society edition which gives a selection from the diary and letters.

LADY MARY COKE (1756-1829)

LETTERS AND JOURNALS, ed. J. A. Home, 4 vols. Edinburgh (1889-96).

MRS LYBBE POWYS (1756-1808)

PASSAGES FROM THE DIARY OF MRS LYBBE POWYS, ed. E. J. Climenson (1898).

MARY BERRY (1763-1852)

EXTRACTS FROM THE JOURNALS AND CORRESPONDENCE OF MISS BERRY from 1783-1852, ed. Lady T. Lewis, 3 vols. (1865).

ELIZABETH, LADY HOLLAND (1770-1845)

JOURNAL, 1791-1811, ed. Earl of Ilchester, 2 vols. (1908).

MARY FRAMPTON (1773-1846)

JOURNAL, 1779-1846, ed. H. G. Mundy (1888).

LADY CHARLOTTE BURY (1775-1861)

THE DIARY OF A LADY IN WAITING, ed. A. F. Steuart, 2 vols. (1908).

ELLEN WEETON (1776-1850)

MISS WEETON: THE JOURNAL OF A GOVERNESS, ed. E. Hall, 2 vols. (1936, 1939)
—covering the years between October 1807 and June 1825.

ELIZABETH FRY (1780-1845)

MEMOIRS, with Extracts from her Journal and Letters. Edited by two of her daughters, 2 vols. (1847).

'GEORGE ELIOT' (1819-80)

GEORGE ELIOT'S LIFE AS RELATED IN HER LETTERS AND JOURNALS, ed. G. W. Cross, 3 vols. (1885).

CAROLINE FOX (1819-71)
—her diary, from March 1835-March 1867, contained in MEMORIES OF OLD FRIENDS, ed. H. N. Pym (1882).

MARGARET SHORE (1819-39)

JOURNAL (1891).

QUEEN VICTORIA (1819-1901)

LEAVES FROM THE JOURNAL OF OUR LIFE IN THE HIGHLANDS (1862).

MORE LEAVES (1883).

THE GIRLHOOD OF QUEEN VICTORIA, by Viscount Esher (1912)
—all these give extracts from the Queen's private diaries of her
domestic and public life between 1832 and 1882.

Bibliographical Series
of Supplements to 'British Book News'
on Writers and their Work

GENERAL EDITOR
Geoffrey Bullough

'Then I began to move into a marvellous dream'

LANGLAND:
PIERS PLOWMAN

by

NEVILL COGHILL

PUBLISHED FOR
THE BRITISH COUNCIL
AND THE NATIONAL BOOK LEAGUE
BY LONGMANS GREEN & CO.

LONGMANS, GREEN & CO. LTD.
48 Grosvenor Street, London, W.1

*Associated companies, branches and
respresentatives throughout the world*

First published 1964
© Nevill Coghill 1964

*Printed in Great Britain by
F. Mildner & Sons, London, E.C.1*

CONTENTS

Frontispiece.—The Valley Thick with Corn, a sepia drawing by Samuel Palmer, is reproduced by permission of the Ashmolean Museum.

Acknowledgements: Thanks are due to the following for permission to quote from copyright material: Chatto & Windus and Atheneum Publishers for material from *The Names and Faces of Heroes* by Reynolds Price, Faber & Faber for material from *Waiting for Godot* by Samuel Beckett, and Longmans, Green for material from *Radcliffe* by David Storey.

For
PRZEMYSŁAW MROCZKOWSKI

LANGLAND:
PIERS PLOWMAN

'The writer of short studies, having to condense in a few
pages the events of a whole lifetime, and the effect on his
own mind of many various volumes, is bound, above all
things, to make that condensation logical and striking . . .
It is from one side only that he has time to represent his
subject. The side selected will be either the one most
striking to himself, or the most obscured by controversy.'
                    Robert Louis Stevenson, *Men and Books.*

I

AUTHORSHIP AND DATE:
SUCH FACTS AS THERE ARE

PIERS Plowman, the greatest Christian poem in our language, comes to us from the second half of the fourteenth
century and is thought, though not unanimously, to be
the work of an unbeneficed cleric, probably in minor
orders, called William Langland. Nothing certain is known
about him; even his name comes doubtfully down to us
by a late tradition. All we know of his personal life is
what he tells us of it in the poem, and that is little enough
and open to doubt. In these uncertainties it is best to begin
by setting out such facts as there are, for they shed a light
helpful to criticism on the poem, on the man who wrote it
and on how it was written and received.

It has survived in fifty-one manuscripts of the fourteenth
and fifteenth century—a very large number, although
The Canterbury Tales tops it with eighty-three—and in one

early printed text; the poem is cast in the form of a series of dream-visions told in the first person, as if Dreamer and Poet were one, and no sensitive reader can escape some impression of his personality and genius, or fail to wonder at the spiritual range and intensity of a mind that can generate a ferociously satirical laughter, a compassion as humane as Lear's upon the heath, and a mystical sense of glory in God's love in the passion and resurrection of Christ. Here and there, among these greater effects, there are other touches, telling us something about the accidents, rather than the substance of his life, and to these touches can be added a few marginal comments with which later fifteenth-century hands have annotated one or two manuscripts, and the brief jottings, gathered by hearsay by Robert Crowley and set down in the early printed text I have mentioned, of which he was the editor, which first appeared in 1550; another version of the same information, more garbled than before, appears in the yet later catalogue of John Bale, *Scriptorum Illustrium Maioris Britanniae Catalogus* (1559).

Before we can consider the author and what is said of him, there is something further to be said of the texts, for they present a complication which bears directly on the author's methods and on the poem's date. The manuscripts fall into three clear classes, offering three distinct versions of the work; they are known as the A, B, and C Texts. Seventeen manuscripts support the first, fifteen and Crowley's text the second, and nineteen the third. A study of these three versions makes it abundantly clear that B is a revision of A, and C of B. It has been doubted whether all three were the work of one mind, and fifty years ago a number of scholars, led by J. M. Manly of Chicago University, persuaded themselves they had reason to believe that no less than five different poets had had a hand in it. But reason that could convince was never shown and critics have now ceased to saw the poet asunder.

The A and B Texts can be dated with some certainty, from references within the poem to contemporary events;

the A Text, for instance, refers unmistakably (A.V.14) to the famous storm that started to blow on the evening of Saturday, 15 January, 1362, which the chronicle-writers also record, and it follows that the first version of the poem was at least later than that. The B Text, which is three times as long as the A Text, describes, with baleful satire, the coronation of Richard II (B. Prologue, 112-209), an event which took place in 1377. The date of the C Text cannot be so clearly established, but Sister Mary Aquinas has shown that it has strongly influenced another work of the late fourteenth century, *The Testament of Love* by Thomas Usk; as he was put to death in 1388, it follows that the C Text must have largely been in being by then. The picture which emerges from these datings is one of a life-time's work-in-progress, seen in its three major stages; they bridge a period of five and twenty years. The poet may have continued to work on it until his death, no date for which is known. He seems not to have written anything else; he was a one-poem man.

When we attack the problem who and what he was, we have to push forward through quagmires of even deeper uncertainty, for the records are late and conflicting. In his own day the poem was famous enough; there is reason to think it had some of the effect of a rallying-cry on the insurgents in the Peasants' Revolt of 1381, for John Ball's famous letter to his followers seems to allude to it; I have italicized the relevant phrases; Ball calls himself Schep (a shepherd) to signify his leadership:

Iohon Schep, som tyme Seynte Marie prest of York, and now of Colchestre, greteth wel Iohan Nameles, and Iohan the Mullere, and Iohon Cartere, and biddeth hem that thei bee war of gyle in borugh [tell them to beware of guile in town] and stondeth togidre in Godes name, *and biddeth Peres Ploughman go to his werk*, and chastise wel Hobbe the Robbere, and taketh with yow Iohan Trewman and alle his felawes, and no mo, and loke schappe you to on heved, and no mo [see that you form together under one head, and no more].

Iohan the mullere hath ygrounde smal, smal, smal;
The Kynges sone of hevene schal paye for al.
Be war or ye be wo; knoweth your freend fro your foe;
Haveth ynow, and seith 'Hoo'!
And do wel and bettre, and fleth synne. . . .

[John the miller has ground fine, fine, fine;
The Son of the King of Heaven shall pay for all.
Beware before you are sorry; know your friend from your
    foe;
Have enough and say 'Ho'!
And do well and better, and flee from sin. . . .]

This would be enough to make a poet cautious in the use of his name and avoid blowing himself up with his own gunpowder; but in any case anonymity was then a common fate for poets; the author of *Sir Gawain and the Green Knight* is unknown, and even Chaucer, though careful to put himself by name into *The Canterbury Tales*, was only mentioned in the official records of his times because he was a trusted servant of the Court, whose work and wages had to be set down in the accounts. William Langland also put his name into his poem, but under the veils of allegory and anagram. There is an ambiguity in the name *William* when it is shortened to *Will*, especially in poems that are involved in moral issues, and even the name Langland or Longland (for they are the same) can be played with:

'I have lyved in *londe*', quod I, 'my name is *longe wille*'[1]
(B.XV.148)

['I have lived in the country', said I, 'my name is long Wil'.]

The Laud manuscript, now in the Bodleian, bears a scribal comment at this line, '*Nota, the name of th'auctour*'. The

[1] All quotations from the A Text are taken, with slight typographical modification, from the edition by G. Kane (1960). Quotations from the B and C Texts are taken, similarly modified, from the editions by W. W. Skeat (Early English Texts Society, 1869, 1873).

fullest scribal note, however, is to be found in a Trinity
College, Dublin, manuscript, in a late fifteenth century hand:

Memorandum quod Stacy de Rokayle pater Willielmi de Langlond,
qui Stacius fuit generosus, et morabatur in Schypton vnder Whicwode,
tenens domini le Spenser in comitatu Oxon., qui predictus Willielmus
fecit librum qui vocatur Perys ploughman.

[To be remembered that Stacy de Rokayle (was) the father of William
of Langlond, and this Stacy was a gentleman, and lived at Shipton-
under-Wychwood in the county of Oxford, a tenant of Lord Despenser,
and this aforesaid William made the book called Piers Plowman.]

This seems circumstantial; the Rokayles are known to
have been involved with the Despensers, who were Lords
of Malvern Chase; business might easily have brought
Stacy over from Shipton-under-Wychwood to Malvern.
It is odd that his son William should have taken the name
Langland if his father's name was de Rokayle, but in the
fourteenth and fifteenth centuries 'there is abundant precedent for younger sons not taking the father's name', as
R. W. Chambers reminds us; it is possible, too, that
William Langland was illegitimate, and that he took his
name from the place of his birth. This last possibility will be
further considered in a moment, but let us first turn to the
testimony of Robert Crowley and John Bale.

This was gathered a hundred and fifty years and more
after the poet's death, a long stretch for the linkages of
human memory; a man born in (say) 1380 might have had
personal knowledge of Langland and have lived on until
(say) 1460; another born in 1450 might have met him in his
last years and learnt from him of the author of Piers Plowman,
then a famous poem, and have passed the information on
in turn, to Robert Crowley in his own old age. I have myself
spoken to a lady who knew Charlotte Brontë's aunt, Miss
Prunty, and who clearly recalled that old lady's contempt
for the change of the family name from Prunty to Brontë,

which she regarded as foreign and finical. And that linkage covers a hundred and fifty years.

For whatever reason Langland changed *his* name, both Bale and Crowley assert him to have been called *Robert Langelande* and say he was a Shropshire man, born 'about eight miles from the Malvern Hills', at 'Cleybirie' says Crowley, at 'Mortymers Clibery' says Bale. Both these authorities, being valiants in the early days of Protestant propaganda, proclaim the poet to have been a champion of their new faith and a follower of Wycliffe: '*contra apertas Papistarum blasphemias adversus Deum*' trumpets Bale; one of those, declares Crowley, who were given the boldness of heart 'to open thir mouthes and crye out agaynste the workes of darckenes, as dyd John Wicklyfe'.

As Langland's poem shows him to have been one of the most orthodox catholics that ever took a sacrament, this opinion is clearly an error; but then all that they say is erroneous. The poet's name was not Robert but William; he never calls himself anything else, and the manuscript note already mentioned confirms this; what is more, the reason for this error is easily found in the line which opens the ninth passus of the A Text: 'Thus, yrobid in rosset, I rombide aboute' which means 'Thus robed in russet', not 'Thus I, Robert, in russet', as no doubt Crowley and Bale conjectured. One manuscript has been found which incorporates this error. Neither Cleobury nor Cleobury Mortimer is eight miles from the Malvern Hills, but something over twenty. These topographical discrepancies can however be reconciled with what appears to be the truth, if we suppose that *Cleobury* was an aural or scribal blunder for *Ledbury*, which is at the right distance from Malvern. This conjecture was first made by A. H. Bright in an exciting book on our subject, *New Light on Piers Plowman*, published in 1928. The Bright family had long lived near Ledbury; local knowledge was their speciality.

We learn from this book that in the parish of Colwall, not far from Ledbury, there lies a great flat meadow called

Longland; the name, says Bright, can be found to describe it in conveyances as far back as 1681. Anyone who takes the main road from Ledbury to Malvern will come upon it, immediately to the left of the road, just below the Duke of Wellington Inn and Chance's Pitch.

As Bright looked up from this field, he was able to see the Herefordshire Beacon towering above him; a little below and to one side, as his local knowledge told him, there lay the moat-like ditches belonging to a vanished Norman keep known as 'Old Castle'; from the Beacon ridge, there flowed several streams, the best of which was known as 'Primeswell'[1] and from this brook could be seen a fine stretch of fields between the site of Old Castle and the Herefordshire Beacon. One had only to go there, thought Bright, and stand by the Primeswell, to recognize instantly the whole landscape that unfolds into a magical allegory in the opening lines of *Piers Plowman*:

> In a somer sesoun whanne softe was the sonne
> I shop me into a shroud as I a shep were;
> In abite as an Ermyte, unholy of werkis,
> Wente wyde in this world, wondris to here.
> But on a May morwenyng on Malverne hilles
> Me befel a ferly, of fairie me thoughte;
> I was wery, forwandrit, and wente me to reste
> Undir a brood bank be a bourne side,
> And as I lay and lenide and lokide on the watris
> I slomeride into a slepyng, it swiyede so merye.
> Thanne gan I mete a merveillous swevene,
> That I was in a wildernesse, wiste I nevere where;
> Ac as I beheld into the Est, an heigh to the sonne,
> I saigh a tour on a toft triyely imakid;
> A dep dale benethe, a dungeoun therinne,
> With depe dikes and derke and dredful of sight.
> A fair feld ful of folk fand I there betwene

[1] Now no longer visible, having been piped to a table-water factory. Bright believed it to be the 'bourne' mentioned in line 8 of the quotation from the opening of the poem, above, beside which the poet lay down to sleep, and beheld his vision.

Of alle maner of men, the mene and the riche,
Worching and wandringe as the world askith.

                                    (A. Prologue.1-19)

[In a summer season when the sun was soft, I got myself into clothes to
look like a shepherd, in the habit of a hermit of unholy behaviour, I went
abroad in the world, to hear of wonders. But on a May morning, on the
Malvern Hills, a marvel befell me, it seemed from fairy-land; I was
weary, having wandered too far, and I went to rest myself under a
broad bank by the side of a brook, and as I lay and leaned and looked
into the waters, I slumbered into sleep, it rippled so merrily. And then I
began to dream a marvellous dream, that I was in a wilderness, I have
no idea where, but as I looked towards the east, high up to the sun, I saw
a tower on a hill-top, well and truly made; a deep dale beneath with a
dungeon in it, with deep ditches and dark ones, and dreadful to see.
A fair field full of folk I found between them, all manner of men, the
middling and the rich, working and wandering as the world asks.]

In the sight of these texts and of this topography it is not
unreasonable to believe, as many scholars now do, that *Piers
Plowman* was written by William Langland, born in the
parish of Colwall by the Malvern Hills, towards the end of
the first half of the fourteenth century. We can even refine
on this a little, for twice in the course of the B Text (B.XI.46
and B.XII.3) he hints in his allegorical way that he is five-
and-forty, and as the date of the B Text cannot be earlier
than 1377, Langland cannot have been born before 1332, if
his hints are to be trusted.

At what date he left the Malverns for London we cannot
know, but go to London he did to seek his fortune, for
he tells us so; the A Text is full of a knowledge of London
and its ways, so he had become a Londoner by the time he
was thirty at least. It is likely, indeed, that he went there
soon after finishing the education he may be presumed to
have had at Malvern Priory, for he had not the physique
for farm work, or so he tells us:

Ich am to waik to worche with sykel other with sythe,
And to long, leyf me, lowe for to stoupe,
To worchen as a workeman, eny while to dure.

(C.VI.23-5)

[I am too weak to work with sickle or with scythe
And too long in the back, believe me, to stoop low,
Or to last any length of time working as a workman.]

But if he could not work as a workman, he could work as a
cleric, for he had had a good education:

'Whanne ich yong was', quath ich, 'meny yer hennes,
My fader and my frendes founden me to scole,
Tyl ich wiste wyterliche what holy wryt menede,
And what is best for the body, as the bok telleth,
And sykerest for the soule . . .'

(C.VI.35-9)

['When I was young', said I, 'many years ago, my father and my friends
paid for my schooling until I assuredly knew what Holy Writ meant,
and what is best for the body, as the Book tells, and what surest for the
soul . . .']

Such a young man would naturally enter Holy Orders,
and that Langland did so is a reasonable certainty, not only
from the deeply-instructed religious cast of the poem, but
from what he tells us of how he earned a living:

The lomes that ich laboure with and lyflode deserve
Ys *pater-noster* and my prymer, *placebo* and *dirige*,
And my sauter som tyme and my sevene psalmes.
Thus ich synge for hure soules, of suche as me helpen
And tho that fynden me my fode vouchen saf, ich trowe,
To be welcome whanne ich come otherwhyle in a monthe. . .

(C.VI.45-50)

['The limbs I labour with and earn my living by are my paternoster and (elementary religious) primer, *Placebo* and *Dirige*, and my psalter sometimes and then my seven psalms. Thus I sing for the souls of such as help me, and those that find me my food are kind enough, I believe, to make me welcome when I come once or twice a month'. *Placebo* and *Dirige* are phrases from Psalms 114 and 5 in the Vulgate version and are used as antiphons in the Office for the Dead. The seven psalms in question are those called the Penitential Psalms, 6, 32, 38, 51, 102, 130, 143.]

As no one would pay a layman to do these offices, it follows that Langland must have taken holy orders of some kind; yet it is almost equally certain he cannot have been a priest, for he tells us he had a wife called Kitty and a daughter called Calotte (C.VI.2 and B.XVIII.426) and I see no reason to disbelieve him. We may conclude he was a *tonsuratus*, an acolyte, who liked wearing the long robe of his profession in which he describes himself, and who went round from patron to patron, praying for them and for their cherished dead, and perhaps (if I may conjecture) reading to them from his poem now and then.

It is a continual source of wonder to any lover of Langland how such a spirit, so learned, so religious, so orthodox and fervent a son of the Church, escaped, or avoided, full priesthood. Perhaps he knew himself to lack the gift, if it is a gift, of continence; for he tells how in his wild youth he gazed into the mirror of middle-earth that Fortune held out before him, telling him to make up his mind what thing he wanted among the wonders of the world, and to go out and grasp it (B.XI.8-10), and instantly in his dream there appeared 'two faire damoyseles', one called *Concupiscencia Carnis*, who 'colled him about the neck' [necked him round the neck], and the other, *Pryde-of-parfyte-lyvynge*; and these:

> badde me, for my contenaunce, acounte clergye lighte

['And bade me, in respect of continence, to take little notice of holy orders.' 'Clergy' means 'learning' but in this passage it refers to holy orders, for the learned were generally ordained. As learning, by itself, is no bar to incontinence, Langland must here be thinking of Ordination.]

and so (he allows us to think) he gave himself over to the flesh and to the lust of the eyes drawn on by 'Fauntelté' [Childishness]. 'Concupiscentia Carnis acorded alle my werkes' (B.XI.42) he confesses, as long as Fortune was his friend. And then he forgot his youth and hastened on into age, and Fortune became his foe, and poverty pursued him (B.XI.61); he lost his hair and his teeth, and was attacked by gout (B.XX.182,190, C.XXIII,191); he went deaf and lost his potency: eld (old age)

> hitte me under the ere, unethe may ich here;
> He buffeted me aboute the mouthe and bette out my tethe,
> And gyved me in goutes, I may noughte go at large.
> And of the wo that I was in, my wyf had reuthe,
> And wisshed ful witterly that I were in hevene.
> For the lyme that she loved me fore, and leef was to fele,
> On nyghtes namely, whan we naked were,
> I ne myght in no manere maken it at hir wille,
> So elde and she sothly hadden it forbeten.

> (B.XX.189-97)

[hit me under the ear, I can hardly hear; he buffeted me about the mouth and beat out my teeth, and gyved me with gout, I could not walk about. And my wife sorrowed for the woe I suffered and most certainly wished I were in Heaven. For the limb she loved and was fond of feeling, especially at night when we were naked, I could in no way make behave in the way she wanted, old age and she, to tell the truth, had so utterly battered it.]

This sardonic glimpse of his latter days is the last we get of Langland the man, and so we may leave him to consider Langland the poet.

II

THE FIRST VISIONS

It is reasonable and attractive to imagine the young cross-grained poet, standing lankily in the big flat field from which he had taken his name and looking up in the May sunshine at the Malvern Beacon, overcome by a moment of great vision. Suddenly he had seen the whole universe, as he knew it, in the configuration of his parish and the hills about it. He had perhaps been helped to this eye-opening instant by seeing miracle plays; that he had seen some cannot be doubted, for he uses their very language at moments. The triple world of the mediaeval theatre, with the mansions of Heaven high on one side and Hell's mouth below and on the other, with man's middle-earth between them, suddenly had bodied itself forth in the Beacon, the ditches of Old Castle and the intervening fields. This was the setting for the first flight of his poem, his first dream-series, known as the *Visio de Petro Plowman*; when it burst upon him, he cannot have foreseen how three further visionary tracts would open up before him and demand to be explored, consequences or sequels to the first, and would be called the *Vita de Do-wel*, the *Vita de Do-Bet* and the *Vita de Do-Best*. Into these four large movements the texts are divided.

The first movement, then, gives the whole poem its name, *Visio de Petro Plowman*; but it is a long time before we meet with Piers in it; Langland had first to depict a world to be saved before he could show a saviour for it. The opening vision of the Field full of Folk is this world as he saw it; it has as much of London in it as of Herefordshire, for we open upon great crowds, busy about the maze of their lives, 'working and wandering as the world asks'. Chaucer shows us England through some thirty sharply individual pilgrims; Langland through surging crowds of shadowy self-seekers, differentiated by their ways of bullying, begging, thieving, tricking and earning a living out of the

Tom Tiddler's Ground of the world; instead of one amiable
and distinguished rogue of a friar, such as Chaucer chooses
as his exhibit, Langland lumps all the Mendicants together,
all the Four Orders, 'preaching the people for the profit of
their bellies' (A.Prologue.56) and we see a swirl of parsons,
pardoners and bishops, barons and burgesses, lawyers and
businessmen, butchers, and brewers, weavers and workmen,
with tinkers and tailors and the idle scum of beggars, sham
hermits and common jugglers, while we hear the shouts of
the tavern-keepers' apprentices advertising their masters'
wares with 'Hot Pies! Good pork and goose! Come and
Dine! White wine from Alsace, red wine from Gascony!'
(A.Prologue.96-108)

In all this rout there are, however, some that quietly and
straitly live by the criterion upon which all Langland's
thought is based—the love of our Lord:

> In preyours and in penaunce putten hem manye,
> all for love of oure lord lyvede wel streite
> In hope for to have hevenriche blisse.
>
> (B.Prologue.25-7)

[Many gave themselves to prayer and penance, and lived austerely
enough, all for the love of our Lord, in hope to have the bliss of the
Kingdom of Heaven.]

One may say that the whole poem is a search for the true
nature of that love. In the last moments of the poem, after
all that has been seen and said, when he finds himself beset
by old age and death, after the attack of Antichrist, and left
alone in the universal desolation of the world, the Dreamer
turns once more to Kynde, that is, to Nature (and perhaps to
God, whose works and will are seen in Nature) who passes
by as he sits in helpless grief and terror:

> And as I seet in this sorwe, I say how kynde passed,
> And deth drowgh neigh me; for drede gan I quake,
> And cried to kynde out of care me brynge.

'Loo! elde the hoore hath me biseye,
Awreke me, if yowre wille be, for I wolde ben hennes.'
'Yif thow wilt ben ywroken, wende into unité,
And holde the there evere, tyl I send for the,
And loke thow conne somme crafte, ar thow come thennes.'
'Conseille me, kynde', quod I, 'what craft is best to lerne?'
'*Lerne to love*', quod kynde, '*and leve of alle othre.*'

                                                (B.XX.198-207)

[And as I sat in this sorrow, I saw how Kynd passed by, and death drew
near me; I began to quake for fear and cried to Kynd to bring me out
of care. 'Look, Old Age the Hoary One has set eyes on me; avenge me
if you will, for I would be out of this.' 'If you would be avenged, go into
Unity (i.e. the Church) and keep yourself there till I send for you;
and see that you learn some craft (trade) before you leave.' 'Advise
me. Kynd', said I, 'what craft is best to learn?' 'Learn to love', said
Kynde, 'and leave all other learning.']

His first lesson in love opens the poem, when the Prologue
is over; it is that Truth and Love are the same, for God is
both; this he learns of Holy Church, the Lady lovely of face,
who comes down from the Tour on the Toft, Truth's
Tower, in the opening vision already quoted:

'Whan alle tresores aren tried', quod she, 'trewthe is the best;
I do it on *deus caritas*, to deme the sothe;

For trewthe telleth that love is triacle of hevene;
May no synne be on him sene that useth that spise,
And alle his werkes he wroughte with love as him liste;
And lered it Moises for the levest thing, and most like to hevene,
And also the plente of pees, moste precious of vertues.
For hevene myghte noghte holden it, it was so hevy of Hymself,
Tyl it hadde of the erthe yeten his fylle.
And whan it haved of this folde flesshe and blode taken,
Was nevere leef upon lynde lighter therafter,
And portatyf and persant as the poynt of a nedle,
That myghte non armure it lette, ne none heigh walles.'

                                                (B.I.85-6/146-156)

['When all treasures are tried', she said, 'Truth is the best; I prove it by
the text "God is Love" . . . For Truth tells that love is the treacle of
Heaven; no sin may be seen on him that uses that spice. And all the
works that He created, He created with love, as it pleased Him, and He
taught it to Moses as the dearest thing, the thing most like Heaven, and
also the plant of peace, most precious of virtues. For Heaven could not
hold it, it was so heavy with Himself, till it had eaten its fill of earth;
and when of this fold of earth it had taken flesh and blood, never was
leaf on linden lighter than it thereafter, and it was portable and piercing
as the point of a needle, so that no armour could keep it out, nor any
high wall.']

Love seen as Truth is the rock of his morality, and in
the first visions of the poem, by this unanswerable criterion,
he measures the actual, contemporary world presented in
them. Truth and Love are the strengths under the rage,
under the irony, under the laughter, under the compassion
of all his poetry. Opposite to Truth is Falsehood, and this is
first pictured for us in the vision of Lady Meed, fountain
of bribery and simony, surrounded by a rout of govern-
mental and ecclesiastical officials, Sherriffs, Deans, Arch-
deacons, Registrars, lawyers and liars; her portrait is drawn
in language that suggests the notoriously venal and luxurious
Alice Perrers, mistress of Edward III in his senility. She is a
colourful figure, robed in scarlet and loaded with jewelry;
her wedding-present is the Lordship of the lands of the Seven
Sins. But presently her wedding is challenged and all her
grotesque followers are put to ignominious flight, riding on
each other's backs. After this sardonic vision of officialdom
and the political world has run its course, and Lady Meed
has met with the reproof of Conscience before the King
—this time an ideal King, certainly not a Plantagenet—
Langland takes us once again to the Field of Folk, and shows
us Reason, with a cross before him, preaching repentance
to the common people. They weep and their Seven Sins come
forward, one after the other, to make their confession, and
are absolved.

These sins are no abstractions, but are seen in terms of shop and pub and fair, false weights, wicked words, watered beer, short measure, slander, ignorance, laziness and a generally sozzled condition. Of the many portraits of the Seven Sins that we have in our literature, these are the most lively, the most scrofulous, the most penitent; and, as they show Langland's satiric art at its best, let us pause over the most famous of them—Glutton on his way to church, to make his confession. Before he gets there Betty the Breweress tempts him into the tavern and there he finds the whole village—Cissy the shoe-maker, Wat the Warrener, Tim the Tinker and two of his apprentices, Hickey the Hackneyman, Clarice of Cockslane, Daw the Ditcher and a dozen others:

> There was laughyng and louryng and 'let go the cuppe!'
> And seten so til evensonge and songen umwhile,
> Tyl Glotoun had yglobbed a galoun and a jille.
> His guttis gunne to gothely as two gredy sowes;
> He pissed a potel in a *paternoster* while,
> And blew his rounde ruwet at his rigge-bon ende,
> That alle that herde that horne held her nose after,
> And wissheden it had be wexed with a wispe of firses.
> He myghte neither steppe ne stonde, er he his staffe hadde;
> ... And whan he drowgh to the dore, thanne dymmed
>   his eighen,
> He stumbled on the thressewolde, an threwe to the erthe.
> Clement the cobelere caughte hym bi the myddel,
> For to lifte hym alofte, and leyde him on his knowes;
> Ac Glotoun was a gret cherle, and a grym in the liftynge,
> And coughed up a caudel in Clementis lappe;
> Is non so hungri hounde in Hertfordschire
> Durst lape of the levynges, so unlovely thei smaughte.
>
> (B.V.344-363)

[There was laughing and scowling and 'Let go the cup!', and they sat so till evensong, singing now and then, till Glutton had englobed a gallon and a gill. His guts began to grumble like two greedy sows;

he pissed a pottle—two quarts—in the time it takes to say a paternoster
and blew his little round horn at his back-bone's end, so that all who
heard that horn, held their noses after and wished it had been wiped
with a wisp of gorse. He could neither step nor stand until he had
his staff . . . and when he drew towards the door, his eyes dimmed
and he stumbled on the threshold and threw to the earth. Clement
the cobbler caught him by the middle, to lift him up, and laid him
across his knees; but Glutton was a great big fellow, grim in the lifting,
and he coughed up a caudel in Clement's lap. There is no hound so
hungry in Hertfordshire that it would dare lap up those leavings, they
tasted so unlovely.]

To the delinquent world thus pictured in the Seven Sins
a penance is given: the penitents are to make a pilgrimage to
St. Truth. For Langland saw sin as a failure in truth and love,
a failure for which a sort of bloody-minded ignorance was
partly responsible, it would seem; but a change of heart
could change the bloody mind, and his sinners showed
themselves eager for their pilgrimage:

> A thousand of men tho throngen togideris,
> Wepynge and weylyng for here wykkide dedis;
> Criede upward to Crist and to his clene Modir
> To have grace to seke Treuthe; God leve that hy moten!
> (A.V.251-4)

[A thousand men then thronged together, weeping and wailing for
their wicked deeds; cried upward to Christ and to his clean Mother,
to have grace to seek Truth. God give them leave to do so!]

But their ignorance remained with them; few were so wise
as to know the way, and they 'blustered forth as beasts over
hills and streams' (A.VI.2), pretty well at random. Presently
they met with a palmer, one of those perpetually globe-
trotting, trophy-laden pilgim-tourists, of the shrine-
collecting type, who seemed to have visited every holy
place on earth; so they ask him the way to St. Truth. He is
the last of Langland's figures of satirical comedy in this part

of the poem, and is here introduced, with a technique typical of mediaeval art, to make an explosion of derisive laughter immediately before a moment of solemnity, thus creating the easy step from the ridiculous to the sublime; for this is the moment for the entry into the poem of Piers Plowman:

> 'Knowist thou ought a corseint,' quath thei, 'that men callen
>   Treuthe?
> Canst thou wisse us the wey where that wy dwellith?'
> 'Nay, so me God helpe', seide the gome thanne.
> 'I saugh nevere palmere with pik ne with scrippe
> Axen aftir hym, er now in this place.'
> *'Petir', quath a ploughman and putte forth his hed,*
> *'I knowe hym as kyndely as clerk doth his bokis.*
> *Clene Conscience and Wyt kende me to his place,*
> *And dede me sure hym sithe to serve hym for evere;*
> *Bothe sowe and sette while I swynke mighte.*
> *I have ben his folewere al this fourty wynter!'*

(A.VI.21-30)

['Do you know a sainted body', said they, 'that people call Truth? Can you inform us of the way to where the creature lives?' 'No, so help me God', said the fellow then, 'I never saw a palmer with staff and scrip ask after him until now and in this place!' *'Peter!' said a plowman, and put forth his head, 'I know him as naturally as a cleric knows his books! Clean Conscience and natural Intelligence told me the way and bound me afterwards to serve him for ever, both to sow and to plant as long as I could work. I have been his follower all these forty winters!'*]

Piers knows the way to Truth, first in the simplest sense of knowing and doing honest, faithful work; but he also knows the more spiritual way through meekness and obedience to the Commandments, that leads to Langland's grand criterion, the love of Our Lord. Piers says:

> 'Ye mote go thorugh meknesse, both men and wyves,
> Til ye come into consience that crist wyte the sothe,
> That ye loue hym levere thanne the lif in youre hertis;

And thanne youre neighebours next in none wise apeire
Otherwise thanne thou woldist men wroughte to thiselve.'
(A.VI.48–52)

[You must go through meekness, both men and women, till you come
into knowledge that Christ knows the truth, that you love him more
dearly than the life in your hearts, and then your neighbours next, in
no way to injure them, or do otherwise that you would wish people
to do unto you.]

If you follow this way, says Piers, you shall come to a
Court as clear as the sun, whose moat is mercy, whose walls
are wit to keep out evil will, whose crenellations are
Christendom and whose buttresses are belief, roofed with
love, guarded by grace; and the tower in which Truth is,
is up towards the sun:

He may do with the day sterre what hym dere likith;
Deth dar not do thing that he defendith.
(A.VI.80–81)

['He may do with the day-star what seems best to him; death dares do
nothing that he forbids.' The day-star, I think, here means Lucifer.]

And if grace grants that you may enter this Court:

Thou shalt se treuthe himself wel sitte in thin herte
And lere the for to love, and hise lawes holden.
(A.VI.93–4)

[You shall see Truth himself truly sitting in your heart, and he shall
teach you how to love, and keep his laws.]

Truth is not only in his heavenly tower, but also in our
hearts, for we are made in His image, and it is He who
teaches us how to love.

The pilgrims find all this too difficult for them, and beg
Piers to be their guide; and he consents, but asks them,
before they set out, to help him plough his half-acre.

So the poem turns from the problem of sin to the problem of hunger in a Christian world, for the 'half-acre' is an emblem of England under the threat of famine, as it was, after the Black Death; and the pilgrims are set to work to provide food for the community. Work is also prayer, and honest work is truth, feeding the hungry is love. As a reward for their work, Hunger is sent away, and Piers receives a Pardon from Truth Himself, for him and his heirs, 'for evermore aftir' (A.VIII.4), a pardon for sin perpetually available.

Then comes the climax, both in drama and significance, of this first great section of the poem; all critics agree as to its striking poetic force; no two wholly agree as to its significance. What happens is this. Piers is standing with the document containing Truth's pardon in his hand, not yet unrolled. A priest in the crowd, supposing him ignorant of Latin, offers to construe it for him into English:

> And Peris at his preyour the pardoun unfoldith,
> And I behynde hem bothe beheld al the bulle.
> In two lynes it lay and nought o lettre more,
> And was writen right thus in witnesse of truethe:
> *Et qui bona egerunt ibunt in vitam eternam;*
> *Qui vero mala in ignem eternum.*

(A.VIII.91-6)

[And Piers at his prayer unfolds the pardon, and I, behind them both, saw the whole bull. In two lines it lay, not a single letter more, and was written exactly thus, in witness of truth: Those who did good shall go into eternal life, but those who did evil into eternal fire.]

This baleful statement (which comes from the end of the Athanasian Creed) is no pardon, as the priest instantly points out; it demands an eye for an eye and a tooth for a tooth. So Piers tore it in pieces.

> And Piers for pure tene pulde it assondir
> And seide '*Si ambulavero in medio umbre mortis,*
> *Non timebo mala, quoniam tu mecum es*'

(A.VIII.101-103)

[And Piers, 'for pure teen' tore it asunder and said 'Though I should walk in the midst of the shadow of death, I shall fear no evil, for thou art with me'.]

What is the meaning of *'pure teen'*? Why did he tear the Pardon asunder? Here begin the enigmas, the inward mysteries of this extraordinary poem, upon which hardly two critics can be found perfectly to agree. *'Teen'* can mean almost any shade of feeling of sorrow, distress, disappointment, anger, or lament. The tearing of the Pardon, which, as a piece of imaginative story-telling, seems so superbly, so unexpectedly fitting, as a piece of allegory bursts with ambiguity. Was it a pardon or was it not? Had Truth really sent it, or was it a cunning fraud, like the pardons of so many Pardoners? And what did Piers think of it? His gesture of tearing it has invited many explanations, and this may be the reason why it is left out in the C Text; for the changes made by Langland in his last revision seem to be made in order to clarify his meanings. Be that as it may, in all three Texts a dispute arises between Piers and the priest, and the noise of it awakes the Dreamer, who finds himself 'meatless and moneyless in the Malvern Hills', wondering, like his readers, what his vision can have meant.

III

DO-WEL, DO-BET and DO-BEST

The poem now leads us through a wilderness of disputation that seeks to solve the overwhelming question posed by the Pardon. If our salvation depends on our 'doing well' (*bona agere*), what does 'doing well' involve? On this quest the Dreamer-poet now sets out, but has no Piers to guide him; for Piers vanishes with his first vision and does not return to comfort and instruct him for many a long Passus.

The first disputants the Dreamer meets with are a couple of Friars, and they remind him, quoting the *Book of Proverbs*, that even the just man sins seven times a day. If he sins, how can he be 'doing well'? If the just are lost, who then can be saved? So what can be the efficacy of the Pardon of Truth? Where is the catch? In his triadic mind the Dreamer's first question now multiplies itself by three, and the quest continues not only for doing well, but also for doing better and doing best. Many are the allegorical phantoms and figures he consults, and his triple question proliferates in their answers and his own conjectures into tissues of theological speculation. What are the merits of the Active, what of the Contemplative Life? Can Learning save the soul? Does not Predestination foredoom us from everlasting to election or to damnation? What are the relative values of Faith and Works? Are the Righteous Heathen (like Aristotle and Trajan) saved? Why? How is it that all Nature obeys Reason, except Mankind? And, as he marvels at the natural world, the tediums of disputation (so fascinating to mediaeval clerisy) are lifted for a moment, and we hear a kind of poetry that Wordsworth, had he known it, might have envied:

> Briddes I bihelde that in buskes made nestes;
> Hadde nevere wye witte to worche the leest.
> I hadde wonder at whom and where the pye lerned
> To legge the stykkes in whiche she leyeth and bredeth . . .
> Moche merveilled me what maister thei hadde,
> And who taughte hem on trees to tymbre so heighe,
> That noither buirn ne beste may her briddes rechen.
> And sythen I loked upon the see, and so forth upon the
>   sterres . . .
> I seigh floures in the fritthe, and her faire coloures,
> And how amonge the grene grasse grewe so many hewes . . .
> Ac that moste moeved me and my mode chaunged,
> That resoun rewarded and reuled alle bestes,
> Save man and his make . . .

(B.XI.336-362)

[Birds I beheld that in bushes made their nests; no man ever had skill enough to make the least of them. I wondered from whom and where the magpie learned to place the twigs in which she lays her eggs, and breeds . . . Much I marvelled who their master was, who taught them to build their nests so high among the trees, so that neither boy nor beast might reach their young. And then I looked out to sea and upwards to the stars . . . I saw the flowers in the forest and their lovely colours, and saw how many shades of colour grew among the grasses . . . but what most moved me, and changed my mood, was that reason rewarded and ruled all animals, except man and his mate.]

Through all these questionings the steady search for a definition of the three good lives continues and gradually their meaning is felt to accumulate into a quite unsystematic yet feeling body of Christian wisdom, in which Conscience takes the lead and the virtues of patience, humility, sincerity and peace of heart have first place, and the acceptance of poverty is commended, for it is the gift of God; and so we move towards the great virtues of Faith and Hope, presented in the shapes of Abraham and Moses, with whom the Dreamer has a long colloquy, till it is interrupted by their coming upon the man who fell among thieves; and there they meet the Good Samaritan, who is Charity.

Faith and Hope, like the priest and Levite in the parable, draw away ('like duck from falcon'), but the Good Samaritan tends the man, wounded by thieves. This wounded man is no other than the human race itself, that fell among thieves in Paradise, being robbed of Eden by Satan; and nothing can cure him:

> Neither Feith ne fyn Hope, so festred ben his woundis,
> Without the blode of a barn, borne of a mayde.
>
> (B.XVII.92-3)

[Neither Faith nor fine Hope, so festered are his wounds, without the blood of a child born of a virgin.]

So, at least, the Samaritan tells the Dreamer; and when he has further instructed him in the trinity-in-unity of God, by images such as that of a candle, its wick and flame, he sets spurs to his mule and rides off like the wind, towards Jerusalem.

Now the long enquiry is over and the Dreamer is readied for the supreme vision. It is Lent, and he sleeps; and in dream he hears the singing of children in the streets of Jerusalem on the first Palm Sunday of all:

> Of gerlis and of *gloria laus* gretly me dremed,
> And how *osanna* by orgonye olde folke songen.
> One semblable to the Samaritan, and some del to Piers the
>   Plowman,
> Barfote on an asse bakke botelees cam prykye,
> Wythoute spores other spere, spakliche he loked,
> As is the kynde of a Knyghte that cometh to be dubbed,
> To geten hem gylte spores, or galoches ycouped.
> Thanne was Faith in a fenestre, and cryde '*A! fili david!*' . .
> Olde Jewes of Jerusalem for joye thei songen
>   *Benedictus qui venit in nomine domini.*
> Thanne I frayned at Faith what al that fare bemente,
> And who sholde jouste in Jherusalem. 'Jhesus', he seyde,
> 'And fecche that the fende claymeth, Piers fruit the
>   plowman.'
> 'Is Piers in this place?' quod I, and he preynte on me,
> 'This Jhesus of his gentrice wole juste in Piers armes,
> In his helme and in his haberioun, *humana natura* . . .'
>   (B.XVIII.8-23)

[Of children and of glory and praise greatly I dreamed, and how old folk sang Hosanna to the sound of an organ. One similar to the Samaritan, and somewhat to Piers Plowman, came riding, unshod, on the back of an ass, without spur or spear; gallant he looked, as is the nature of a Knight coming to be dubbed, to win his gilt spurs and his slashed shoes. Then Faith was in a window and cried 'Ah, Son of David!' Old Jews of Jerusalem sang for joy 'Blessed is he that comes in the name of the Lord!' Then I asked Faith what all this fuss was about and who should joust in Jerusalem. 'Jesus', he said, 'and he will fetch the fruit of Piers the Plowman which the Fiend claims.' 'Is Piers in this place?' said I, and he gazed at me: 'This Jesus, of his nobility, will joust in Piers' armour, in his helmet and habergeon, human nature . . .']

The sublimity of vision and colloquialism of language unite to carry us vividly to the scene described, and onwards to the trial before Pilate and to the crucifixion itself, which has the stamp of a gospel's authority:

> '*Consummatum est*', quod Cryst, and comsed forto swowe,
> Pitousliche and pale as a prisoun that deyeth;
> The lorde of lyf and of lighte tho leyed his eyen togideres.
> The daye for drede withdrowe, and derke bicam the sonne,
> The wal wagged and clef, and al the worlde quaved . . .
> Some seyde that he was goddes sone that so faire deyde,
> > *Vere filius dei erat iste*.
>
> > > > (B.XVIII.57-68)

['It is finished', said Christ, and began to swoon, piteously and pale, like a prisoner dying; the Lord of life and of light laid his eyelids together. Day withdrew in dread and dark became the sun; the wall shook and cleft in two, and the whole world trembled. Some said it was God's son that died so fairly, 'truly this was the son of God'.]

But this triumph of eye-witness poetry, that reaches back towards *The Dream of the Rood*, five centuries before, and is, in this description, an equal masterpiece, now moves on to an even greater effort of imagination, in picturing the harrowing of Hell. Thither the Dreamer descends, and sees Christ's approach to Hell's barriers, as a Voice speaking from a light, shining upon that darkness. So it is also seen in the Apocryphal Gospel, known as *The Acts of Pilate*, where Langland undoubtedly found it:

> Efte the Lighte bad unlouke, and Lucifer answered,
> What lorde artow?' quod Lucifer, '*quis est iste?*'
> '*Rex glorie*', the Lighte sone seide,

'And lorde of myghte and of mayne, and al manere vertues
   dominus virtutum:
Dukes of this dym place, anon undo this yates,
That Cryst may come in, the Kynges Sone of Hevene.'
And with that breth helle brak, with Beliales barres;
For any wye or warde, wide opene the yatis.
Patriarkes and prophetes, *populus in tenebris,*
Songen Seynt Johanes songe, *Ecce Agnus Dei.*
Lucyfer loke ne myghte, so lyghte hym ableynte.
And tho that Owre Lorde loved, into his lighte he laughte,
And seyde to Sathan, 'Lo, here my soule to amendes
For alle synneful soules, to save tho that ben worthy;
Myne thei be and of me, I may the bette hem clayme . . .
                              (B.XVIII.313-327)

[Again the Light bade them unlock, and Lucifer answered: 'What Lord
ar thou?' said Lucifer, 'what is this one?' 'The King of Glory', the Light
soon said, 'and Lord of might and of power, Lord of all virtues. Dukes of
this dim place, open the gates at once, that Christ may come in, Son of
the King of Heaven.' And with that breath, Hell broke, with Belial's
bars; wide open were the gates, in spite of man or guard. Patriarchs and
prophets, the people that sat in darkness, sang St. John's song, 'Behold
the Lamb of God'. Lucifer could not look, the Light so blinded him.
And those that Our Lord loved, he caught up into his light, and said to
Satan 'See here my soul in amends for all sinful souls, to save those that
are worthy; mine they are, and of me, I may claim them the better.']

The Passus ends with jubilation in Heaven; Mercy and
Truth meet together, Righteousness and Peace kiss each
other, and these four 'wenches', as Langland calls them
in his salubrious style when they first appear, are left
dancing till Easter dawns, when the poet wakes, and calls
to his wife and daughter:

Tyl the daye dawed this damaiseles daunced,
That men rongen to the resurexioun, and right with that
   I waked,
And called Kitte my wyf, and Kalote my daughter—
'Ariseth and reverenceth goddes resurrection,

And crepeth to the crosse on knees, and kisseth it for a
    juwel!
For goddes blissed body it bar for owre bote,
And it afereth the fende, for such is the myghte,
May no grusly gost glyde ther it shadweth!'

                           (B.XVIII.424-31)

[Till the day dawned these damsels danced, and men rang the bells for
the resurrection, and instantly I awoke and called Kitty my wife and
Calotte my daughter—'Rise, and reverence God's resurrection, and
creep to the cross on your knees, and kiss it for a jewel! For it bore God's
blessed body for our good, and it puts fear into the fiend; such is its
power that no grisly spirit may glide where it overshadows!']

The eighteenth Passus of the B Text is the top of Langland's
writing in this vein, our greatest Christian poetry: yet, when
you compare it with Glutton in the ale-house, you hear the
same vigorous voice, uttering things as sharply seen and
heard, in the same simple vigorous speech. The line 'Lucyfer
loke ne myghte, so lyghte hym ableynte' is in the same
tone of language as that which describes Glutton in a somewhat similar condition:

And whan he drowgh to the dore, thanne dymmed his eighen,
He stumbled on the thresshewolde, an threwe to the erthe.

The blinding of Lucifer by the blaze of Christ is as realistic a
detail, in an apocalyptic mood, as that of Glutton, by mere
drunkenness, in a mood of sardonic satire. It is the range of
mind supported by an equal strength of speech that makes
this poet and his poem unlike any other; he has both lion
and lamb in him, and hyena too. To take other examples,
here he is describing the theological sophistries of well-fed
dons on their dais at dinner:

Thus thei dryvele at her deyse the deite to knowe,
And gnawen god with the gorge whan her gutte is fulle.

                           (B.X.56-7)

[Thus they drivel on their dais, discussing the deity, and gnaw God in their throats when their gut is full.]

and this triumphant poetical rage issues from the same Christian ferocity as Langland's tenderness, in the same language of colloquial power:

> The most needy aren oure neighebores, an we nyme good
>   hede,
> As prisones in puttes, and poure folke in cotes,
> Charged with children and chef lordes rente,
> That thei with spynnyge may spare, spenen hit in hous-hyre,
> Bothe in mylk and in mele to make with papelotes,
> To aglotye with here gurles, that greden after fode . . .
>
>   (C.X.71-6)

[The most needy are our neighbours, if we take careful heed, such as prisoners in pits, and poor folk in hovels, charged with children and rent to their landlords, so that what they can spare out of spinning they must spend on house-hire, and on milk and meal to make a sort of porridge with, to glut their children, crying out for food.]

With the Harrowing of Hell (as it is called) ends Do-Bet, and the poem moves on to the Resurrection; once again Christ is seen in Piers, for the Dreamer, falling asleep, suddenly dreams that he is in church hearing Mass, and that Piers the Plowman comes in, painted in blood, with a cross in his hand, before the common people:

> And righte lyke in alle lymes to owre lorde Jhesu;
> And thanne called I Conscience to kenne me the sothe.
> 'Is this Jhesus the Juster?', quod I, 'that Juwes did to deth?
> Or is it Pieres the Plowman? Who paynted hym so rede?'
> Quod Conscience, and kneled tho, 'thise aren Pieres armes,
> His coloures and his cote-armure, ac he that cometh so blody
> Is Cryst with his crosse, conqueroure of crystene'.
>
>   (B.XIX.6-14)

[And right like, in all his limbs, to our Lord Jesus; and then I called Conscience to know the truth. 'Is this Jesus the Jouster?' I said, 'Or is it Piers the Plowman? Who painted him so red?' Said Conscience then, and knelt, 'These are Piers' arms, his colours and coat-armour, but he that, comes so bloody is Christ with his cross, conqueror of Christians'.]

And it is by the power of that conquest that the Church is built; Jesus, fighting in the armour of Piers, has done well, done better and done best; by his victory the sacrament of Pardon is established:

> And whan this dede was done, *Dobest* he taughte,
> And yaf Pieres power and pardoun he graunted,
> To alle mannere men, mercy and foryyfnes,
> And yaf hym myghte to assoylye men of alle manere
>   synnes*
> In covenant that thei come, and knowleche to paye,
> To Pieres pardon that plowman, *redde quod debes*.
>   (B.XIX.177-82. The asterisked line from C.XXII.185,
>   as the B Text is here corrupt.)

[And when his deed was done he taught Do-Best, and gave Piers power, and granted pardon to all manner of men, mercy and forgiveness, and gave power to absolve men of all manner of sins, on condition that they come, and acknowledge to pay the debt which you owe to the Pardon of Piers Plowman.]

And so the enigma of the Pardon sent to Piers is solved; Truth had bought it on Calvary, and had granted it to the race that fell among thieves, to wipe away their sins, *provided* that they did their share, and paid their debt of confession, and whatever else they owed to the sacraments and the Church; that done, they would be doing well, however many times a day they, like the just man, had fallen. But they must do their part too. Grace would be with them.

After the Ascension comes the descent of the Dove 'in the likeness of lightning', upon Piers and his companions; for Christ, having put on Piers, 'our suit' of human nature,

now puts it off, leaving Piers on earth, to build the barn
that is to hold his harvest of souls; the Holy Spirit directs
the building of this barn: it is to be called 'Unity'—Holy
Church in English:

> 'Ayeines thi greynes', quod Grace, 'begynneth for to ripe,
> Ordeigne the an hous, Piers, to herberwe in thi cornes.'
> 'By God! Grace', quod Piers, 'ye moten yive tymbre,
> And ordeyne that hous ar ye hennes wende.'
> And Grace gave hym the crosse, with the croune of
>   thornes,
> That cryst upon Calvarye for mankynde on pyned,
> And of his baptesme and blode that he bledde on Rode
> He made a maner morter, and mercy it highte.
> And therewith Grace bigan to make a good foundement,
> And watteled it and walled it with his peynes and his
>   passioun,
> And of al holywrit he made a rofe after,
> And called that hous Unité, holicherche on Englisshe.
>
> (B.XIX.313-25)

['Against the time when your grains begin to ripen', said Grace,
'ordain yourself a house, Piers, to garner your corn.' 'By God, Grace',
said Piers, 'you must give me timber and ordain that house before you
go away.' And Grace gave him the cross with the crown of thorns on
which Christ suffered for mankind on Calvary; and of his baptism and of
the blood that He bled on the cross, he made a kind of mortar, and it was
called Mercy. And with it Grace began to make a good foundation, and
wattled and walled it with His pains and passion, and of all holy writ
he made a roof afterwards and called that house Unity, Holy Church in
English.]

And so the simple Peter Ploughman of the first vision, in
virtue of The Incarnation and of Pentecost, has become
Peter, the rock on which Christ founded his church, and is
to make of it a barn to store the grain of christian souls,
from fields that are white to harvest.

With such a climax many poets would have felt they had
reached the end of their vision and would be ready to lay

down their pens. But Langland saw further; he was not celebrating a victory but a desolation. For Antichrist was still to come, with his seven allies, the seven sins, and with Old Age and Death and all the terrors of eschatology at his heels, to upturn and destroy the House of Unity and drive out the fools that had taken refuge in it. He is the great enemy of Truth, and the Friars are in his following:

> . . . anon ich fel asleope,
> And mette ful merveilousliche that, in a mannes forme,
> Antecrist cam thenne, and al the crop of treuthe
> Turned tyte up-so-doun, and overtilte the rote,
> And made fals to springe and sprede, and spede menne
>   neodes.
> In eche cuntreie ther he cam, he cutte away treuthe,
> And gert gyle growe ther as he a god were.
> Freres folweden that feonde, for he yaf hem copes,
> And religiouse reverencede hym, and rongen here belles . . .
>   (C.XXIII.51-9)

[. . . presently I fell asleep, and I dreamed most marvellously that, in a man's form, Antichrist then came and at once turned upside down all Truth's crop, and overturned the root, and made False to spring and spread and suffice men's needs. In each country he came to, he cut away Truth, and caused Guile to grow there, as if he were a god. Friars followed that fiend, for he gave them copes and the Religious reverenced him and rung their bells.]

In this destruction and betrayal of the church the poem ends, and Conscience is left to walk 'as wide as the world lasts' to seek Piers Plowman, who once again has vanished from the poem:

> 'Bi cryste', quod Consience tho, 'I wil bicome a pilgryme,
> And walken as wyde as al the worlde lasteth,
> To seke Piers the Plowman that pryde may destruye,
> And that freres hadde a fyndyng that for nede flateren,
> And contrepleteth me, Conscience. Now Kynde me avenge,

And sende me happe and hele til I have Piers the Plowman!'
And sitthe he gradde after grace, til I gan wake.

(B.XX.378-84)

['By Christ', said Conscience then, 'I will become a pilgrim, and walk
as wide as the whole world lasts to seek Piers the Plowman who can
destroy Pride, and that Friars may have a maintainance who now must
flatter to supply their needs and counter-plead me, Conscience. Now,
Nature, avenge me, and send me luck and health until I have Piers
Plowman!' And then he cried out for Grace, and I awoke.]

It is hard in our days to see Friars as Langland saw them.
We need Chaucer's help, and that Chronicler's byword
sneer, *Hic est mendicans, ergo mendax* (This is a friar, therefore
a liar). But the rest of this vision we can see well enough, a
world in moral ruin, seeking some way of good life, and
seeking someone who knows how to live and teach it. For
Langland, at least, all was to do again; the pilgrimage to
Truth had to begin once more from the beginning; and
Conscience sets about it, as the Dreamer awakes.

IV

PIERS HIMSELF

It is uniquely fortunate for us that two writers of first
genius, but of contrasted natures, almost exactly contemporary with each other, should both have given us a portrait
of their Age, in the terms of the two high centres of their
culture, the Court and the Church, showing us the best
things and thoughts of their day in the two languages of
English poetry, the old and the new, alliteration and rhyme,
at their last and first greatness. Both writers were learned in
what most concerned them: Chaucer in all the flowerings of
the humane spirit from Ovid to Boccaccio, Langland in all
that touched on Holy Writ: Chaucer intent on the evolving

nuances of personality, Langland on the needs and qualities of the soul. Chaucer's art centred itself on romantic love, Langland's utterance on the love of Our Lord; they were both Christians, but Chaucer shows himself as pious rather than religious, with more feeling, let us say, for the Blessed Virgin than for the Holy Ghost; Langland shows little piety or sentiment, but much religious passion. He does not seek comfort but grace. In almost all things each other's opposite, they seem exactly complementary. Together they express a spiritual civilization in being; and they lived the kinds of life they describe. They have passed on the inheritance, enriching it.

They are alike in one rare faculty, though each exercises it in his own manner: the faculty for irony; Chaucer's irony is urbane, sophisticated, *nuancé*, Langland's blazing like a Hebrew prophet's, anger sauced with laughter. The objects of the great ironists are always the same in their satires —affectation and hypocrisy—and we find the same rogues and frauds held up to unfading mockery in both Langland and Chaucer—monks, friars, pardoners, summoners, and other tricksters and double-talkers. Most of these characters have now disappeared from the English scene, or at least into other professions; but the power to see them as they appeared to the searching secular eye of Chaucer and the no less searching, but mystical eye of Langland, gives us a binocular, stereoscopic vision of the body and soul of their Age.

Chaucer, however, has left us no character, among all his many, that embodies the whole duty of man or woman. Rulership may perhaps be seen in his Duke Theseus, wife-manship in his Wife of Bath; a diffused aristocratic principle of *largesse* runs through all he wrote, less as a principle for us to follow than as a noble infection for us to take, if we are capable of it. He has made no myth for us unless, unknowingly, the myth of 'Merry England'. In all other ways he has out-classed Langland easily enough during the six centuries between us and them; everything has gone his way—the language, the verse, the literary conventions, the attitudes and interests, secularization, humanism, the cult of character, romance, everything. He is an early modern, Langland a late mediaeval, wrapped up in marvellous but outdated allegories, as if by the mists of Malvern Hills. He seems a poet mainly for mediaevalists, at first sight.

Yet these are superficial contrasts, and greatness in poetry is not affected by any of them; Langland is a great poet too, and in one respect has a greater hold on our imaginative attention, in that he faces despair. He ends his poem in a desolation as ruinous as that in *The Waste Land*; the Church has tumbled down, the faithful are scattered, bamboozled or seduced, and nothing is left but the individual conscience, by itself, seeking grace 'as wide as the world lasts', crying out for Piers Plowman.

What is this enigmatic figure whose identity so strangely merges with that of Christ and of St. Peter? To what reality in experience does it correspond? From the character of the poem and from the number of its manuscripts, one would infer some spiritual need that many felt, but which died away or found satisfaction in some other image in the seventeenth century, when *Piers Plowman* sank into oblivion. Milton knew of it, but its language was too difficult and its matter too gothic to suit the taste of that time.

It is tempting to think of Piers as a mediaeval image comparable to the image of *The Dance of Death*, so popular in the fifteenth century, or like those double-decker family tombs of the same period, where angels support a weight of heraldry in honour of some alabaster lord or lady recumbent on the upper storey, while below there lies the sculpture of a rotting corpse, to show what six months of death will do, even to princes. If these images are parallel to that of Piers, we may think of him as an emblem from an age gone by that can no longer satisfy any more serious need than a wish to understand the art of the later middle ages. And I think that if *Piers Plowman* had never under-

gone revision, that is how we would think of him. He
would seem no more than what he is in the A Text, an ideal
farmer, a noble peasant, another manifestation of the convention that gave us the virtuous Plowman of Chaucer's
Prologue, but carried it rather further in its claims for his
usefulness to society and for the purity of his vision of God.

But when Langland revised his poem to touch Piers with
divinity, he lifted it out of Time, so that the convention of
an Age became a universal and the noble Christian peasant
a type of Christ. By this he gave form to an idea often re-
asserted in his poem, that man is made in God's image of
Truth and Love (their fountain-head his heart), and the
corollary faith that at one point in history God was made in
man's image. The *Imitatio Christi* is a thought to which
Western imagination perpetually returns for renewal; it
tells us 'what we need to be', and this is especially true of
Ages that have a keen sense of spiritual need. The idea of
life as a pilgrimage makes good sense with it, for Christians
claim of Christ that he is the Way as well as the Truth; these
concepts are embodied in Langland's imagery: Do-well,
Do-Better and Do-Best, for which Piers stands, are ways of
life that Christ himself had lived, so Langland tells us
(B.XIX.104-89); the pilgrimage towards them is our quest
for Piers, under the guidance of Grace.

Chaucer's use of the imagery of pilgrimage is not so ur-
gent: he makes of it a happy human holiday, something in
the manner of Chesterton's poem; he is casual and confident that it is possible

> To shewe yow the wey, in this viage,
> Of thilke parfit glorious pilgrimage
> That highte Jerusalem celestial,

while not neglecting the fact that 'there is good news yet
to hear and fine things to be seen, Before we go to Paradise
by way of Kensal Green'. Langland's urgency has only once
been matched, in *The Pilgrim's Progress*. Langland's pilgrim-

age is a quest, Bunyan's an escape.

From the furthest extremes of Christian theology, these great poets meet in their knowledge of the world and of the soul's need in the struggle of light with darkness; it is a Light that harrows Hell, and, at the crucifixion 'Lyf and deth in this derknesse, her one fordoth her other' (B.XVIII.65) [Life and death in this darkness, each is destroying the other], and it is 'Life, life, eternal life' that Christian seeks, as he thrusts his fingers in his ears and flees from the City of Destruction. Both Langland and Bunyan see the world as a wilderness and dream of a remedy, a salvation: many are the parallels and the contrasts between their dreams. Bunyan's pilgrim is allowed to reach and enter the Gate of the Celestial City: 'Then I heard in my Dream that all the Bells in the City Rang for Joy.' Langland's pilgrims are dispersed in their desolated world, in which Conscience is left alone, calling after Grace in the search for Piers.

For all the differences between them, Langland and Bunyan are natural Christian poets of an equal urgency and an equal vision of man and his soul in the wilderness of the world, that is also Vanity Fair, the Fair Field of folk; where Langland overgoes Bunyan is that he has shown us Christ in Piers and Piers in Christ, a thing we need to see.

We see a third, and a more modern, picture of the world's wilderness in Samuel Beckett's *Waiting for Godot* (1956), for we are back to that basic vision once again, though the urgency is lost, since the hope is lost. Yet if the old hope is lost, the old criterion remains:

Vladimir: Your boots. What are you doing with your boots?
Estragon: (*turning to look at his boots*) I'm leaving them there. (*Pause*) Another will come, just as . . . as . . . as me, but with smaller feet, and they'll make him happy.
Vladimir: But you can't go barefoot!
Estragon: Christ did.
Vladimir: Christ! What's Christ got to do with it? You're not going to compare yourself to Christ!
Estragon: All my life I've compared myself to him.

It seems that in our Age there are others that have Estragon's criterion in mind; I quote from a recent short story from America:[1]

'What do people mean when they say somebody is their personal hero?'
It comes sooner than I expect. 'Your hero is what you need to be.'
'Then is Jesus your hero?'
'Why do you think that?'
'You say you are scared of dying. Jesus is the one that did not die.'
...'I think your hero has to be a man. Was Jesus a man?'
'No sir. He was God disguised.'
'Well, that's it you see. You would not stand a chance of being God —need to or not—so you pick somebody you have got half a chance of measuring up to.'

A like and yet a different return to the same image can be seen in David Storey's *Radcliffe* (1963).

'But if Christ came to earth as man, why didn't He come as a man we know? Why didn't He use His sex? Isn't it from sex that all our problems and frustrations arise? Yet He refused to acknowledge it by His own example.'

Can eighteenth or nineteenth century fiction or drama show parallels for these three passages? I do not think so. No one, outside the pulpit, seems to have felt the need for questionings so extreme. *Piers Plowman* was not republished between 1561 and 1842, and was even then considered as little more than an obscure curiosity of literature; and it remained so until Skeat's great editions began to make it famous once again. It has reawakened in a world more ready for it; in those glossier days before our century began, the need for an image of man raised to the power of Christ may not have been so generally felt. But now the time gives it proof.

[1] Reynolds Price, 'The Names and Faces of Heroes', New York and London (1963).

LANGLAND: PIERS PLOWMAN

A Select Bibliography

(Books published in London, unless stated otherwise)

Editions:

THE VISION OF WILLIAM CONCERNING PIERS THE PLOWMAN, TOGETHER
WITH VITA DE DOWEL, DOBET ET DOBEST BY WILLIAM LANGLAND, ed.
W. W. Skeat
—in the Early English Text Society, Original Series, Nos. 28, 38, 54.
'A' Text, 1857. 'B' Text, 1869. 'C' Text, 1873.
THE VISION OF WILLIAM CONCERNING PIERS THE PLOWMAN IN THREE
PARALLEL TEXTS, TOGETHER WITH RICHARD THE REDELESS (about
1362-1399), ed. W. W. Skeat. Oxford (1886)
—edited from numerous manuscripts. Contains a Preface, Notes, and
a Glossary. Still the standard texts for 'B' and 'C'.
PIERS THE PLOWMAN, A CRITICAL EDITION OF THE 'A' VERSION, ed. T. A.
Knott and D. C. Fowler. Baltimore (1952)
—contains an Introduction, Notes, and a Glossary.
PIERS PLOWMAN: THE 'A' VERSION. WILL'S VISIONS OF PIERS PLOWMAN AND
DO-WELL, ed. G. Kane (1960)
—an edition in the form of Trinity College, Cambridge MS.R.3.14,
corrected from other manuscripts, with various readings.

Extended Studies:

PIERS PLOWMAN, A CONTRIBUTION TO THE HISTORY OF ENGLISH
MYSTICISM, by J. J. Jusserand (1894).
NEW LIGHT ON PIERS PLOWMAN, by A. H. Bright (1928)
—an enquiry into the topography of the poem. Contains a Preface by
R. W. Chambers.
ALLITERATIVE POETRY IN MIDDLE ENGLISH, 2 vols., by J. P. Oakden.
Manchester (1930-35).
AN ATTEMPT TO APPROACH THE 'C' TEXT OF PIERS PLOWMAN, by F. A. R.
Carnegy (1934).
THE RELATIONS BETWEEN THE SOCIAL AND DIVINE ORDER IN WILLIAM
LANGLAND'S 'VISION OF WILLIAM CONCERNING PIERS THE PLOWMAN',
by F. A. R. Carnegy. Breslau (1934).
PIERS PLOWMAN, AN INTERPRETATION OF THE 'A' TEXT, by T. P. Dunning.
Dublin (1937)
—an illuminating enquiry into the theology of the poem.

PIERS PLOWMAN AND CONTEMPORARY RELIGIOUS THOUGHT, by G. Hort [1938].

PIERS PLOWMAN, THE 'C' TEXT AND ITS POET, by E. T. Donaldson. New Haven (1949)

—this authoritative study also contains a Bibliographical Index that includes all important articles on the poem published before 1949.

PIERS PLOWMAN AND THE SCRIPTURAL TRADITION, by D. W. Robertson and B. F. Huppé. Princeton (1951)

—a study of the poem that enriches it with illustration from mediaeval scriptural glosses.

PIERS PLOWMAN AND THE SCHEME OF SALVATION, by R. W. Frank Jr. New Haven (1957).

PIERS THE PLOWMAN, LITERARY RELATIONS OF THE 'A' AND 'B' TEXTS, by D. C. Fowler. Seattle (1961).

PIERS PLOWMAN, AN INTRODUCTION, by E. Salter. Oxford (1962).

PIERS PLOWMAN, AN ESSAY IN CRITICISM, by J. Lawlor (1962)

—a detailed interpretation of the poem as a whole, with critical chapters on its rhythms, imagery and word-play.

Shorter Studies:

Up till fairly recently, most of the critical writing on this poem has been in the form of essays and articles in learned journals. A selection from among these is offered below, but the reader is advised to supplement it from the very full article by M. W. Bloomfield, 'The Present State of Piers Plowman Studies', in *Speculum*, xiv, 1939, and from the Bibliographical Index already mentioned at the end of E. T. Donaldson's book on the 'C' Text (see above).

'Piers Plowman and its Sequence', by J. M. Manly. [In *CHEL*, vol. ii. 1908.]

—this was the first essay to suggest multiple authorship of the poem, and it led to many rejoinders, the most important of which are published in the Early English Text Society under the title *The Piers Plowman Controversy* (Extra Issue, No. 139, 1910).

'The "A" Text', by R. W. Chambers and M. Grattan. *MLR*, iv, 1909–1910.

'The Authorship of Piers Plowman', by R. W. Chambers *MLR*, v, 1910.

'Long Will, Dante and the Righteous Heathen', by R. W. Chambers. *Essays and Studies*, ix, 1924.

'The Date of the "C" Version of Piers the Plowman', by Sister Mary Aquinas. *Abstract of Theses, University of Chicago, Humanistic Series*, iv, 1928.

'The Construction of Piers Plowman', by H. W. Wells. *PMLA*, xliv, 1929.

'The Text of Piers Plowman', by R. W. Chambers and H. Grattan. *MLR*, xxvi, 1931.

'The Character of Piers Plowman', by N. Coghill. *Medium Aevum*, ii, No. 2, 1933.

'The Philosophy of Piers Plowman', by H. W. Wells. *PMLA*, liii, 1938

—Wells' essay of 1929 and this essay were the first to show a structural and intellectual organization of the poem.

'Piers Plowman: A Comparative Study', by R. W. Chambers. [In *Man's Unconquerable Mind*, 1939.]

—contains what is perhaps the best short account of the poem yet published.

POETS AND THEIR CRITICS: LANGLAND AND MILTON, by R. W. Chambers (1942)

—British Academy Warton Lecture, 1941.

'Langland and the Salvation of the Heathen', by T. P. Dunning. *Medium Aevum*, xii, 1943.

'The Date of the "A" Text of Piers Plowman', by J. A. W. Bennett. *PMLA*, lviii, 1943.

THE PARDON OF PIERS PLOWMAN, by N. Coghill (1946)

—British Academy Gollancz Memorial Lecture, 1945.

'Justice and Charity in "The Vision of Piers Plowman"'. by G. Mathew. *Dominican Studies*, i, 1948.

'Langland's Piers Plowman', by D. Traversi. [In *The Age of Chaucer*, 1954 (vol. i of the Pelican *Guide to English Literature*, ed. B. Ford).]

LADY MEED AND THE ART OF PIERS PLOWMAN, by A. G. Mitchell (1956)

—Chambers Memorial Lecture, University College London, 1956.

'The Structure of the "B" Text of Piers Plowman', by T. P. Dunning. *RES, NS*, vii, 1956.

'The Imaginative Unity of Piers Plowman', by J. Lawlor. *RES, NS*, viii, 1957.

'The Audience of Piers Plowman', by J. Burrow. *Anglia*, lxxv, 1957.

Translations:

THE VISION OF PIERS PLOWMAN, by H. W. Wells (1935)
—reprinted 1945. In alliterative verse, complete. With an Introduction by N. Coghill.

VISIONS FROM PIERS PLOWMAN, by N. Coghill (1949)
—in alliterative verse. Selections covering the whole poem.

THE BOOK CONCERNING PIERS THE PLOWMAN, by D. and R. Attwater (1957)
—in alliterative verse. In the Everyman edition.

PIERS THE PLOWMAN, by J. F. Goodridge (1959)
—reprinted 1960. Prose version, with an Introduction. In the Penguin edition.

Background:

ENGLISH WAYFARING LIFE IN THE MIDDLE AGES, by J. J. Jusserand (1889)
—frequently reprinted.

ENGLAND IN THE AGE OF WYCLIFFE, by G. M. Trevelyan (1899)
—4th edition, 1929.

THE WANING OF THE MIDDLE AGES, by J. Huizinga (1924)
—Pelican edition, 1955.

LITERATURE AND PULPIT IN MEDIAEVAL ENGLAND, by G. R. Owst. (1933).

MEDIAEVAL PANORAMA, by G. G. Coulton (1938).

CHAUCER'S WORLD, by E. Rickert, with C. Olson and M. Crow (1948).

THE FOURTEENTH CENTURY, by M. McKisack. Oxford (1959).

Bibliographical Series
of Supplements to 'British Book News'
on Writers and Their Work

GENERAL EDITOR
Geoffrey Bullough

RICHARD PERKINS

From an engraving after a portrait in Dulwich College Picture Gallery

A leading actor of the Queen's Men praised by Webster for his performance in *The White Devil*, probably as Flamineo

JOHN WEBSTER

by

IAN SCOTT-KILVERT

PUBLISHED FOR
THE BRITISH COUNCIL
AND THE NATIONAL BOOK LEAGUE
BY LONGMANS, GREEN & CO.

LONGMANS, GREEN & CO. LTD.
48 Grosvenor Street, London, W.1

Associated Companies, branches and representatives
throughout the World

First Published 1964
© Ian Scott-Kilvert 1964

Printed in Great Britain
F. Mildner & Sons, London, E.C.1

JOHN WEBSTER

I

TRAGEDY deals in absolutes. The typically tragic image
is that of Thomas Hardy's poem, 'The Convergence
of The Twain', which describes the collision of the
Titanic with its fated iceberg. The typically tragic situation
is the act of self-will pursued, whether in ignorance or
knowledge, *à outrance*, the determination of the tragic hero,
Oedipus or Faustus or Macbeth, to refuse compromise and
to hold his course. Comedy accepts our weaknesses as
ultimately controllable within a human norm: tragedy
springs from the paradox that men's desires and ambitions
vastly exceed their limitations. Tragedy's central theme is
the meaning of suffering and the mystery of evil—'Is there
any cause in nature that makes these hard hearts?' But it is
not, as John Dennis, the Augustan critic believed that it
should be, 'a very solemn lecture, inculcating a particular
Providence, and showing it plainly protecting the good and
chastising the bad'. It is not a sermon nor a philosophical
enquiry, but an art which strives to arouse a particular kind
of emotion, and only certain kinds of situation will produce
this effect—neither the downfall of an innocent hero nor
of an out-and-out villain, for example. The true material of
tragedy is the fate, in the Aristotelian phrase, of 'the man in
the middle', the hero who is allowed no unsullied choice,
but is torn by conflicting impulses, and is forced to act, to
suffer, to bear the load of guilt, and finally to attain self-
knowledge. Thus tragedy makes its impact not as doctrine
but as discovery, however unwelcome or unpleasant, by
virtue of its truth to our experience and its uncompromising
confrontation of the worst that life can do to man. But in
order to arrive at this knowledge, it is necessary that the
conflict between the forces of good and evil should be left
free to play itself out, not be pre-determined in the interests
of divine or poetic justice.

So at least it seems to the modern reader, but this freedom

of the imagination has not been acceptable to every age. Restoration audiences could not endure the ending of *King Lear*, and the death of Cordelia was banished from the English stage for a century and a half. But the drama is above all a communal art, a sharing of experience, and the tragic writer is concerned with the extremes of human potentiality. Among the Elizabethans and Jacobeans we find the desire to explore the heights and depths of men's conduct, to encompass the mysterious contradictions of human nature, more highly developed than in any other dramatic literature. The inspiration of the early Elizabethan drama springs from the Renaissance mood of delight in the splendour of the mortal world, and its exhilaration at the sense of power derived from the newly won knowledge of the time. Marlowe's *Tamburlaine* echoes the Renaissance boast, 'Men can do all things if they will', for the intellectual vitality of the age led directly from enquiry to action. But this impulse to rise above man's 'middle state' soon turns to disillusion at the discovery of his limitations.

Such, in crude outline, was the spiritual crisis which brought English tragedy to its maturity, and the period in which its distinctive masterpieces were created was as short-lived as it was rich in achievement. It is preceded by a decade or more of plays such as *The Spanish Tragedy*, *The Jew of Malta*, and *Titus Andronicus*, pieces created to satisfy the robust appetites of a confident society; it is succeeded by a drama of indifference, exemplified in the tragi-comedies and romances of Beaumont and Fletcher and their successors. The great era includes—apart from Shakespeare's four major tragedies—*Timon*, *Coriolanus*, *Antony and Cleopatra*, Tourneur's *The Revenger's Tragedy* and *The Atheist's Tragedy*, Chapman's Bussy and Biron plays, and Webster's *The White Devil* and *The Duchess of Malfi*, together with plays of such near-tragic outlook as *Troilus and Cressida*, *Measure for Measure*, *Volpone* and *The Malcontent*, and it is concentrated within the first dozen years of the seventeenth century. Middleton's work belongs essentially to the same period, though he does not begin to write tragedy until late in his career. Shakespearean tragedy pursues a more profound, less nihilistic line of development, but in the work of his immediate juniors, such as Tourneur and Webster, we see the fulfilment of the process already foreshadowed in the later plays of Marlowe. The upward, aspiring, humanistic conception of man is replaced by a downward, realistic, satirical estimate, and the dominant tragic theme becomes the misdirection of humanity's most admired qualities, authority, courage, love, intelligence in men; beauty, devotion, civilization in women. *Troilus and Cressida* gives warning of the fearful consequences to mankind 'when degree is shak'd', but what Shakespeare's successors call in question is the fitness of the human hierarchy itself. These writers, in Professor Leech's phrase, know little of heaven, much of hell, and the kind of consolation which their tragedy offers might be summed up in Webster's line from *The White Devil*:

> Through darkness diamonds spread their richest light.[1]

II

The re-birth in Western Europe of the pagan literary form of tragedy was in itself an indication of a much wider historical process—the replacement of the theocratic values of the Middle Ages by a conception of life based partly upon the re-discovered ideals of the ancient world, partly upon man's growing sense of mastery over nature. In particular the revival of tragedy bore witness to the revolution which had taken place in men's beliefs concerning death, the after-life and the power of the individual to shape his own destiny. The attitude of the Greek tragedians had been

---

[1] Act III, scene i. Quotations from *The White Devil* and *The Duchess of Malfi* are taken from *Webster and Tourneur* (1959), in the Mermaid series. All other quotations from Webster are taken from *The Complete Works of John Webster*, ed. F. L. Lucas, 4 vols. (1927).

paradoxical—at once rational and fatalistic. Solon's famous warning, 'Call no man happy until he is dead', at least implied that if man refrained from excess and *hubris*, he had a chance of avoiding calamity. On the other hand disaster, when it came, had to be accepted as the will of the gods, although, as with Oedipus or Hippolytus, the punishment might be out of all proportion to the offence.

The mediaeval view is conveniently summarized for us in Chaucer's *Prologue to The Monk's Tale:*

> Tragedie is to seyn a certeyn storie,
> As olde bokes maken us memorie,
> Of hym that stood in greet prosperitee,
> And is y-fallen out of hegh degree
> Into myserie, and endeth wrecchedly.

In other words, man is merely the victim of the unpredictable movements of Fortune's wheel. But behind this simple definition lies the far more important Christian belief that death is a punishment for man's sin, that it represents not the end but the beginning of the true life, and hence that earthly triumphs and disasters are of no account, save as a preparation for the world to come. Thus a mediaeval drama such as *Everyman* is not a tragedy, because the hero, although sorely tried, knows that his salvation is assured provided that he makes himself the willing instrument of God's purposes, and hence the tribulations of this life are seen as no more than the first act of a 'Divine Comedy', in the sense that Dante uses the term. But tragedy foreshortens as it were the perspective of the hereafter, and deliberately creates the impression of finality: every action seems eternal and irrevocable, and although we are conscious of the influence of higher powers, we believe that the hero is to a great extent responsible for his choice and so for its consequences.

As the new learning spread, so the assumptions of mediaeval Christianity were first challenged, then undermined. In statecraft, in commerce and the use of wealth, in science and the arts, in short in every sphere of human intercourse, the new education encouraged a civilized and active self-development which began to compete more and more insistently with the contemplative ideal. The doctrines of <u>Machiavelli</u>, transmitted to England in a distorted form, came to exercise a peculiar fascination upon the Elizabethans, and seemed to provide a technique for overcoming the vicissitudes of fortune and the hazards of the struggle for power. At the same time the Stoic philosophy, with its emphasis upon dying well, especially as it is presented in the plays of Seneca, offered yet another guide to conduct in misfortune. Very few Elizabethan dramatists could read Greek, and the inspiration which they drew from the great themes of the ancient drama—the jealousy of Medea, the pride of Oedipus, the revengeful cruelty of Atreus—reached them almost entirely through the medium of Seneca. Seneca draws upon much the same mythological material as the Greeks, but he gives it an altogether coarser, more crudely theatrical treatment. His taste for realistic descriptions of bloody actions and physical torture, combined with his sententious moralizing, appealed strongly to the Elizabethans, and his most popular plays were those in which he dramatized a spectacular sequence of crime and revenge, such as the *Thyestes*, the *Agamemnon* and the *Medea*. The consolation he offers is philosophical rather than religious. While the Greeks had believed that calamity might be avoidable through right action, Seneca regards it as inseparable from the human condition and seeks rather to find a way of triumphing over it. The new element which he introduces into tragedy is the defiant courage of the hero, which enables him to preserve his integrity, and thus win a Pyrrhic victory over an unjust fate:

> Though in our miseries Fortune have a part,
> Yet in our noble sufferings she hath none:
> Contempt of pain, that we may call our own.
> (*The Duchess of Malfi*, V. iii.)

It is worth noting that the influence of Seneca in England is closely connected with that of Machiavelli, for Senecan tragedy became known to the Elizabethans not only in Latin but through the plays of Seneca's Italian imitators. It was these dramatists, and especially Giraldi Cinthio (from whom Shakespeare borrowed the plot of *Othello*), who first created the character of the Machiavellian intriguer, and who thus provide the link between the Senecan tyrant (Atreus or Lycus) and the Elizabethan Machiavellian villain.

All these conceptions played a vital part in the creation of the tragedy of the period. But perhaps its most exceptional characteristic is its almost obsessive preoccupation with death. Of course death is always likely to provide the climax of a tragedy, but to the Elizabethans and Jacobeans it was often the play's very *raison d'être*, the end of human achievement and the embodiment of the final and the terrible. They regarded a man's attitude towards death as a uniquely significant clue to his character, and they explored every means to dramatize the sight of death upon the stage. Death haunted the imagination of the Elizabethans to a degree which it is difficult for us to appreciate. The emblems and disguises of death, the *memento mori* encountered in the jewellery, the churches, the public signs and many other everyday objects were familiar to every member of the audience. These associations enabled the playgoer to follow the poet without difficulty on the furthest flights of his imagination, from the simple images of the skull, the worm, and the taper to the 'fell sergeant' of Shakespeare's *Hamlet*, or, strangest of all, the 'lean, tawny-face tobacconist' of Dekker's *Old Fortunatus*.

III

Apart from the approximate dates of publication of his works we know very little about Webster's life. It is unlikely that he can have been born much later than 1580:

the first mention of his dramatic career is dated 1602, in which year an entry in Henslowe's Diary refers to his collaboration with Middleton, Drayton, Munday and others in the play *Caesar's Fall*. For the next six or seven years he worked for a variety of companies. Later in 1602 he collaborated with Dekker, Heywood and Chettle in *Lady Jane*—a historical drama concerning the ill-fated Lady Jane Grey—and *Christmas Comes But Once A Year*. Two years later we find him working with Dekker on two comedies of city life, *Westward Ho* and *Northward Ho*, and in the same year he published the Induction to Marston's *The Malcontent*. This was a comic 'curtain-raiser' written in prose and full of topical jokes, somewhat in the manner of the Induction to Shakespeare's *Taming Of The Shrew*. In 1607 he was again collaborating with Dekker, and published *Sir Thomas Wyatt*, possibly a revised version of *Lady Jane*. By this time he may already have begun work on *The White Devil*, which is believed to have taken him several years to write. The early months of 1612 are the most likely date for the first performance, which was given by the Queen's Men at the Red Bull, a surprisingly 'low-brow' playhouse for a piece of this kind. In his note to the first edition Webster pays tribute (the first time that a poet had ever done so) to the playing of an actor: this was Richard Perkins, then at the beginning of his career and later to become the most famous member of the company. 'The worth of his action', writes Webster, 'did crown both the beginning and the end', which makes it almost certain that he played the part of Flamineo.

The production of *The White Devil* evidently enhanced Webster's reputation, and at the end of 1612 he published 'A Monumental Column', an elegy inspired by the death of the eighteen year old Prince Henry, James I's much admired eldest son. Both the dramatic technique and the versification of *The Duchess of Malfi* suggest that Webster's two great tragedies were written in close succession, and it is likely that *The Duchess* belongs to the year 1613. His next work was probably the lost historical play *The Guise*, while in 1614 he contributed a new set of Characters to the highly successful volume of this title which had been posthumously published for Sir Thomas Overbury. The *Characters* are a collection of epigrammatic, often satirical prose portraits of contemporary types; they are modelled on the *Ethical Characters* of the Greek philosopher Theophrastus, a work which had been translated into Latin by Casaubon and enjoyed great popularity at this period. Webster's last indisputably independent play, a tragi-comedy of bourgeois life (again placed in an Italian setting) entitled *The Devil's Law-Case* followed some two years later, and he is also the author of 'Monuments of Honour', an elaborate occasional poem written on behalf of the Merchant Taylors' Company for the Lord Mayor's Pageant and published in 1624. After this his most notable work is the Roman tragedy *Appius and Virginia*, which some scholars have ascribed to the earliest phase of his career, while others judge it to have been written in partnership with Heywood in the late 1620's. Other plays in which Webster's collaboration is discernible are *Anything For A Quiet Life*, a comedy originally attributed to Middleton, which Mr. Lucas dates about 1621, *The Fair Maid Of The Inn*, shared with Massinger and Ford, and *A Cure For A Cuckold* with Rowley, both these latter pieces probably belonging to the year 1625. Recent research by Professor R. G. Howarth claims several new attributions for Webster, notably *A Speedy Post* (1624), *The Valiant Scot* (1637) and several more of the Overburian Characters.

Our picture of Webster's life remains conjectural in the extreme. The sequence of his published works suggests that he was not a particularly inventive playwright, but was influenced by current theatrical fashion. After writing his two great tragedies he seems to have experimented with a variety of topical themes, but never again found a subject which could rekindle his inspiration: certainly in his later plays of bourgeois life his interest seems to be engaged only in an intermittent and perfunctory fashion. The closing years of his life are again veiled in obscurity, but there is at least a strong presumption that the dramatist was the John Webster who died on 10 March, 1637, and was buried in the churchyard of St. James, Clerkenwell, which was also the resting place of his colleagues Dekker and Rowley.

IV

The years of Webster's apprenticeship in the theatre coincided with a period of intense disillusion in the national life. The decline of landed wealth and the pursuit of money-making in its place, the downfall of the brilliant but erratic Earl of Essex, the death of Queen Elizabeth and the conspicuous absence of the magic of sovereignty in her successor, the disgrace and imprisonment of Raleigh, the series of conspiracies aimed at the throne and culminating in the Gunpowder Plot—these and many parallel events combined to produce a sense of the breakdown of established standards and beliefs, which was quickly reflected in the drama. Shakespeare and Chapman, survivors of the Elizabethan age, approach tragedy by way of the historical play, and we find them at all times keenly aware of the sanctity of kingship and the hierarchy of degree. Their protagonists are men and women of unquestioned authority, whose public life is brought to ruin by private weaknesses. The tragedy of Othello or of Antony lies not only in the hero's betrayal—real or imaginary—by his beloved, but in the collapse of his soldiership.

But with the younger generation of tragedians, Marston, Webster, Tourneur and Middleton, we feel at once the absence of this ideal order. The new playwrights are oppressed by an apparently irreconcilable conflict between the world of earthly experience and the world of the spirit:

> While we look up to heaven, we confound
> Knowledge with knowledge. O, I am in a mist!
>
> (*The White Devil*, V. vi.)

Humanity, they are compelled to recognize, is no better for its new-found knowledge, but rather more inhuman: indeed what marks out the tragedy of this period is the ingenuity and elaboration of the dramatists' conception of evil. The bond of nature is cracked, and the pragmatic creed of Machiavelli, with its assumption of the natural weakness and wickedness of men and its insistence upon *la verità effetuale della cosa*, has become the reality which forces itself upon the playwright's vision. Beyond this code of self-seeking, all is uncertainty, 'a mist' as Webster repeatedly describes it; the divine powers are indifferent, and the heavens high, far off and unsearchable.

By comparison with the Elizabethan approach, the new dramatic poetry is noticeably more sceptical, more sophist-icated, more aware of inner contradictions. The very title, *The White Devil*, contains a multiplicity of meanings, which begin with the Elizabethan proverb, 'the white devil is worse than the black', and may be applied not only to Vittoria but to the hero, Bracchiano, and indeed to the society in which the play is set. The new poetry is also more condemnatory and satirical in tone, and in the case of Webster (though not of Marston and Tourneur, who caricature and distort to intensify the effect of their satire) it is more naturalistic in its handling of character and event. For Webster's audience *The White Devil* was a strikingly topical play: the actions which it depicts had taken place barely a quarter of a century before. And just as a subject which is remote in legend or history seems to emphasize the influence of fate upon the outcome, so the choice of a modern theme creates the opposite illusion: the more contemporary the characters, the greater their apparent freedom of action. Certainly by comparison with plays such as *Romeo and Juliet* or *Othello* the plots of Webster's tragedies owe very little to chance: at first glance his characters strike us as wilful to the last degree in courting their own downfall. Of course freedom and compulsion are necessarily the coordinates upon which all tragedy is plotted,

and every dramatist of consequence discovers as it were a
new equation for the act of choice, which is the starting
point for a tragic situation. But a closer study suggests that
Webster differs from most of his contemporaries in choosing
not to make this issue explicit. When Bosola exclaims

> We are merely the stars' tennis-balls, struck and bandied
> Which way please them
>
> (*The Duchess of Malfi*, V. iv.)

we know that this is only a half-truth in the design of the
tragedy, and in fact the continuous uncertainty as to whether
fate or chance rules the world contributes powerfully to the
horror which the play inspires in us.

What perhaps most astonishes the modern reader of
Jacobean tragedy is the divergence between the avowed
purpose of the dramatists and the actual effect of the drama,
between the impression intended and the impression conveyed. Both the poets and the critics of the time were
convinced that Renaissance tragedy was more improving
than Greek. They found fault with the latter for its
rebellious protest against divine providence, and praised
the former for demonstrating, in Puttenham's phrase, 'the
just punishment of God in revenge of a vicious and evil
life'. Similarly the playwrights constantly defend the theatre
against the attacks of the Puritans by stressing its reformative
value. Yet in *The White Devil* it is perfectly clear that
Webster's sympathies are strongly drawn towards the
guilty lovers, while in *The Duchess of Malfi* the sufferings
inflicted upon the heroine are out of all proportion to her
offence. It was this discrepancy between the precept and the
practice of Elizabethan and Jacobean tragedy which
prompted Rymer's indignant question—which he might
as well have applied to Webster's tragedies as to *Othello*—
'If this be our end, what boots it to be virtuous?' Webster's
sympathy, not only in his tragedies but also in his later
plays, consistently goes out to what he calls 'integrity of

life', that is the determination to remain what you are, in the face of suffering, misfortune and death: admiration for this quality can scarcely be reconciled with conventional notions of good and evil.

V

Webster's contribution to the comedies written with Dekker is hardly distinguishable from his collaborator's. But in his first independent play, *The White Devil*, he suddenly emerges as a highly sophisticated writer who has succeeded in forging an original masterpiece out of the theatrical fashions of the moment. *The White Devil* brings together an astonishing number of these. It is in part a tragedy of revenge, with the customary accompaniments of ghosts, madness, treachery and sudden violence: it is in part a tragedy of love, centred upon the brilliant figures of a Renaissance prince and a renowned adulteress. It is also an Italianate tragedy, complete with Machiavellian plotters, and new and horrifying methods of assassination. It has something of the pageantry of a chronicle play, with its Papal election and its dramatic trial scene. Finally, it provides a satirical commentary upon courtly life by means of the fashionable creation of a malcontent observer, the total effect being seasoned with the type of formal moralizing, the 'elegant and sententious excitation to virtue', which the serious writers and critics of the day regarded as indispensable to tragic writing.

It was a recognized convention of the period that tragedy should be based upon incidents taken from real life, the theory being that audiences would be more deeply impressed by a catastrophe based upon fact than by an invented plot. The events described by Webster in *The White Devil* were drawn from a recent *cause célèbre* in Italian history. The play's heroine, Vittoria Accorombona, was a strikingly beautiful girl who had been married at the age of sixteen to

Francesco Peretti (Camillo), a nephew of Cardinal Montalto (Monticelso), who later became Pope Sixtus V. The Duke of Bracchiano, Paolo Orsini, a member of one of the noblest Roman families and a soldier who had distinguished himself at Lepanto, met Vittoria in Rome in 1580, when she was twenty-three, and fell passionately in love with her. He was believed to have murdered his wife Isabella on the ground of her infidelity, and he now procured the murder of Vittoria's husband and soon afterwards married her in secret. The suspected couple were expressly forbidden to marry by Pope Gregory XIII, Peretti's murder was investigated, and Vittoria arrested. But she was soon released, and when Pope Gregory died in 1585, Bracchiano married her openly. On the same day Cardinal Montalto, the uncle and protector of Peretti, was elected Pope and lost no time in excommunicating Bracchiano. Later in that year the Duke fell sick and died, but not before making generous provision for Vittoria. The Orsini family were determined to deprive her of this legacy in the interests of the young heir (Giovanni), and when Vittoria resisted their efforts, she was brutally murdered in Padua by a band of assassins led by one of Bracchiano's kinsmen, the Lodovico of the play.

These events were recorded in innumerable chronicles of the time. The Swedish scholar, Dr. Gunnar Boklund, has traced over a hundred separate accounts—the most interesting, and one which shows many correspondences with minor incidents of the play, being a newsletter written in German for the famous banking house of Fugger. But whatever Webster's source, which has never been conclusively identified, he drastically re-shaped both the details and the motivation of the original straggling narrative. Lodovico, who is credited with a secret passion for Bracchiano's murdered wife, is transformed from a minor character into the principal agent of retribution, whose consuming desire for revenge hangs over the play from beginning to end. The young Peretti is given the unsympathetic role of a middle-aged cuckold, Isabella becomes a virtuous wife, while Bracchiano, far from dying peacefully in his bed, is first poisoned by mercury smeared on the mouth-piece of his helmet and then strangled on his death-bed by assassins disguised as Capuchin friars, a horrifying scene which provides one of the climaxes of the action.

But by far the most important addition to the play is the character of Vittoria's brother. The roles of Flamineo in this play and of Bosola in *The Duchess of Malfi* are peculiarly Websterian creations and represent two of his most original contributions to Jacobean tragedy. Each is in one sense a topical character, a Renaissance 'forgotten man', who is amply endowed with intelligence and courage, but lacks preferment. Each is in critical parlance 'a tool villain', who, as in other Jacobean plays, bears a grudge against his master, but whose motives have been subtly humanized, and who thus brings a new dimension to the tragedy, because he is capable of the pangs of conscience:

> I have lived
> Riotously ill, like some that live in court,
> And sometimes when my face was full of smiles,
> Have felt the maze of conscience in my breast.
>
> (*The White Devil*, V. iv.)

Each is also given the role of satirical observer: he exercises an important influence upon the action and the emotional tone of the play, but at the same time stands apart, mocking, criticizing, and uttering many of the dramatist's sharpest comments upon the other characters and the human condition in general.

Elizabethan drama commonly achieves its most powerful effects by violent contrasts, the contrast between Hamlet and the gravediggers, Cleopatra and the clown, murders which take place on wedding-nights. The first impression left by *The White Devil* is that Webster is aiming at a similar kind of contrast between outward magnificence and inward corruption. His purpose, as implied in the play's title, is

apparently to juxtapose the splendour and the horror of a
Renaissance court, and to exploit the paradox, so potent in
the minds of his audience, that the loveliest and most
civilized country in the world was also as a contemporary
describes it, 'the Academie of manslaughter, the sporting-
place of murther, the Apothecary's shop of poyson for all
Nations', where a man such as Lodovico could pride himself upon a murder as a work of art. *The White Devil* is a
tragedy of worldliness, of the desires of the flesh embraced
with the courage of utter abandon. Abandon is the keynote
of Bracchiano's first speech, 'Quite lost, Flamineo!', and it
is clear from the outset that here there will be no struggles
of conscience, no question of a noble character weakened
or overthrown by misfortune. The protagonists of this play
are bent on earthly pleasures and rewards, and they show
themselves to be shameless and often heartless: they may
appeal to our reluctant admiration, but not to our pity.
Perhaps the sharpest irony of the play is found in its message
that man, even at his most calculating and self-willed,
cannot be master of his fate. Bracchiano, the soldier-prince
of the Cinquecento, still represents in our eyes something
of the magnificence and assurance of his age, but the
poisoned helmet which reduces this former hero of Lepanto
to delirium and an unsanctified death, may be seen as an apt
symbol for the spiritual corruption which had infected the
Renaissance ideal of greatness.

As soon as the play is studied more closely, the contradictions and ambiguities of its values begin to appear. In the
opening scenes we find Lodovico, a man of blood already
guilty of several murders in Rome, swearing vengeance
before any crime has been committed. Francisco, the
brother of the murdered Isabella, pursues his revenge with
such Machiavellian lack of scruple that he taints the justice
of his cause, and at the end of the play is condemned by his
young nephew Giovanni, whose rights he is supposed to be
vindicating. On the other hand, when Isabella and Camillo
are murdered, Webster by representing their deaths in

dumb-show contrives to distance the crime and diminish its horror, and thus to avoid alienating our sympathy for Bracchiano and Vittoria. In the trial scene we are shown for the first time the full measure of Vittoria's courage, when alone and abandoned by her lover, she not only faces but dominates a completely hostile court. At the same time we know that this is the courage of impenitence and bravado, not of a clear conscience, for there is little doubt that even if she has not actually procured her husband's murder, she is at least an accessory after the fact. Yet when she shows herself equally undaunted by the lawyer's pedantry and the Cardinal's animosity, admiration for her courage proves stronger than the evidence, so that the audience can almost accept her denials:

> For your names
> Of whore and murderess, they proceed from you
> As if a man should spit against the wind
> The filth returns in's face . . .
>
> (*The White Devil*, III. ii.)

or the outrageous profession of innocence with which she greets her sentence of imprisonment in a house of correction:

> It shall not be a house of convertites.
> My mind shall make it happier to me
> Than the Pope's palace, and more peaceable
> Than thy soul, though thou art a cardinal.
>
> (*The White Devil*, III. ii.)

In this play Webster takes up a position which is quite different from that of Kyd or of Shakespeare in their revenge tragedies, where the duel between the avenger and his antagonist can quickly be identified as a struggle between good and evil, and there is in fact a fundamental difference in his conception of tragedy. In *Hamlet* the avenger is not only technically the hero, but in a very real sense the moral centre of the play. In *The White Devil* there is no moral centre, and no set of values is held up as the right one. Yet the play, its author might well argue, possesses a strongly moral theme, which is stated in the opening lines, the theme of 'courtly reward and punishment'. Where Webster differs from Shakespeare is in pursuing his moral purpose by condemnation and exposure, by focussing attention not upon the hero but upon the social setting, the corruption of which is held up as a warning, in short by teaching man 'wherein he is imperfect'. The play is much concerned with the situation of prince and courtier and the vicious nature of their relationship. On the prince's side power leads to ruinous extravagance, the guilty recollection of which haunts Bracchiano on his death-bed, and to tyrannous injustice: he refuses to reward Flamineo's faithful service, but heaps privileges upon Mulinassar, who is in reality his deadly enemy, the Duke of Florence, in disguise. On the courtier's side the system encourages unscrupulous flattery and disloyalty at the first opportunity: Bracchiano is mocked and ignored the moment that he is dead.

In spite of the powerful impetus of the action, this satirical approach produces a discordant and at times disjointed impression both in the construction and the characterization, with the result that individual scenes are intensely vivid but the total effect is confused. In its general design the plot lacks the unifying power of a single dominant motive: it moves forward in a succession of loosely connected episodes and with the help of casually introduced supernumeraries such as the doctor, the conjuror, the lawyer and the ambassadors. The poetry displays abrupt changes of feeling and a perpetual conflict of moods, so that the most eloquent and passionate protestations may be called in question or rendered ambiguous by some ironical comment, which makes us doubt the motives of the speaker.

This ambiguity applies principally to the character of Vittoria. Here, as the play's title suggests, Webster has aimed at creating an image of fatal fascination, a character who combines treachery and loyalty, cowardice and courage, infidelity and devotion to a degree which baffles judgement. But equally the minor characters are not what they at first appear: we find on closer scrutiny that Isabella is by no means totally unselfish, and that even Cornelia and the upright Marcello are quite ready to accept Bracchiano's patronage. Above all this ambivalence makes itself felt in the relationship between Bracchiano and Vittoria. The Duke's 'Quite lost, Flamineo!' leaves us in no doubt as to the depth of his infatuation, but this declaration is immediately followed by Flamineo's sneers, which cheapen not only Bracchiano's passion in itself but Vittoria as the object of it. Later in the play the effect of the otherwise moving quarrel and reconciliation scene in the house of convertites is offset by our knowledge that the lovers have themselves been outwitted by Francisco. And in Bracchiano's death scene, the audience's sympathy for Vittoria, at first aroused by the tenderness of the Duke's

> Where's this good woman? Had I infinite worlds
> They were too little for thee: must I leave thee?
> *(The White Devil*, V. iii.)

is later dispelled by his delirious ravings, which repeatedly hint at her wantonness and falsehood, and from this point onward Webster offers no hint that theirs is a union which can transcend death. When Vittoria faces her own end, the quality which emerges supreme is her defiant courage, not her tenderness. The love which she and Bracchiano have shared is destructive in its essence, and in the superb simile with which she confronts her fate,

> My soul, like to a ship in a black storm,
> Is driven I know not whither,
> *(The White Devil*, V. vi.)

it may not be fanciful to detect a parallel to Dante's image of the lovers in the second circle of the Inferno, who have abandoned salvation for passion, and who, yielding to the

strength of their desires, are forever 'blown with restless
violence about the pendent world'. Paradoxically *The
White Devil* offers us the most brilliant and spirited picture
of 'the busy trade of life' that Webster ever created. Compared with its successor it gives off a vitality, a confidence
and a dramatic impetus which he could never afterwards
sustain through a whole play. But it remains a tragedy of
despair.

VI

The Duchess of Malfi was first performed not later than
the end of 1614. It clearly belongs to the same creative phase
as *The White Devil*, for Webster's powers, unlike Shakespeare's, did not pass through a prolonged and many-sided
development: his art rose swiftly to its zenith and swiftly
declined. In *The Duchess of Malfi* there are many striking
parallels with its predecessor, but the contrast in tone and
in tempo is unmistakable. These resemblances, it may be,
are the product of Webster's peculiar and laborious methods
of composition, which often led him to re-fashion or to
transpose situations which he had already handled. Thus he
once more takes for his theme a woman's passion pursued
in defiance of the social code, the unwritten law of 'degree'.
On this occasion the heroine marries beneath her station
rather than above it, but the result is the same: she suffers
the persecution of powerful enemies, namely her brothers
(again a Cardinal and a Duke) who act as the supposed
champions of moral orthodoxy and family interest. Once
more the author dwells upon the corruption of high place,
and once more he gives a major role to a satirical malcontent,
a down-at-heel scholar and soldier, who is forced by poverty
to make himself the creature of an unscrupulous patron.

But from the outset the mood of the play is more
chastened and melancholy, the texture of the poetry more
delicate, less rhetorical, the tempo of events less strenuous,

more world-weary. *The White Devil* delivers a crushing
indictment of courtly society, but at the same time it depicts
a world of exuberant animation and self-assertion. Although
its characters fail in their worldly ambitions, they still desire
passionately to live. By contrast, the Cardinal as he dies asks
to be laid by and never thought of, and Antonio reckons
life but the good hours of an ague. A malevolent stillness and
secrecy brood over the action and behind it lurk the terrors
of madness, witchcraft and the supernatural. The play
seems to be set in a sombre half-world, poised between
death and life, and this oppressive atmosphere is intensified
by the nightmarish rhythm of the Duchess's persecution,
which seems to be now suspended, now pursued with
demoniac cruelty. The Duchess's torment of being
continually watched and prevented from sleeping was a
recognized method of dealing with witches. Ferdinand,
when he vows never to set eyes on her more, is in effect
calling down a curse upon his sister. The Duchess in the
agony of her imprisonment solemnly curses her brothers,
and elsewhere we learn of the hereditary curse which
dooms the House of Aragon. By comparison with the
earlier tragedy, in which man is seen as a sinning but
potentially magnificent creature, his stature has terrifyingly
shrunk: 'deformity' is a key-word in Webster's vocabulary
for this play.

The plot is based on historical events, but it reached
Webster in fictional form through one of Bandello's novels
adapted into French by Belleforest: this version was in turn
translated into English by William Painter and included in
his *Palace of Pleasure*, published in 1566, which was Webster's
direct source. Painter treats his subject as a cautionary tale,
the story of a woman of royal birth who, after being
widowed early in her youth, 'was moved with that desire
that pricketh others that be of flesh and blood', and contracted a secret marriage to her steward, a commoner. In
doing this she chose to ignore the wishes of her family, and
so, the novelist concludes, her fate was not undeserved.

Webster, however, found in this tale of suffering a further development of his conception of tragedy. Previously he had shown his admiration for the courage which was the saving grace of characters who were otherwise unscrupulous or morally insensitive. Here the ordeal he imposes on his heroine is not confined to violence and death: it is a remorseless attempt to annihilate her soul, and the courage of the Duchess is the more spiritually profound because she is capable of self-judgement. None of the characters of *The White Devil* had possessed sufficient self-judgement to be capable of altering the course of his life. Webster's moral scheme demanded that the Duchess's murder should be avenged, and he proves the keenness of his moral sense by his control of Bosola's gradual awakening to the iniquity of his service. Bosola's dying words,

> Let worthy minds ne'er stagger in distrust
> To suffer death or shame for what is just:
> Mine is another voyage,
>
> (*The Duchess of Malfi*, V. v.)

contain the agonized discovery that *he* has suffered death and shame to no purpose. But dramatically speaking the pursuit of the Duchess's murderers introduces a shift of interest which is fatal to the unity of the play, and after the greatness of the fourth act the closing scenes are inevitably felt as an anti-climax.

A great deal of critical comment has been devoted to the motives of the Cardinal and of Ferdinand in persecuting their sister, and again to the question of how far Webster considered the Duchess's conduct as blameworthy. The Cardinal is, no doubt, concerned in his aloof and haughty fashion with the question of family honour, and the news of the Duchess's feigned pilgrimage to Loreto can rouse him to anger. But he never speaks to her save in Ferdinand's company, and his behaviour is so much that of the self-sufficient Machiavellian that it is difficult at times to remember that he is her brother at all. With Ferdinand the case is very different. It is he who takes the initiative and invents every refinement of cruelty in the torture of his sister. It is he who obscenely threatens her in the first scene, and who is thrown into a frenzy of rage at every mention of the pleasures of her marriage. Certainly Webster hints at an intense physical awareness of his sister, which some critics have gone so far as to interpret as an incestuous passion. But while Webster repeatedly stresses the pain and the fury which lie behind Ferdinand's outbursts, he consistently declines to interpret them, and it is at least arguable that the peculiar effect of terror and suffering which he sought to convey demanded that this issue should remain a mystery: in fact the Duchess's ordeal becomes the more horrifying because of the very lack of an explicit motive on the part of her tormentors.

As for the Duchess, a modern audience naturally tends to see her as the innocent victim of her brothers' jealousy, suspicion and greed. The fact remains, however, that in choosing to disregard their warnings and marry beneath her she compromises her integrity and finds herself involved with Antonio in a web of deceit and subterfuge from which she is delivered only by her imprisonment. According to the public opinion of the time she had not only flouted the secular and religious concept of degree, but had added to her offence by concealing it. Besides this, there was a strong current of disapproval against the re-marriage of widows; Webster in his 'Character of a Virtuous Widow' indicates the strength of this sentiment:

> For her children's sake she first marries, for she married that she might have children, and for their sakes she marries no more. She is like the purest gold, only employed for Princes' medals, she never receives but one man's impression . . .

The Swedish scholar Inga Stina Ekblad has put forward the theory, supported by a close analysis of the text, that the consort of madmen introduced by Ferdinand as a final torment for his sister was intended as a masque in mockery of her marriage to Antonio, and that its form is derived from the *Charivari* or 'marriage-baiting', a ceremony of French origin, which dates from the late Middle Ages and was performed as a gesture of public disapproval of a reprehensible or unequal marriage. This interpretation certainly lends a deeper and more intelligible purpose to an episode which has often been criticized as a crude attempt to intensify the horror of the Duchess' 'mortification by degrees'. According to the same theory Bosola's famous dirge:

> Hark, now everything is still
> The screech-owl and the whistler shrill
> Call upon our dame aloud
> And bid her quickly don her shroud . . .
>
> Strew your hair with powders sweet:
> Don clean linen, bathe your feet,
> And (the foul fiend more to check)
> A crucifix let bless your neck:
> 'Tis now full tide, 'tween night, and day
> End your groan, and come away,
>
> (*The Duchess of Malfi*, IV. ii.)

represents both in its context and its imagery a mock epithalamion, performed to bring the Duchess not to her wedding-chamber but to her death.

Nevertheless, in this play there is far less moral ambiguity than we find in *The White Devil*. In the character of the Duchess Webster creates for the first time a tragic figure who in the process of suffering develops in stature. At the beginning of the play we are made aware of her youthful beauty, her grace, her impulsiveness, her craving for love and her isolation, while the scene in which she woos and marries Antonio strikes a note of tenderness and devotion which is entirely new in Webster's work. Throughout her relation-

ship with Antonio it is the Duchess's courage which keeps
the initiative, and when her secret is discovered it is she
who faces her brother's dagger and contrives Antonio's
pretended disgrace. The turning point in her development
is reached with her separation from Antonio, when she
declares that 'nought made me e'er Go right but Heaven's
scourge-stick . . .' and this scene leads directly to the fourth
act which may claim to be regarded as one of the supreme
achievements of Jacobean drama.

Here the play suddenly opens into a wider universe
which transcends common experience: the action moves
on the psychological plane to the frontiers of madness, and
on the spiritual to a limbo of suffering in which the Duchess
undergoes her purgatory. As in the storm scenes of *Lear*,
time and place seem to be suspended, and in these few pages
it is as if the Duchess passes through a lifetime. The conflict
within her nature between 'the spirit of greatness' and 'the
spirit of woman', which has persisted throughout the play,
is now brought to its climax. When she is deprived of all
that she cherishes most, her husband, her children, her
position, her very identity, she loses all desire to live, her
mind totters, and it is Bosola's deliberate alternation of
mockery and compassion which helps her to cling to sanity
and to see her situation without illusion. She has passed
beyond the state of defiant self-assertion, which had earlier
wrung from her the Senecan outcry 'I am Duchess of Malfi
still',[1] and in her last words to the executioners who are to
strangle her, she has put behind her not only despair but
pride:

> Pull, and pull strongly, for your able strength
> Must pull down Heaven upon me:
> Yet stay; Heaven-gates are not so highly arched
> As princes' palaces; they that enter there
> Must go upon their knees.
>
> (*The Duchess of Malfi*, IV. ii.)

[1] An echo of a famous phrase from Seneca's *Medea*: 'Medea superest'.

This declaration of humility stands out in contrast to the self-conscious resolve shown by Webster's other heroes and heroines in the face of death, and it is unique in Webster's writing: it suggests that in the creation of the Duchess he lays hold for once of a spiritual assurance and exaltation which elsewhere escape him.

VII

In the history of literature tragedy is generally regarded as an exceptionally stable form, which has somehow preserved throughout the centuries a recognizable resemblance to its Greek originals. But these resemblances are deceptive. Greek drama is essentially religious. Its primary concern is not to study the personality of the hero but to interpret the regulation of human affairs by the actions of the gods: its plots are drawn from a single body of mythology and its form is rigidly stylized. Elizabethan tragedy is essentially secular. The playwrights abandoned the scriptural or allegorical material which had supplied the themes of the mediaeval drama, and turned their attention instead to English and Roman histories or French and Italian *novelle*. The mysteries which they explore are those

> Of fate and chance and change in human life

and this change of direction has never been reversed. But if Elizabethan and modern tragedies share some resemblances in theme, they share very few in form or technique, and the reader will be led far astray if he expects the Elizabethan play to conform to the dramatic methods of Ibsen and his successors, themselves strongly influenced by the techniques of modern fiction.

The vital point to be grasped here—admirably developed by Miss M. C. Bradbrook in her *Themes and Conventions of Elizabethan Tragedy*—is that the Elizabethan playwright did not set out to devise a plot in the form of a logical or internally consistent narrative. The essential ingredients for his drama were striking episodes and memorable language. He could not, as his modern counterpart can, conceal his lack of poetic inspiration by attention to the details of construction. Yeats's criticism of the speech of modern dramatic characters is well-known: 'When they are deeply moved, they look silently into the fire-place', and he was referring to the modern playwright's assumption that he can achieve his emotional effect through the placing and sequence of events, rather than through the eloquence of his dialogue. To Elizabethan audiences eloquence was the very breath of drama, and they were interested above all in how a character spoke and acted in a moment of crisis rather than in how he arrived there. In this respect an Elizabethan tragedy is more like the score of an opera than the text of a novel. The elements of place and time, for example, are treated as freely and flexibly as possible. If they lend themselves to dramatic exploitation, well and good, but they possess few rights of their own. Much of the sustained effect of terror and anguish which is built up in the fourth act of *The Duchess of Malfi* depends on the vagueness of the location and the suspension of time during the Duchess's imprisonment.

This is not to say that the Elizabethans were incapable of the kind of mechanical dexterity which was so much admired by William Archer. Shakespeare achieves something of this cog-wheel effect in *Othello*, and Jonson in *Volpone*, while Beaumont and Fletcher were still more adroit in the plotting of their material. But most of the playwrights of the period were not thinking along the lines of the Aristotelian whole, and it would be difficult to select any play as a typical specimen of Elizabethan or Jacobean dramatic structure. Since the source material varied so widely, and since plays tended to be conceived as a series of striking situations, every major playwright developed a dramatic form of his own, the mould of which was shaped by the nature of his poetic gifts. At its best the imaginative pressure and concentration of the language of Jacobean tragedy sweeps away the problems of dramatic illusion. The poets created a speech which could be simple or ceremonious by turns, and was at once direct in its elementary sense and rich in secondary meanings. In *The White Devil*, for example, Webster achieves one of the most powerful openings in the whole range of Jacobean drama. Lodovico's cry of 'Banish'd!' not only sums up the initial situation of the play and casts the shadow of the revenger over all that follows, but in a deeper sense it suggests the self-excommunication of this blood-crazed figure from the normal instincts of humanity. It is at once followed by other metaphors central to the play's meaning, such as those which hint at Vittoria's career—'Fortune's a right whore' and 'an idle meteor soon lost i'th'air'. The best of Webster's poetry, like that of Shakespeare, Tourneur, Middleton and other contemporaries, possesses this power of prefiguring the action by means of dramatic images which leap from the particular to the general and reveal the moral universe that surrounds the characters and the setting.

VIII

Webster is one of those rare dramatists who in his first independent play achieves at a single bound the height of his poetic powers. *The White Devil* offers us Jacobean verse in its full maturity: here Webster is exploiting after his own fashion many of the developments in style and versification which Shakespeare had first introduced into his great tragedies. The end-stopped blank verse pentameter has been completely remoulded, passages of any length are frequently enjambed, the rhythms of colloquial speech are counterpointed against the regular beat of the line, and the style and tone of the dialogue clearly reflects the demand for

a greater naturalism in expression and performance. Like
the best of his rivals in the theatre Webster quickly establishes
a dramatic idiom which is unmistakably his own. Unlike
his fellow satirists Marston and Tourneur, he shows himself
sympathetic even to the most villainous of his characters
and keenly aware of their individual and unpredictable
qualities, and he shares something of Shakespeare's gift for
coining images which can project a character within a single
line of verse or prose.

The tone of his verse is at once witty, sardonic, allusive,
full of nervous energy. His handling of metre is often as
harsh and irregular as Donne's, and his frequent habit of
introducing resolved feet reflects the complexity or deliberate outlandishness of his figures of speech:

> Mark her, I prithee: she simpers like the suds
> Acollier hath been washed in . . .
>
> (*The White Devil*, V. iii.)

Elsewhere when he aims at a sententious effect he produces
a *rallentando* through a sequence of heavily stressed mono-
syllables:

> This busy trade of life appears most vain
> Since rest breeds rest, where all seek pain by pain.
>
> (*The White Devil*, V. vi.)

If he lacks the architectonic sense, he comes nearest of all
his contemporaries to Shakespeare in his power to produce
striking yet subtle variations of mood, of strength and of
pace within a scene. Some of his finest effects are achieved
by sudden transformations of this kind, as in *The White
Devil* with the entry of the boy Giovanni in mourning for
his mother immediately after the passion and tumult of the
court scene, or with Ferdinand's eavesdropping upon the
careless jesting of the lovers in *The Duchess of Malfi*. While
other dramatists employ song to great effect, Webster in

The White Devil and *The Duchess of Malfi* without invoking the aid of music uses the dramatic lyric in a completely original fashion to introduce a different emotional dimension. Of Cornelia's lines:

> Call for the Robin-red-breast and the wren,
> Since o'er shady groves they hover,
> And with leaves and flowers do cover
> The friendless bodies of unburied men
>
> (*The White Devil*, V. iv.)

Lamb wrote:

I never saw anything like this dirge, except the ditty which reminds Ferdinand of his drowned father in *The Tempest*. As that is of the water, watery, so this is of the earth, earthy. Both have that intenseness of feeling which seems to resolve itself into the elements which it contemplates.

These achievements represent the peaks of Webster's art. On the other hand he is curiously unenterprising in his use of the soliloquy, which he normally employs merely to give notice of his characters' intentions rather than to explore their inmost qualities. And besides his didactic habit of rounding off an episode with a conventional platitude, he is apt to interrupt the progress of a scene with a tedious moral fable, thus destroying much of the tension which he has carefully built up.

This habit brings us to his borrowings from other authors. Commentators long ago remarked that his plays, especially *The White Devil* and *The Duchess of Malfi*, contain many sentiments, images and even whole sentences which have been lifted from contemporary writers, in particular from Montaigne, Sidney, and the Scottish dramatist William Alexander. Of course originality was less highly prized in Webster's age than it is today. Quotation or adaptation from classical or foreign authors was regarded as a mark of erudition, and plagiarism was even to some extent encouraged by the educational system of the time which required students to keep a commonplace book. Mr. F. L. Lucas defends Webster's imitation and contends that he almost always transmuted what he borrowed into something different and better. This is often the case, but it does not tell us the whole story. Certainly Webster excels in the final stroke, the expansion of some hitherto unremarked detail, which transforms a second hand perception into a touch of perfect aptness. He was not the kind of author who plagiarized in order to save himself mental effort. On the contrary he was an exceptionally laborious artist who took great pains to weave his borrowings into the texture and atmosphere of his plays. Nevertheless his borrowings so far exceeded the normal that they came to affect his methods of composition. If we analyse the sequence of his dialogue in passages where the borrowing can be traced, it becomes clear that his imagination was often prompted by what he had read rather than by his own invention. This habit of working from a commonplace book explains the peculiarly conceit-laden and disjointed style which Webster employs in a passage such as the following, which contains images drawn from three different authors:

Thou shalt lie in a bed stuffed with turtle-feathers, swoon in perfum'd linen like the fellow was smothered in roses. So perfect shall be thy happiness that as men at sea think land and trees and ships go that way they go, so both heaven and earth shall seem to go thy voyage. Shalt meet him, 'tis fixed with nails of diamonds to inevitable necessity.

(*The White Devil*, I. ii.)

In the same way his longer verse passages do not flow as Shakespeare's do with an opulent succession of metaphors, in which each image springs naturally from its predecessor. Instead they often consist of a series of undeveloped metaphors or similes so loosely strung together that any one might be removed without damage to the rest, and the borrowing habit also seems to be responsible for the abrupt transitions of thought and feeling which so often occur in his verse. But when all this has been said, the fact that Webster's finest flights are often launched with the help of a borrowed idea does not diminish their effect. The study of his sources is valuable not in a derogatory sense, but because the identification of the original often helps to penetrate a meaning, clarify a dramatic effect, or define the qualities of a character which the commentators have missed.

Webster's use of figures of speech is closely related to his conception of tragedy, and his imagery throws much light upon the inner meaning of his plays. Both *The White Devil* and *The Duchess of Malfi*, for example, are pervaded by images of the fair show that masks inward corruption or poison, and the calm weather that hides an impending storm, and each of these sequences of metaphor is skilfully woven into the play so as to suggest the deceitfulness of fortune. The Elizabethan delight in the familiar objects and traditional beauties of the created world lies far behind him, and in his choice of metaphor and simile he deliberately singles out the curious, the grotesque and the sinister. His universe is a place of fear—it is noticeable that he is one of the few Elizabethans who does not celebrate the sublime and healing qualities of music. The birds which figure in his poetry are visualized in captivity or awaiting death, and when he describes the characteristics of plants or minerals it is the deformed and the deadly which fascinate him—witness his references to hemlock, mildew, poison, snakes and the mysterious properties of the mandrake. Often his visual symbols suggest a fearful immediacy, an icy touch, a suffocating embrace, a physical contact with the horrible. He strives to express and reconcile incongruity, above all that of the mortality of the graveyard and the sensuality of the living body. The symbolic act to which his imagination continually returns is that of tearing away the mask and uncovering the dreadful shape in the effort to resist the horror of death.

His poetry and prose follow two distinct styles of expression. The first is sophisticated, intellectually agile, staccato and restless in rhythm. In the second we find his imagination working at white heat, for he is a poet of brief and blinding insight rather than of steady illumination. This is the style which is reserved for the climaxes of his plays and which pervades his most highly wrought passages:

> Your beauty! O, ten thousand curses on't
> How long have I beheld the devil in crystal!
> Thou hast led me, like an heathen sacrifice,
> With music and with fatal yokes of flowers
> To my eternal ruin. Woman to man
> 　either a god or a wolf.
>
> 　　　　　　　　　　　　　(*The White Devil*, IV. i.)

> I am not mad yet, to my cause of sorrow:
> The Heaven o'er my head seems made of molten brass,
> The earth of flaming sulphur, yet I am not mad.
> I am acquainted with sad misery
> As the tanned galley-slave is with his oar;
> Necessity makes me suffer constantly
> And custom makes it easy.
>
> 　　　　　　　　　　　　　(*The Duchess of Malfi*, IV. ii.)

At these moments Webster's language is unadorned. His vocabulary becomes predominantly Anglo-Saxon, enriched by the rare Latin word, his rhythm steady, his tone prophetic: his words seem to wield an absolute power, with which they suddenly gather together the thought and emotions of the whole play, state the tragic issue and create the moment of vision.

IX

Webster's contribution to the Overbury collection of *Characters* is of interest because the Character as a literary genre noticeably influenced the dramatic writing of the time. Theories of psychological classification such as the doctrine

of the humours were in the air, and Theophrastus's treatise
aroused an interest in a similar analysis of manners and
sociology. Bishop Hall was the pioneer of the form and in
his *Characterismes of Vertues and Vice* he handles the subject
in broader and more concrete terms than his Greek model.
Thus while Theophrastus remarks that 'The Flatterer is a
person who will say as he walks with another, "Do you
observe how people are looking at you?" ' Hall individual-
izes his portrait as follows: 'The Flatterer is blear-eyed to
ill and cannot see vices . . . Like that subtle fish, he turns
himself into the colour of every stone . . . He is the moth
of liberal men's coates, the earewig of the mightie, the bane
of courts, a friend and slave to the trencher, and good for
nothing but to be factor for the Divell.'

Webster develops his character-writing along similar
lines. Clearly the form was congenial to him: it demanded
a mannered, compressed, carefully cadenced prose, gave
scope for ingenious and extravagant imagery and lent itself
equally to satirical commentary and moral exhortation. It
is noticeable that in his two major tragedies Webster puts
almost all this type of prose into the mouths of his two
satirical commentators, Flamineo and Bosola. Among the
Overbury *Characters* connoisseurs of Webster's powers of
invective will appreciate his sketch of 'A Jesuit', and of
'A Rimer' ('A Dung-Hille not well laid together'), but in
general he succeeds better in praise than in blame. The best
pieces written in his happier vein are the characters of 'An
Excellent Actor', 'A Franklin', and—a surprising contribution for Webster—'A Fayre and Happy Milke-Mayd'. This
last may be seen as the complete antithesis of his tragic
heroines, and in fact Bosola, when he finally urges the
Duchess to lay aside her youth, her beauty and her desire
to live, tells her (IV. iii):

Thou art some great woman sure, for riot begins to sit on thy fore-
head (clad in grey hairs) twenty years sooner than on a merry milk-
maid's.

X

Webster's drama is often criticized as episodic and lacking in architectonic power. Certainly the plots of *The White Devil* and *The Duchess of Malfi* are overloaded with detail, and there are moments when the playwright wilfully abandons dramatic truth for the sake of an immediately striking effect. Nevertheless each of these tragedies embodies a dramatic idea which is sufficiently powerful to hold it together. It is impossible to say the same of his later plays. At least five years separate *The Duchess of Malfi* from Webster's next play, and in that interval the changing mood of the theatre has been at work. Both Jacobean tragedy and comedy at their best had been bent on the pursuit of reality. The characteristics of the 'new wave' of tragi-comedy, of which the most skilful practitioners were Beaumont and Fletcher, had been sketched as early as 1609 in the latter's preface to *The Faithful Shepherdess:*

> A tragie-comedie is not so called in respect of mirth and killing, but in respect it wants deaths, which is inough to make it no tragedie, yet brings some near it, which is inough to make it no comedie.

This was a formula with insidious possibilities. Shakespeare, it is true, turns it to sublime use in his final romances. There he contrives to raise the action to a higher plane, on which at the end of each play the confused purposes of sinful humanity are transcended by a divine forgiveness. But in other hands the new mode suggests little more than a weary longing to lay aside the ultimate questions and seek relief from the painful integrity of great art, whether tragic or comic. Suspense or surprise in an exotic setting, sudden reversals of situation or transformations of sentiment—in short entertainment of an agreeably romantic kind—now become the dramatist's principal aim, and to achieve the unforeseen he must be prepared to distort character, confuse motive and ignore the normal consequences of human actions. These tendencies become increasingly apparent in Webster's later plays, the more regrettably so, because his genius was obviously so unsuited to satisfy the new taste. John Fletcher, the originator of the tragi-comic mode, was a sufficiently ingenious and versatile playwright to make this irresponsible treatment of the drama plausible. When Webster attempts such effects the result seems as unnatural as it is clumsy: in fact, as one might expect, the scenes which redeem his post-tragic plays are those in which his instinct prompts him to work against the prevailing fashion.

This division of purpose is most apparent in his last independent play, *The Devil's Law-Case*. Here he abandons courtly for bourgeois life and makes no attempt to draw a coherent moral. Nevertheless, a number of recognizable characteristics survive from his earlier work. Once again it is a woman's passion which dominates the plot and asserts an even more astonishing defiance of conventional standards. The play opens with Leonora, a sixty year old widow, cynically arranging with her son Romelio a marriage of convenience for her daughter Jolenta. Mother and son are well aware that Jolenta is in love with another aristocratic wooer, Contarino, but have no compunction in allowing a duel to take place between the suitors. But when Romelio tries to make certain of the wounded Contarino's death by disguising himself as a Jewish physician and stabbing his supposed patient, it transpires that Leonora has fallen in love with Contarino, and in revenge hires an unscrupulous lawyer to prove her own son illegitimate and thus disinherit him. The climax is reached in the trial scene—Webster excels throughout his career in the drama of the court-room —in which the corrupt eloquence of the prosecuting lawyer is matched by the resource of Romelio and the perspicacity of the upright advocate Crispiano. Leonora's case collapses, but this does not prevent a grotesque *dénouement* whereby she is matched 'happily ever after' with the young Contarino, Jolenta with her prescribed husband Ercole, and Romelio with a nun whom he had seduced years before.

The figure who dominates the play and links it with the world of the tragedies is the Neapolitan merchant Romelio. This character represents yet another of Webster's Machiavellian studies, shrewder and more experienced than Flamineo, as quick-witted and resolute as the Cardinal. When he disguises himself as a Jewish physician, Webster is clearly evoking the memory of Marlowe's Barabas, the Jew of Malta, and appears to be depicting Romelio as a thorough-paced villain. But later when he is visited in prison by a Capuchin friar to prepare him for death—an episode strongly reminiscent of the death-cell scene in *Measure for Measure*—the humour and steadiness of temper which underlie Romelio's courage make a powerful appeal to our sympathy:

> *Friar:* Pray tell me, do you not meditate of death?
> *Rom:* Phew, I tooke out that lesson
> When once I lay sicke of an Ague: I do now
> Labour for life, for life! Sir, can you tell me
> Whether your Toledo or your Millain blade
> Be best temper'd?
> *(The Devil's Law-Case,* V. iv.)

Romelio is by far the most vital of Webster's tragi-comic creations and it is certainly the role into which he poured the best of his later dramatic poetry.

Anything For a Quiet Life, a comedy written mainly in prose in collaboration with Middleton, is the least interesting play of any in which Webster took a hand. It makes fun of the marriage of an elderly knight to a young, capricious and self-willed girl. Lady Cressingham bullies her husband into parting with his estate, disinheriting his eldest son and sending away his younger children, but at the end of the play she is suddenly presented in a completely different light as a sensible wife, who has rid her husband of his ruinous obsessions with alchemy and gambling. *A Cure for A Cuckold,* attributed to Webster and Rowley and probably written some four years later, at least provides more dramatic tension. The hero, Lessingham, is told by his mistress that he will succeed in his wooing only if he kills his best friend for her sake. Although he is prepared to comply, both parties contrive to evade this harsh condition, and the unscrupulousness of Lessingham's action is forgotten in a conventionally happy ending. The play is chiefly memorable for its duelling scene on Calais sands, for its sequel when Lessingham pretends that he has fulfilled his mistress' command, and last but not least for Rowley's comic creation of the returned mariner, Compass. In the following year appeared *The Fair Maid of the Inn*, which is generally regarded as the joint work of Webster, Massinger and Ford. In this play Webster returns to a theme which resembles that of *The Devil's Law-Case*, the disowning of a son (Cesario) by his mother (Mariana), though on this occasion the object is to save him from danger. But once again we find a hero whose shifts of affection and equivocations in his dealings with the heroine are finally rewarded by marriage. Webster's contribution to this play is mainly limited to the second act and the last three scenes, and his sardonic style shows itself most plainly in a satirical creation, the fantastic charlatan Forobosco.

With *Appius and Virginia* Webster returns finally to tragedy—that is if we follow those scholars who place the play at the end rather than the beginning of his career. There is evidence for either conclusion, but Mr. Lucas makes a strong case when he argues that the portrait of the Roman lawyer in this play is such an accomplished creation that it is far more likely to have followed the equally so-phisticated Cantilupo of *The Devil's Law-Case* than to have preceded the crude caricature of an advocate that we find in *The White Devil*. There is also the argument from topical allusion, which suggests that the starving of the Roman army, which plays an important part in the plot, refers to the scandalous neglect and hardships suffered by an English contingent despatched to the Low Countries in the year

1624-5. Those critics who prefer the later date attribute only a minor share of collaboration to Heywood. The play reflects something of the blunt, unsophisticated quality of early Roman history. The action is straightforward, the sequence of emotions easily predictable, the characters drawn with rigid, somewhat elementary strokes: in particular the character of the martyred Virginia possesses far too little freedom of choice to stand comparison with Webster's earlier heroines. But amidst the artificiality of Caroline tragedy the rough simplicity of Virginius's farewell to his daughter stands out powerfully. And in Appius's speech before execution, Webster expresses for the last time the tribute he can never withhold from courage—especially in a villain:

> Think not, lords
> But he that had the spirit to oppose the gods
> Dares likewise suffer what their powers inflict . . .
> Now with as much resolvéd constancy
> As I offended will I pay the mulct . . .
> Learn of me, Clodius,
> I'll teach thee what thou never studies't yet
> That's bravely how to dy . . .
>
> (*Appius and Virginia*, V. ii.)

XI

> Webster was much possessed by death
> And saw the skull beneath the skin

writes T. S. Eliot. Certainly in his tragedies the menace and the mystery of death become the preoccupation which in the end overpowers all others, so that the dramatist seems deliberately to hold his characters on the brink of eternity as he questions them in their dying moments. Time and again his imagination returns to study the different responses

of humanity to this ordeal that none can escape: now it is
the sudden, uncontrollable dread voiced by Bracchiano:

> O thou soft natural death, that art joint-twin
> To sweetest slumber: no rough-bearded comet
> Stares on thy mild departure: the dull owl
> Beats not against thy casement: the hoarse wolf
> Scents not thy carrion. Pity winds thy corse
> Whilst horror waits on princes

and

> On pain of death, let no man name death to me,
> It is a word infinitely terrible.
>
>   (*The White Devil*, V. iii.)

or Flamineo's wry mockery, which masks a total and
desperate uncertainty in all things spiritual:

> *Lod:* What dost think on?
> *Fla:* Nothing; of nothing: leave thy idle questions
>   I am i'th' way to study a long silence.
>   To prate were idle, I remember nothing.
>   There's nothing of so infinite vexation
>   As man's own thoughts . . .
>   We cease to grieve, cease to be fortune's slaves
>   Nay cease to die by dying . . .
>
>   I do not look
> Who went before, nor who shall follow me;
> No, at myself I will begin and end
>   (*The White Devil*, V. vi.)

or the Duchess of Malfi's resolution and assurance:

> What would it pleasure me to have my throat cut
> With diamonds, or to be smothered
> With cassia, or to be shot to death with pearls?
> I know death hath ten thousand several doors

For men to take their exits: and 'tis found
They go on such strange geometrical hinges
You may open them both ways: any way, for heaven's sake
So I were out of your whispering: tell my brothers
That I perceive death, now I am well awake,
Best gift is they can give, or I can take.
I would fain put off my last woman's fault,
I'll not be tedious to you

(*The Duchess of Malfi*, IV. ii.)

or, as a final comment, the stoical fatalism of Bosola:

Yes, I hold my weary soul in my teeth,
'Tis ready to part from me . . .
O, I am gone.
We are only like dead walls or vaulted graves
That, ruined, yield no echo. Fare you well—
It may be pain, but no harm to me to die
In so good a quarrel: O this gloomy world,
In what a shadow, or deep pit of darkness
Doth womanish and fearful mankind live.
Let worthy minds ne'er stagger in distrust
To suffer death, or shame, for what is just
Mine is another voyage.

(*The Duchess of Malfi*, V. v.)

Webster was also 'possessed' by the contrast between the
wilful pretensions and desires of men and women and the
reality which lies in wait for them. He does not follow
Shakespeare's conception of tragedy as a fateful and exceptional conjunction of character and circumstance, whereby
a man

Carrying, I say, the stamp of one defect . . .
His virtues else, be they as pure as grace . . .
Shall in the general censure take corruption
From that particular fault

(*Hamlet*, I. iv. 30-35)

for to Webster corruption is a matter of the general doom, not the particular fault. The world, as he sees it, is a pit of darkness through which men grope their way with a haunting sense of disaster, and the ordeal to which he submits his characters is not merely the end of life but a struggle against spiritual annihilation by the power of evil: it is noticeable that none of them, however intolerable the blows of fate, seeks refuge in suicide. The nature of this struggle is beset by a terror which is Webster's most original contribution to tragic art. At the end of a Shakespearean tragedy the forces of evil have spent themselves, the hero has in some measure learned wisdom. At the end of *The White Devil* death merely interrupts the worldly concerns of the protagonists, leaving them face to face with damnation. Only in *The Duchess of Malfi* do we receive a suggestion of a further vision, a hint that the spiritual chaos of the early seventeenth century is not eternity.

Webster is not an easy dramatist to appreciate, nor does he yield up his best at a first reading. His plots lack the unity and the impetus which are the reward of devotion to a single dominant theme. But judged by his individual scenes he remains, after Shakespeare, the most profound and theatrically accomplished tragedian of his age, who excels equally in the sudden *coup de théâtre* or in the gradual heightening of tension and the capacity to play upon the nerves of his audience. He surpasses Middleton and Ford in the imaginative depth and concentration of his poetry, and Chapman and Tourneur as a creator of living men and women and of roles which can still hold the stage. He succeeds better than any of his contemporaries in re-creating the colour and the spiritual climate of Renaissance Italy— in *The White Devil*, as Mr. Lucas says, we know at once that we have crossed the Alps. On the strength of his two great plays he stands in the history of English tragedy as second only to Shakespeare.

JOHN WEBSTER

A Select Bibliography

(Place of publication London, unless stated otherwise)

Bibliography:

A BIBLIOGRAPHY OF THE ENGLISH PRINTED DRAMA TO THE RESTORATION, by W. W. Greg, 4 vols. (1939-1959).

A CONCISE BIBLIOGRAPHY, by S. A. Tannenbaum. New York (1941).

Collected Works:

THE WORKS OF J. WEBSTER, ed. A. Dyce (1830)
—reprinted 1857.

THE DRAMATIC WORKS OF J. WEBSTER, ed. W. C. Hazlitt (1857)
—reprinted 1897.

THE COMPLETE WORKS OF JOHN WEBSTER, ed. F. L. Lucas, 4 vols. (1927)
—the standard edition and a monument of scholarship. Vols. I and II, which contain *The White Devil* and *The Duchess of Malfi* but omit *The Devil's Law-Case*, were reprinted in 1958. This edition includes revisions of the introduction, text of vols. I and II, and commentary, but the introduction and bibliography of the original edition are drastically abridged.

Selections:

WEBSTER AND TOURNEUR, ed. J. A. Symonds (1888)
—in the Mermaid series. Contains *The White Devil* and *The Duchess of Malfi*. 2nd impression 1903; reset 1959. The New Mermaid series announces publication of separate paperback editions, with revised text and notes, of *The Duchess of Malfi* (1964) and *The White Devil* (1965).

WEBSTER AND FORD (1954)
—in the Everyman's Library series. Contains *The White Devil* and *The Duchess of Malfi*.

Separate Works:

COMMENDATORY VERSES PREFIXED TO THE THIRD PART OF MUNDAY'S TRANSLATION OF PALMERIN OF ENGLAND (1602).

ODE PREFIXED TO S. HARRISON'S ARCH OF TRIUMPH ERECTED IN HONOUR OF JAMES THE FIRST (1604).

THE MALCONTENT . . . with the additions plaied by the King's majesties servants (1604). *Drama*

—includes Webster's Induction. This is also included in *The Works of John Marston*, ed. A. H. Bullen, 1887.

THE FAMOUS HISTORY OF SIR THOMAS WYAT. WITH THE CORONATION OF QUEEN MARY AND THE COMING IN OF KING PHILIP (1607). *Drama*

—the title-page attributes the play to Dekker and Webster. Reprinted in W. J. Blew, *Two Old Plays*, 1876; Tudor Facsimile Texts, 1914.

WEST-WARD HOE (1607). *Drama*

—the title-page attributes this play to Dekker and Webster. Probably first performed 1604. Reprinted, Tudor Facsimile Texts, 1914.

NORTH-WARD HOE (1607). *Drama*

—the title-page attributes this play to Dekker and Webster. Probably first performed 1605. Reprinted, Tudor Facsimile Texts, 1914.

THE WHITE DIVEL, OR THE TRAGEDY OF PAULO GIORDANO URSINI, DUKE OF BRACHIANO. WITH THE LIFE, AND DEATH, OF VITTORIA COROMBONA, THE FAMOUS VENETIAN CURTIZAN (1612). *Drama*

—reprinted 1631, 1665, 1672. Edited by G. B. Harrison, 1933, Temple Dramatists; by G. H. W. Rylands, 1933, in *Elizabethan Tragedy;* by J. R. Brown, 1960, Revels Plays. The last provides a valuable supplement to F. L. Lucas's edition.

COMMENDATORY VERSES. PREFIXED TO HEYWOOD'S APOLOGY FOR ACTORS (1612).

A MONUMENTAL COLUMN. ERECTED TO THE LIVING MEMORY OF THE EVER-GLORIOUS HENRY, LATE PRINCE OF WALES (1613). *Verse*

NEW CHARACTERS (DRAWNE TO THE LIFE) OF SEVERALL PERSONS, IN SEVERALL QUALITIES (1615)

—a group of thirty-two Characters added, with a separate title-page, to the sixth edition of the Overbury collection. Included in *The Miscellaneous Works in Prose and Verse of Sir Thomas Overbury, Knt.*, ed. E. F. Rimbault, 1856. Reprinted 1890.

THE TRAGEDY OF THE DUTCHESSE OF MALFY (1623). *Drama*

—reprinted 1640, 1664, 1668 and 1708. Edited by C. Vaughan, 1896, Temple Dramatists; by F. Allen, 1921: with introductory essays by G. H. W. Rylands and C. Williams, 1945; by A. K. MacIlwraith in *Five Stuart Tragedies*, 1953, World's Classics.

MONUMENTS OF HONOUR (1624). *Verse*

—the poem commissioned by the Merchant Taylors Company for the Lord Mayor's Show of 1624.

THE FAIR MAID OF THE INN (1647). *Drama*
—published in the Beaumont & Fletcher First Folio, 1626. Reprinted
in their Second Folio, 1679, and included in *The Works of Beaumont
& Fletcher*, ed. A. Glover and A. R. Waller (the standard edition),
1905-12. Lucas accepts the view of H. D. Sykes that the play is a
work of collaboration between Massinger, Webster and Ford.

APPIUS AND VIRGINIA (1654). *Drama*
—the title-page attributes this play to Webster alone, but most
modern scholars accept Heywood's collaboration. Probably first
performed between 1625 and 1627. Reprinted in 1659 and 1679.

A CURE FOR A CUCKOLD (1661). *Drama*
—the title-page attributes this play to Webster and Rowley. Probably
first performed about 1625.

ANYTHING FOR A QUIET LIFE (1662). *Drama*
—the title-page attributes this play to Middleton, but Sykes and Lucas
assign most of the scenes to Webster. It is included in *The Works of
Thomas Middleton*, edited by A. Dyce, 1840; and by A. H. Bullen,
1885.

Note:

R. G. Howarth assigns to Webster *A Speedie Poste* (1624) and *The
Valiant Scot* (1637). Webster's dedication to *The Devil's Law-Case*
(1623) mentions *The Guise*, a lost play probably written 1614-23,
among his other works. Other references of the period mention
Webster's collaboration in the following lost plays: *Caesar's Fall*
(Munday, Middleton, Drayton, Webster); *Christmas Comes But
Once a Year* (Heywood, Dekker, Chettle, Webster); *The Late Murder
in Whitechapel* or *Keep the Widow Waking* (Ford, Webster, Dekker,
Rowley).

Some Critical Studies:

SPECIMENS OF ENGLISH DRAMATIC POETS, by C. Lamb (1808).

LECTURES ON THE DRAMATIC LITERATURE OF THE AGE OF ELIZABETH, by
W. Hazlitt (1821).

VITTORIA ACCORAMBONI, [by] D. Gnoli. Florence (1870)
—an important study of the historical background of *The White
Devil*.

JOHN WEBSTER, by E. E. Stoll (1905).

COLLECTANEA, by C. Crawford (1906)
—reprints from *Notes & Queries*.

GIOVANNA D'ARAGONA, DUCHESSA D'AMALFI, [by] F. Morellini. Cesena (1906)
—the standard work on the historical background of *The Duchess of Malfi*.

THE AGE OF SHAKESPEARE, by A. C. Swinburne (1908).

JOHN WEBSTER AND THE ELIZABETHAN DRAMA, by Rupert Brooke (1916)
—a pioneer work, now rather out of date in its literary judgements.

THE OLD DRAMA AND THE NEW, by W. Archer (1923).

SIDELIGHTS ON ELIZABETHAN DRAMA, by H. D. Sykes (1924)
—contains essays on *Appius and Virginia*, *The Fair Maid of the Inn* and *Anything for a Quiet Life*.

A CABINET OF CHARACTERS, by G. Murphy (1925)
—a useful introduction to the Overbury collection of Characters.

SELECTED ESSAYS, by T. S. Eliot (1932)
—the essays on 'Four Elizabethan Dramatists', 'Seneca in Elizabethan Translation' and 'Shakespeare and the Stoicism of Seneca' are particularly relevant.

THEMES AND CONVENTIONS OF ELIZABETHAN TRAGEDY, by M. C. Bradbrook (1934).

THE JACOBEAN DRAMA, by U. M. Ellis-Fermor (1936).

ELIZABETHAN REVENGE TRAGEDY, by F. T. Bowers (1940).

STUART DRAMA, by F. S. Boas (1946).

SHAKESPEARE'S TRAGEDIES AND OTHER STUDIES IN SEVENTEENTH CENTURY DRAMA, by C. Leech (1950).

JOHN WEBSTER, by C. Leech (1951).

THE TRAGIC SATIRE OF JOHN WEBSTER, by T. Bogard (1955).

'Tourneur and the tragedy of revenge', by L. G. Salingar. In *The Age of Shakespeare* (1955). *The Pelican Guide to English Literature*, ed. B. Ford, vol. 2.

THE SOURCES OF THE WHITE DEVIL, by G. Boklund (1957).

JACOBEAN THEATRE, ed. J. R. Brown and B. Harris. *Stratford-upon-Avon Studies*, I (1960)
—contains an interesting study of *The White Devil* and *The Duchess of Malfi* by J. R. Mulryne.

JOHN WEBSTER'S BORROWING, by R. W. Dent (1960)
—an important study of Webster's methods of composition and
indebtedness to other authors.

ELIZABETHAN DRAMA: MODERN ESSAYS IN CRITICISM, ed. R. Kaufmann
(1961)
—contains essays on Webster by H. T. Price and I. Ekblad.

THE DUCHESS OF MALFI: SOURCES, THEMES, CHARACTERS, by G. Boklund
(1962).

Bibliographical Series
of Supplements to 'British Book News'
on Writers and Their Work

GENERAL EDITOR
Geoffrey Bullough

¶ Robert Southey was born in Bristol on 12 August 1774. He died on 21 March 1843.

ROBERT SOUTHEY

Detail from a painting by Sir Thomas Lawrence *in the*
National Gallery of South Africa

ROBERT SOUTHEY

by

GEOFFREY CARNALL

PUBLISHED FOR
THE BRITISH COUNCIL
AND THE NATIONAL BOOK LEAGUE
BY LONGMANS, GREEN & CO.

LONGMANS, GREEN & CO. LTD.
48 Grosvenor Street, London W.1

*Associated companies, branches and
representatives throughout the world*

First published 1964
© Geoffrey Carnall 1964

*Printed in Great Britain by
F. Mildner & Sons, London, E.C.1*

ROBERT SOUTHEY

I

ROBERT Southey saw himself as a dominating figure in the England of his day. He was the author of several major poems, and an intrepid innovator in his subjects and his metres. His literary achievement had been publicly recognised when he was made Poet Laureate—the King's own poet. As a prominent contributor to the *Quarterly Review*, he exercized a powerful influence on public life. As an historian, he was a pioneer in recording the development of the vast new nation of Brazil. In his *History of the Peninsular War*, he celebrated what seemed to him the most inspiriting event of his time—the Spaniards' general and simultaneous insurrection against the mighty military power of Napoleon's France.

Southey shared to the full in that restless energy so characteristic of the Napoleonic era. It was a time of grandiose political and philosophical systems, and was prolific in plans for treatises, histories, and epic poems. The results were often disappointing, and Southey would certainly have been disappointed at the relatively small part assigned to him in English literary history. His most memorable work is seldom even thought of as his. Few people associate 'The Story of the Three Bears' with his name. His *Life of Nelson* is still being reprinted, but it is for the great admiral's sake, not Southey's. 'The Battle of Blenheim' and 'The Inchcape Rock' have almost acquired the anonymity of folklore. If Southey is remembered as a man, it is as the ridiculous figure in Byron's 'Vision of Judgement'. He is still a stock example (partly because of his association with Wordsworth and Coleridge) of the ardent young reformer who is corrupted and turns conservative. Social historians, however, sometimes honour him as an early critic of the evils which the new factory system brought to early nineteenth-century Britain. He made a

5

notable protest against the commercial spirit, regarding it as deeply injurious to the kindly and generous feelings of human nature. Yet his protests are no longer read as those of Carlyle and Dickens are.

He was endowed with a strong sensibility—too strong, in fact. His senses, he confessed, were perilously acute: 'impressions sink into me too deeply. . . . I fly from one thing to another, each new train of thought neutralizing, as it were, the last.' Such a method of writing would seem to guarantee a failure to achieve fully satisfactory expression. Yet his work constantly betrays the feelings which he found almost unendurable. This is particularly true of his copious and unguarded correspondence; but from nearly all his work the attentive reader will learn something of the stresses under which men lived in his time: a time of exceptionally rapid social change and insecurity.

II

Southey was born in Bristol on 12 August, 1774. He came from a family of farmers and tradespeople, his own father being a linen-draper. Much of his childhood was spent under the capricious care of a maiden aunt with some pretensions to gentility, Miss Tyler. She utterly dominated his mother: 'never', Southey wrote later, 'did I know one person so entirely subjected by another.' This early experience of domestic despotism probably helped to create the rather bleak view of life that casts a shadow over nearly all his writings. He was a sensitive child, and his family enjoyed making him cry by forcing him to listen to sad songs and dismal stories. He reacted against this overmastering sensibility by developing military ambitions. At the age of nine, he read Shakespeare's history plays, concluded that England was now once again on the brink of civil war, and made up his mind to take a leading part in the conflict. In order to enlist followers, he set up as an interpreter of dreams, referring his schoolfellows' dreams to the coming great civil wars and the appearance of a very great man—meaning himself.

The stratagem was ingenious, but apparently did not work. His literary ambitions developed later, and were much more successful. Being an enthusiastic admirer of Spenser's 'Faerie Queene', he decided to finish the poem. Before he was fifteen, he had sketched a plan based on every hint he could gather from the six books which Spenser himself had completed. Southey actually wrote three cantos of this projected continuation. Nothing, he said, ever gave him so much delight as the dream of what he intended to do in it.

The predominant impulse in this and other early projects seems to have been one of constructing a world of his own, in which the menacing forces outside him could be contended with on terms more advantageous than everyday life often allowed. The appeal of the remote and exotic is specially apparent in the plan he formed to illustrate various national mythologies, each with its own heroic poem. His later epics were in part a fulfilment of this scheme.

Southey was fifteen when the French Revolution began, and he soon became a passionate sympathizer with the revolutionary cause. He was expelled from Westminster School for writing an attack on flogging (he proved it to be an invention of the Devil). Later, at Balliol College, Oxford, he felt himself increasingly at odds with the course of life arranged for him. His uncle, the Rev. Herbert Hill, who was Chaplain to the British Factory at Lisbon, wanted his nephew to become a clergyman. But Southey had little relish for this. Modern geology and Gibbon's history had undermined his belief in the Bible. As a democrat he objected to a system which gave bishops incomes of £10,000 a year. As an enthusiastic reader of Goethe's *Werther* he was inclined to question the ethical doctrines of Christianity. It is true that he learned to reject the sensibility of *Werther* for the fortitude and self-control of stoicism as interpreted by Epictetus. But this was not enough to over-come his distaste for the Church. He could see only one way out. He must emigrate.

The idea of emigration took a firm shape in 1794, when he met Samuel Taylor Coleridge, then an undergraduate at Cambridge. Between them they evolved a plan for a settlement in America (first Kentucky, and later Pennsyl-vania), to be run on egalitarian, 'pantisocratic' principles. Although the plan came to nothing, for a time it had an intoxicating effect on both men. They lived in Bristol, and took a prominent part in radical agitation there. They gave lectures, and wrote propagandist pieces. The one which became most famous in the end was Southey's poetic play about Wat Tyler. This leader of the Peasants' Revolt in the fourteenth century had become a type of the spirit of radical reform. Southey affected to regard him as an ancestor: was not his genteel aunt a Miss Tyler? Inspired by this personal association, he denounced the aristocrats with uninhibited enjoyment:

> Be he villain, be he fool,
> Still to hold despotic rule,
> Trampling on his slaves with scorn!
> This is to be nobly born.

As the prospect of emigration receded, however, his revolutionary ardour cooled. It no longer seemed so difficult to make a living in England. A school-friend, Charles Wynn, gave him an annuity, and the Bristol bookseller Joseph Cottle, who later published the *Lyrical Ballads* of Wordsworth and Coleridge, issued a handsome edition of Southey's first epic poem, 'Joan of Arc'. This soon gained him a considerable literary reputation. After some desultory efforts to study law, he gradually settled into the life of a professional man of letters: a vocation which was confirmed when in 1803 he went to live at Greta Hall in Keswick, in the Lake District of the north of England. Coleridge was already staying there. He had married Sarah Fricker, a sister of Southey's wife Edith; and the two families formed the nucleus of a large household, of which Southey's letters give a pleasant picture.

Before this final settlement in Keswick, he spent two considerable periods with his uncle in Portugal. It was here that he developed his interest in Portuguese and Spanish history and literature, a subject on which he became the leading English authority. His first impressions of the country, indeed, were unfavourable. He found the squalid poverty repulsive, and had little good to say for the Roman Catholic Church. Still, he preferred Catholicism to the Calvinistic forms of protestantism which he knew in England, because it did more to kindle and satisfy the feelings and the imagination:

Bad indeed must the sinner be who will not be burnt white at last! Every prayer at a crucifix helps him—and a Mass on purpose is a fine *shove* towards Paradise. It is a superstition of hope.

The power lent by Catholic belief, in alliance with the strong national feelings of the people, enabled the Spaniards to resist the French after the invasion of 1808. Southey heard country people talk of their old heroes, and 'witnessed the passionate transfiguration which a Spaniard underwent when recurring from the remembrance of those times to his own'. In the chivalric literature of Spain, much of which Southey translated into English, it was possible to find an antidote to the sense of weakness which he found so difficult to tolerate. As the Cid smote down his enemies, so Southey delighted to trample on his.

He never found any difficulty in provoking opposition. 'Joan of Arc' is a calculatedly controversial poem: English readers were not used to seeing their heroic King Henry V consigned to hell. His shorter poems and ballads, like Wordsworth's, are particularly concerned with the common people and their sufferings. In his 'Botany Bay Eclogues' he enters sympathetically into the condition of convicts who had been transported to Australia. He exploits popular traditions, and deliberately avoids sophistication. As the Scots critic Francis Jeffrey remarked, the new sect of poets had a 'perverted taste for simplicity' and a 'splenetic and idle discontent with the institutions of society'. Southey's most scoffed-at poems were his experiments in metres borrowed from Greek and Latin poetry. The trouble was that he wrote about subjects his readers found ludicrously unclassical —beggars and screaming babies.

Thus, although Southey was no longer the young revolutionary of 1794, he was still seen by the public as an unorthodox poet, hostile to the established order of things. After 1810, however, he acquired a very different reputation. He became a warm partisan of public order, an outspoken Tory. His views changed in the first instance because of political controversies over the Peninsular War. When the Spaniards rose against the French in 1808, the news was enthusiastically welcomed in Britain, eager for new allies in the long and exhausting war with France. Southey's joy was unbounded. All that the chivalry of Spain had meant to his imagination seemed now to be realized in political action. As the Spanish campaign dragged on, however, and Napoleon continued to dominate Europe, a mood of war-weariness began to increase in Britain. The opposition parties took a gloomy view of the war in Spain, and Southey came to feel that only the conservative government of Spencer Perceval could be relied on to back the Spaniards. Hence Wat Tyler's apologist was converted to support for the unreformed British Constitution, which may have kept power in the hands of a few rich men, but did at least ensure a strong administration. Any reform which gave more influence to the middle and lower classes would be intolerable.

It was not only the war that made Southey conservative. He was also alarmed at the increasingly turbulent state of British politics. The industrial system had shattered traditional social loyalties. It had created a society which was callous and irresponsible. He was appalled by the conditions of life in towns like Birmingham and Manchester, and especially by the employment of children in factories. 'I thought', he wrote in his *Letters from England*, 'that if Dante had peopled one of his hells with children, here was a scene worthy to have supplied him with new images of torment.' Prosperity was founded on the brutalization of the great mass of the people. As he put it once in the *Quarterly Review*, the modern industrial system

carries in itself the sure cause of its own terrible destruction. That physical force which it has brought together as an instrument of lucration —a part of its machinery—will one day explode under high pressure.

There would be a terrible war of the poor against the rich. With serious riots in London in 1810, the 'Luddite' machine-breaking in some factory areas in 1812, and above all, in the same year, the assassination of the Prime Minister, Spencer Perceval, it looked as though violent revolution were an immediate danger. Southey's own radicalism had been violent, and he detected the same mood in the reform movement as a whole. Many well-disposed friends of order were not, he felt, sufficiently disturbed by the trend of events. From his retreat in Keswick Southey sought to sound the alarm, and to point out the means of reforming society so that the pressures making for revolution could be contained and removed.

From its first number in 1809, he had been a leading contributor to the *Quarterly Review*, a journal closely associated with Perceval's administration. It was here that he expounded his views on the measures necessary to save the country. Strong government was the first need: trouble-makers should be transported to Australia, where they would have less scope for mischief. But his articles were not mere pleas for repression. He recognized that social inequality like that found in England was utterly wrong. He sympa-thized with the pioneering socialist plans of Robert Owen,

seeing in them a practical application of the ideals of panti-
socracy, to which he still felt a strong attachment. He even
commended the revolutionary society of 'Spencean philan-
thropists', insofar as they aimed at building experimental
socialist communities. His main interest, however, was in
universal education (on sound and law-abiding principles),
and in assisted emigration.

Southey's services to public order and social reform were
not confined to journalism. In 1813 he agreed to accept the
office of Poet Laureate. The duties of this office consisted
mainly in supplying poems for royal weddings and other
court occasions, and Southey's immediate predecessor had
been a poet of very modest talents, Henry James Pye. For a
reputable man of letters it required much boldness to undertake the work at all. But Southey had conceived the idea of
using his laureate poems to strengthen the spirit of order and
true patriotism. The Poet Laureate was to give utterance to
the soul of the nation. He wrote irregular odes to keep up
the people's will to win the war, to commend schemes of
welfare, and to deplore insane faction, rabid treason, and
erring zeal. When the Princess Charlotte married, he wrote
a 'Lay of the Laureate' in which her royal duties were
clearly detailed, and her latter end plainly set before her:

> Is this the Nuptial Song? with brow severe
>   Perchance the votaries of the world will say:
> Are these fit strains for Royal ears to hear?
>   What man is he who thus assorts his lay,
> And dares pronounce with inauspicious breath,
> In Hymeneal verse, the name of Death?

A year later the Princess was indeed dead—and Southey
wrote a decorous Funeral Song. His most ambitious, and
most disastrous, laureate poem was inspired by the death (in
1820) of George III. 'A Vision of Judgement' relates how the
poet witnesses the king's triumphant entry into heaven—a
ceremony which the powers of darkness would like to
prevent, but cannot. George, rejuvenated and restored to

sanity, is greeted by his royal ancestors, and by great Englishmen of the past. Southey is particularly delighted to catch a glimpse of Spenser, whose poetry caught him up into a world of romance which made the real world 'weary, and stale, and flat'. Indeed, the Poet Laureate was so eager to join the departed worthies that he pressed forward to enter the Gates of Heaven—but in vain. The poem ends, as it began, with Southey listening to a church bell tolling for the king's death.

In a controversial preface, Southey attacked what he called the 'Satanic school' among modern poets. Their work, he said, was sometimes lascivious, sometimes loathsome, and was 'more especially characterized by a Satanic spirit of pride and audacious impiety, which still betrays the wretched feeling of hopelessness wherewith it is allied'. The poet whom Southey had chiefly in mind here was Byron, who retaliated with truly diabolical effectiveness. The 'Satanic' poet's 'Vision of Judgement' broadly accepts Southey's account of what happened before the gates of heaven, but gives it an interpretation much less flattering to George III and the Laureate. Southey alleged that the Devil had put up two of the King's chief antagonists to testify against him—John Wilkes and the mysterious Junius; but they were ashamed of themselves, and held their tongues:

> Caitiffs, are ye dumb? cried the multifaced Demon in anger.
> Think ye then by shame to shorten the term of your penance?
> Back to your penal dens! . . . And with horrible grasp gigantic
> Seizing the guilty pair, he swung them aloft, and in vengeance
> Hurl'd them all abroad, far into the sulphurous darkness.

Byron agrees that they refused to testify, but attributes Wilkes's refusal to his habitual good-nature, and Junius's to disdain. He also agrees that Southey was snatched up to the gates of heaven on this occasion—but the snatching was done by the devil Asmodeus, anxious to have Southey damned forthwith for scribbling as though he were 'head clerk to the Fates'.

There undoubtedly was something irresistibly ludicrous about Southey's attempt to be the National Poet. He was not particularly deferential himself to those in authority, and he had too much of a radical past to live down: a fact neatly underlined in 1817 when his youthful poetic drama 'Wat Tyler' made its first appearance (in a pirated edition) before a delighted public. After 1822, moreover, he stood for a point of view which became steadily more remote from political realities. It was a time of accelerating reform. Some of this was acceptable to him: Peel, for example, was drastically cutting down the number of offences punishable by death. But Southey was wholeheartedly against letting Roman Catholics enter the British Parliament—an attitude which could not be maintained in the face of mounting pressure from Ireland. In 1829 'Catholic Emancipation' was accepted by Parliament, and the following year a new government came into power, pledged to a general reform of the House of Commons. It seemed to Southey that the 'state Omnibus' was rolling smoothly 'down an inclined plane, and towards a precipice'. When he was in London in the autumn of 1830, he met the Duke and Duchess of Kent and their young daughter, the future Queen Victoria, who was brought in to tell him that she had read his *Life of Nelson*. The whole family seemed to Southey to be 'as unconcerned about the state of affairs, and passing their days as pleasantly, as Marie Antoinette in her time of coming troubles'.

He was not as disheartened by politics in his later years as some of his gloomy predictions might suggest. He became a friend of Lord Ashley (afterwards Lord Shaftesbury), and saw in him the type of man who would come forward, after the revolution had run its course, to re-edify the Constitution. Southey encouraged him in his interest in factory reform, the more so as most Conservatives in Parliament neglected the issue. ('Verily, verily', said Southey, in a moment of exasperation, 'they seem to be demented.') He warned Ashley, however, against actually visiting the manufacturing districts for fear that his health might suffer from 'the distressful recollections which would be impressed upon you and *burnt in*'. Even now, Southey had evidently not lost his overmastering sensibility.

He himself took no active part in politics. Nothing could tempt him to quit his retreat in Keswick: certainly not the offer he once received to join *The Times* newspaper, nor the seat in Parliament that Lord Radnor wanted him to take in 1826. Apart from his occasional journeys, he spent his life in quiet and constant literary work. He was a model father of his family, a kindly and diplomatic president of a small pantisocratic republic, where no servant was allowed to address the children as Master or Miss. The atmosphere of the place is suggested by a letter which Southey wrote in 1812, when Keswick was alarmed by the presence of 'ugly fellows': unemployed labourers from neighbouring industrial towns. He was asking a friend to send two pistols and a watchman's rattle. The rattle was to give the alarm when the ugly fellows arrived, but Southey looked forward to 'the glorious tunes, the solos and bravuras, that I shall play upon that noble musical instrument before any such fellow makes his appearance'. Southey's son Cuthbert comments gravely that 'these musical anticipations were fully realized'.

Unfortunately the ills of life were not always to be warded off so cheerfully. He was tenderly attached to his eldest son Herbert, and had great hopes of him. But he died in 1816, when only nine years old. Southey was so deeply distressed that his spirits never fully recovered. His wife was even more severely affected by the death ten years later of their daughter Isabel, and eventually lost her reason. After her death (in 1837), Southey married the poet Caroline Bowles, but shortly afterwards his own mind began to fail. He became incapable of recognizing his friends, or of reading. It can be said, however, that he never lost his love of books. He was to be seen in his magnificent library, patting his books affectionately, like a child. He died on 21 March, 1843.

III

Is Southey's poetry still worth reading?

He himself put a high value on his long narrative poems. They have had their admirers, it is true, including Shelley and Cardinal Newman, but readers generally have agreed to ignore them. Richard Porson remarked, with a fine ambiguity, that ' "Madoc" will be read—when Homer and Virgil are forgotten'; and, as Byron was careful to explain, *not till then.*

If Southey's epics fail to hold the attention, it is because he so often fails to involve himself deeply enough in the situations he describes. He lived in a time of appalling political earthquakes, and the subjects of his poems reflect this quite explicitly—too explicitly. In such an epoch, Southey believed, the indispensable virtue was courage, the willingness to act; and action sometimes depends on shutting out perceptions that might be disconcerting. More than once he remarked that 'composition, where any passion is called forth, excites me more than it is desirable to be excited'. The writing of poetry could make his face burn and his heart throb. The real themes of his poetry haunted the threshold of his consciousness, but seem always to have been held back, except when disguised in comic forms. He recorded many of his dreams, and these are sometimes illuminating. In one dream he was haunted by evil spirits. He tried to reason himself into a belief in their unreality, but the horrors continued to increase:

At length an arm appeared through the half-opened door, or rather a long hand. Determined to convince myself that all was unsubstantial and visionary, though I saw it most distinctly, I ran up and caught it. It was a hand, and a lifeless one. I pulled at it with desperate effort, dragged in a sort of shapeless body into the room, trampled upon it, crying out aloud the while for horror.

His cries were real enough, and woke up his wife, who in turn woke him, thus delivering him from the most violent fear that ever possessed him. He felt, he said, like a mediaeval monk engaged in a contest with the Devil—though one imagines that a devil with horns and tail would have been less frightening than this shapeless horror. Only the annihilation of the feared object would give him a feeling of security, or so it seemed during the dream.

Southey rarely explored the sense of impotence that haunted him in this nightmare, though there is a fine example in his *History of the Peninsular War*. In 1808, Ferdinand of Spain went to Bayonne and thus entered a trap prepared for him by the French:

Confused and terrified as Ferdinand was, and feeling himself in the power of the French, the only ease he could find was by endeavouring implicitly to believe their protestations of friendship.

Southey could hardly have endured this story if he had not known there was to be a happy ending. A power lay dormant in Spain of which the possessors themselves had not suspected the existence until the insurrection broke out. 'The holiest and deepest feelings of the Spanish heart were roused, and the impulse was felt throughout the Peninsula like some convulsion of the earth or elements.'

'The sense of power', Southey said of one of his heroes, 'revived his heart.' Much of his poetry was written to reinforce that sense of power, and his epics glorify the man who never loses his nerve in unpredictable and frightful situations. They are, above all, poems of violence. The domestic pieties, and what he calls 'the healing power of nature', are evident enough, but it is the battle scenes which really engage his poetic energies. This is already clear in his earliest major poem, 'Joan of Arc'. It is best read in the first edition of 1796, where the author's revolutionary sentiments have not been toned down. Not that any revisions could ever do much to soften an English epic which presents the English as wolfish invaders. But later editions somewhat moderate the 'fierce and terrible benevolence' of the original:

> To England friendly as to all the world,
> Foe only to the great blood-guilty ones,
> The masters and the murderers of mankind.

The poem is informed with a faith that the oppressed can be roused to

> Dash down his Moloch-idols, Samson-like,
> And burst his fetters—only strong whilst strong
> Believed.

The climax comes with Joan's address to the newly-crowned King of France. She bids him rule justly, assuring him that

> hireling guards,
> Tho' flesh'd in slaughter, would be weak to save
> A tyrant on the blood-cemented Throne
> That totters underneath him.

The burning of Joan of Arc, although at one time Southey thought of writing a play on the subject, is not given any prominence. Passive suffering was too uncongenial to his imagination. If an innocent maiden were condemned to be burnt alive, his natural impulse was to save her by miracle and blast the perpetrators of the wicked deed: as he contrived to do in one of his shorter poems, 'The Rose'. But with Joan, history would not permit this.

In 'Thalaba the Destroyer' (1801) the shackles of history are cast aside. The hero is an Arabian youth destined to destroy the evil magicians who live in the Domdaniel Caverns 'underneath the roots of Ocean'. The magicians try to destroy Thalaba first, but are always cheated by the courage and piety inspired by his sense of mission, or by the direct intervention of providence. Thus, Abdaldar seeks to stab Thalaba while the latter is prostrate in prayer. The hot blast of the Simoom passes just at the right moment, and Abdaldar is suffocated while the pious worshippers remain unharmed beneath the poisonous whirlwind. At one point Thalaba is taunted with trusting in the magic powers of a ring he took from Abdaldar's corpse. He replies:

> Blindly the wicked work
> The righteous will of Heaven!
> Sayest thou that diffident of God,
> In Magic spells I trust?
> Liar! let witness this!

And he throws the ring into the abyss, where it is caught by a skinny hand. Thus to renounce the aid of magic is no great sacrifice, because high-wrought feeling

> Infused a force portentous, like the strength
> Of madness through his frame

and he is able to throw his antagonist after the ring.

The poem ends with Thalaba's mysteriously-guided journey to the Domdaniel Caves. He travels in a dog-sleigh, and then in a little boat: a part of the poem which delighted the young Shelley, whose 'Alastor' is plainly indebted to it. Thalaba is parachuted down a deep cavern to the roots of Ocean, and there stabs the Giant Idol of the magicians' god, Eblis. The ocean-vault falls in, destroying the magicians along with Thalaba himself, whose soul is immediately translated to paradise.

Cardinal Newman greatly admired the 'irrepressible onward movement' of this poem, leading as it did to a 'tremendous catastrophe in which the hero dying achieves his victory'. What is surprising in this judgement is Newman's feeling that the catastrophe is 'tremendous'. The perils of Thalaba's adventures are so readily overcome that it is difficult to feel much concern about them. For Newman, perhaps, this was one of the poem's merits.

The perils in 'Madoc' (1805) are felt much more intensely. It tells the story of a mediaeval Welsh prince who left the feuds of his native land to settle in America. The first part, 'Madoc in Wales', describes the hero's recruitment of a party of emigrants; the second part, 'Madoc in Aztlan', describes the merciless struggle with the people of Aztlan— ancestors of the Mexicans whom the Spaniards discovered in the sixteenth century. The climax of the poem is the night when Aztec priests and people wait for the sun to rise at the beginning of a new era—wait with a torturing fear that it may never rise again:

> Oppressive, motionless,
> It was a labour and a pain to breathe
> The close, hot, heavy air. Hark! from the woods
> The howl of their wild tenants! and the birds,
> The day-birds, in blind darkness fluttering,
> Fearful to rest, uttering portentous cries!

What follows in fact is a devastating volcanic explosion:

> Anon, the sound of distant thunders came:
> They peal beneath their feet. Earth shakes and yawns,
> And lo! upon the sacred mountain's top,
> The light . . . the mighty flame! A cataract
> Of fire bursts upward from the mountain head, . . .
> High, . . . high, . . . it shoots! the liquid fire boils out;
> It streams in torrents down!

Even though the Aztecs are presented as an exceedingly dangerous enemy, Southey allows his imagination to overwhelm them here with a violence understandable only when one remembers the shapeless horror of his nightmare.

'The Curse of Kehama' (1810) is closer to the manner of 'Thalaba'. The exotic subject, suggested by Southey's reading of Hindu myth and legend, gives considerable scope to his predilection for images of power. Power in this poem is concentrated in the great and wicked figure of Kehama. By the performance of prescribed sacrifices, he has attained semi-divine status, and is attempting to consolidate his conquest of the lower regions of the universe. His son Arvalan had tried to rape Kailyal, a peasant girl, but had been killed in the attempt by her father, Ladurlad. Ladurlad is condemned to the severest torture Kehama can devise: a total deprivation of all satisfactions of the senses. He can never sleep, and must endure an everlasting fire in his heart and brain. To linger out the punishment, Ladurlad is protected by a charm from all possible causes of death. He is thus enabled to thwart Kehama's will, intervening to desecrate the great sacrifice which was to have made Kehama absolute master of hell and earth and the lower heavens. The setback is only temporary, for at the end of the poem Kehama appears to be achieving the final step to omnipotence by drinking the amreeta cup. In fact he is condemning himself to an eternity of torment. Three statues already support the throne of judgement in the underworld: one is the first man who heaped up superfluous wealth, another the first king and conqueror, and another the first deceiving priest. Kehama is transformed into the fourth statue. Ladurlad is then released from the curse, while his daughter joins a beautiful spirit, the Glendoveer, with whom she lives in heaven happy ever after.

Kehama was for Southey a type of the presumptuous will and intellect that threatened old pieties and released infernal energies to devastate the world. In his letters he compares Kehama to Napoleon, and the poem itself makes clear the alliance between Kehama and demonic subversion. In Padalon, the Hindu hell, the rebel spirits lie in chains, but Kehama has filled them with hope. Gigantic demons are constantly having to rivet the rebels' chains to repress their rage:

> Loud around,
> In mingled sound, the echoing lash, the clash
> Of chains, the ponderous hammer's iron stroke,
> With execrations, groans, and shrieks and cries
> Combined in one wild dissonance, arise;
> And through the din there broke,
> Like thunder heard through all the warring winds,
> The dreadful name. Kehama, still they rave,
> Hasten and save!
> Now, now, Deliverer! now, Kehama, now!
> Earthly Almighty, wherefore tarriest thou?

The stoic resistance and domestic piety of Ladurlad and his daughter, the ethereal daring of the Glendoveer, can offer no decisive act of resistance to Kehama. But their firm conviction that 'they who suffer bravely save mankind' enables them to co-operate with the ultimately beneficent purposes of providence. Kehama is defeated in the end only by the mightiest of the gods: Seeva, the Destroyer.

The fifth of Southey's epic poems, 'Roderick, the Last of the Goths', has a wider range of feeling than any of its predecessors. He was more genuinely involved in this Spanish subject than he had been in the others. It tells the story of the Moorish invasion of Spain in the eighth century, and is obviously inspired by Southey's admiration for Spanish and Portuguese resistance to the French during the Peninsular War. It appeared, indeed, in 1814, not long after the end of the fighting. The theme of resistance to misbelievers is combined with others which deeply interested him. Roderick, the last Gothic King of Spain, raped Count Julian's daughter. Count Julian called in the Moors to avenge the wrong, and thus led to the subjection of his country. Roderick, repentant, travelled about Spain in disguise as a priest, helping the forces that were consolidating behind Prince Pelayo, until the first victories against the Moors were achieved. In the battle at the end of the poem, Roderick revealed himself, thus adding to the confusion of the Moors, but afterwards disappeared again.

The poem is exceptional in the extent of the interest that Southey shows in the relationship between Roderick and Count Julian's daughter, Florinda. He is not usually much attracted to love as a subject for poetry, and once remarked that he would like to see the tales which Jean-Pierre Camus, Bishop of Belley, wrote to inspire horror and disgust for the passion. Although Southey does not go so far as the bishop, he certainly tends to relate the passionate forms of love to pain and destruction. If he puts Sappho into one of his early monodramas, she is about to commit suicide. If the beautiful Laila, in 'The Lovers' Rock', runs away with her lover

Manuel from her Moorish home, they are trapped on the way and throw themselves down a precipice rather than risk dying separately. In three major poems, 'Wat Tyler', 'The Curse of Kehama', and 'Roderick', rape or attempted rape forms a conspicuous part of the plot. In 'Roderick', however, the guilty man is a sympathetic character. We come to see that the rape is hardly a rape at all: Florinda was in love with Roderick, and she resisted him on account of a rash vow she had made to live as a hermit.

As in all the other epics, however, it is the violence which impresses itself most memorably. The experience which Southey finds unendurable is the sense of 'joyless, helpless, hopeless servitude', not only to the Moors, but to the very nature of things. In fighting the Moors, the Spaniards are comforted and reconciled to life, above all at a moment like the Battle of Covadanga, when the Moorish army is lured into a deep valley, and then crushed by a landslide set in motion by Pelayo's force:

> The Asturians shouting in the name of God,
> Set the whole ruin loose! huge trunks and stones,
> And loosen'd crags, down, down they roll'd with rush
> And bound, and thundering force.

The poem reaches its climax in the battle where Roderick throws off his disguise, rejoicing in his strength. He lays about him with his good sword,

> and smote
> And overthrew, and scatter'd, and destroy'd,
> And trampled down.

Much as Southey might enjoy celebrating battles in poetry, he did not care for the real thing. In the late summer of 1815, he visited the field of the Battle of Waterloo. He was much distressed by the condition of the soldiers who were recovering from their wounds, and remarked that he had never before seen the real face of war so closely:

'God knows!' he added, 'a deplorable sight it is.' His laureate poem on the subject, 'The Poet's Pilgrimage to Waterloo', is a resolute attempt to digest this melancholy experience. After an account of his visit, he dreamed that he met a tempter who argued that life was sickening and meaningless, undirected by any purpose:

> The winds which have in viewless heaven their birth,
>   The waves which in their fury meet the clouds,
> The central storms which shake the solid earth,
>   And from volcanoes burst in fiery floods,
> Are not more vague and purportless and blind,
> Than is the course of things among mankind!

Southey recovers his optimism when the Heavenly Muse reassures him that human progress is real, and that Britain's civilizing mission in the world will make a great contribution to it. The earlier doubts are suppressed by a firm effort of the will, however, rather than through any deeply-felt assurance.

The most pleasing of his longer poems is also the most unreservedly sombre. This is 'A Tale of Paraguay', which was published in 1825. It tells of a small family who were the only survivors of a smallpox epidemic in a tribe of Guarini Indians. Mother, son, and daughter were eventually brought into one of the Jesuit settlements, where, although kindly treated, they soon died. The poem is Southey's most extensive and deliberate account of the insecurity to which human life is exposed. Disease, war, predatory animals—all help to make men's hold on life a frail one. Settlement in the Jesuit 'reduction' appears to remove the most apparent causes of insecurity, but in fact the change in the way of life of 'these poor children of the solitude' proves more deadly than anything else. Dobrizhoffer, the Austrian Jesuit who ruled the reduction, was deeply grieved when first the mother, then the daughter died: but neither of them felt distress. The daughter saw him weep,

and she could understand
The cause thus tremulously that made him speak.
By his emotion mov'd she took his hand;
A gleam of pleasure o'er her pallid cheek
Pass'd, while she look'd at him with meaning meek,
And for a little while, as loth to part,
Detaining him, her fingers lank and weak,
Play'd with their hold; then letting him depart
She gave him a slow smile that touch'd him to the heart.

Something is expressed here of Southey's own most painful experiences—the deaths of his children. It was made bearable for him by the remoteness of the subject, and by the feeling that it was better for these Indians to die under Dobrizhoffer's benevolent care than to survive his expulsion along with the other Jesuits in 1767, when 'all of good that Paraguay enjoy'd' was overthrown 'by blind and suicidal Power'.

Impressive in its own way as 'A Tale of Paraguay' is, however, it is not resilient enough to be fully characteristic of Southey. His buoyancy finds its most natural expression in many of his shorter poems, especially those in which the Devil plays a part. There is St. Romuald, for example, who used to fight with Satan 'all through a winter's night' until

his face became
All black and yellow with the brimstone flame,
And then he smelt—O Lord! how he did smell!

While Southey usually contrives to keep the Devil at bay, some of his most memorable ballads re-enact the nightmare of being overpowered by an alien will. This experience could be made palatable by attributing great wickedness to the victim, as in 'God's Judgement on a Wicked Bishop'. It is mere poetic justice to be eaten by thousands of rats when you have just burned a barn crowded with women and children. 'The Old Woman of Berkeley' is a little more disquieting. It tells how a witch was carried off by the Devil in spite of the devoted efforts of a large company of priests, choristers, and bellmen, and the protection of a stone coffin fastened by iron bars and tied down by three chains, blessed and sprinkled with holy water. The Old Woman may be a witch, but one cannot help feeling for her—or at least for the priest her son and the nun her daughter, who labour so diligently for their mother's salvation, and to no effect. This ballad is said to have been translated into Russian, and its publication prohibited, because children were frightened by it.

By contrast, the Russian authorities would have found a poem that Southey wrote some thirty years later positively edifying. This was 'The Young Dragon'. It was founded on a Spanish legend about Antioch in early Christian days. Satan was alarmed at the number of conversions to Christianity there, and hatched out a dragon to punish the city. This dragon required a Christian virgin every day, and when a certain Marana was chosen, her father (a pagan) took active measures to save her life. He stole the thumb of John the Baptist, preserved as a relic in Antioch, and just as the dragon was about to devour his daughter, lobbed it down the dragon's throat. The effect was remarkable:

> A rumbling and a tumbling
>   Was heard in his inside,
> He gasp'd, he panted, he lay down,
>   He roll'd from side to side:
> He moan'd, he groan'd, he snuff'd, he snor'd,
> He growl'd, he howl'd, he rav'd, he roar'd;
>   But loud as were his clamours,
> Far louder was the inward din,
> Like a hundred braziers working in
>   A caldron with their hammers.

His body swelled up, rose slowly from the ground, and, when three miles up, exploded with a sound that could be heard a hundred leagues away. The débris was dispersed like the fall-out from a nuclear explosion, and the Holy Thumb ascended to heaven.

Southey's best work is often his most playful, as is shown by 'The Story of the Three Bears'.[1] It is a beautifully poised treatment of the theme of the unamiable protagonist whose sins get her into trouble. (The amiable Goldilocks belongs to a decadent version.) The impudent old woman, who eats the little bear's porridge, pushes the bottom out of his chair, and goes to sleep in his bed, is surely well-advised to jump out of the window when the bears discover her. But nothing worse happens than complaints from the Great Huge Bear in his great rough, gruff voice—represented by 𝕲𝖗𝖊𝖆𝖙 𝕳𝖚𝖌𝖊 𝕲𝖔𝖙𝖍𝖎𝖈 𝕿𝖞𝖕𝖊.

The story belongs to a world which Southey did not generally believe in: a golden world where bears do nobody any harm, and never suspect that anybody will harm them. A more characteristic view of life is suggested in that famous early poem 'The Battle of Blenheim'. Here he is content to juxtapose the world of domestic decency with the dreadful world of power. It reflects both sides of his character: his inborn kindliness and sensitivity, and his unwilling conviction that the world is a savage place. Old Kaspar, talking to Peterkin and Wilhelmine about the many thousand bodies that 'lay rotting in the sun', makes Southey's point with a fine economy:

> 'Great praise the Duke of Marlbro' won
>   And our good Prince Eugene.'
> 'Why 'twas a very wicked thing!'
>   Said little Wilhelmine.
> 'Nay—nay—my little girl', quoth he,
> 'It was a famous victory.'

IV

Southey's prose is vigorous, direct, and covers much ground in little time. 'My way', he said once, 'is when I see

[1]First published in Vol. IV of his desultory novel *The Doctor*, in 1837.

my object, to dart at it like a greyhound.' Unfortunately he
often pays for this vigour by oversimplifying the issues. He
is too anxious to reach an assured position to have time to
unravel complexities. He does not suppress the contra-
dictory feelings that influence his views, but they appear as
fluctuations of opinion and feeling, not as constituents of a
consistent attitude. When he was considering Roman
Catholicism in the context of current British politics, he used
language of unqualified hostility:

Wherever the Roman Catholic superstition predominates, it offers only
these alternatives:— Unbelief, with scarce a decent covering of hypocrisy, and all the abominations of vice, as exhibited in Italy and France,
among the higher ranks; or base, abject, degrading destructive bigotry
in all, as in Spain, Portugal, and the Austrian States. These are the
effects which always have been, and always must be, produced by a
Catholic establishment.

Edinburgh Annual Register for 1808.

Southey wrote these words while he was working on
'Roderick', a poem which might have come from the pen
of a Catholic apologist. 'A Tale of Paraguay' and the
History of Brazil show how warmly he felt towards the
Jesuits of South America. It might be possible to reconcile
the various opinions that Southey expresses so vehemently;
but Southey himself did not make any very adequate
attempt.

The same is true of his attitude towards the protestant sect
of the Quakers. He was united with them in steadfast
opposition to slavery, in their warm but undogmatic
religious feeling, in their stoic discipline of life, and their
practical goodwill. He once expressed a wish that he could
bring up his son Herbert as a Quaker. In some moods he
could feel that pacifism was a practical policy. He believed
that the Quakers of Pennsylvania had shown that 'a people
whose principle it is never to resist evil, and always to bear
testimony against it, cannot be crushed by any exertion of
human power short of universal massacre'. At one time he

supported the abolition of all capital punishment, on the ground that this example would produce a more general reverence for life. He also proposed that the management of British prisons should be entirely handed over to the Quakers. But even at the time of his greatest sympathy with Quakerism, around 1807, he was apt to express warlike and unquakerly views. Quakerism, he told someone, is the true system of the Gospel, 'but I want to have the invasion over before I allow it to be so'.

His attitude towards John Wesley and the Methodist movement was more consistent, and his *Life of Wesley* is in many ways a valuable contribution to the religious history of Britain in the eighteenth century. Southey was well versed in Methodist literature, and reduces a mass of documentation to a clear and workmanlike narrative. But he is not fully in sympathy with his subject. His imagination could be deeply stirred by Catholicism; he could contemplate bringing up his best-loved son as a Quaker. He felt no such involvement with this predominantly working-class religious movement. Originally fiercely hostile to it, he gradually developed an attitude of measured respect. He recognized that Wesley had reclaimed many from a course of sin, supported many in poverty, sickness, and affliction, and imparted to many a triumphant joy in death. But one continually feels that Southey has a certain distaste for the Methodists, and the book leaves one with a sense of having surveyed Methodism from the outside, not with having gained much understanding of the inner dynamics of the movement.

In his *Letters from England*, however, this kind of detachment is turned to good account. It was published (in 1807) as the work of a Spanish traveller, Don Manuel Alvarez Espriella, and Southey enters spiritedly into the part of a Catholic and a foreigner. He speaks of fashions in dress, furniture, and religion, of quackery and dishonesty of many kinds. He is deeply impressed by 'the ingenuity, the activity, and the indefatigable watchfulness of roguery in England'.

He visits the picturesque Lake District, and tells of the cheap boarding schools in Yorkshire—later to be pilloried by Dickens in *Nicholas Nickleby*. There is an eloquent account of the evils of life in industrial Manchester. He is interested in crowd behaviour, and gives several striking examples of it. He goes into great detail about the religious underworld, seeing here evidence of a deep social current flowing he knows not where. Southey is obviously fascinated by incidents like Joanna Southcott's debate with the Devil: it is a subject he might have used in a ballad. The book lives because of its vivid presentation of the surface of life in early nineteenth-century England; but it is a surface which invites the reader to speculate, with Don Manuel, about what is going on below.

His critique of industrial society is more fully developed in a series of imaginary conversations between himself and the ghost of Sir Thomas More which he published in 1829: the *Colloquies on the Progress and Prospects of Society*. In spite of More's Catholicism, Southey felt deeply in sympathy with him. Had he not conceived the original Utopia? And might not Southey himself have resisted the protestant reformation if he had been a contemporary of More's? 'I resisted opinions', he makes More say, 'which in their sure consequences led to anarchy in all things.' Southey's own revulsion against anarchy led him to endorse the co-operative projects of Robert Owen, and to revive the idea of a protestant order of Sisters of Charity. His book is a notable monument of the nineteenth-century rebellion against 'the devouring principle of trade'.

None of Southey's other prose works, however, has quite the vitality of the *Life of Nelson*. There was a real sympathy of spirit between the poet and the admiral. Southey saw in this man who could not bear tame or slow measures a superb example of the leadership needed in such portentous times as his. Vexed and disappointed as he might sometimes unavoidably be, Nelson had the resilient spirit that Southey valued in himself. Nelson, he said, had 'that lively spring of hope within him, which partakes enough of the nature of faith to work miracles in war'. Once he was engaged in action, 'his conversation became joyous, animated, elevated, and delightful'. Even in his death agonies during the Battle of Trafalgar, the same spirit persisted. When the surgeon asked him whether his pain was very great, 'he replied, "So great, that he wished he was dead. Yet", said he, in a lower voice, "one would like to live a little longer too!" ' The affinity to Thalaba and Roderick is evident: but Southey's Nelson is a finer creation than his other heroes. None of them combines so convincingly the qualities of courage and kindliness:

He governed men by their reason and their affections: they knew that he was incapable of caprice or tyranny; and they obeyed him with alacrity and joy, because he possessed their confidence as well as their love. 'Our Nel', they used to say, 'is as brave as a lion, and as gentle as a lamb.' Severe discipline he detested, though he had been bred in a severe school: he never inflicted corporal punishment if it were possible to avoid it and when compelled to enforce it, he, who was familiar with wounds and death, suffered like a woman.

On his own initiative, Southey would not have made one of his heroes irritable through 'fatigue, and anxiety, and vexation at the dilatory measures of the commander-in-chief'. Not that such irritation was outside his experience. On the contrary, Southey the *Quarterly* reviewer was constantly complaining that his most effective blows were spoiled by the cowardly editor. Nelson among the Neapolitans plainly looked, in Southey's eyes, just like himself among the politicians who controlled the *Quarterly Review*. Nelson, he said,

saw selfishness and knavery wherever he looked; and even the pleasure of seeing the cause prosper, in which he was so zealously engaged, was poisoned by his sense of the rascality of those with whom he was compelled to act.

But Southey did not write poetry about such complexities.

He has been much criticized for his censorious comments on Nelson's attachment to Lady Hamilton. It is true that irregular love-affairs were as uncongenial to Southey as the finer points of tactics, but he admired Lady Hamilton in her rôle as encourager of heroism, and acknowledges her 'uncommon intellectual endowments'. Her worst sin, from Southey's point of view, was undue devotion to the Neapolitan court. He thought this was about the worst government that had ever existed. If the revolutionary spirit of the 1790's had been allowed to sweep away such rotten régimes—if Britain had not interfered in their favour—Southey would have been well pleased. When Lady Hamilton appeared to him to act as the agent of such a government, no words of condemnation could be too strong. It must be admitted, however, that Southey's considered opinion of Lady Hamilton is as difficult to assess as his considered opinion of the Roman Catholic Church.

V

Southey himself is not much easier to sum up. There can be no doubt of his kindness, his willingness to help, and the utter reliability that made such help really useful. But there is an unmistakable element of hardness in his character. He could be a severe judge of other people, especially if political issues were involved. Once outside the security of his domestic life, he felt himself to be in a world where ruthlessness was necessary to survival. He was always at the mercy of his emotions. Even in his sixties he would still blush with pleasure like a girl, or turn slate-coloured with anger. 'How has he not been torn to pieces long since', Thomas Carlyle asked himself, 'under such furious pulling this way and that?' He could be extraordinarily timid, too— at least in unfamiliar situations. In 1834 John Lingard summoned Wordsworth and Southey to give evidence on a literary point in a lawsuit. Wordsworth spoke boldly, looking the very figure of a robust mountaineer, 'his shirt unbuttoned in the front, disclosing a tough and hairy breast'. But there was nothing so robust about Southey. He could be brought to say no more than that he agreed with Wordsworth's testimony.

Southey often contemplated the idea of emigrating, thinking not only of North America, but at various times of Switzerland, Portugal, Brazil, and Australia. A similar impulse prompted his enthusiasm for projects of large-scale emigration for the working classes, as well as for the transportation of seditious journalists and politicians. Anything that relieved the menacing pressure of life in industrial England was welcome. The appeal of emigration was purely ideal, of course, so far as he himself was concerned. Keswick served well enough as a retreat, and his library of 14,000 volumes was a secure vantage-point for viewing the problems of man and society—as he did in his *Colloquies* with the ghost of Sir Thomas More. Southey's poems and histories are inspired by current events and feelings, but the source-materials (cited in notes which often crowd out the text) interpose a thick screen between the world and his sensibility:

> My days among the Dead are pass'd;
>   Around me I behold,
> Where'er these casual eyes are cast,
>   The mighty minds of old . . .

The 'casual' is significant. Here at least Southey could afford to take his ease. Downstairs young Herbert might be playing at Apollyon in the *Pilgrim's Progress*, roaring at his sisters like a lion seeking whom he might devour: but that was as near as the Devil, and the alarming energies that he symbolized, ever got to Greta Hall. Except in dreams.

ROBERT SOUTHEY

A Select Bibliography

(Place of publication London, unless stated otherwise)

Bibliography:

THE EARLY LIFE OF ROBERT SOUTHEY, by William Haller. New York (1917)

—Appendix A is a detailed descriptive list of Southey's works, but does not include contributions to periodicals.

THE ENGLISH ROMANTIC POETS AND ESSAYISTS: A REVIEW OF RESEARCH AND CRITICISM. ed. C. W. Houtchens and L. H. Houtchens. Modern Language Association of America, New York (1957)

—the chapter on Southey, by Kenneth Curry, is the fullest bibliographical guide available.

Collected Works:

THE POETICAL WORKS OF ROBERT SOUTHEY, COLLECTED BY HIMSELF. 10 vols. (1837-38)

—reprinted several times in one volume.

POEMS OF ROBERT SOUTHEY, ed. M. H. Fitzgerald (1909)

—contains bibliographical notes, but omits 'Joan of Arc', 'A Vision of Judgement', and some minor poems.

SELECT PROSE OF ROBERT SOUTHEY, ed. Jacob Zeitlin. New York (1916)

—selected passages only.

Separate Works:

THE FALL OF ROBESPIERRE: AN HISTORIC DRAMA, by S. T. Coleridge. Cambridge (1794). *Verse*

—Coleridge wrote Act I, Southey Acts II and III.

POEMS: . . . BY ROBERT LOVELL, AND ROBERT SOUTHEY. Bath (1795).

JOAN OF ARC, AN EPIC POEM. Bristol (1796)

—revised editions in 1798, 1806 and 1812. Some further revisions were made in the *Poetical Works* of 1837-38.

POEMS, BY ROBERT SOUTHEY. Bristol (1797)

—a second, revised, edition appeared in 1797, and a second volume in 1799.

LETTERS WRITTEN DURING A SHORT RESIDENCE IN SPAIN AND PORTUGAL. Bristol (1797).

THALABA THE DESTROYER. 2 vols. (1801). *Verse*

MADOC (1805). *Verse*

METRICAL TALES AND OTHER POEMS (1805).

LETTERS FROM ENGLAND: BY DON MANUEL ALVAREZ ESPRIELLA. 3 vols. (1807)

—there is a modern reprint, edited by Jack Simmons (1951).

THE CURSE OF KEHAMA (1810). *Verse*

HISTORY OF BRAZIL. Vol. 1 (1810)

—vol. 2 appeared in 1817, vol. 3 in 1819.

OMNIANA, OR HORAE OTIOSIORES. 2 vols. (1812)

—by Southey and Coleridge.

THE ORIGIN, NATURE, AND OBJECT OF THE NEW SYSTEM OF EDUCATION (1812).

THE LIFE OF NELSON. 2 vols. (1813)

—revised editions in 1814 and 1830. The best modern edition is by Geoffrey Callender (1922). The text of the first edition is available in Everyman's Library and Nelson Classics.

RODERICK, THE LAST OF THE GOTHS (1814). *Verse*

ODES TO HIS ROYAL HIGHNESS THE PRINCE REGENT, HIS IMPERIAL MAJESTY THE EMPEROR OF RUSSIA, AND HIS MAJESTY THE KING OF PRUSSIA (1814).

CARMEN TRIUMPHALE, FOR THE COMMENCEMENT OF THE YEAR 1814 (1814).

THE MINOR POEMS OF ROBERT SOUTHEY. 3 vols. (1815)

—reprints *Poems* and *Metrical Tales*.

THE POET'S PILGRIMAGE TO WATERLOO (1816). *Verse*

THE LAY OF THE LAUREATE. CARMEN NUPTIALE (1816).

WAT TYLER (1817). *Verse*

A LETTER TO WILLIAM SMITH, ESQ., M.P. (1817).

THE LIFE OF WESLEY; AND THE RISE AND PROGRESS OF METHODISM. 2 vols. (1820)

—there is a modern reprint, edited by M. H. Fitzgerald (1925).

A VISION OF JUDGEMENT (1821). *Verse*

THE EXPEDITION OF ORSUA; AND THE CRIMES OF AGUIRRE (1821).

HISTORY OF THE PENINSULAR WAR. Vol. 1 (1823)

—vol. 2 appeared in 1827, vol. 3 in 1832.

THE BOOK OF THE CHURCH (1824).

A TALE OF PARAGUAY (1825). *Verse*

VINDICIAE ECCLESIAE ANGLICANAE. LETTERS TO CHARLES BUTLER, ESQ., COMPRISING ESSAYS ON THE ROMISH RELIGION AND VINDICATING THE BOOK OF THE CHURCH (1826).

ALL FOR LOVE; AND THE PILGRIM TO COMPOSTELLA (1829). *Verse*

SIR THOMAS MORE: OR, COLLOQUIES ON THE PROGRESS AND PROSPECTS OF SOCIETY. 2 vols. (1829).

ESSAYS, MORAL AND POLITICAL. 2 vols. (1832).

LIVES OF THE BRITISH ADMIRALS. vols. 1 and 2 (1833)

—vol. 3 appeared in 1834, vol. 4 in 1837. Reprinted as *English Seamen*, edited by David Hannay (1895).

LETTER TO JOHN MURRAY, ESQ., 'TOUCHING' LORD NUGENT (1833).

THE DOCTOR. Vols. 1 and 2 (1834)

—vol. 3 appeared in 1835, vol. 4 in 1837, vol. 5 in 1838, and vols. 6 and 7 in 1847. There is a modern (abridged) edition by M. H. Fitzgerald (1930).

THE LIFE OF THE REV. ANDREW BELL. 3 vols. (1844)

—vol. 1 by Southey, vols. 2 and 3 by his son C. C. Southey.

OLIVER NEWMAN: A NEW-ENGLAND TALE (UNFINISHED): WITH OTHER POETICAL REMAINS (1845).

ROBIN HOOD: A FRAGMENT. BY THE LATE ROBERT SOUTHEY, AND CAROLINE SOUTHEY (1847). *Verse.*

SOUTHEY'S COMMON-PLACE BOOK, ed. J. W. Warter. 4 vols. (1849–51).

JOURNAL OF A TOUR IN THE NETHERLANDS IN THE AUTUMN OF 1815, ed. W. Robertson Nicoll (1903).

JOURNAL OF A TOUR IN SCOTLAND IN 1819, ed. C. H. Herford (1929).

JOURNALS OF A RESIDENCE IN PORTUGAL, 1800–1801 AND A VISIT TO FRANCE, 1838, ed. Adolfo Cabral. Oxford (1960).

See also the following section for Southey's biographies of Kirke White, John Bunyan, Isaac Watts, and William Cowper.

Works Edited or Translated by Southey:

ON THE FRENCH REVOLUTION, BY MR. NECKER. 2 vols. (1797)

—vol. 2 translated from the French by Southey.

THE WORKS OF THOMAS CHATTERTON. 3 vols. (1803)

—edited by Southey and Joseph Cottle.

AMADIS OF GAUL, BY VASCO LOBEIRA. 4 vols. (1803)

—translated from the Spanish.

THE REMAINS OF HENRY KIRKE WHITE. 2 vols. (1807)

—includes a short biography by Southey. Vol. 3 appeared in 1822.

PALMERIN OF ENGLAND, BY FRANCISCO DE MORAES. 4 vols. (1807)

—translated from the Portuguese.

SPECIMENS OF THE LATER ENGLISH POETS. 3 vols. (1807).

CHRONICLE OF THE CID. (1808)

—translated from the Spanish.

THE BYRTH, LYF, AND ACTES OF KING ARTHUR. 2 vols. (1817).

THE PILGRIM'S PROGRESS. WITH A LIFE OF JOHN BUNYAN (1830).

ATTEMPTS IN VERSE, BY JOHN JONES, AN OLD SERVANT: WITH . . . AN INTRODUCTORY ESSAY ON THE LIVES AND WORKS OF OUR UNEDUCATED POETS (1831)

—the *Essay* was reprinted in 1925, edited by J. S. Childers.

SELECT WORKS OF THE BRITISH POETS, FROM CHAUCER TO JONSON, WITH BIOGRAPHICAL SKETCHES (1831).

HORAE LYRICAE. POEMS . . . BY ISAAC WATTS . . . WITH A MEMOIR OF THE AUTHOR (1834).

THE WORKS OF WILLIAM COWPER. . . . WITH A LIFE OF THE AUTHOR. 15 vols. (1835-37).

Contributions to Periodicals:

Number 5 of the *Flagellant*, 1792, contained Southey's attack on flogging.

Contributions from Southey appeared in the *Monthly Magazine*, 1796-1800; the *Morning Post* (poems), 1798-9; the *Critical Review*, 1798-1803; the *Annual Anthology* (edited by Southey), Bristol, 1799-1800; the *Annual Review*, 1802-8; the *Athenaeum*, 1807-9; the *Edinburgh Annual Register*, Edinburgh, 1808-11, to which Southey contributed the 'History of Europe'; and the *Foreign Review*, 1828-30. For his contributions to the *Quarterly Review*, 1809-39, see *The Quarterly Review under Gifford*, by H. Shine and H. C. Shine. Chapel Hill (1949); and *Life and Correspondence of Robert Southey*, by C. C. Southey, vol. 6 (1850), pp. 400-2 (incomplete). Southey also contributed poems to Annuals like the *Literary Souvenir*, 1826-8, the *Amulet*, 1829, the *Anniversary*, 1829, and the *Keepsake*, 1829.

Letters:

MEMOIR OF THE LIFE AND WRITINGS OF THE LATE WILLIAM TAYLOR, by J. W. Robberds. 2 vols. (1843).

THE LIFE AND CORRESPONDENCE OF ROBERT SOUTHEY, by C. C. Southey. 6 vols. (1849-50).

SELECTIONS FROM THE LETTERS OF ROBERT SOUTHEY, ed. J. W. Warter. 4 vols. (1856).

WALTER SAVAGE LANDOR: A BIOGRAPHY, by J. Forster. 2 vols. (1869).

THE CORRESPONDENCE OF ROBERT SOUTHEY WITH CAROLINE BOWLES, ed. E. Dowden. Dublin (1881).

LAMB'S FRIEND THE CENSUS-TAKER: LIFE AND LETTERS OF JOHN RICKMAN, by O. Williams (1911).

NEW LETTERS OF ROBERT SOUTHEY, ed. K. Curry. 2 vols. New York (1964).

Some Biographical and Critical Studies:

Review of 'Thalaba the Destroyer', by F. Jeffrey, *Edinburgh Review*, 1802

—reprinted in *Famous Reviews*, edited by R. Brimley Johnson (1914).

Review of 'The Curse of Kehama', by John Foster, *Eclectic Review*, 1811

—reprinted in Foster's *Contributions to the Eclectic Review*, vol. 2 (1844). An evangelical-Christian critique.

THE VISION OF JUDGEMENT, by Lord Byron (1822).

THE SPIRIT OF THE AGE, by W. Hazlitt (1825).

Review of *Colloquies of Society*, by T. B. Macaulay, *Edinburgh Review*, 1830

—reprinted in Macaulay's *Critical and Historical Essays*, vol. 1 (1843).

EARLY RECOLLECTIONS, by J. Cottle. 2 vols. (1837)

—revised as *Reminiscences of Samuel Taylor Coleridge and Robert Southey* (1848).

'Lake Reminiscences, from 1807 to 1830. No. IV—William Wordsworth and Robert Southey', by T. De Quincey, *Tait's Edinburgh Magazine*, 1839

—reprinted in De Quincey's *Works*, edited by David Masson, vol. 2. Edinburgh (1889). Also in *Recollections of the Lake Poets*, edited by E. Sackville-West (1948).

SOUTHEY, by E. Dowden (1879).

REMINISCENCES, by T. Carlyle, vol. 2 (1881).

ESSAYS IN ENGLISH LITERATURE, series 2, by G. Saintsbury (1895)

—the essay on Southey is reprinted in Saintsbury's *Collected Essays and Papers*, vol. 1 (1923).

STUDIES OF A BIOGRAPHER, by L. Stephen, vol. 4 (1902).

LECTURES ON THE RELATION BETWEEN LAW AND PUBLIC OPINION IN ENGLAND DURING THE NINETEENTH CENTURY, by A. V. Dicey (1905)

—lecture 7 briefly relates Southey to 'Tory philanthropy'.

THE ROMANTIC MOVEMENT IN ENGLISH POETRY, by A. Symons (1909)

—'Southey had a small but genuine talent of a homely and grotesque order.'

'Robert Southey und Spanien', von L. Pfandl, *Revue hispanique* (1913) —an exhaustive study.

THE EARLY LIFE OF ROBERT SOUTHEY, by W. Haller. New York (1917) —the fullest study of Southey as poet.

A HISTORY OF BRITISH SOCIALISM, by M. Beer, vol. 1 (1919) —Southey as critic of capitalism.

THE LAUREATESHIP. A STUDY OF THE OFFICE OF POET LAUREATE IN ENGLAND, by E. K. Broadus. Oxford (1921).

POLITICAL IDEAS OF THE ENGLISH ROMANTICISTS, by Crane Brinton (1926) —Chapter 2.

LA LITTÉRATURE PORTUGAISE EN ANGLETERRE A L'ÉPOQUE ROMANTIQUE, par F. Walter. Paris (1927) —Chapter 3.

THE NOBLE SAVAGE, by H. N. Fairchild. New York (1928) —Chapter 6.

EDMUND BURKE AND THE REVOLT AGAINST THE EIGHTEENTH CENTURY, by A. Cobban (1929) —Southey's political and social thinking related to that of Burke, Wordsworth, and Coleridge.

'Southey's Relations with Finland and Scandinavia', by H. G. Wright, *Modern Language Review*, 1932.

THE TRANSITION IN ENGLISH HISTORICAL WRITING, 1760-1830, by T. P. Peardon. New York (1933) —Southey's place in the development of historiography.

'Southey and Brazil', by J. de Sousa Leão, *Modern Language Review*, 1943.

SOUTHEY, by J. Simmons (1945) —the standard biography.

HUMAN DIGNITY AND THE GREAT VICTORIANS, by B. N. Schilling New York (1946) —chapter 4. Southey as opponent of orthodox political economy.

THE FIRST ROMANTICS, by M. Elwin (1947) —biographical account of Wordsworth, Coleridge, and Southey.

GUIDE THROUGH THE ROMANTIC MOVEMENT, by E. Bernbaum. Second edition. New York (1949) —excellent brief study and bibliography.

THE POETS LAUREATE, by K. Hopkins (1954).

THE SILENT REBELLION: ANGLICAN RELIGIOUS COMMUNITIES 1845-1900, by A. M. Allchin (1958)
—emphasizes Southey's contribution to the revival of the idea of Sisters of Charity.
CULTURE AND SOCIETY 1780-1950, by R. Williams (1958)
—brief discussion of Southey's critique of modern industrial society.
SOUTHEY E PORTUGAL 1774-1801, by A. Cabral. Lisbon (1959)
ROBERT SOUTHEY AND HIS AGE: THE DEVELOPMENT OF A CONSERVATIVE MIND, by G. Carnall. Oxford (1960).
THE ENCHANTED FOREST, by W. W. Beyer. Oxford (1963)
—Appendix V: 'Southey, Orientalism, and *Thalaba*.'

Bibliographical Series
of Supplements to 'British Book News'
on Writers and Their Work

GENERAL EDITOR
Geoffrey Bullough

SIR WALTER RALEGH

from a painting by an unknown artist in the
National Portrait Gallery

SIR WALTER RALEGH

by

AGNES M. C. LATHAM

PUBLISHED FOR
THE BRITISH COUNCIL
AND THE NATIONAL BOOK LEAGUE
BY LONGMANS, GREEN & CO.

LONGMANS, GREEN & CO. LTD.
48 Grosvenor Street, London W.1

*Associated companies, branches and
representatives throughout the world*

First published 1964
©Agnes M. C. Latham, 1964

*Printed in Great Britain by
F. Mildner & Sons, London, E.C.1*

CONTENTS

¶Sir Walter Ralegh was born at Hayes Barton, Devonshire, in 1554. He was condemned to death and executed at Westminster on 29 October 1618.

SIR WALTER RALEGH

I

INTRODUCTION

Sir Walter Ralegh is valued above all as a man of action. His intellectual and literary gifts were an added ornament, proper to the Renaissance concept of a fully developed personality. Conversely, his many and varied occupations as soldier, seaman, courtier and explorer, seem to have increased his stature as a man of letters. His writings were almost always a by-product of his active life, designed to recommend his projects, to call attention to their success or to excuse their failure. He wrote because he had something he very urgently wanted to say, and this intimate personal urgency is one of the dominant characteristics of his work. It is reflected in the poignant, melancholy rhythms of *The History of the World* and the passionate disarray of his verse, and equally in the direct, near-colloquial narrative of *The Last Fight of the Revenge* and *The Discovery of Guiana*. He never uses fine writing for its own sake but rises to meet what seems to him a great occasion. Because he was living a full life in an expanding world he often met with great occasions. Adverse critics contend that he manufactured them—that he used his literary gifts to heighten any difficulties he encountered and to distort the truth in his own interest. Nobody denies him imagination, but it is perhaps true that he lacked judgement.

Walter Ralegh was born in 1554, a younger son of a Devonshire gentleman, with his own way to make in the world, backed by a host of West Country kinsfolk who were doing the same thing. As a young man he fought on the Protestant side in the French Wars of Religion and in the Desmond Rebellion in Ireland. When he was not fighting he spent some time in residence at Oriel College, Oxford, and at the Inns of Court, in London. All the time his eyes were fixed upon Court favour, the highest prize which any fortune hunter could possibly hope to win, and by 1580 he had made it his. He became first favourite of the Queen. That same vitality and vigour, charm and intelligence, that personal urgency which still survives in his written work, must have had twice the force when embodied in the man himself. Elizabeth could not resist it.

He flourished in her grace, but it was a full-time occupation, and personal adventure was for the moment in abeyance. In 1592 his fortunes took a spectacular turn for the worse, on the discovery that he had secretly married one of the Queen's maids-of-honour, a treachery his royal mistress could not forgive. The young Earl of Essex, who had been disputing with him for the Queen's affection, was there to fill his place. Ralegh was left to strive for distinction in the war at sea, taking part in maritime expeditions against Spain and leading a voyage of exploration to South America, where he hoped to found an English colony in Guiana, to be the nucleus of an overseas empire. As reigning favourite, arrogant and acquisitive (he had very expensive tastes, founding colonies being one of them) he had been far from popular. After his fall from favour he could be openly abused and derided. He was suspected of engineering the downfall of Essex, but that rash young nobleman suffered more from the encouragement of his friends than from the machinations of Sir Walter Ralegh.

When, in 1603, the old Queen died and King James VI of Scotland became King James I of England, Ralegh was marked down for destruction. His enemies wanted to finish with him and James did not want to start. The King was content to accept the popular estimate, enhanced by a deliberate whispering campaign in high circles. Before long Ralegh was charged with complicity in a plot to dethrone the King, make peace with Spain and exact tolerance for Roman Catholics. The nature and extent of his complicity in these ill-organized projects has never been made clear. They do not seem such as would appeal to him, but there was sufficient evidence, largely supplied by his friend, Lord

Cobham, to convict him. King James accorded him a last-minute reprieve and confined him for thirteen years in the Tower, while he made peace overtures to Spain in his own good time.

The new policy of appeasement was not too well liked. There were those who thought that Elizabeth's long struggle with King Philip should end in a knock-out blow rather than in a negotiated peace. Subjected to increasing pressure, James in 1616 agreed to release though not to pardon his prisoner, who for some time had been offering to open a gold mine in Guiana without giving just cause of offence to Spain. The Spanish Ambassador intimated strongly that he was offended even before the expedition sailed. No compensating mine was found. The English destroyed a Spanish outpost which lay in their way, protesting that they had not known it was there, though there was every reason why they should have known and they probably did. Ralegh's young son was shot dead in the skirmish.

Ralegh himself was in no position to exercise authority, though he had to bear the blame for everything that happened. He had been near to dying of a tropical fever during the voyage and stayed at Trinidad, while his lieutenant, Lawrence Keymis, led the prospectors inland. On his return, Ralegh reproached him bitterly for not opening the mine, whereupon Keymis retired to his cabin and took his own life. Ralegh returned empty-handed to an England which was deeply curious about the venture and not wholly unsympathetic. His defence of his proceedings was eagerly read. His letters home, recounting the disasters of the voyage, were copied and passed from hand to hand, together with the verses he was said to have written on the fly-leaf of his Bible the night before he was beheaded. For James did not spare him, and his death took on the air of a martyrdom, or at any rate of a tragedy, in which he played his central part to admiration.

He appealed to the middle seventeenth century as a victim of Stuart tyranny. They saw him as anti-Spanish, anti-

Catholic, and even anti-royalist, a witness in *The Discovery of Guiana* to England's colonial future and in *The History of the World* to a divine providence guiding events. Thus, in a way which would have amazed contemporaries, accustomed to hearing him called 'damnable atheist' and 'mischievous Machiavel', he became a hero. A small sheaf of minor works circulated as the *Remains of Sir Walter Raleigh*. Modern research has inevitably modified the picture. Sir Julian Corbett has queried his naval expertize. S. R. Gardiner is convinced of his guilt in 1618, and has some damaging documents to show relating to the last Guiana voyage. Mario Praz finds his policy machiavellian, and he is credited with presiding over a club of freethinkers called the School of Night. The latter charges do nothing to dim the vivid colours in which he is usually presented. The many biographies which attempt to unravel the riddle of his personality testify to its enduring fascination.

II

POET

Ralegh's poetry has survived only in stray pieces, sifted from the anthologies and commonplace books of the time, with subscriptions of dubious value. He preserved his anonymity more jealously than most Elizabethans, anxious as they were to appear gentlemen, with minds above money. He had more reason. The lady he adored was the greatest lady in the land. Much poetry was addressed to the Queen in her public character. Ralegh addressed her personally and privately in the character of platonic mistress. This was not matter for the book-stalls. His poetic reputation was confined to a select circle. It included George Puttenham, who had some firsthand knowledge of his verses, since he quotes from them in his *Art of English Poetry* (1589), describing Ralegh's vein as 'most lofty, insolent and passionate'. Spenser was also among the privileged few. In 1589 Ralegh visited him in Ireland and listened to readings from un-published verse, after which he read in exchange some of his own. It was, says Spenser,

> all a lamentable lay,
> Of great unkindness, and of usage hard,
> Of Cynthia the Ladie of the sea,
> Which from her presence faultless him debarr'd . . .
> Right well he sure did plain:
> That could great Cynthia's sore displeasure break,
> And move to take him to her grace again.
>   'Colin Clouts Come Home Againe' (1595)

The character of Timias, who loves the maiden-huntress Belphoebe though he can never possess her, and is banished her sight when he turns momentarily aside, is Spenser's idealized picture, in the third book of *The Faerie Queene*, of Ralegh and Elizabeth. He gives the story a happy ending, with Timias forgiven, and it would appear that in 1589 Ralegh, who had retired to Ireland in temporary disfavour, did indeed soothe the Queen's vexation with some plaintive verses which have not survived outside Spenser's description of them. In 1592 there came a rift which verses could not heal. Elizabeth Throckmorton, one of the Queen's maids of honour, gave birth to a son. Ralegh was the father and Essex the godfather. Before long it was common knowledge that Cynthia's devoted servant was a married man. It is possible to sympathize with both sides. He was a man approaching forty who wanted a home and children, she a woman of sixty, burdened with the crown of England, who felt that she had been fooled with sweet words. Ralegh tried to heal the wound, as he had before, with more words. Among the Cecil Papers at Hatfield House there is a manu-script fragment of some five hundred lines in his hand entitled 'The Eleventh and Twelfth Books of the Ocean to

Cynthia'. Presumably he hoped that his friend Sir Robert
Cecil might find occasion to show them to the Queen and
that he could perform again the feat of 1589. It was a far-
fetched hope which failed. If the verses seem inordinately
passionate, it is worth reflecting how very much Ralegh
lost when he lost the Queen's regard.

The Hatfield fragments remain almost the only undoubted
specimens of Ralegh's verse. The title suggests that they are a
continuation of the 'lamentable lay' known to Spenser,
though it is difficult to imagine how ten earlier books could
have been filled with matter so abstract. There is no
narrative thread. The lines display only a perpetual flux and
reflux of contrary feeling, as the poet remembers happier
days and then recalls the painful present, only to deny the
reality of present pain and grief in the contemplation of an
eternity of beauty to which he must needs respond with an
undying affection. Sensual love and sensual beauty, which
are ephemeral, are strongly contrasted with their opposites:

> And though strong reason hold before mine eyes
> The images and forms of worlds past
> Teaching the cause why all those flames that rise
> From forms external, can no longer last
>
> Than that those seeming beauties hold in prime,
> Love's ground, his essence, and his empery,
> All slaves to age, and vassals unto time,
> Of which repentance writes the tragedy;
>
> But this, my heart's desire could not conceive,
> Whose love outflew the fastest flying time;
> A beauty that can easily deceive
> Th'arrest of years, and creeping age outclimb,
>
> A spring of beauties which time ripeth not,
> Time that but works on frail mortality,
> A sweetness which woe's wrongs outwipeth not,
> Whom love hath chose for his divinity,

A vestal fire that burns but never wasteth,
That loseth naught by giving light to all,
That endless shines eachwhere, and endless lasteth,
Blossoms of pride that can nor fade nor fall.

In spite of its vague and transcendental manner the poem
plainly relates to the current situation. It tells of 'the tokens
hung on breast and kindly worn', the showers of grace

Which now to others do their sweetness send ...
Filling their barns with grain and towers with treasure,

and how, when the writer attempted

To seek new worlds, for gold, for praise, for glory,
To try desire, to try love severed far,
When I was gone she sent her memory
More strong than were ten thousand ships of war

To call me back, to leave great honour's thought,
To leave my friends, my fortune, my attempt,
To leave the purpose I so long had sought ...

The last book 'Entreating of Sorrow' breaks off in the middle
of a line and the fragment as a whole though it is copied in a
fair hand is disorderly, reflecting what is perhaps an in-
tentionally assumed desperation. The writer would like the
reader to think that he is half crazy and that his lines are
something overheard rather than formally stated. They have
a cloudy magnificence and power but along with it a
curious limpness. The poet seems to be inviting the emotion
to take him where it will and attempts little control.
C. S. Lewis speaks of 'the monotony, the insanity, and the
rich, dark colours of an obsessive despair'. Metrically the
verse is extremely fluent. There is a vaguely pastoral frame-
work, perhaps continuing something in earlier books, much
imagery of trees and fruit and corn and flowers, and some
bold similes.

The lax construction and the absence of anything resembling climax are not characteristic of Ralegh's writing. His manner in lyrics tends to be terse, pointed and epigrammatic. An instance is 'Conceit begotten by the eyes', in which he treats his favourite theme of ephemeral passion:

> As ships in ports desired are drowned,
> As fruit once ripe, then falls to ground,
> As flies that seek for flames, are brought
> To cinders by the flames they sought:
> So fond Desire when it attains,
> The life expires, the woe remains.

A poem which is notable for its abrupt, contemptuous rhythms is 'The Lie', in which he savagely reveals the corruptions of society and forces upon it again and again the ultimate insult of 'the lie':

> Go soul, the body's guest,
>   Upon a thankless errand,
> Fear not to touch the best,
>   The truth shall be thy warrant;
> Go, since I needs must die
>   And give the world the lie.

The tradition that he was the author of this not very typical poem is possibly a tribute to his personality, his supposed disrespect for established sanctities. It is the kind of poem people could imagine him writing. A similar tradition assigns to him a much stranger poem, 'The passionate man's pilgrimage', in which the speaker is about to be beheaded and imagines his journey to a better land, where justice is not corrupt,

> For there Christ is the King's Attorney:
>   Who pleads for all without degrees
>   And he hath angels, but no fees.

If it is his, it must represent his feelings when in 1603 he awaited the headsman's axe and reflected upon the injustice and brutality of his trial. Where 'The Lie' shocks with its matter, this shocks by its manner, the irregular verse form, the odd juxtaposition of legal terms and eschatology, the way the writer abandons himself in a kind of trance to chance rhythms and word associations:

> And by the happy blissful way
> More peaceful pilgrims I shall see,
> That have shook off their gowns of clay,
> And go apparelled fresh like me.
> I'll bring them first
> To slake their thirst,
> And then to taste those nectar suckets
> At the clear wells
> Where sweetness dwells,
> Drawn up by saints in crystal buckets.

It is hard to judge poetry written under stress, which may not be characteristic of the author's normal manner. One of the interesting things about Ralegh's verse is the number of times he seems to be writing under the pressure of strong emotion, with a rather strange abandon. An instance, close in both matter and manner to the last books of *Cynthia*, is the little colloquy he devised upon the basis of the ballad of Walsingham:

> She hath left me here all alone,
>   All alone as unknown,
> Who sometimes did me lead with herself,
>   And me loved as her own.

The verses which he wrote in 1618, in expectation of death, are in another category, completely controlled. This time his sentence came as no surprise to him, and he met it with great gallantry. The verses were just one gesture among many. Sympathizers, who made endless copies of them,

might not have been so much impressed had they realized
that he was recalling a stanza of an earlier poem, to which he
has added a staid and devout couplet:

> Even such is time which takes in trust
> Our youth, our joys, and all we have,
> And pays us but with age and dust:
> Who in the dark and silent grave
> When we have wandered all our ways
> Shuts up the story of our days.
> And from which earth and grave and dust
> The Lord shall raise me up I trust.

The earlier piece lamented the passing of youth and beauty
and sensuous delight and offered no comfort for it. It is a
not uncommon mood with Ralegh, and is displayed
perfectly in his answer to Marlowe's 'Passionate Shepherd':

> Time drives the flocks from field to fold,
> When rivers rage, and rocks grow cold,
> And Philomel becometh dumb,
> The rest complain of cares to come.
>
> The flowers do fade, and wanton fields
> To wayward winter reckoning yields,
> A honey tongue, a heart of gall,
> Is fancy's spring, but sorrow's fall.

Too little of his poetry has survived for it to be easy to
make any general assessment of it, to trace influences or
suggest sources. It changes before the reader's eyes from the
stilted angry couplets prefaced to Gascoigne's satire,
The Steel Glass, in 1576, through the smoothness of 'Nature
that washt her hands in milk' and the terseness of 'Conceit
begotten by the eyes', to the turbulence of 'The Books of
the Ocean's Love to Cynthia' and the startling free associations of 'The passionate man's pilgrimage', to the grave
serenity of 'Even such is Time'. The one quality these pieces

have in common is their disillusion. Contemporaries stress their sweetness. To Spenser Ralegh's verse was 'honied' and 'with nectar sprinkled'. It has in addition qualities of violence and of concentrated scorn, and a note of deep melancholy. Tucker Brooke has described it as 'the froth that rises where unplumbed waters break on adamant'.

III

SEAMAN

The problem of establishing a reliable canon affects Ralegh's prose as well as his poetry. It has too long been taken for granted that all the pieces collected and published under his name in the mid-seventeenth century (one of them, *The Cabinet Council*, by John Milton) were his. These doubts, however, do not arise in regard to his three best known works, *The Last Fight of the Revenge*, *The Discovery of Guiana*, and *The History of the World*.

The first two are propaganda pieces. Ralegh was early convinced that England, threatened by the might of Catholic Spain, should not defend herself by sending reluctant recruits to fight land battles in France, Ireland and the Low Countries, but should open a naval offensive concentrated upon cutting Spanish trade routes to the New World. It was not to be expected that the Queen and her more conservative ministers would have much grasp of advanced naval strategy. Even today historians contend that England's first line of defence was the continental coast, and that it would have been most ill-advised to exchange the European land-theatre for the experimental hazards of the Atlantic. Nonetheless Elizabeth was not averse to a supplementary policy of naval pressure, the more so because the seamen could pay themselves out of the profits of their privateering. Her Majesty, Ralegh complained long after, 'did all by halves'.

In 1591, Lord Thomas Howard was awaiting the home-coming of the Spanish treasure fleet, which had been forced for fear of English commerce-raiders to winter at Havana. He was watering and cleaning his ships at the Azores, when he was surprised by an armada from Spain, which was King Philip's very expectable retort to English depredations among his merchantmen. The largest ship in Howard's squadron, the *Revenge*, was commanded by Ralegh's Cornish cousin, Sir Richard Grenville. Grenville was the last to get away, and finding himself cut off from his commander by the Spanish fleet, elected to sail through the middle of it with all his guns blazing rather than to turn and run before the wind. To run would have been an entirely proper naval manoeuvre in no way parallel to 'running' in a land battle. Grenville, always something of a fire-eater, preferred the other course and after a prolonged battle against spectacular odds lost the Queen's best ship to the enemy.

Ralegh's pamphlet, published anonymously, followed so promptly upon the action that he was still ignorant of the fact that Grenville had died of wounds and been buried at sea, after which a cyclone of exceptional violence had battered the Spanish ships, thus indicating that either God or the devil was on Grenville's side. The pamphlet was called *A Report of the Truth of the Fight about the Isles of Azores this last Summer betwixt the Revenge, one of Her Majesty's Ships, and an Armada of the King of Spain*, but is generally known by its running head as *The Last Fight of the Revenge at Sea*. Hakluyt reprinted it with his *Voyages* in 1598 and acknow-ledged Ralegh as the author. It would be natural to think that he was writing specifically in defence of his cousin but the text does not bear this out. Though Grenville, with great skill and plausibility, is transformed from a hothead into a hero, Ralegh's main concern is with the honour of England, the morale of her seamen, and the importance of the war at sea. Whoever had commanded the *Revenge* (for a time he was hoping to command her himself), he would have made the same case with the same urgency. He is not expert yet in the handling of prose. His sentences are often top-heavy and repetitive, but he is already a master of the telling phrase and gives a very strong sense of first hand participation in the events he is describing. Through the incidents he selects and the emphasis he lays on them, he contrives to impose an epic pattern upon what might in hostile hands have been a sorry tale of the loss of a capital ship, elevating it, as Bacon puts it, 'even to the height of an heroical fable'. A plainness and directness in the writing, together with a convincing show of impartiality and fair-mindedness (except towards the enemy, who could not expect it) give the narrative great power. All that can be objected against Grenville is in fact stated, but the reader responds in spite of it to the gallantry of the unequal encounter. Grenville need not have exposed his ship:

The other course had been the better, and might right well have answered in so great an impossibility of prevailing. Notwithstanding, out of the greatness of his mind, he could not be persuaded.

Thereafter the battle is described in a narrative calculated to make a 'pure navy' man wince. Grenville had wilfully exchanged the new strategy of long range gunnery and manoeuvrable ships for a hand-to-hand encounter through the night. This was exactly the kind of fighting which the Spaniards expected and for which they were equipped. Nonetheless, he held them off for an astonishingly long time, and Ralegh's rhetoric is equal to his theme. In its way and before its time, it is a piece of brilliant journalism:

But as the day increased, so our men decreased: and as the light grew more, by so much more grew our discomforts. For none appeared in sight but enemies, saving one small ship called the *Pilgrim*, commanded by Jacob Whiddon, who hovered all night to see the success; but in the morning bearing with the *Revenge*, was hunted like a hare among many ravenous hounds, but escaped. All the powder of the *Revenge* to the last barrel was now spent, all her pikes broken, forty of her best men slain, and the most part of the rest hurt. In the beginning of the fight she had but one hundred free from sickness, and four score and ten sick, laid in hold upon the ballast. A small troop to man such a ship, and a weak garrison to resist so mighty an army. By those hundred all was sustained, the volleys, boardings and enterings of fifteen ships of war besides those which beat her at large.

The statement that the ammunition was exhausted does not tally with the last phase of the story, in which the survivors successfully bargained for their lives in exchange for the ship, after locking the master gunner in his own gun-room lest he should obey Sir Richard's orders to split and sink her. Since he seemed only too ready to do so, he clearly had some powder at his disposal. Ralegh has no fault to find with the men, who had fought a good fight. Rehearsing their commonsense arguments, he tranquilly observes that these won the day, 'it being no hard matter to dissuade men from death to life'. This double vision is characteristic of him. He could see the practical necessities that coexist with heroic potentialities. His idealism is the stronger for being based in fact and shot with a faint astringent cynicism. He used his imagination as an instrument for discerning truth as well as for heightening and manipulating it. It is because of this paradoxical clearsightedness that he could make poetry out of disillusion.

A lively and very partisan account of the expedition against Cadiz, in which Ralegh served under Essex in 1596, exists in manuscript and was printed in 1700. Various manuscript fragments relate to the navy and naval affairs. Ralegh projected a full-scale naval history for Prince Henry, but it is doubtful if he advanced far with it.

IV

EMPIRE BUILDER

The Discovery of Guiana illustrates very plainly Ralegh's double mastery of fact and fiction. It gave him a bad name among contemporaries, as well as enchanting the world, then and ever since. It is a very much more substantial work than the pamphlet on the *Revenge*. It was published in 1596, with his name on the title page, and is based upon his own experience. It might appear at first sight to be purely personal propaganda, but the plan Ralegh recommends was well beyond the resources of any private individual. Quite simply, he proposed that England should take over South America, beginning with the only region not effectively colonized by Spain: the country watered by the Orinoco and its tributaries, then known as Guiana. The terrain which Ralegh actually traversed, from the mouth of the Orinoco to the Caroni river, is now part of Venezuela. It was a further step in the Spanish war, and required the support of Queen and country. No such support was forthcoming and we should perhaps be thankful, for it would have been a tremendous undertaking, and there is no doubt that here as elsewhere Ralegh's optimism leapt ahead of rational expectation. He was not ignorant of colonizing, having twice dispatched settlers to Virginia. Their fate—the first came home and the second mysteriously disappeared in the wilderness—might have given him pause. Yet on his behalf it must be admitted that the Virginian venture was ultimately successful, though not before it had passed into the hands of a merchant syndicate.

When Ralegh colonized Virginia he was settling new-found land. His policy in Guiana was more aggressive. He had come to realize that casual commerce-raiding would never effectively stop the flow of gold and silver to Spain. What England needed was what Spain had in abundance, land bases from which to operate. He had reason to think that behind the dense forests of the Orinoco lay a secret empire of the Incas. Its capital city, Manoa, situated on a vast inland sea, was known to the Spaniards as El Dorado. He had carefully studied Spanish chronicles, read Spanish letters seized at sea, and sifted the gossip of West Country ports. The exploits of Cortez and Pizzaro provided encouraging parallels. And yet the whole idea was a myth, which with a few days to spare Ralegh himself could have exploded. The great lake had no existence apart from seasonal floods in the high valleys. Objects of wrought gold produced by obliging Indians were relics of the Chibcha civilization of Colombia, out of which the Spaniards had already carved the Kingdom of New Granada. There was no truth in the story that some of the Inca princes had escaped and founded a new empire as rich as the old.

Ralegh's strategic plan was bold and brilliant. He intended to invade the Inca empire with the help of the borderers, who claimed to have been dispossessed. Then, having established a benevolent rule, the English could lead all Guiana against the Spanish colonies to the west of it, mobilizing the deep resentment of the natives against the brutal conquistadores. This meant that Ralegh's own conduct, in contrast, had to be kindly and protective. He sang Elizabeth's praises—and who could do it better than he? She was stronger than the hated *Castellani* and had freed many nations from their tyranny. 'The like and a more large discourse I made to the rest of the nations both in my passing to Guiana, and to those of the borders, so as in that part of the world', he reports delightedly, 'her majesty is very famous, whom they now call *Ezrabeta Cassipuna Aquerewana,* which is as much as Elizabeth, the great princess, or greatest commander.'

One of the pleasantest aspects of the *Discovery* is Ralegh's sympathy with the native Indians and his crusading fervour on their behalf. Their inferiority is in no way stressed, for they were to be enlisted as allies. In 1618, his argument that Guiana was English was based largely upon their power to enter into contracts and dispose of their own land by treaty with Europeans. He was genuinely charmed by their simple dignity. 'The tawny women', he noted, were 'excellently favoured, which came among us without deceit, stark naked.' Old chief Topiawari was touching in his grief for an only son lost in battle and he proved unexpectedly shrewd in council. His picturesque phraseology was worth reproducing:

He remembered in his father's time when he was very old, and himself a young man, that there came down into that large valley of Guiana a nation from so far off as the Sun slept (for such were his own words), with so great a multitude as they could not be numbered nor resisted, and that they wore large coats and hats of crimson colour, which colour he expressed by showing a piece of red wood wherewith my tent was supported, and that they were .... those that had slain and rooted out so many of the ancient people as there are leaves in the wood upon all the trees.

Significantly, Ralegh never reproaches the Indians with their barbarous religion nor congratulates himself upon the prospect of saving souls. He takes an intelligent interest in their customs and recounts them with tolerant understanding. It surprised him to find that they warred for women and not for gold, but he thought it over and saw that it made sense in a sparsely populated country.

The native *caçiques*, on their side, were captivated by his persuasive tongue. He could address them in their own heroic terms, and not without that necessary component of primitive heroism, much practical good sense. All the time, he carefully concealed the gold lust which was going to attract colonists, and freely distributed English coins as tokens from the Queen. An attempt to recoup by sacking the Spanish settlement at Cumaná was beaten off with heavy losses. This was an uncomfortable incident which Ralegh touches on lightly. The expedition, in consequence, came home little the richer and was early discredited. Ralegh may have convinced himself too easily that he could preserve good relations with the natives once Guiana was thrown open to English settlers, but it is plain, nonetheless, that he was thinking in terms larger than petty gain.

Part of *The Discovery of Guiana* is narrative, part descriptive (in terms which range from the geographical to the lyrical), part is a defence against charges of deliberate deceit and gross gullibility, and part is an eloquent statement of policy. By 'discovery' Ralegh means the opening and exploring of the country. He was not claiming to be the

first to enter it. On the contrary, he rehearses the history of
early Spanish expeditions with a strong sense of the drama
inherent in them. He owed a good deal to current literature
of the New World with which he was very familiar. His
personal narrative presumably originated in some kind of
journal of the voyage.

Though it has often been challenged, the book is basically
accurate. If there is deceit, the writer had first deceived himself. Ralegh believed in the 'mighty, rich and beautiful
empire of Guiana', and it is very hard for the reader not to
share his delusion, as he confidently retails the information
he had gathered from the border tribes, and from Antonio
de Berrio, Governor of Trinidad, who spent a lifetime
seeking El Dorado and died still believing in it. Ralegh
admits that his own party never entered the secret empire
and he does not claim to have spoken face to face with
anyone who had been in Manoa. He dallies pleasurably with
stories of Amazons, remote sisters of *Ezrabeta Cassipuna
Aquerewana*, which may well have had some foundation in
tribal custom as well as in classical history. He gives details
of the Ewaipanoma, 'the men whose heads do grow
beneath their shoulders', much in the spirit that modern
explorers report on the Abominable Snowman. He was
struck by the unanimity with which the Indians asserted
their existence, and the odd way in which it corroborated
Sir John Mandeville. But he goes no further than giving the
reader his own reasons for crediting these wonders. He does
not pose as an eye-witness.

His suppressions are in fact more dangerous than his
assertions. E. G. M. Taylor accuses him of concealing 'the
twofold climatic pulse—the change of season marked by the
onset of the rains, and by the dangerous swelling of the
waters, yet not by any cooling of the air'. The health of his
party seems nonetheless to have been excellent. They were a
close knit and efficient company, nearly all from the
West Country. Ralegh praises the food available—fish,
game, fruit, maize, cassava bread and native wines. He finds

hammocks comfortable and convenient. His interest in new drugs is excited by native balsams and by the lethal arrow-poison, curare. Any hint that the rocks are metalliferous is exploited for rather more than it is worth, but he knows how gold occurs, in hard white spar or else in alluvial deposits.

The book went through many editions and was translated into Latin, Dutch and French. It was read as an up-to-the-minute news item, as a story of adventure, as a description of a strange country and as a practical prospectus for fortune hunters. But over and above all these it has an enduring charm, supplied by the same hand which shaped *The Last Flight of the Revenge* into a heroic paradigm. This time it was not epic but a kind of exotic pastoral. The land, the beauty of the land and the promise of the land are what stay in the reader's mind, the brightness and newness of the brave New World. Every corner turned is in itself a small discovery:

I never saw a more beautiful country nor more lively prospects, hills so raised here and there over the valleys, the river winding into divers branches, the plains adjoining without bush or stubble, all fair green grass, the ground of hard sand easy to march on either for horses or foot, the deer crossing every path, the birds toward the evening singing on every tree with a thousand several tunes, cranes and herons of white, crimson, and carnation perching on the river's side, the air fresh with a gentle easterly wind, and every stone that we stooped to take up promised gold or silver by his complexion.

The unspoiled country, the courtesy of its inhabitants, the golden city always just behind the next mountain range entered into the English imagination, to be reflected in Prospero's enchanted island and in Milton's Eden.

In 1617 Ralegh set sail once more, in a magnificently equipped vessel called the *Destiny*, which had cost him rather more than he had, and with a number of none too reliable consorts, the nature of the voyage and of its leader being not such as to attract sober spirits. It would appear from the available evidence that he was not going to be too particular how he got gold provided he got it. There was talk of his being joined by Flemish ships, and he certainly planned to use Frenchmen. If these took to privateering or burned a Spanish outpost, they could account for it to governments less tied than that of England to policies of appeasement. The question of what mine or mines he aimed at, how soundly grounded his hopes were, and whether he had intended from the beginning to take to privateering if the mines failed, still provide subjects for hot debate, as does his excuse for the destruction of the town of San Thomé, which barred the way to a mine previously said to be in unoccupied territory.

The documents relative to the last Guiana expedition have been printed in one volume by V. T. Harlow. They include the letters Ralegh wrote to his wife and sponsors, his famous *Apology for the Voyage to Guiana*, and the co-called *Little Apology*, which was a letter to his cousin Sir George Carew. All these circulated freely in manuscript at the time. The note of personal urgency and personal commitment is naturally at its strongest in them. *The Apology* was written in great haste, under cover of a simulated bout of sickness. The arguments, recast in 1889 and shorn of emotion, were used as part of the British answer to territorial claims by Venezuela and as such they failed to convince. Harlow prints from a large number of Spanish documents which were officially transcribed at this time and which reveal curious and unexpected aspects of the expedition. What the Venezuelan case amounts to in sum is that exploration and colonization are two different things. The English never settled in the country. In 1618 it was not too late to claim that they were in process of settling and that they had the good will of the native *caçiques*, whereas the Spaniards had effected no more than a precarious military occupation. The country has in fact yielded gold in fair quantity and some diamonds. At present it is exploiting rich deposits of iron. The flooding of the rivers, which so hampered Ralegh's party, has proved a serious hindrance to progress.

V

HISTORIAN

The History of the World was composed during Ralegh's thirteen years' imprisonment in the Tower. He was allowed to have his books and to employ secretaries and amanuenses. Inevitably there was some envious gossip, to which Ben Jonson contributed, suggesting that he had done little of the work himself or had not made his indebtedness sufficiently plain. Contemporaries, anxious only to have their own contributions recognized, did not criticize his reliance upon compendiums already published, which was considerable in places, and indeed is hardly surprising. He had no Hebrew and not much Greek, reading Greek authors as much as possible in Latin translations. His French was fluent. He read and presumably spoke Spanish and he cannot have been without Italian. He had time on his hands and we know from his friend Sir Robert Cecil that he could 'toil terribly'.

His plan was comprehensive, beginning with the Creation. He intended, after he had dealt with the ancient world, to concentrate chiefly upon his own country and to come as near as he dared to modern times. In the event, the work breaks off in the third century A.D. He was, he says in his Preface, uneasy about the reception of a modern history and disheartened by the death in 1612 of James's heir apparent, Prince Henry, whose interest in the project had supported and encouraged him.

The work, in its incomplete form, was published in 1614. It is carefully printed, with an engraved allegorical frontispiece and a number of maps and diagrams, and it fills nearly 800 pages in folio. It is one of the few works to which Ralegh put his name and he was promptly rebuked for his presumption. On the King's orders all copies were recalled some months after publication and not released until the title-page had been removed. Ralegh, a prisoner under sentence of death, had no business to present himself as an author. Such at least is the common interpretation of the affair, based on a theory that there was a titlepage in the first edition, as well as the engraved frontispiece, on which no author's name appears. It has recently met a lively challenge from John Racin, Jr., who cannot believe an excision would be feasible or could be effected without leaving traces in surviving copies.

Nor would the suppression of the author's name, which in any case was an open secret, have satisfied King James, who is known to have condemned the book as 'too saucy in censuring princes'. It was an article of faith with James that kings were God's vice-gerents. From this unexceptionable place he liked to move on to the respect which was therefore their due from loyal subjects. Ralegh moved in another direction. The power of kings, he delighted to point out, however great they may look in the small theatre of the world, is as nothing beside the power of God, who will exact satisfaction for all their sins. James is personally extolled as an admirable ruler, gentle of disposition and free of ancient blood-guilt, but the glib comments are lost in the grand pattern of the book, which is designed so that 'it may no less appear by evident proof than by asseveration, that ill-doing hath always been attended with ill success'.

Ralegh traces this pattern very clearly in the summary history of the kings of England which he inserts in his Preface. He found it ready made in the English chronicles, but whereas they are directed towards establishing a particular dynasty in divine favour and disestablishing rivals, Ralegh when he comes to deal with world history is more impartial. If it exasperated King James to be invited to look at himself through the wrong end of a telescope and see himself of no account, it must have been infinitely soothing to Ralegh, the prisoner in disgrace, to reduce the whole world to a scale where there was very little distinction between himself and his oppressors, except insofar as the very act of reduction, the detached clarity of vision, made him their superior. It is not for nothing that the Preface became known as *A Premonition to Princes*, and that the book ends with the famous apostrophe to Death, the Leveller:

It is therefore Death alone that can suddenly make man to know himself. He tells the proud and insolent that they are but abjects, and humbles them at the instant; makes them cry, complain and repent, yea even to hate their forepassed happiness. He takes the accounts of the rich and proves him a beggar—a naked beggar, which has interest in nothing but the gravel that fills his mouth. He holds a glass before the eyes of the most beautiful, and makes them see therein their deformity and rottenness; and they acknowledge it. O eloquent, just and mighty Death! Whom none could advise, thou hast persuaded; what none hath dared, thou hast done; and whom all the world hath flattered, thou only hast cast out of the world and despised. Thou hast drawn together all the far-stretched greatness, all the pride, cruelty, and ambition of man, and covered it all over with these two words *Hic Jacet*.

While Ralegh belittles man and undermines worldly values, he sets all within the structure of God's Providence. There is an order in this world, even if it is the sad one of sin and retribution. It is for this reason, and not from any idle pedantry, that he begins with the Creation and the Fall of Man. They are basic to his thesis. Thereafter he spends a long time on Bible history, since the Bible is revealed truth and makes a particularly plain demonstration of the working out of God's will. His strenuous efforts to clarify the chronology of the Old Testament and to relate it to what is otherwise known of the ancient world resulted in a series of intricate and impressive tables reproduced as an appendix to the book. From Jewish history he goes on to the Persians, the Greeks and the Romans, always following the fortunes of kings and leaders of men, the people who inaugurate policy and whose deeds have been recorded. If these, the greatest, are found wanting, it is not suggested that there will be much for which to commend their inferiors. Man is judged by his rulers. He may suffer pitiably at their hands but he shares their nature and in a position of power would not behave much differently:

Only those few black swans I must except, who having the grace to
value worldly vanities at no more than their own price, do by retaining
the comfortable memory of a well-acted life, behold death without dread
and the grave without fear; and embrace both as necessary guides
towards endless glory.

Contemporaries were delighted by the comprehensive-
ness of the history and did not miss, as the modern reader
must, the sense of intimate participation with which Ralegh
could imbue a narrative of events which fell within his own
experience. This is to some extent compensated by his
readiness to comment, generalize and digress. He will
analyze character and motive, assess policy and dilate upon
the moral implication of events, giving not only a picture of
the past but of the mind of the Renaissance judging the
past. He retains his power to highlight the drama of events,
and if he omits the small, revealing details, it is because they
have not for the most part been preserved by the earlier
annalists he consulted. From time to time, though not so
often as one might wish, he notes parallels in modern times
and speaks of matters with which he is personally acquainted
—of refugees smoked out of caves in the French wars, of
the existence of Amazons in South America, of naval tactics
or of the fighting qualities of the English soldier. But the
main purpose of his narrative is far from that of a modern
historian. It gives a view of history which is theocentric and
providential, and a pessimistic assessment of man. It has
therefore been dismissed by critics as conventional,
'rabbinical' and little better than mediaeval. This was not the
opinion of contemporaries. Throughout the seventeenth
century it was highly valued, because it presented a picture
of life in consonance with the feeling of the times. Milton as
well as Ralegh derived all history from the Creation and the
Fall of Man.

In the eighteenth century it was beginning to lose ground
as a historical work, though it was still valued for its piety
and its excellent prose style. As a piece of writing it is the

best thing Ralegh did. Ben Jonson, who was not easy to please, commended his prose, and Samuel Johnson, an equally severe critic, found it acceptable a hundred and fifty years later and distinguished it as 'elegant'. The *History* gave Ralegh considerable practice in summary narrative and terse comment. The vitality and robustness of the man are in the style, together with a detachment, due in part to his isolation from the world and from his subject matter, and in part natural to him. It is the same cool, calculating but not unsympathetic attitude that he took to the native civilizations of America, applied now to the world at large. His plainness has lost its initial awkwardness, but it derives much of its vigour from the fact that he never in his life had taken much count of formal propriety and correctness. He has no fear of sinking, and this in an age which tended to write uneasily and with excessive care.

The same absorption in direct communication ensures that when he rises it is not an empty tumescence. It is easy to select passages and label them 'purple' but it is not fair to the writer—if indeed it is fair to any good writer. At its most magnificent, Ralegh's prose still echoes his own speaking voice. It is not a falsetto. It changes because his subject has changed. His high style is at its most sustained in the Preface, its melancholy purged of excess sentiment by the note of cold disillusion. The rhythms of the long brooding sentences are extremely subtle—worthy to be set beside Donne, Browne and Milton, yet demonstrably not quite like any one of them. The mood, characteristic of its time, is a sombre stoicism, intensified rather than lightened by a vision of divine order enforced by a remote and retributive deity.

VI

'ATHEIST'

The publication of *The History of the World*, with its pronounced if melancholy piety, removed the stigma of atheism from Ralegh's name to the satisfaction of contemporaries. Sentencing him in 1618, his judge observed, 'Your faith hath heretofore been questioned, but I am resolved you are a good Christian, for your book, which is an admirable work, doth testify as much'. One of the crowd which listened attentively to his last speech from the scaffold reported afterwards that he spoke 'not one word of Christ, but of the great and incomprehensible God, with much zeal and adoration'. The comment could be extended to *The History of the World*. Ralegh is there concerned with the source of ultimate power and ultimate order rather than with saving grace, but it is a question of emphasis not of orthodoxy.

Even a cursory glance through his writings should absolve him of the charge of atheism, which so deeply shocked his own time. It was not, however, directed against a man of letters with published work to his credit but against a royal minion, an arrogant and extravagant upstart. Ralegh had a public image upon which mud of almost any kind would stick. The Queen had given him positions of authority which he could not exercise without offence to somebody. A major cause of his unpopularity was the number of trade monopolies which had been assigned to him. He was known to be very rich. The jewels on his shoes alone were said to be worth more than £6,000. It was easy to claim that he lived in luxury at the expense of the poor and honest man. To the more obvious motives for envy and dislike, his enemies were able to add the sinister connotations of the word 'atheist'. It was used at the time as an indiscriminate term of reproach, often with no very exact theological implications. A bad man is manifestly no Christian. It could be applied as simply as that. But there were sides to Ralegh's character which on a superficial level might appear to give better justification for it. It would not otherwise have hung about him for so many years, with its murky suggestions and brimstone odour, to be exploited relentlessly in the treason trial of 1603.

The first to use it was the Jesuit, Robert Parsons, in an

unflattering portrait of Elizabeth's court. His Latin pamphlet
was widely read. A summary in English, published in 1592,
speaks of 'Sir Walter Ralegh's school of atheism and the
conjuror who is master thereof and of the great diligence
used to draw young gentlemen to this school'. The writer
seems to have been reflecting on Ralegh's interest in the
physical sciences, in particular mathematics, as taught by a
notable scholar, Thomas Harriot. Mathematical studies
followed naturally from his practical concern with naviga-
tion and cartography. Harriot, whom he maintained as a
member of his household, can be plausibly identified as his
'conjuror'. He was one of the most advanced astronomers of
his day and carried to his grave the odium which tended to
accompany a man who probed God's mysteries in the
physical universe.

As well as being a patron of Harriot, Ralegh was said to
have been one of those to whom Marlowe 'read the atheist
lecture', and upon this slender foundation there has been
built a supposition that he and Marlowe were closely
acquainted. A theory with more substance is that both men
were involved in a libertine circle known as the School of
Night. This has recently become a critical commonplace. It
is worth examining the foundation upon which it is built.
Father Parsons, in a hostile pamphlet, spoke of Ralegh's
'school of atheism'. So much is fact. From there the commentators go on to equate 'school of atheism' with the
phrase 'school of night', which is used by Shakespeare in
Love's Labour's Lost, buried deep among some rather obvious
pleasantries upon the hackneyed theme of fair and dark
beauty. Biron is mocked because he has fallen in love with a
Dark Lady. 'Fie', cries the King of Navarre,

> black is the badge of Hell,
> The hue of dungeons, and the School of night.

This solitary, unemphatic, rather mysterious phrase has been
used, with the help of much ingenious argument, to prove

the play a satire upon Ralegh and his associates and their scientific studies. The argument, in fact, can stand without reference to 'the school of night', though it is harder without it to bring in Ralegh. Shakespeare mocks pedants, who as plodders and killjoys have never found favour in comedy, and suggests that young men find their stars in women's eyes. The question may then be propounded whether he had any particular person or persons in mind, who they were and what kind of audience would understand and enjoy sallies at their expense.

In 1594, rumours of atheism followed Ralegh to Dorset where he had retired to his country house at Sherborne. An ecclesiastical commission was sent to investigate, perhaps to protect rather than to convict him. Anyhow, no prosecution followed, nor did the evidence warrant it. The heart of his offending seems to have been that at a dinner party he and his brother Sir Carew baited a conventional parson, the Rev. William Ironside. Ralegh took up the position, theologically unexceptionable, that man cannot define the substance of the soul. The parson, unwilling to be put down by a layman, retorted with logic, and Ralegh proceeded to tie him in knots. Ernest Strathmann thinks that in essence the dispute was concerned with the validity of Aristotelian logic and hardly with theology at all, and that Ironside knew the local gossips had misinterpreted it. The consequences show that Ralegh was playing a dangerous game and it is not likely to have been the first time he had played it. He enjoyed argument and had a gift for it. He would have done well to walk more circumspectly, but circumspection was never a characteristic of his. Infinitely plausible and warmly sympathetic when he was so disposed, he could on occasion be tactless and wantonly indiscreet. He had the intelligent man's confidence that truth speaks for itself and he was contemptuous of commonplace minds.

Ralegh was interested in the problems propounded by the nature of God, of creation and of the image of God in man. They bulk largely in *The History of the World*, especially in the second chapter. *A Treatise of the Soul*, said to be his work, was printed from a manuscript copy in 1820. A minor piece called *The Sceptick* was one of the first of his papers to be published and appeared regularly with his *Remains*. It is a collection of notes from Sextus Empiricus, and is confined to showing the imperfections of human knowledge. A philosophical position such as this can very easily be accompanied by faith in an inscrutable deity. Indeed it was regularly used by polemists to throw man back upon God, all human props having been proved fallible. It is peculiarly liable to be misconstrued by narrow minds. Ralegh had a dangerous kind of disengagement, a tolerance when confronted with alien ideas and an intellectual boldness. It is not hard to imagine him listening to Marlowe reading 'the atheist lecture'.

Over and above this, his own beliefs are marked by an austerity unlikely to recommend them to simpler minds and warmer hearts. He is constant, for instance, in his assertion that immortal souls are completely severed from all human concerns:

But hereof we are assured, that the long and dark night of death . . . shall cover us over till the world be no more. After which, and when we shall again receive organs glorified and incorruptible, the seats of angelical affections: in so great admiration shall the souls of the blessed be exercised as they cannot admit the mixture of any second or less joy, nor any return of foregone or mortal affection, towards friends, kindred, children. Of whom whether we shall retain any particular knowledge, or in any sort distinguish them, no man can assure us: and the wisest men doubt.

In his farewell letter to his wife, when he awaited the death-stroke in 1603, this became 'As for me, I am no more yours, nor you mine. Death hath cut us assunder: and God hath divided me from the world, and you from me.' Gentle and practical, he begs her not to have scruples about marrying again, 'For that will be best for you: both in respect of God and the world'.

It is not always realized how profoundly unsentimental Ralegh was, even to hardness. This comes out very clearly in his brief *Instructions to his Son*, which almost all readers find too apt to recommend self-interest. In politics he had a kind of machiavellian realism, in which he differs from his fellow Elizabethans only in being more articulate. Many of his actions seem to contradict it. He was not a very shrewd politician and allowed himself to be outmanoeuvred. He stood by the old Queen, for instance, when self-interest should have sent him where the rest were going, to her probable heir. They quietly and industriously undermined him. In popular belief machiavellian craft was as characteristic of him as atheism. He was the arch-plotter. Melodrama lit him luridly. At his trial he was addressed as 'monster', 'viper' and 'spider of hell'. Yet he had done much to advance his country and help his countrymen, notably the seamen and the west-country tinners. He was concerned with tin mining as Lord Warden of the Stannaries. As Vice-Admiral of Devon and Cornwall he had charge of the Admiralty Courts. He had served his time as a member of parliament, where he spoke up for the underprivileged, against witch-hunts among nonconformists and against taxing the poor. It was a matter of regret to him that he was never a member of the Privy Council.

During his imprisonment he wrote some able treatises upon current affairs. *The Prerogative of Parliaments* is an imaginary discussion in which a Justice of the Peace shows a rather haughty Councillor that an English king must rule through his parliament or disregard it at his peril. As advice to a reigning Stuart, trying his best to bypass his parliaments, it was more timely than tactful. It appeared in 1628 under a foreign imprint. Prince Henry asked him to summarize the arguments against the pro-Spanish marriages which were proposed for the prince and his sister. These pamphlets are vigorous, orderly and spare, not without the flash of anecdote or phrase with which Ralegh almost always lights up his arguments. It is he, for instance, who tells how

Essex fatally alienated the Queen by blurting out in a temper that 'her conditions were as crooked as her carcase'. Elsewhere he regrets that she had not 'believed her men of war, as she did her scribes' for then they would have made the kings of Spain 'Kings of Figs and oranges, as in old times'. A very Raleghan discourse, on a wider and more general subject, is *The Miseries of War*. It is typical of the disillusioned historian seeing through the pretences of mankind. The Ralegh who none the less urged the exploitation of Guiana and pressed the war with Spain was, on his own admission, no more than human. 'Of a long time my course was a course of vanity', he said in his last speech from the scaffold. 'I have been a seafaring man, a soldier, and a courtier, and in the temptations of the least of these there is enough to overthrow a good mind, and a good man.'

His character is far from simple, and though much information is available about his life it is often too fragmentary to solve the contradictions, which may lie at deep levels. In his writing he combines cynicism with idealism, truth with fiction, and a sombre pessimism with a contagious zest for life.

SIR WALTER RALEGH

A Select Bibliography

(Place of publication London, unless stated otherwise)

Bibliography:

A BIBLIOGRAPHY OF SIR WALTER RALEGH, by T. N. Brushfield, 2nd edition. Exeter (1908).

Collected Works:

JUDICIOUS AND SELECT ESSAYES AND OBSERVATIONS UPON THE FIRST INVENTION OF SHIPPING; THE MISERY OF INVASIVE WARRE; THE NAVY ROYALL AND SEA-SERVICE [authorship queried, see H. E. Sandison, *Arthur Gorges*, 1928]; WITH HIS APOLOGIE FOR HIS VOYAGE TO GUIANA (1650).

THE SCEPTICK, OR SPECULATIONS; OBSERVATIONS OF THE MAGNIFICENCY AND OPULENCY OF CITIES; HIS SEAT OF GOVERNMENT; ALSO HIS DEMEANOR BEFORE HIS EXECUTION [i.e. his last speech]; AND LETTERS TO THE KING'S MAJESTIE, AND OTHERS OF QUALITIE [and also three poems: i. 'The Passionate Man's Pilgrimage'; ii. 'Even Such is Time'; iii. 'On the Snuff of a Candle'] (1651)
—subsequently reprinted as *The Remains* (see next entry).

THE REMAINS OF SIR WALTER RALEIGH (1651-1702)
—the editions between 1651 and 1702 contain in various combinations the items in the 1651 volume together with *His Instructions to his Sonne; and The Son's Advice to his aged father* [first published 1632, the second item almost certainly spurious]; *Maxims of State* [first published 1642]; *Observations touching Trade and Commerce with the Hollander* [first published 1653. Authorship queried, see A. Buff, *Englische Studien* 1877); *The Prerogative of Parliaments in England* [first published Middelburg and Hamburg 1628].

THREE DISCOURSES : I. OF A WAR WITH SPAIN AND OUR PROTECTING THE NETHERLANDS; II. OF THE ORIGINAL AND FUNDAMENTAL CAUSE OF NATURAL, ARBITRARY AND CIVIL WAR; III. OF ECCLESIASTICAL POWER (1702)
—the last two discourses appeared in 1650 as *The Misery of Invasive War*. The section in discourse II on *Civil or Unnatural War* is new.

WORKS. POLITICAL, COMMERCIAL AND PHILOSOPHICAL: TOGETHER WITH HIS LETTERS AND POEMS. TO WHICH IS PREFIX'D A NEW ACCOUNT OF HIS LIFE by T. Birch. 2 vols. (1751)

—does not include the *History of the World*, but adds to works previously collected some new poems and letters and *The Cabinet Council containing the Cheif Arts of Empire and Mysteries of State* (1658), published as *Aphorisms of State* (1661) and as *The Arts of Empire and the Secrets of Government* (1697). [Authorship queried by E. Strathmann, *Times Literary Supplement*, 13 April 1956]; *A Discourse touching a Match propounded by the Savoyan, between the Lady Elizabeth and the Prince of Piedmont; A Discourse touching a Marriage between Prince Henry of England, and a Daughter of Savoy* [first published as *The Interest of England with regard to Foreign Alliances* 1750]; *A Voyage for the Discovery of Guiana; An Introduction to a Breviary of the History of England with the Reign of King William the I.* [First published 1693, authorship queried].

THE WORKS OF SIR WALTER RALEGH, KT. NOW FIRST COLLECTED; TO WHICH ARE PREFIXED THE LIVES OF THE AUTHOR BY WILLIAM OLDYS AND THOMAS BIRCH. 8 vols. Oxford (1829)

—Volume I. *Lives*. Volumes II-VII. *The History of the World*. Volume VIII contains all the minor works in the edition of 1751 with some smaller pieces, including *A Relation of Cadiz Action*, (first printed with the abridged *History of the World*, 1700); *A Treatise of the Soul*

—the collection of poems is supplemented from Sir E. Brydges's unreliable Lee Priory Press edition (see below).

Selected Works:

POEMS, ed. Sir E. Brydges (1813)
—printed at the editor's Lee Priory Press.

POEMS BY SIR HENRY WOTTON, SIR WALTER RALEIGH AND OTHERS, ed. J. Hannah (1845)
—Pickering's attractively printed anthology.

THE COURTLY POETS FROM RALEIGH TO MONTROSE, ed. J. Hannah (1870).

SELECTIONS, ed. G. E. Hadow. Oxford (1917)
—contains excerpts from *The History of the World*, the whole of *The Last Fight of the Revenge, Cadiz Action* and some letters.

POEMS, ed. A. M. C. Latham (1929)
—revised and supplemented, 1951. The standard text.

Separate Works:

A REPORT OF THE TRUTH OF THE FIGHT ABOUT THE ISLES OF AÇORES, THIS LAST SUMMER. BETWIXT THE REVENGE ONE OF HER MAIESTIES SHIPPES AND AN ARMADA OF THE KING OF SPAINE (1591)

—reprinted in Hakluyt's *Voyages*; Vol. II (1599) and in Arber's *English Reprints* (1908). Not included by Birch or in the Oxford *Works*.

THE DISCOVERIE OF THE LARGE, RICH, AND BEWTIFUL EMPIRE OF GUIANA. (3 edns. 1596)

—reprinted in Hakluyt's *Voyages;* Vol. III (1598). Edited by R. H. Schomburgk with valuable topographical notes, a transcript of Ralegh's autograph journal of the voyage, and 'Considerations on the Voyage to Guiana' said to be by Ralegh but more probably by Lawrence Keymis (1848). Edited by V. T. Harlow, 1928, with an excellent introduction, transcripts from Spanish documents, and a reproduction of one of Ralegh's maps, BM Add. MS 17940 A.

THE HISTORY OF THE WORLD. IN FIVE BOOKES. (1614)

—9 editions before 1700. Reprinted by W. Oldys. 2 vols, 1736. Abridged as *The Marrow of Historie* (1650) and as *An Abridgment of Sir Walter Raleigh's History* (1698)

Some Biographical and Critical Studies:

FRAGMENTA REGALIA, by Sir R. Naunton (1641).
—ed. E. Arber, 1895.

THE ARRAIGNMENT AND CONVICTION OF SIR WALTER RAWLEIGH, by Sir T. Overbury (1648).

THE LIFE OF SIR WALTER RALEGH, by W. Oldys (1736)
—prefixed to *The History of the World*, reprinted in *Works*, 1829.

THE LIFE OF SIR WALTER RALEGH, by T. Birch (1751)
—prefixed to *Collected Works*, reprinted in *Works*, 1829.

THE LIFE OF SIR WALTER RALEGH, by A. Cayley. 2 vols. (1805).

COMPLETE STATE TRIALS, ed. T. B. Howell. Vol. II (1809).

'The Case against Sir Walter Ralegh', by S. R. Gardiner. *Fortnightly Review*, 1867.

THE LIFE OF SIR WALTER RALEGH, TOGETHER WITH HIS LETTERS, by E. Edwards. 2 vols. (1868)
—a standard work, well documented, providing the only substantial collection of Ralegh's letters.

DRAKE AND THE TUDOR NAVY, by J. C. Corbett. 2 vols. (1899).

SIR WALTER RALEGH, by W. Stebbing. 2nd edition, Oxford (1899)
—one of the best of the biographies of Ralegh.

SUCCESSORS OF DRAKE, by J. C. Corbett (1900).

SIR WILLIAM MONSON'S NAVAL TRACTS, ed. M. Oppenheim. 5 vols.
(1902).

'Sir Walter Ralegh's *History of the World*', by C. Firth. *Proceedings of the
British Academy*, 1917-18
—reprinted in *Essays Literary and Historical*, 1938.

'The Battle of Flores', by G. Callender. *History*, 1919.

WILLOBIE HIS AVISA, ed. G. B. Harrison (1926)
—prints in full the evidence before the commission enquiring into
atheism in Dorset.

RALEGH'S STAATSTHEORITISCHE SCHRIFTEN: DIE EINFÜHRUNG DES
MACHIAVELLISMUS IN ENGLAND, von N. Kempner. Leipzig (1928).

'Un machiavellico Inglese: Sir Walter Raleigh', di M. Praz. *La
Cultura*, 1929.

RALEGH'S LAST VOYAGE, by V. T. Harlow (1932)
—reprints all available documents.

ATHEISM IN THE ENGLISH RENAISSANCE, by G. T. Buckley. Chicago
(1932).

'La Religion de Sir Walter Ralegh', par J. Beau. *Revue Anglo-
Américaine*, June 1934.

LATE TUDOR AND EARLY STUART GEOGRAPHY, by E. G. R. Taylor (1934).

RALEGH, THE LAST OF THE ELIZABETHANS, by E. Thompson (1935).

THE SCHOOL OF NIGHT, by M. C. Bradbrook (1936).

'Sir Walter Ralegh as Poet and Philosopher', by C. S. Tucker Brooke.
English Literary History (1938)
—reprinted in *Essays on Shakespeare*, 1948.

'The Sixteenth-Century Lyric in England', by Y. Winters. *Poetry,
Chicago*, 1938-9.

'The Textual Evidence for The School of Night', by E. A.
Strathmann. *Modern Language Notes*, 1941.

RALEIGH AND THE BRITISH EMPIRE, by D. B. Quinn (1947)
—for Ralegh's Virginian Colony, see the same author's *The Roanoke
Voyages*, 2 vols., 1955.

'Sir Walter Ralegh's Goldmine', by A. M. C. Latham. *Essays and Studies*, 1951.

SIR WALTER RALEGH: A STUDY IN ELIZABETHAN SKEPTICISM, by E. A. Strathmann. New York (1951)
—an admirably detailed and documented study.

'The Working Papers for The History of the World', by W. F. Oakeshott. *The Times*, 29 November 1952.

SIR WALTER RALEGH, by P. Edwards (1953)
—this is the only general study of Ralegh as a literary figure.

English Literature in the 16th Century, by C. S. Lewis. Oxford (1954).

'Two Elizabethan Poets: Daniel and Ralegh', by P. Ure. In *The Age of Shakespeare*, vol. II of *The Pelican Guide to English Literature*, ed. B. Ford, 1955.

'A Reading of The Ocean's Love to Cynthia', by D. Davie. *Elizabethan Poetry*, ed. Brown and Harris, 1960
—the original MS of this fragmentary poem survives at Hatfield House.

THE QUEEN AND THE POET, by W. F. Oakeshott (1960)
—a detailed study of Ralegh's poetry against the background of his life.

ENGLISH LITERATURE IN THE EARLIER SEVENTEENTH CENTURY, by D. Bush. 2nd edition, Oxford (1962).

'Ralegh and the Revolutionaries', by C. Hill. The *Listener*, 21 June 1962
—the influence of Ralegh's writings upon the later seventeenth century.

RALEGH AND THE THROCKMORTONS, by A. L. Rowse (1962)
—contains decisive evidence of Ralegh's marriage. See also F. Sorensen, 'Sir Walter Ralegh's Marriage', *Studies in Philology*, 1936, and P. Lefranc, 'La date du mariage de Sir Walter Ralegh *Etudes Anglaises*, 1956.

'The Early Editions of Sir Walter Ralegh's *The History of the World*' by John Racin, Jr. *Studies in Bibliography*, 1964.

Bibliographical Series
of Supplements to 'British Book News'
on Writers and Their Work

GENERAL EDITOR
Geoffrey Bullough

Tho: Moor Lᵈ Chancelour

SIR THOMAS MORE

from a drawing of 1526 by HANS HOLBEIN *in the Windsor Castle Collection
reproduced by gracious permission of H.M. the Queen*

SIR THOMAS MORE

by

E. E. REYNOLDS

PUBLISHED FOR
THE BRITISH COUNCIL
AND THE NATIONAL BOOK LEAGUE
BY LONGMANS, GREEN & CO.

LONGMANS, GREEN & CO. LTD.
48 Grosvenor Street, London, W.1

*Associated companies, branches and
representatives throughout the world*

First published 1965
© E. E. Reynolds, 1965

*Printed in Great Britain by
F. Mildner & Sons, London, E.C.1*

CONTENTS

CONTENTS

SIR THOMAS MORE

SIR Thomas More's political ideas, his religious convictions and the crisis of conscience that led to his martyrdom in 1535, are not the concern of this essay; they cannot be completely separated from a consideration of his work for they were the essence of his life, but the emphasis in these pages will be placed on his literary achievement.

I. LIFE

Thomas More, the son of a lawyer, was born in London in 1478. He was educated at St. Anthony's School and in Cardinal Morton's household, followed by two years at Oxford. His legal training began in 1494 and he was called to the Bar at Lincoln's Inn in 1501. For a time he felt drawn to the contemplative life in the Charterhouse, but found that he had no vocation. He was learned in Latin and Greek and in the works of the Early Fathers; he gave public lectures on St. Augustine. Among his close friends were John Colet, William Grocin, William Lily, William Latimer and Thomas Linacre, all of whom had studied in Italy. In 1499 he met Erasmus and they became lifelong friends. More was elected to Parliament in 1504 and in the following year he married Jane Colt. They made their home in Bucklersbury. There were four children: Margaret, Elizabeth, Cecily and John. More became an Under-Sheriff of London in 1510 and was again returned to Parliament. Jane More died in 1511, and he then married a widow, Alice Middleton; her daughter Alice, Margaret More's foster-sister Margaret Giggs, and a ward Anne Cresacre became members of the family and were educated with More's children under his direction. Others joined them to form what has been called More's School. No distinction was made between boys and girls.

More soon gained a reputation with the City Companies for his legal ability and for his skill in negotiations; he was

7

also in demand as a Latin orator at official receptions. His services were used on a commercial embassy to Flanders in 1516, and again to Calais a year later. So successful was he that, reluctantly, he became a member of the King's Council in 1517. The king and queen enjoyed his conversation so much that he accompanied them to their various manors and, for a time, acted as the king's secretary. His learning and wit made him a delightful companion. He was present at the Field of Cloth of Gold in 1520, and, in the following year, was made Under-Treasurer and was knighted. His daughter Margaret married William Roper in 1521, and they, with her sisters and brother when they married, all formed what was a patriarchal household.

Thomas More became Speaker of the House of Commons in 1523; other honours that came to him at this period were his appointment as Chancellor of the Duchy of Lancaster and as High Steward of both Universities. By 1524 his household had outgrown the home in Bucklersbury, so he built a new house at Chelsea. On two occasions he accompanied Wolsey on important embassies, in 1521 to Calais and in 1527 to Amiens. His last embassy was in 1529 when, with his friend Cuthbert Tunstal, he shared in the negotiations that resulted in the Peace of Cambrai. Meanwhile, the king had asked his support in his divorce proceedings, but More felt unable to agree with the king's opinion. In spite of this, he succeeded Wolsey as Lord Chancellor on 23 October 1529. The divorce proceedings made the office burdensome and he resigned on 16 May 1532. When the Act of Succession was passed early in 1534, he refused to take the oath, as it implied a repudiation of papal authority. He was sent to the Tower on 17 April 1534. During his fifteen months' imprisonment, the king assumed the title of Supreme Head of the Church of England. As More could not accept this break from the Roman See, he was indicted under a new Act of Treason for refusing to the king one of his titles. He was tried on 1 July 1535 and was executed five days later. The Roman Catholic Church canonized him in 1935.

II. EARLY WRITINGS

In his character sketch of his friend Thomas More, Erasmus tells us that, 'as a young man he wrote and acted in some little comedies. He rejoices in brilliant sallies, seasoned with true wit, and a clever retort delights him, even when against himself. Hence it was that in youth he amused himself composing epigrams and took special pleasure in Lucian. His first years were given to poetry. Then for a long time he worked hard to acquire a flexible prose style, making experiments of all kinds.' Those 'little comedies' have not survived, but when he was a boy in Cardinal Morton's household he was noted for his ready improvisations in Interludes; this characteristic was preserved in London legend in the unacted Elizabethan play, *The Booke of Sir Thomas Moore*.

The epigrams were translated from Greek into Latin and in these he vied with his friend and fellow-student, William Lily, the first high-master of St. Paul's School. More and Erasmus were both attracted to Lucian and they translated into Latin several of the dialogues. The satire, the mockery and fantastic humour of Lucian were congenial to them, and his influence can be traced in much of their work, notably in *The Praise of Folly*, and *Utopia*. This devotion to classical studies places More in the group of Christian humanists who were his friends.

Some of More's English verses have been preserved but they rarely rise above mediocrity. The best poem is *A ruful lamentacion* on the death of Henry VII's Queen in 1503. It takes the form of a monologue by the dying woman:

> Adew myne owne dere spouse, my worthy lorde,
> The faithfull love, that dyd us both combyne,
> In mariage and peasable concorde,
> Into your handes here I cleane resyne,
> To be bestowed uppon your children and myne,
> Erst wer you father, & now, must ye supply,
> The mothers part also, for lo now here I ly.

In this poem and in a number of others, More used Chaucer's seven line stanza (later known as rime royal), but frequently with six instead of five accented syllables in the last line. In the *English Works* of 1557 his verses are described as having been written 'in his youth for his pastime', but I suspect his hand in *Twelve Merry Jests of one called Edyth* printed in 1525 by his brother-in-law, John Rastell, and ascribed to Walter Smyth, More's personal servant.

It is interesting to recall that Dr. Johnson, in the 'History of the English Language' prefaced to his Dictionary, gave over eight folio pages out of twenty-seven to extracts from More; a long passage from *Richard III* filled three pages, but no fewer than five were from these early poems. Johnson's concern was with the vocabulary, not the quality, of the verses. Such a selection seems strange to us, but it points to what may be called their Englishness. They show no classical influences. More's liking for the Chaucerian stanza has been noted; there are a number of references in his books to Chaucer and there are echoes of Chaucerian phrases. This stanza was also favoured by John Skelton, and More's *Merry Jest* is written in a verse form more regular than the Skeltonic but with the same lively movement:

> It happed so,
> Not long a go,
> A thrifty man there dyed,
> An hundred pounde,
> Of nobles rounde,
> That had he layd a side:
> His sonne he wolde,
> Should have this golde,
> For to beginne with all:
> But to suffise
> His chylde, well thrise,
> That money was to smal.

To what extent More and Skelton were acquainted is not known; the only record of their meeting also brings Erasmus

and More together for the first time; this was in the summer
of 1499. Skelton was then tutor to Henry, Duke of York,
and More took Erasmus to Eltham to present him to the
Duke.

When Erasmus heard of the execution of Thomas More
thirty-five years later, he exclaimed, 'I feel as if I had died
with More so closely were our two souls united'. It was a
fruitful friendship. There was not only the stimulus of
contact between two men of keen intelligence and quick wit,
but More was brought into the main stream of European
scholarship, and his circle of friends was extended. It was
during Erasmus' second visit to England in 1505 that the
two friends made their translations from Lucian. A collection of these was published in Paris in 1506; they were
reprinted nine times during More's lifetime. Another
translation, this time into English, had probably been made
a few years earlier, but it was not published until about 1510.
This was a free adaptation of a Latin life of Pico della
Mirandola (1463-1494). More was attracted to this young
Italian humanist because they shared a love of learning and a
longing for the cloister which neither was able to satisfy.
The book also included translations of some of Pico's
letters, and some verses, again in Chaucerian stanzas, composed by More on themes suggested by Pico's writings.
More's prose had not yet freed itself from the influence of
classical rhetoric, and, while the verses have lost some of the
early raciness, they had a more serious intention.

Among More's 'experiments' mentioned by Erasmus, may
be included the unfinished *History of King Richard the Third*,
written about 1513. The first reliable text was published in
the *English Works* in 1557, with this note, 'which worke hath
bene before this tyme printed in Hardynges Chronicle and
in Hallys Chronicle: but very muche corrupte in many
places'. In the Hardynge-Grafton Chronicle (1543) *Richard
III* appeared anonymously; in Hall's Chronicle (1548) the
author's name was given, as it was also in Holinshed's
Chronicle (1577) which followed the text of 1557. More

also wrote a Latin version, and the indications are that he worked on both concurrently. The 'experiment' here was in historical narrative with perhaps Sallust in mind. For such a purpose More had excellent material in hand. As a boy he had lived through the reign of Richard III and he could recall stories told by Cardinal Morton; best of all, he could draw upon the recollections of his own father and those of his contemporaries, some of whom had held office under Richard. The influence of classical rhetoric is early shown in the invented declamation 'The Oration of the King in his Death-bed', but as the writer gets into the swing of his narrative and begins to enjoy the story he is telling, so the classical pattern becomes less discernable. Much has been written on the derivation of More's prose, but any discussion must be largely speculative as we know so little about his reading in English. We know more of his classical and patristic studies, but there are few references in his books to native prose literature. We know that he had read the works of such spiritual writers as Richard Rolle and Walter Hilton, but had he read Caxton's translations, or Malory? The question cannot be answered, nor perhaps does it matter very much since he was attempting an historical narrative for which there was no close precedent in English. The Chronicles were pedestrian records and there was no vernacular tradition of historical biography. English prose was still in its formative stage and More had therefore to follow his own genius both in form and expression. The result was a notable innovation. It was a great loss that he did not complete his book; indeed he had something more ambitious in mind, for he hinted that he might write of 'the time of the late noble Prince of famous memory King Henry the Seventh, or percase that history of Perkin [Warbeck]'.

This is not the place to discuss the value of *Richard III* as history; there are some errors of fact but More used to the full his chance of talking with those who had played their parts in those dangerous times, and he could therefore record the oral tradition while it was still forming. His view of Richard was the popularly accepted one, and it was adopted and perpetuated by Shakespeare, and no amount of research seems able to destroy it.

The narrative moves easily but an occasional unevenness comes when a long and involved sentence is used in explaining policy or the significance of events. It soon becomes clear that More is happiest when he is recording action or writing dialogue, when, that is, he is writing dramatically. This is apparent in many scenes. There is, for instance, the account of the meeting between Queen Elizabeth and Cardinal Bourchier when she resisted as long as she could the request that she should allow her younger son to leave sanctuary at Westminster to join his brother. At last she gave way:

And therewithal she said unto the child: 'Farewell, my own sweet son, God send you good keeping. Let me kiss you once yet ere you go, for God knoweth when we shall kiss together again.' And therewith she kissed him and blessed him, turned her back and wept and went her way, leaving the child weeping as fast.

When the Lord Cardinal and these other lords with him had received this young Duke, they brought him into the Star Chamber, where the Protector took him in his arms and kissed him, with these words: 'Now welcome, my lord, even with all my very heart.' And he said in that of likelihood as he thought. Thereupon forthwith they brought him to the King, his brother, unto the Bishop's Palace at Paul's, and from thence through the city honourably into the Tower—out of which after that day they never came abroad.

More's sense of the comic is uppermost in such an incident as Dr. Shaw's sermon at St. Paul's Cross. This had been planned to lead up to the appearance of Richard, but Shaw misjudged the timing and when he gave the cue, 'This is the father's own figure', Richard failed to answer it; so Shaw had to carry on as best he could, and when the Protector at last arrived, the preacher repeated the cue.

But the people were so far from crying 'King Richard!' that they stood as they had been turned into stones, for wonder of this shameful sermon. After which once ended, the preacher got him home and never after durst look out for shame but keep him out of sight like an owl.

A sense of pity is shown in the account of Jane Shore, Edward IV's last mistress:

I doubt not some shall think this woman too slight a thing to be written of and set among the remembrances of great matters: which they shall specially think, that haply shall esteem her only by that they now see her. But meseemeth the chance so much the more worthy to be remembered, in how much she is now in more beggarly condition, unfriended and worn out of acquaintance, after good substance, after as great favour with the Prince, after as great suit and seeking to with all those that those days had business to speed, as many other men were in their times, which be now famous only by the infamy of their ill deeds. Her doings were not much less, albeit they be much less remembered because they were not so evil. For men use, if they have an evil turn, to write it in marble; and who so doth us a good turn, we write it in dust: which is not worst proved by her, for at this day she beggeth of many at this day living, that at this day had begged if she had not been.

More had gone some way towards forming a personal style. His liking for alliteration may be noted. 'Men mused what the matter meant.' 'People diversely divining upon this dealing.' 'Wise ways to win favours.' At times he achieved epigrammatic quality and he could use antithetic phrasing:

Every man answered him fair, as though no man mistrusted the matter which, of truth, no man believed.

Very faithful and trusty enough, trusting too much.

George, Duke of Clarence, was a goodly noble prince, and at all points fortunate, if either his own ambition had not set him against his brother, or the envy of his enemies, his brother against him.

Richard III should be regarded not so much as an historical inquiry as a dramatic evocation.

III. *UTOPIA* AND *THE FOUR LAST THINGS*

Between 1513 and 1529 More's writings, apart from official letters, were in Latin, with the exception of another unfinished manuscript, *A Treatise on the Four Last Things*. He leapt into European fame by the publication of *Utopia* at the end of 1516. The third edition (Basle, 1518) also contained More's *Epigrams*. *Utopia* was in Latin, but as his name and the title of the book have become almost synonymous, it is impossible to ignore *Utopia* in a consideration of his position as an English author. Moreover the book drew the attention of the learned world to the fact that there were scholars even in England! Books written by Englishmen and circulating in Europe were rare, and one of the services More did for his country was to make it more widely known. *Utopia* was not translated into English until 1551, sixteen years after More's death, by Ralph Robinson. His work cannot be included among the outstanding Tudor translations, but it has held its own, and most people know the book in this version. The only rival is the more accurate rendering by Bishop Gilbert Burnet, first published in 1684 and frequently reprinted. The book was written in Latin because More was addressing himself to the learned world and in his day a knowledge of English was a rare accomplishment. It is to our loss that he did not produce a parallel version in English as he had done for *Richard III*.

The book has proved a stimulus to political thought but some queer ideas have been fathered on More that would have astonished and amused him. Some of those who have found what they were seeking in *Utopia*, have ignored its form and intention. Erasmus, who was staying with More when the First Book was being written, had no doubt of the author's purpose. He urged a friend to read the book 'if you ever want to see the sources from which almost all the ills of the body politic arise'. *Utopia* is not a Utopia! The word has come to mean an ideal state, but we must not read that meaning into More's intention. In describing an imagined state, he was criticizing contemporary society. The form is dramatic. The First Book is a dialogue, and the Second a monologue or discourse by the fictional Hythlodaye; it is therefore as hazardous to deduce More's own opinions from *Utopia* as it is to deduce those of Shakespeare from his plays. We must make allowance for the dramatic irony and for More's love of fun. Those who ignore these Lucianic elements soon get into difficulties and some over-solemn interpreters have been more amusing than convincing. An instance of the danger of taking seriously everything More wrote is worth giving. *Utopia* is prefaced by a dedicatory letter to Peter Gilles of Antwerp, who was the friend of More and Erasmus. He figures in the dialogue. In his letter More asked if his friend could recall what Hythlodaye said about the position of Utopia, as a learned divine wished to go there as a missionary. Gilles entered into the spirit of More's letter and replied that unfortunately he could not help as he had had a fit of coughing just when Hythlodaye was telling them the situation of the island. Ralph Robinson solemnly added a note that the divine was Rowland Philips, the Vicar of Croydon. Robinson shows no trace of a sense of humour and he failed to see the joke, and he was not the last to do so.

Utopia was an island where everything was owned in common under an elected magistracy. Great care was given to the education of the children and of their parents, no distinction being made between the sexes. Each man was taught a trade, but life was divided between town and country so that all shared in work on the land. The houses had gardens and the towns were well planned and sanitary. Hospitals were provided for the sick and aged. They had no use for money and despised personal adornment. The Utopians were deists who believed in immortality; their few priests were carefully chosen and could marry. All forms of religion were respected, but if anyone caused civil disturbance by the violence of his advocacy, he was banished or made a slave. Games and sports, but not hunting, were encouraged, and all were trained in military exercises, but they preferred to employ mercenaries in their wars, which were defensive only.

This bare outline of the polity of Utopia is sufficient to indicate the problems that arise as soon as the details are studied; these problems have been discussed by many commentators, but cannot be adequately considered here.

Those who are bored with descriptions of imaginary disciplined states will find that the First Book of *Utopia* has qualities of its own. The greater part is devoted to two topics: why do men become thieves, and, should a philosopher take service under a prince? The first reflects More's experience as an Under-Sheriff, or magistrate, in London during the previous five years when he had to deal summarily with the rogues and vagabonds of the City. The second was an immediate problem, as, following More's success in an embassy to the Low Countries, during which he had written the Second Book of *Utopia*, Wolsey suggested that he should become a King's Counsel, which would mean putting himself at the service of the Crown. The discussions in the First Book of *Utopia* probably reflected conversations with Erasmus, who was strongly opposed to More concerning himself with 'the busy trifles of princes', as this would prevent him from contributing to the advance of 'bonae litterae'. For the time being More refused the invitation, but, after another successful embassy in 1517, he agreed to become a King's Counsel. As Erasmus predicted, this meant that More had little leisure for scholarship. In 1520 he published a long letter in Latin to a monk who had attacked Erasmus, after which there was a silence of nine years, save for the unfinished *Four Last Things* written in 1522 but not printed until after his death.

This meditation, as it may be described, on Death, Judgement, Heaven and Hell was written for his children and other young people who formed his 'school'; they were now growing up and Margaret had just married William Roper. She also wrote on the same theme but her work is not extant. *The Four Last Things* is the most sombre of More's writings and, though there are passing references to Cicero and Plutarch, it shows little trace of classical influence. We think of More as a Christian humanist, but he cannot be confined to a pigeon-hole. This work is as mediaeval as the Dance of Death painted on the cloister walls of St. Paul's. As we read, we are reminded of the hellfire sermons of the friars. The nearest contemporary parallel was the series of sermons on *The Penitential Psalms* preached by his friend Bishop John Fisher and one of the popular devotional books of the day.

More did not complete his consideration of even the first subject, Death; he discussed the sins of pride, envy, covetousness, gluttony, and, in part, sloth, and then broke off. Had he carried out his intention on the same scale, he would have produced a substantial volume. The text was taken from Ecclesiastes, 'Remember the last things, and thou shalt never sin', but for the portion that was finished the appropriate text would have been, *Sic transit gloria mundi*. Grim as it is, the meditation abounds, as all More's work does, with images drawn from common life:

If thou shouldst perceive that one were earnestly proud of the wearing of the gay golden gown, while the lorel [rogue] playeth the lord in a stage play, wouldst thou not laugh at his folly, considering that thou art very sure that when the play is done he shall go walk a knave in his old coat? Now thou thinkest thyself wise enough while thou art proud in thy player's garment, and forgettest that when thy play is done, though shalt go forth as poor as he. Nor thou rememberest not that thy pageant may happen to be done as soon as his.

We shall leave the example of plays and players which be too merry for this matter. I shall put thee a more earnest image of our condition, and that not feigned similitude but a very true fashion and figure of our worshipful state. Mark this well, for of this thing we be very sure, that old and young, man and woman, rich and poor, prince and page, all the while we live in this world we be but prisoners, and be within a sure prison, out of which there can no man escape. And in worse case be we than those that be taken and imprisoned for theft. For they, albeit their heart heavily harkeneth after the sessions, yet have they some hope either to break prison the while, or to escape there by favour, or after condemnation some hope of pardon. But we stand all in other plight: we be very sure that we be already condemned to death, some one, some other, none of us can tell what death we be doomed to, but surely can we all tell that die we shall.

Even the humour can be grim:

Think ye not now that it will be a gentle pleasure, when we lie dying, all our body in pain, all our mind in trouble, our soul in sorrow, our heart all in dread while our life walketh awayward, while our death draweth toward, while the devil is busy about us, while we lack stomach and strength to bear any one of so manifold heinous troubles, will it not be, as I was about to say, a pleasant thing to see before thine eyes and hear at thine ear a rabble of fleshly friends or rather of flesh flies, skipping about thy bed and thy sick body, like ravens about thy corpse, now almost carrion, crying to thee on every side, 'What shall I have? What shall I have?' Then shall come thy children and cry for their parts; then shall come thy sweet wife, and where in thine health haply she spake thee not one sweet word in six weeks, now shall she call thee sweet husband and weep with much work and ask thee what she shall have; then shall thine executors ask for the keys, and ask what money is owing thee, ask what substance thou hast, and ask where thy money lieth. And while thou liest in that case, their words shall be so tedious that thou wilt wish all that they ask for upon a red fire, so thou mightest lie one half hour in rest.

The Four Last Things reminds us that the mainspring of Thomas More's life was a profound religious faith; it explains his thoughts of becoming a Carthusian monk, the chapel he built at Chelsea, his service at the altar, the hairshirt he wore, and his death.

IV. CONTROVERSIAL WRITINGS

More may have left this meditation unfinished because he was called upon to defend Henry VIII against Luther, who in 1520 had finally broken from Rome by, among other writings, his pamphlet entitled *The Babylonish Captivity of the Church*, in which he argued that contrary to Catholic teaching there were three, not seven, sacraments. Henry VIII decided to reply to Luther; his book *Assertio Septem Sacramentorum* was published in 1521; it was for this that the Pope conferred on the royal author the title of Defender of the Faith. It was not a recondite argument but a statement that a well-instructed layman, as the king was, could write. After the theologians had read the manuscript, the king asked Thomas More to edit the book and see it through the press. Luther replied in terms that were unusually scurrilous even for those days. It was beneath the dignity of the king to notice such an attack, so More answered it under the pseudonym of Gulielmus Rosseus; his reply was published in 1523. We need not here discuss the controversy, but it has its importance because it marked the opening of a new phase in More's writings. From that date until he went to the Tower in 1534, his writings were controversial, all, happily, written in English. He was not, however, closely involved until 1528 when his old friend Cuthbert Tunstal, Bishop of London, urged him to undertake the defence of the Church against Lutheranism. William Tyndale's translation of the New Testament was smuggled into England in 1526, to be followed two years later by his *Obedience of a Christian Man*. So Tunstal wrote to Thomas More:

Because, dear brother, you are able to rival Demosthenes in our vernacular tongue no less than in Latin, you cannot spend your leisure hours, if you can steal any from your official duties, better than in writing in our own language such books as may show simple and unlearned men the cunning malice of these heretics.

The first fruit of this labour was *A Dialogue of Sir Thomas More . . . Wherein be treated divers matters . . . with many things touching the pestilent sect of Luther and Tyndale*. This was printed by his brother-in-law, John Rastell, and published in June 1529, six months before Sir Thomas More became

Lord Chancellor. The original title was shortened in the *English Works* of 1557 to *A Dialogue concerning heresies and matters of religion.*

This *Dialogue* is the most readable of More's controversial works and the nearest to Tunstal's suggestion that it should be addressed to the 'simple and unlearned'. He was able to write it in the comparative leisure of the period before he was burdened by the duties of high office and was not yet oppressed by the problems created by the king's desire to break his marriage and to control the Church in England.

More imagines that a friend has sent him an inquirer, the tutor of his sons, who is perturbed by the teaching of Luther and wishes to discuss the doubts that have come into his mind. So the book takes the form of a dialogue between More and this Messenger, carried on partly in More's study and partly in his garden. A fortnight elapsed between Book Two and Book Three; during this interval the Messenger discussed his problems with an old university friend. There is no problem here, as in *Utopia*, of distinguishing More's views for he speaks in his own person. It is a true dialogue since the Messenger is allowed to put his points fully; he is not invented simply to put up a series of Aunt Sallies to be knocked down, though, inevitably, in the end he is persuaded that Luther and Tyndale were heretics. Indeed, anyone who wishes to understand the opening phases of the Catholic-Protestant dispute cannot do better than read this contemporary record written before the atmosphere became too warm for calm discussion. The tone is genial and the argument is persuasive. The following passage illustrates the freedom allowed to the Messenger, and will serve also as an example of More's style:

Surely the thing that maketh in this matter the clergy most suspect, and wherein, as it seemeth, it would be full hard to excuse them is this, that they not only damn Tyndale's translation (wherein there is good cause) but over that do damn all other, and as though a layman were no Christian man, will suffer no layman to have any at all. But when they find any in his keeping, they lay heresy to him therefore. And thereupon they burn up the book, and sometime the good man withal, alleging for the defence of their doing a law of their own making and constitution provincial, whereby they have prohibited that any man shall have any upon pain of heresy. And this is a law very provincial, for it holdeth but here. For in all other countries of Christendom the people have the scripture translated into their own tongue, and the clergy there findeth no such fault therein. Wherefore either our people be worst of all people, or else our clergy is worst of all clergies. But, by my troth, for ought I can see here, or perceive by them that have been elsewhere, our lay people be as good and as honest as be anywhere. And if any be otherwise, the occasion and example cometh of the clergy, among whom we see much more vice than among ourself. Whereas they should give us an example of virtue and the light of learning, now their examples, what they be, we see. And as for learning, they neither will teach us but seldom and that shall be but such things as pleaseth them, some glosses of their own making, nor suffer us to learn by ourself, but by their constitution pull Christ's gospel out of Christian people's hands, I cannot well see why, but lest we should see the truth.

More's style is uneven; he can get involved in long sentences that need close reading. At the end of this *Dialogue*, for instance, there is a sentence of seven hundred and fifty words that leaves the reader breathless. This may be paralleled with a six hundred word sentence in Latin to be found in *Utopia*. Both are exceptionally long but they show the irregular quality of More's prose. One who wrote Latin with ease, as More did, was inevitably influenced by its syntax when turning to the vernacular. It was when he was writing narrative that More was able to use his native language most effectively. An example of this occurs early in this *Dialogue*. The Messenger alleged that some miracles were fraudulent. More agreed, and in illustration told the story of a blind beggar who went to St. Alban's Abbey during a visit of Henry VI. The man declared that St. Alban had restored his sight:

So happened it, then, that Duke Humfrey of Gloucester, a great wise man and very well learned, having great joy to see such a miracle called that poor man unto him. And first shewing himself joyous of God's glory, so shewed in the getting of his sight, and exhorting him to meekness, and to none ascribing of any part the worship to himself nor to be proud of the people's praise which would call him a good and godly man thereby. At last he looked well upon his eyen, and asked him whether he could never see nothing at all in all his life before. And when as well his wife as himself affirmed fastly no, then he looked advisedly upon his eyen again, and said, I believe you very well, for me thinketh that ye cannot see well yet.

Yes, Sir, quod he, I thank God and his holy martyr, I can see now as well as any man.

Ye can, quod the Duke. What colour is my gown? Then anon the beggar told him.

What colour, quod he, is this man's gown? He told him also, and so forth without sticking, he told him the names of all the colours that could be shewed him. And when my lord saw that, he bade him walk faytoure [imposter], and made him be set openly in the stocks. For though he could have seen suddenly by miracle the difference between divers colours, yet could he not by sight so suddenly tell the names of all these colours but if he had known them before, no more than the names of all the men that he should suddenly see.

Soon after he had finished this *Dialogue*, More must have begun his second controversial work; this was a reply to *A Supplication of the Beggars*, a savage attack on the clergy by a lawyer, Simon Fish, in the form of a petition to the king from the beggars of England; this short pamphlet was in circulation by the end of 1528. More's book, entitled *The Supplication of Souls*, was published in September 1529. In this he adopted the form of Erasmus' *Praise of Folly*, which is a discourse by Folly herself. More's book is a declamation on behalf of the souls in purgatory in which they plead that they should not be deprived of the prayers of the living. The charges made by Fish against the clergy are examined, but the emphasis is put on the teaching of the Church, especially on the doctrine of purgatory. Within this framework, More was able to give play to his dramatic sense, and his humour lightens what could have been a pedestrian theological exposition. So the Souls see their widows, 'waxen wanton and forgetting us their old husbands':

Yet we hear sometimes our wives pray for us warmly; for in chiding with her second husband, to spite him withal, 'God have mercy', saith she, 'on my first husband's soul, for he was a wise and honest man, far unlike you'. And then marvel we much when we hear them say so well of us, for they were ever wont to tell us far otherwise.

More did not limit himself to Fish's complaints but used the opportunity for some ironical comments of his own. He represented the Souls as regretting the lavish funerals they had ordered:

For some hath there of us, while we were in health, not so much studied how we might die penitent and in good Christian plight, as how we might be solemnly borne out to burying, have gay and goodly funerals, with heralds at our hearses, and offering of our helmets, setting up our escutcheon and coat armours on the walls, though there never came harness on our backs, nor never ancestor of ours ever bare arms before.

In *Utopia*, by contrast, where the dead were cremated,

when any die cheerfully and full of hope, they do not mourn for them, but sing hymns when they carry out their bodies, commending their souls very earnestly to God.

The controversialist seems doomed to follow a path that gets dustier and dustier. At first he steps out with a light step, but he soon discovers that whatever he says, his opponent can always find something further to say. This was the course to which More found himself committed. He had a formidable opponent in William Tyndale, who, at his best, could put his arguments into clear English. His *Answer unto Sir Thomas More's Dialogue* was published in the spring of 1531. To this More replied with a *Confutation of Tyndale's Answer;* Books I-III were published in 1532, and Books

IV-VIII in 1533. A ninth book, unfinished, was published after his death. The first volume was issued about the time More resigned the Chancellorship (16 May 1532). He was now freed from public duties, and 1533 saw the publication, in addition to the second volume of the *Confutation*, of *The Apology*, *The Debellation of Salem and Bizance*, and the *Letter impugning John Frith;* in 1534 came his last controversial work, *Answer to the First Part of the Poisoned Book*. These works fill eight hundred pages of the folio edition of 1557, in all, about eight hundred thousand words. Allowance must be made for his practice of quoting his opponent's statements, always with scrupulous accuracy, but, even so, this vast output is astonishing. It is not surprising that at the end of a letter to Thomas Cromwell in March 1534, he wrote: 'I pray you pardon me, that I write not unto you with my own hand, for verily, I am compelled to forbear writing for a while by reason of this disease of mine, whereof the chief occasion is grown, as it is thought, by the stooping and leaning on my breast, that I used in writing.'

It would be out of place here to review this group of writings, but some characteristics may be noted. More's prolixity weakened the effect of his arguments; he let his pen run on as the thoughts poured from his mind; at times the impression is given that he had not planned his books, nor could he have had time for revision and pruning. By contrast the argument of his *Dialogue against Heresies* had clearly been thought out, with the result that the book has a unity that is lacking in others. The dialogue form imposed some restraint on the writer. More was criticized for his longwindedness in his lifetime. In his *Apology* he defended himself:

Howbeit, glad would I have been if it might have been much more short for then should my labour have been so much the less. But they will, if they be reasonable men, consider in themselves that it is a shorter thing and sooner done to write heresies than to answer them. For the most foolish heretic in a town, may write more false heresies in one leaf, than

the wisest man in the world can well and conveniently by reason and
authority soyle [answer] and confute in forty.

By contrast Tyndale showed skill in marshalling his ideas
at reasonable length. His books were therefore easier to read
and did not demand the same staying power that More
expected from his readers. The 'simple and unlearned men'
of whom Tunstal wrote, must have been deterred from
tackling a book of the length of the *Confutation*. More's
shorter books made a wider appeal, though even *The
Supplication of Souls* was ten times the length of Simon Fish's
A Supplication of the Beggars. The reader with some experience
of More's work would be encouraged to persevere in the
certainty that the author's love of an anecdote or of a
homely illustration, and his quick sense of humour, would
be some compensation for the heavier pages, and it is in
these passages that More's English becomes lively and
nearer the spoken language. At times he even attempted
dialect. Here from the *Dialogue*, for instance, is a Kentish
labourer speaking:

Nay, by our Lady, masters, yche [I] cannot tell you well, why, but chote
[I wote] well it hath. For, by God, I knew it a good haven till that steeple
was builded, and by the Mary mass, cha [I have] marked it well, it never
throve since.

These stories were often short and pithily told, as for
example the following taken from *The Supplication* about
'a lewd gallant and a friar':

Whom when the gallant saw going barefoot in a great frost and snow, he
asked him why he did take so much pain. And he answered that it was
very little pain if a man would remember hell. 'Yea, friar', quoth the
gallant, 'but what an there be none hell, then art thou a great fool'.
'Yea, master', quoth the friar, 'but what an there be hell, then is your
mastership a much more fool.'

This use of the anecdote was not unusual at that period.
Moral tales had long been a recognized part of the preacher's

equipment, and collections, such as the *Gesta Romanorum*, were in common use. More's stories were always apposite, but they were not too pointedly edifying in the preacher's sense. Here is another example, taken this time from the *Debellation*:

And as for the railing fashion—if I durst tell so sad a man a merry tale, I would tell him of the friar that, as he was preaching in the country, spied a poor wife of the parish whispering with her pewfellow; and he, falling angry thereto, cried out unto her aloud, 'Hold thy babble, I bid thee, thou wife in the red hood'. Which when the housewife heard, she waxed as angry again, and suddenly she start up and cried out unto the friar again, that all the church rang thereon, 'Marry, sir, I beshrew his heart that babbleth most of us both. For I do but whisper a word with my neighbour, and thou hast babbled there all this hour.'

V. DEVOTIONAL WRITINGS

There are signs of weariness as the *Confutation* 'drags its slow length along'. At the end of his Preface, More advised his readers to ignore both the books of the heretics and his own, and to read 'such English books as most nourish and increase devotion'. He suggested the *Imitation of Christ* and Walter Hilton's *Scale of Perfection*. His controversial writing ended when, on 17 April 1534, he was committed to the Tower where he was to remain for fifteen months without trial. For the greater part of that time he was allowed his books, pen, ink and paper; he used them not for belabouring heretics but for works that are primarily devotional. 'Calm of mind, all passion spent', he produced his finest and most typical work, *A Dialogue of Comfort Against Tribulation*, with the whimsical explanation that it was 'made by an Hungarian in Latin, and translated out of Latin into French, and out of French into English'. The speakers were the aged Anthony and his nephew Vincent; the background of their conversation was the danger threatening Christendom by the advance of the Turks into Hungary. This figured the spread of heresy in Europe, but the parallel is not unduly pressed. The main part of the work is a disquisition on one of the Compline Psalms, 'He that dwelleth in the secret place of the most High shall abide under the shadow of the Almighty'.

The book has all the attractive qualities of More's works: he calls up pictures of the past with glimpses of his family and of his experiences in state affairs; there are anecdotes from many sources; references to the Fathers and to classical authors show his wide reading, and, above all, his frequent scriptural quotations are evidence of his close knowledge of the Bible. Though he gives no names, it is not difficult to identify some of the characters. For instance, it is Wolsey who is described in this sentence: 'But glorious [vain-glorious] was he very far above all measure, and that was great pity, for it did harm, and made him abuse many great gifts that God had given him.' Then follows an ironical account of a competition among guests at the Cardinal's table to see who could give him the most lavish praise.

Some of More's shortcomings as a writer are not so noticeable in this serene book; there are few involved sentences, and his love of alliteration is kept under control, though it has its fling occasionally. 'Yet are there some fools so fed with this fond fantasy of fame', and, 'peevish pastimes of purpose to put . . .' We may note too his liking for a triad of terms:

Captivity, bondage or thraldom, what is it but the violent restraint of a man, being so subdued under the dominion, rule and power of another.

The whole book is the expression of a mind and spirit that had come to terms with life. He even hinted at the possibility of reaching an understanding with the Lutherans and their doctrine of justification by faith:

As we, I say, grant unto them these things, so this one thing or twain do they grant us again, that men are bound to work good works if they have time and power, and that whoso worketh in true faith most, shall be most rewarded.

So he declared: 'Therefore will I let God work and leave off contention; and nothing shall I now say, but that with which they that are themself of the contrary mind shall in reason have no cause to be discontented.'

This book was not the only fruit of More's solitude in the Tower, a solitude that brought him back, as it were, to his earlier longing for the life of the cloister. He wrote a *Treatise to receive the Blessed Body of our Lord*. This, short as it is, contains a recollection of the king's visit to him at Chelsea:

For if we will but consider, if there were a great worldly prince which for special favour that he bare us would come visit us in our own house, what a business we would then make, and what a work it would be for us, to see that our house were trimmed up to every point, to the best of our possible power, and everything so provided and ordered, that he should by his honourable receiving perceive what affection we bear him, and in what high estimation we have him.

Another work, a *Treatise upon the Passion of Christ*, was unfinished; shortly before his trial (1 July 1535), his books and writing materials were removed from his cell. He began to write this treatise in English and then continued it in Latin, an interesting return to his love of that language. At his first interrogation in the Tower by members of the Council, he declared that he had 'fully determined with myself neither to study nor to meddle with any matter of this world, but that my whole study should be upon the passion of Christ and mine own passage out of the world'. That this was indeed his intention is shown by this treatise which is of some length. The first group of meditations was on the Fall and the Redemption; he then commented on the Gospel story of the Passion, going into great detail and supporting his exposition by quotations from the Greek and Latin Fathers. A passage on martyrdom has a poignant interest in view of his own perilous situation:

For many of truth have there been that at the first brunt have fearfully shrunk and fainted, and yet afterward valiantly passed through all the pain that was put upon them. Now albeit, I cannot deny but that the example of them that suffer death with a bold and hardy courage is a right expedient for a great many to hearten them to do the like; yet, on the other side, forasmuch as all the sort of us in effect be timorous at the coming of death, who can tell how many take good by these folk too, which though they come to it, as we see, with much anguish and dread, do yet in conclusion manfully pass through those horrible strong stops of weariness, fear, and heaviness, and so, stoutly breaking through all those violent lets [hindrances], do gloriously conquer death, and mightily get up into heaven.

A Dialogue of Comfort was first published in 1553. The other Tower writings in English were first printed in the collected *English Works* of 1557, the Latin ones in 1563.

VI. LETTERS

No account of Thomas More's writings would be complete without some notice of his letters. Most of these were in Latin but there is an important group in English belonging to the last two years of his life. These concern the troubles that were gathering around him. First there was the attempt to implicate him in the prosecution of the Nun of Kent; then followed the king's anger at More's refusal to approve of the annulment of the king's marriage. On both these subjects he wrote to the king and to Thomas Cromwell; the two long letters to the latter are of primary biographical importance, but they do not make easy reading. The involved sentences call for close attention if the full meaning is to be extracted. More, in fact, was not a ready letter-writer and in those that are extant he shows little of the facility and humour of Erasmus. The letters he wrote from the Tower, especially those to his daughter Margaret, are charged with an emotion that gives them a place apart. So we come to 'the last thing that he ever wrote'. It was the eve of his execution. 'Our Lord bless you good daughter and your good husband and your little boy and all yours and all my children and all my godchildren and all my friends.'

VII. MORE AND ENGLISH PROSE

It is impossible to assess the influence of Thomas More's English works on the development of our prose. Only one book, the *Dialogue against Heresies*, went into a second edition during his lifetime. The size of each edition is not known, but the total number could probably be reckoned in hundreds, not thousands. His execution in 1535 followed by sermons up and down the country denouncing him and John Fisher for sedition, effectively stopped further publication. It was not until Mary Tudor's reign that his nephew William Rastell was able to publish in one volume in 1557 *The Works of Sir Thomas More, Knight, Written by Him in the English Tongue*. As this did not appear until the end of the Queen's reign, it had small chance of becoming known. Queen Elizabeth, daughter of Anne Boleyn, was not likely to favour the dissemination of the writings of Thomas More. It was almost by chance that one of his works, *Richard III*, continued to be printed. As we have seen, it was included anonymously, in the Hardynge-Grafton Chronicle and so passed into chronicle literature. Appearing as it did amid a hotch-potch of indifferent material, it could not fail to impress the reader with its vivid writing and dramatic appeal. Dr. Tillyard expressed the opinion that

the effect of More's history was very great and largely incalculable. Through being incorporated in later chronicles it escaped the anti-Catholic feeling that might have prejudiced its popularity if it had been lumped with the rest of his work. I should guess that it not only set the pattern of Shakespeare's *Richard III* but was a direct incitement to him to write dramatically rather than anecdotally. Anyhow there it was, one of the two pieces of original English historical writing apt actively to incite an Elizabethan dramatist to get close to his matter and to treat it primarily as human happenings and only secondarily as a repertory of morals or a mere series of events. (*Shakespeare's History Plays*, p. 39.)

The second piece referred to is the *Life of Cardinal Wolsey* by George Cavendish, who married a niece of Sir Thomas More.

High claims have been put forward for More's prose and its place in the development of the written language. As we have seen, it varied in quality; that is not surprising, for English prose had yet to take shape, and it was to go through several phases before a standard was achieved. More undoubtedly made his contribution, and an important one, to this movement, but it is hard to define the nature of that contribution. It may have been his genius for telling a story in a direct and dramatic manner that had most influence on his readers; the incidents were vividly narrated, and the characters, even if sketched with but a few bold lines, were alive. Nor is it fanciful to suggest that had he been an Elizabethan, he would have been a dramatist.

There is another form of influence that should be noted since it was the fruit of that religious conviction for which he died. The meditations and prayers he composed in the Tower were widely known and used for long after his death. They were printed again and again in Catholic manuals of devotion and repeated by many who were unaware of their origin. Their language places them beside some of the great collects in the Anglican Book of Common Prayer:

Good Lord, give me the grace so to spend my life, that when the day of my death shall come, though I feel pain in my body, I may feel comfort in my soul; and with faithful hope of thy mercy, in due love towards thee and charity towards the world, I may, through thy grace, part hence into thy glory.

SIR THOMAS MORE

A Select Bibliography

(Place of publication London, unless stated otherwise)

Bibliography:

MOREANA, by F. & M. P. Sullivan. Part A-F, Los Angeles (1964) in progress.

A PRELIMINARY BIBLIOGRAPHY, by R. W. Gibson (1961).

Collected Editions:

THE WORKES OF SIR THOMAS MORE WRYTTEN BY HIM IN THE ENGLYSH TONGE (1557)

—edited by More's nephew, W. Rastell.

LUCUBRATIONES. Basel (1563)

—the first collection of More's Latin writings.

THE ENGLISH WORKS, ed. W. E. Campbell, R. W. Chambers, and A. W. Reed.

    I.   Early Poems; Life of Pico; Richard III; Four Last Things (1931).
    II. The Dialogue Concerning Tyndale (1931)

—a facsimile reproduction from the 1557 folio is given in each volume, followed by a modern transcript; no further volumes issued.

YALE EDITION OF THE COMPLETE WORKS, ed. R. Sylvester and others.

    I. English and Latin Poems. 2. Richard III (1964). 3. Life of Pico; Four Last Things. 4. Utopia (1964). 5. Responsio ad Lutherum. 6. Dialogue Concerning Heresies; Supplication of Souls; Letter vs. Frith. 7. & 8. Confutation. 9. Apology; Debellation. 10. Answer to a Poisoned Book: Dialogue of Comfort. 11. Treatise on the Passion: On the Blessed Body; Devout Instructions. 12. & 13. Correspondence

—in progress. A shorter series, based on the above, will be issued in modern spelling. Proposed volumes: *Selected Letters* (1961); *Utopia* (1964); *Richard III*, etc.; *Polemical Works*; *Dialogue of Comfort*; *Devotional Works.*

Selections:

SIR THOMAS MORE: SELECTIONS FROM HIS ENGLISH WORKS, ed. P. S. and H. M. Allen. Oxford (1924).

Letters:

THE CORRESPONDENCE OF SIR THOMAS MORE, ed. E. F. Rogers. Princeton
and Oxford (1947)
—this does not include More's letters (in Latin) to Erasmus, which are
to be found in *Opus Epistolarum Des. Erasmi Roterodami*, ed. P. S.
and H. M. Allen, 11 vols., Oxford (1906-1947).

Separate Works:

LIBELLOS VERE AUREUS DE OPTIMO REIP. STATU, DEQUE NOVA INSULA
UTOPIAE. . . [Louvain, 1516]
—the first edition of *Utopia:* the original Latin text. Latin and English texts, Yale Edition, 1964.
A FRUTEFUL AND PLEASAUNT WORK OF THE NEWE YLE CALLED UTOPIA
(1551)
—the first English version; translated by R. Robinson. The standard
edition to date of *Utopia* (Robinson's translation, with the Latin
text) is that of J. H. Lupton, Oxford, 1895.
A DIALOGUE OF COMFORT AGAINST TRIBULATION (1553)
—included in the Everyman edition of *Utopia*, 1910. Also edited
separately by P. E. Hallett, 1937.
UTOPIA, translated by G. Burnet (1684)
—edited (with English poems) by S. Lee. 1906.
HISTORY OF KING RICHARD III
—early versions of More's *History of King Richard III* are to be found
in the Chronicles of Hardyng and Hall. It was edited by J. R.
Lumby, Cambridge, 1883. See Yale edition, 1964.
THE APOLOGYE (1533)
—ed. A. I. Taft, Early English Text Society, 1929.
THE FOUR LAST THINGS, ed. D. O'Connor (1935).
ENGLISH PRAYERS, ed. P. E. Hallett (1938).
HISTORY OF THE PASSION, ed. P. E. Hallett (1941).
LATIN EPIGRAMS, ed. L. Bradner and C. A. Lynch. Chicago (1943).

Some Biographical and Critical Studies:

LIFE AND DEATH OF SIR THOMAS MORE, by Cresacre More [1626]
—ed. J. Hunter, 1828.
THE OXFORD REFORMERS OF 1498, by F. Seebohm (1867)
—Colet, More, Erasmus.
LIFE AND WRITINGS OF BLESSED THOMAS MORE, by T. E. Bridgett (1891).
SIR THOMAS MORE, by H. Brémond, trs. H. Child (1904).

EARLY TUDOR DRAMA, by A. W. Reed (1926).

THE SAGA AND MYTH OF SIR THOMAS MORE, by R. W. Chambers (1927)
—British Academy lecture.

SIR THOMAS MORE, by T. Stapleton, translated by P. E. Hallett (1928).

LIFE AND DEATH OF SIR THOMAS MORE, by N. Harpsfield, ed. E. V.
Hitchcock. E.E.T.S. (1932).

THOMAS MORE AND HIS FRIENDS, by E. M. G. Routh. Oxford (1934).

SIR THOMAS MORE, by C. Hollis (1934).

LIFE OF SIR THOMAS MORE, by W. Roper, ed. E. V. Hitchcock.
E.E.T.S. (1935).

THOMAS MORE, by R. W. Chambers (1935).

A PORTRAIT OF SIR THOMAS MORE, by A. Cecil (1937).

ACTA THOMAE MORI, ed. H. de Vocht. Louvain (1947).

INTRODUCTION TO UTOPIA, by H. W. Donner (1947).

ERASMUS, TYNDALE AND MORE, by W. E. Campbell (1949).

THE TRAGEDY OF THE LOLLARD'S TOWER, by A. Ogle. Oxford (1949).

UNDER GOD AND THE LAW, ed. R. O'Sullivan. Oxford (1949)
—studies of More by various hands.

LIFE OF SIR THOMAS MORE, by Ro. Ba., ed. E. V. Hitchcock. E.E.T.S.
(1950).

MORE'S UTOPIA, by J. H. Hexter. Princeton (1952).

SAINT THOMAS MORE, by E. E. Reynolds (1953).

HUMANISM AND POETRY IN THE EARLY TUDOR PERIOD, by H. A. Mason
(1959).

MARGARET ROPER, by E. E. Reynolds (1960).

LIVES OF SAINT THOMAS MORE, by W. Roper and N. Harpsfield (1963)
—Everyman's Library.

THE LIKENESS OF THOMAS MORE, by S. Morison (1963).

THE TRIAL OF ST. THOMAS MORE, by E. E. Reynolds (1964).

Note: The Amici Thomae Mori (29 rue Volney, Angers, France),
publish a Journal, *Moreana*, devoted to More Studies.

Bibliographical Series
of Supplements to 'British Book News'
on Writers and Their Work

GENERAL EDITOR
Geoffrey Bullough

WILLIAM · WYCHERLEY

from a portrait after LELY *in the*
National Portrait Gallery

WILLIAM WYCHERLEY

by

P. F. VERNON

PUBLISHED FOR
THE BRITISH COUNCIL
AND THE NATIONAL BOOK LEAGUE
BY LONGMANS, GREEN & CO.

LONGMANS, GREEN & CO. LTD.
48 Grosvenor Street, London W.1

*Associated companies, branches and
representatives throughout the world*

First published 1965
© P. F. Vernon 1965

*Printed in Great Britain by
F. Mildner & Sons, London, E.C.1*

CONTENTS

¶William Wycherley was born in Hampshire, probably on 28 May 1641, and died in London on 31 December 1716, he was buried in St. Paul's Church, Covent Garden.

WILLIAM WYCHERLEY

I. LIFE

'WILLIAM WYCHERLEY A Shropshire Gentleman, who has excell'd all Writers in all Languages, in Comedy'—a partial view undoubtedly, yet by no means extraordinary in the dramatist's lifetime, when he was generally considered to be the greatest English comic writer since Ben Jonson. He lived in turbulent times, however, when social and moral attitudes were shifting rapidly; and after his death these changes began to undermine his reputation. In the second half of the eighteenth century the theatres would accept only tame adaptations of his comedies which had cut out their satiric bite. His work then disappeared completely from the stage. By the middle of the nineteenth century Restoration comedy was commonly regarded as a scandalous and barely mentionable chapter in the history of English literature. Wycherley was singled out as the most obnoxious offender. Macaulay compared his work to a skunk, protected from the critics because too filthy to handle. In the early part of the present century critics began to take a new and sympathetic interest in Restoration drama, but Wycherley's status remained somewhat ambiguous. The typical comedy of manners was now felt to be cynical, detached and amoral, a view which probably helped to widen the popularity of Restoration comedy after the first world war. But Wycherley, with his obvious fondness for moralizing, seemed something of a misfit; he had now become too moral. His comedies did not catch on as readily as those of William Congreve, the other major comic dramatist of the period. They are still rarely performed and relatively little known. This is a pity, for of all the Restoration and eighteenth-century dramatists Wycherley comes closest in temper to the theatre of the present day, while regular performance of his work would do much to dispel the widespread rumour that Restoration comedy is trivial and irresponsible.

Although greatly admired by his contemporaries, Wycherley did not lead a particularly happy life. His father, Daniel, was born in the town of Clive, near Shrewsbury in Shropshire, where members of the family had lived comfortably for over two centuries. He became High Steward in the Marquess of Winchester's household at Basing House in Hampshire and there married Bethia Shrimpton, lady-of-honour to the Marchioness. William, the first of six children, was probably born on 28 May 1641; the date is not absolutely certain. Less than two years later civil war broke out. In 1645 Basing House was destroyed by parliamentary forces under Cromwell, the Marquess was imprisoned, his estates confiscated. Daniel acted as his deputy until the Restoration of the monarchy in 1660 and during this time managed to set aside for himself a large sum of money with which he later bought substantial property in his native county. He eventually became a barrister, spending much of his time and the greater part of his fortune on lengthy law suits; a fact which helps to explain his son's lifelong contempt for the legal profession. When about fifteen years old William was sent to study in France. While living in the Charente district he seems to have been deeply impressed by the conversation of the Marchioness de Montausier, daughter and disciple of the celebrated Madame de Rambouillet, whose salons had fostered the cult of refined manners and 'Platonic' love known as *préciosité*. Thus at an early age he came into direct contact with a literary movement which deeply influenced English drama both before and after the Restoration. He became a Roman Catholic; but on his return to England in 1660 he was sent to Oxford for a short while and there reconverted to Protestantism. Towards the end of the same year he took up legal studies at the Inner Temple in London.

Nothing much is known of his activities during his twenties. He may well have spent some time in Madrid in the household of the poet-ambassador, Sir Richard Fanshawe, and he probably took part in the naval battle of 1665 against the Dutch. In 1669 his first work was published anonymously, an irreverent verse burlesque of the Hero and Leander story. Feeble as they seem now, burlesques of this kind were popular when the Greek and Roman classics had almost the status of sacred texts in the educational syllabus. Two years later his first comedy, *Love in a Wood, or, St James's Park*, was performed by the actors known as the King's Men at the Theatre Royal in Bridges Street. The London theatres at this time catered for an intimate and privileged social circle; so the success of Wycherley's first play did more than spread his name. It also secured his position among the select group of leading writers and wits who moved within the court circle; gained him the friendship of such important figures as the Earl of Rochester and the Duke of Buckingham; and eventually led to the favour and patronage of King Charles II himself. His next work, *The Gentleman Dancing-Master*, was put on in 1672 by the rival company of actors at the new and splendid Dorset Garden Theatre, as the Theatre Royal had been burnt down earlier in the year. It was a comparative failure. But early in 1675 at the new Theatre Royal in Drury Lane Wycherley scored a triumph with *The Country-Wife*, one of the most influential plays of the century. At the end of the following year *The Plain-Dealer* was produced at the same theatre. The play apparently puzzled the first-night audience and its fate seemed uncertain until the balance was tilted in its favour by the enthusiastic applause of Buckingham and his friends. It soon became the most admired of Wycherley's works and earned him the nickname of 'plain dealer' or 'Manly' from the name of the principal character. But those who knew him always insisted that the dramatist resembled the rude and surly Manly only in his truthfulness and courage, his own manner being courteous and charming.

Wycherley was to live some forty years longer, but he wrote nothing further for the theatre. Already he was suffering from the ill-health which was to trouble him for the rest of his life, and soon other problems were to occupy his mind. He had by now whole-heartedly adopted the habits and outlook of the wealthy gentlemen whose lives centred on the theatres, the coffee-houses and the other places of wit and entertainment to be found in the capital. He despised the mercenary values of the business world and the unsophisticated life of the country, even though these had provided the means for his education. Yet the life led by a London gentleman demanded money, and Wycherley had no secure source of income. In an age when it was considered undignified to write for profit he never escaped from the endless struggle to make ends meet. The King helped him to spend the winter of 1678-9 in the healthier climate of France, and on his return proposed that he should become tutor to the young Duke of Richmond. This plan, which would have brought a permanent pension, came to nothing when it was discovered that in the autumn of 1679 Wycherley had secretly married the recently widowed Countess of Drogheda. It was an unfortunate marriage from every point of view. His wife not only made him miserable by her violent jealousy while she lived; she even failed to leave him, when she died, the fortune for which he had married her. At her death a mere two years after the marriage the legal disputes over her first husband's will, which were to last for more than fifteen years, had only just entered the preliminary stages. Meanwhile Wycherley's debts overwhelmed him, and in 1682 he found himself in a debtors' prison, where he remained until early in 1686 when the new King, James II, helped to clear his debts and promised him a pension after influential friends had arranged a performance of The Plain-Dealer at court. When James fled the country less than three years later the dramatist was again left penniless.

After this he lived modestly, partly in London, partly in Shropshire, with occasional visits to Bath to improve his health. He did not lose contact with the literary world, however. When in London he was the accepted leader of the men of letters who gathered at Will's Coffee House. He had many friends and admirers among the younger writers, including the dramatist William Congreve and the critic John Dennis. He had been writing poems off and on throughout his life, and some time before 1696 he decided to bring out a collection consisting mainly of new verse. The volume was ready by 1699, but, owing to difficulties with the publisher, did not appear until 1704. It was poorly received. Wycherley's memory was now failing, and many of the poems suffer from repetitiveness and appalling metrical lapses. At about this time Wycherley met Alexander Pope, then only sixteen years old, and, impressed by the elegance of the young poet's early pieces, asked him to polish up some of his own poems. Pope at first welcomed the task as an honour, but, finding it more and more troublesome, eventually told the dramatist to continue his revision himself. For a while the warm friendship between the two cooled, though Pope kept in touch with the dramatist until the latter's death.

At the age of seventy-four Wycherley married again. The whole affair reads like the plot of one of his own comedies. In 1715 a cousin, Captain Thomas Shrimpton, suggested that Wycherley might marry a young woman who could offer a cash dowry large enough to pay off his debts. She would benefit in turn from the jointure provided by old Daniel's will, should his eldest son remarry. The woman proposed by Shrimpton was, in fact, his own mistress. According to the servants, this unscrupulous fortune-hunter used every possible kind of pressure to force the old dramatist's consent, from getting him drunk to threatening him with the debtors' prison. Seriously ill, Wycherley protested that he needed a panel of doctors rather than a wife. Some time before this he had been reconverted to Catholicism and, his condition worsening, he received the last sacrament. Shrimpton intensified his efforts. Worn out and indifferent, if fully conscious of what was happening, the old man eventually put his signature to the marriage contract. 'Matrimony is plac'd after Extreme Unction in our Catechism, as a kind of Hint of the Order of Time in which they are to be taken'—Wycherley would have appreciated Pope's dry comment. Eleven days after the marriage on 31 December 1715, he died. He was buried in St. Paul's Church, Covent Garden. Shortly afterwards Shrimpton married the now wealthy widow.

II.   SATIRE AND SOCIAL CRITICISM

A first glance at Wycherley's comedies reveals one striking characteristic: his fondness for maxims. The dialogue, particularly in his later comedies, is often made up entirely of an exchange of these terse moral generalizations. This suggests something of his whole approach to comedy. In the first place he set out quite openly to teach his audience. On the titlepage of *The Gentleman Dancing-Master* he placed a motto from Horace which begins, 'It is not enough to make the listener laugh aloud'. He took it for granted that the highest function of comedy was to instruct. Secondly, he shared the common concern of his age for the simple, general truths of experience. Like Descartes, Hobbes and the other influential philosophers of his time, like the scientists and artists who founded the Royal Society after the Restoration, he felt confident that the universe contained an underlying order, a strictly determined pattern of cause and effect. His comedies try to reveal something of this order, to make clear some of the basic principles of human behaviour. In their very structure they give the impression of careful design rather than of spontaneous, accidental growth. Most European comedy displays a 'classical' regularity of this kind, but readers brought up on some of the less disciplined Elizabethan plays often feel that formal symmetry is bound to curb the imagination and lead to superficiality. In fact the art of establishing connections offers plenty of scope for subtlety and imaginative depth.

As a satirist, for instance, Wycherley could not be content simply to judge the things he disliked according to some accepted moral standard. Anti-social behaviour, he assumed, must arise from some confusion in thinking, from some simple inconsistency which people would avoid if only they could be made to think logically. Like Ben Jonson, a dramatist with whom he had a great deal in common, he had a clear, incisive mind which enabled him to seek out the false premises underlying various social habits and to pursue them relentlessly in his comedies to an extreme conclusion where everyone could see how absurd they were.

Wycherley differs from other Restoration dramatists both in his seriousness and in his artistic consistency. Sharp, pointed, bold, masculine, strong—these were the words his contemporaries chose when describing his work. They suggest both sound judgement and acute penetration. His dramatic method is exceptionally purposeful. He begins with a clear end in view and rarely loses sight of it. Consider these opening sentences: 'Not a Husband to be had for money' (*Love in a Wood*); 'To confine a Woman just in her rambling Age! take away her liberty at the very time she shou'd use it!' (*The Gentleman Dancing-Master*). These plunge the audience straight into the problems the plays are about to consider. Everything then turns upon the central themes. The characters are not rounded individuals: once introduced, they do not reveal new and suprising facets of personality. They are rather illustrations in an argument, pruned of all irrelevant features. The audience knows exactly how they will behave; yet they do not seem to be mere puppets manipulated by their creator. This is because their actions follow logically from the attitudes they hold. In this sense the plots are plausible and 'natural', even though they would often be impossible in real life. The dialogue, though it suggests colloquial speech, is quite unlike ordinary conversation. Crammed with imagery, witty aphorisms, similes and double meanings, it is designed as an indirect commentary for the benefit of the audience, rather than as an imitation of the way people really talk.

Despite their neatness and order, Wycherley's comedies retain something of the crowded vigour of earlier English comedy. He will combine in a single play incidents which his older French contemporary, Molière, found sufficient for two or even three separate comedies. But he always succeeded in fusing the separate strands of an action, so that they seemed only related aspects of a single problem. His young friend, John Dennis, one of the most perceptive commentators on his work, noted that he was 'almost the only Man alive who has made Comedy instructive in its Fable; almost all the rest, being contented to instruct by their Characters'. Indeed, although he borrowed the rough outlines of nearly all his plots from other writers, one of his chief excellences lay in his ability to construct a plot in which even the smallest detail had some significance.

Recent studies have abstracted from his work a body of ideas similar to much of the naturalistic and sceptical thinking of the period; but his comedies actually deal with particular social problems rather than with philosophy in the narrow sense. Their themes, generally speaking, concern the preservation of traditional ideals in a changing society. Capitalism, at this time, continued to develop at a rapid pace, despite the apparent set-back of the Restoration. Wycherley regarded the loosening of rigid class divisions, the growing influence of the business community and the spread of acquisitive values as a serious threat to the humane and civilized level of personal relationships achieved, or at least aimed at, by the most intelligent among the upper-class group for whom he wrote. What particularly worried him was the effect of mercenary competition on friendship and sexual relations. The breakdown of family ties, which disturbed the Elizabethan dramatists so much, left him unmoved. 'FRIENDSHIP', he wrote, 'is a greater Tye on Faith than Blood, and free Love than Marriage-Bonds.'

Marriage was a favourite topic with the Restoration dramatists, and it is the main butt of Wycherley's satire.

To understand why, it is necessary to remember what marriage involved in seventeenth-century England. Marriage was not then a private and wholly voluntary contract between two individuals. As in many parts of the world today, it was felt to be the concern of the family group. Matches were generally arranged by the heads of families, by fathers or by elder brothers. An entry in Samuel Pepys's diary concerning his brother's marriage illustrates the typical attitude fairly well:

My chiefest thought is now to get a good wife for Tom, there being one offered by the Joyces, a cozen of theirs, worth £200 in ready money.
(31 December 1661)

Among the wealthy classes such matters as fixing a dowry and jointure and preserving or enlarging family estates took priority. The wishes of those about to be married were not entirely ignored, but normally had to take second place. Women seldom had much say in the choice of their partners. Traditionally they were conceded the right to refuse a proposed husband, but, as Richardson's novel *Clarissa* in the mid-eighteenth century shows so vividly, refusal might well involve a more than average degree of heroism. Men were allowed greater freedom of choice, but would rarely risk offending relatives on whom they depended financially. Parents still sometimes arranged marriages between young children in this period; young women were often coupled with middle-aged men, and Wycherley's personal experiences of marriage show that there were many other ways in which money could destroy the faintest chance of a happy married relationship.

This was, of course, no new state of affairs. For centuries European writers had been expressing their frustrated desire for a love free from the social ties of arranged marriage; nowhere more intensely than in the imaginary 'Platonic' world of the French aristocratic romances and the closely related English court drama under Charles I. But after the

Restoration, plaintive escapism of this kind was stiffened with a good measure of down-to-earth thinking. The traditional code of family conduct had always been intimately linked with political theory and practice. The revolution and the execution of Charles I had forced all thinking men to make a thorough re-assessment of the relations between ruler and subject, and now some of them felt the need to re-examine the bonds which held the miniature state of the family together. They began to question the right of a father to dictate to his adult sons and daughters; began to challenge the absolute sovereignty of husband over wife, and even to doubt the binding force of marriage vows which were not freely contracted. Reasoning of this kind lies behind many of the comic situations in Restoration drama; it is the very fabric of Wycherley's work. His attack on the contemporary marriage of convenience does not, therefore, necessarily imply a criticism of all marriage. For him 'free love' did not have its modern meaning; it meant rather a freely chosen partnership based on mutual attraction and respect. In his comedies he always implied that this partnership could work within the framework of marriage.

Wycherley's emphasis on free choice in personal relationships is clearly related to the new individualism of the century. But he saw himself as a conservative, defending what he believed to be traditional values against the economic effects of individualism. Forced marriage, fortune hunting, jealousy, indifference and inconstancy—all these he considered to be the evil results of treating people as if they were property, and he blamed them, not always fairly, on the rise of the middle class. But he was also interested in other aspects of social climbing. His comedies are crowded with fops and would-be wits, men who have bought titles or try in other ways to edge themselves into the highest social circles. At first sight it may seem as though he is breaking butterflies upon a wheel, that his affected fools are too insignificant to deserve the ridicule he heaps upon them. But

Wycherley sensed danger in their feeble and superficial attempts to imitate the culture of true gentlemen. It was not just that they lacked correct manners; Wycherley always connected their emphasis on display, on external accomplishments, with a crippling moral deficiency which led to selfishness and treachery in their relations with others. His defence of social and literary decorum forms part of that long tradition of satiric writings which includes Dryden's 'MacFlecknoe' and reaches its highest point in Pope's 'Dunciad' where it appears most clearly as a struggle for the survival of an entire way of life and thought.

Wycherley's comedies are also concerned with changes which were taking place in the lives of upper-class women. With the spread of capitalist methods of business organization, the longer periods spent by noblemen in London away from their country estates, and the greater number of servants, women who would formerly have held important responsibilities in the family were leading a life of increasing idleness. In London and the big spas an exclusive feminine social life was developing, trivial, affected and inward-looking. Wycherley attacked this world of card games and scandal with its false veneer of prudery as yet another obstacle in the way of intelligent, open and equal relationships between men and women.

These interests place Wycherley firmly in the main stream of English satirists from Ben Jonson to Swift and Pope. Like all Restoration comedy, however, his work differs from the masterpieces of these great satirists in its narrower scope. It expresses the interests and the limited vision of a small social group. One soon becomes aware of an inability to reach out imaginatively to the motives and needs of other classes, even to see far beyond the limits of the court at Westminster and the fashionable districts of the capital. Wycherley was deeply affected by the major political and social changes of his time, but was able to judge them only by their effect on the personal lives of a privileged group. Yet the class he represented was in many respects enlightened, and its way of life contained qualities worth preserving: qualities which allowed him to see serious limitations in the forces which were altering society. One may miss in his work the breadth of vision revealed in any one of Jonson's finest comedies, or in the total output of Molière, but his analysis of a smaller field is remarkably acute.

III.   *LOVE IN A WOOD*

When the public theatres reopened at the Restoration after a long period of enforced silence, it almost seems as though the dramatists consciously set out to search for some fruitful comic tradition they could build upon. As the taste for spiteful satires on the Puritans dwindled, they turned for inspiration to Molière in France, to the Spanish comedy of intrigue, to Beaumont and Fletcher, to Ben Jonson and to other earlier English writers. Almost everything they handled was reduced to undistinguished farce. John Dryden and Sir George Etherege obtained the most promising results by developing elements in the comedies of Brome and Shirley, written before the civil wars. They combined in various ways satire on fops and false wits, the intrigues of cunning cheats, the trials and adventures of romantic heroes and heroines and, most important, witty quarrels between upper-class lovers who, like Beatrice and Benedick in Shakespeare's *Much Ado About Nothing*, after a show of reluctance finally join together in marriage. Wycherley in his first play, *Love in a Wood*, grafted on to this loose comic form an adaptation of a Spanish cloak and sword drama[1] to produce a comedy which, though complicated, had greater unity and more serious meaning than any recent work for the stage.

It is fascinating to see Wycherley's clear mind forcing order out of apparent chaos. The play contains two quite distinct worlds. The first, presented satirically, contains fortune hunters, social climbers and bawds who cheat one

---

[1] Calderón's *Mañanas de abril y mayo* (*April and May Mornings*).

another in a series of intrigues and counter-intrigues which reminds one of Jonson's *Volpone* or *The Alchemist*. The second, more benevolent and urbane in manner, following the Spanish play, consists of true lovers from a higher social class. These two separate strands have at first sight so little in common that, despite the skilful weaving of the plot, they seem doomed to fall apart. But Wycherley cleverly turned this apparent weakness to advantage by making a moral contrast between the two a central part of his play's meaning. Every incident, every joke indeed, has some bearing on the main theme, which is the importance of trust and esteem in love, courtship and marriage.

All the characters in the satiric intrigues are linked by a common weakness; they have all, in some way or another, allowed money to sully their approach to love. Unknown to one another they are all manipulated by a cunning bawd and matchmaker, a fitting representative of the forces which poison love by mixing it with greed for money. She alone prospers as interests clash, plots become entangled and the biters themselves are bit.

The dialogue in these scenes, though vigorous and colloquial, is stuffed with meaningful images which form a continuous, indirect commentary. A succession of references to card-sharpers and confidence tricksters, for example, creates the atmosphere of an underworld of crooks. Whenever the Puritan miser, Gripe, appears, witty play with religious phrases underlines his hypocrisy. In the following episode he is visiting a mistress in her poor lodgings. The bawd, Mrs. Joyner, tries to force him to spend freely, while he invents pious excuses not to do so. Notice how, in his last speech, images connected with food suggest the coarseness of his real emotions:

Joyn. What do you look for, Sir?
Gripe. Walls have ears, Walls have ears; besides, I look for a private place to retire to, in time of need; oh here's one convenient.
[*Turns up a Hanging, and discovers the slender provisions of the Family*]

Joyn. But you see poor innocent Souls, to what use they put it, not to hide Gallants.

Gripe. Temperance is the nurse of Chastity.

Joyn. But your Worship may please to mend their fare; and when you come, may make them entertain you, better than, you see, they do themselves.

Gripe. No, I am not dainty, as I told you; I abominate Entertainments; no Entertainments, pray, Mrs. *Joyner.*

Joyn. No!   [*Aside.*

Gripe. There can be no entertainment to me, more Luscious and Savoury, than the communion with that little Gentlewoman; will you call her out, I fast till I see her.[1]   (III.iii)

The two pairs of upper-class lovers, who put genuine feeling before financial interests, provide a decent alternative to fortune-hunting and prostitution. But this is true only at the end of the play. At the start their relationships suffer from serious flaws which plunge them temporarily into the atmosphere of mistrust which surrounds the inferior group. One of the gentlemen is a libertine, the other is absurdly jealous. Wycherley relates both faults to a lack of faith in the intelligence and integrity of their mistresses which comes close to the view held by the other characters, that women can be treated as a form of property. An entertaining sequence of comic disasters finally purges them of their mistaken attitudes.

It is in his use of the stage setting to bind the action together that Wycherley shows most originality.[2] St. James's Park, which gives the play its sub-title and where many of the incidents take place, looms over the whole action. The main

[1] Here the words 'communion' and 'fast' have both religious overtones and associations with food. Quotations from Wycherley's works follow the first editions, with slight alterations in spelling and punctuation where the originals might present difficulty. The figures in brackets refer to the acts and scenes in which quotations occur, according to the divisions in the Mermaid edition.

[2] The Restoration stages, unlike those on which Shakespeare's plays were first acted, used painted scenery which could be changed during performance.

title is itself a pun, for the phrase 'in a wood' at this time meant 'in confusion', and in the play the wooded park at night becomes a symbol of the confusion caused by the various intrigues which take place within it. Wycherley makes the new fashion of rambling in the park stand for the latest patterns of sexual behaviour. St. James's Park had only recently been opened to the public; previously it had been a royal game preserve. How typical of modern life, Wycherley suggests. Gone are the old deer hunts, and instead men and women are now chasing one another in the park. It is a racy idea, handled with wit and subtlety. Wycherley made excellent dramatic use of darkness in his three finest comedies; and here a group of words such as 'see' and 'blind', in the metaphorical senses of 'realize' and 'deceived', give added meaning to the imaginary blackness of the stage. The various characters, muttering about the lack of light, keep mistaking one another in the dark, and in this way the stage scene gradually comes to represent a deeper misunderstanding. The park thus links up all the different forms of deception in the play, including the self-deception of the true lovers. The final confusion in the darkness unravels their mistakes, leading them 'out of the dark' and away from the winding alleys between the trees, the by-paths of love 'where we are still way-lay'd, with Surprizes, Trapans,[1] Dangers, and Murdering disappointments'; leaving the rest to grope their way through the gloomy wood of mistrust.

As one might expect, the play shows signs of inexperience. The dialogue is stiff in places; there are too many set pieces which have not been worked smoothly into the action. Above all, the plot contains unnecessary duplication. Wycherley had a great deal to say and had not yet learnt the importance of sacrificing detail for the sake of clarity. Yet *Love in a Wood* was a break-through: a fully integrated comedy with a consistent, serious purpose.

---

[1] *Trapans:* traps, tricks.

IV.   *THE GENTLEMAN DANCING-MASTER*

The Gentleman Dancing-Master did not fulfil this early promise. A gayer work, more full of laughter, it is also more superficial. Were it not for the attack on 'senseless Plays' in the *Prologue*, one might be tempted to dismiss it merely as pleasant farce. The basic ingredients of the simple plot come from the common Restoration stockpot; some of the flavouring again comes from Spain.[1] The daughter of a wealthy merchant thwarts his scheme to marry her to a rich fool and wins a gentleman of her own choosing. It is not hard to see why the familiar story appealed to Wycherley. He hammers the implied message home:

> When Children marry, Parents shou'd obey,
> Since Love claims more Obedience far than they.   (V.i)

Though there is plenty of farce, the action does have point: the incidents bring out effectively the connection between the father's sternness, the proposed bridegroom's unworthiness and the daughter's rebellion. Whenever he can, Wycherley darts in with a sharp satiric thrust, such as this reply by the heroine, Hippolita, to her guardian aunt, Mrs. Caution:

> *Mrs. Caut.* Well, Malapert! I know you hate me, because I have been the Guardian of your Reputation. But your Husband may thank me one day.
> *Hipp.* If he be not a Fool, he would rather be oblig'd to me for my vertue than to you, since, at long run he must whether he will or no. (I.i)

The richest comedy springs from the supposed naïvety of Hippolita, who is underestimated by every other character, including her lover, Gerrard. The love scenes show Wycherley at his most charming; the mood of tenderness is enchanced by gentle humour and good sense:

[1] Wycherley developed a hint he found in Calderón's *El maestro de danzar* (*The Dancing Master*).

Ger. How's this? you surprise me as much as when first I found so much Beauty and Wit in Company with so much Innocency. But, Dearest, I would be assur'd of what you say, and yet dare not ask the question. You h—— do not abuse me again, you h—— will fool me no more sure.

Hipp. Yes, but I will sure.

Ger. How! nay, I was afraid on't.

Hipp. For I say you are to be my Husband, and you say Husbands must be Wittols[1] and some strange things to boot.

Ger. Well, I will take my Fortune.

Hipp. But have a care, rash man.

Ger. I will venture.

Hipp. At your peril, remember I wish'd you to have a care, forewarn'd, fore-arm'd.

Pru. Indeed now that's fair; for most men are fore-arm'd before they are warn'd.

Hipp. Plain dealing is some kind of honesty however, and few women wou'd have said so much.

Ger. None but those who wou'd delight in a Husband's jealousie, as the proof of his love and her honour.

Hipp. Hold, Sir, let us have a good understanding betwixt one another at first, that we may be long Friends; I differ from you in the point, for a Husband's jealousie, which cunning men wou'd pass upon their Wives for a Compliment, is the worst can be made 'em, for indeed it is a Compliment to their Beauty, but an affront to their Honour.

Ger. But, madam ——

Hipp. So that upon the whole matter I conclude, jealousie in a Gallant is humble true Love, and the height of respect, and only an undervaluing of himself to overvalue her; but in a Husband 'tis arrant sawciness, cowardise, and ill-breeding, and not to be suffer'd.

Ger. I stand corrected gracious Miss.   (V.i)

Hippolita's sophisticated wit may seem unlikely in a middle-class girl of fourteen, but Wycherley needed her youth to emphasize the naturalness of her disobedience, and in his eyes no woman could be really desirable without a mature intelligence.

[1] *Wittol:* a contented cuckold, a man who willingly accepts his wife's infidelity.

Paris, the proposed bridegroom, is among the best of the many Frenchified fops in Restoration comedy. With less malice than most of Wycherley's fools, he gives plenty of scope for the pathetic brand of clowning. Colley Cibber, the actor-dramatist immortalized in Pope's 'Dunciad' has given a lively description of James Nokes, the actor who almost certainly played the part on the first night:

In the ludicrous distresses, which by the laws of comedy, folly is often involv'd in; he sunk into such a mixture of piteous pusillanimity, and a consternation so rufully ridiculous and inconsolable, that when he had shook you, to a fatigue of laughter, it became a moot point whether you ought not to have pity'd him. When he debated any matter by himself, he would shut up his mouth with a dumb studious powt, and roll his full eye into such a vacant amazement, such a palpable ignorance of what to think of it, that his silent perplexity (which would sometimes hold him several minutes) gave your imagination as full content as the most absurd thing he could say upon it.

Given this style of acting, one can imagine the effect of the scene where Paris, who has been ordered to change into Spanish clothes, enters wearing a fantastic mixture of French and Spanish costumes and then, struggling to stop himself swearing in French, pleads to be allowed to keep just his favourite French cravat.

Wycherley learnt some useful lessons in writing this play. He now knew how to keep his action clear and uncluttered. The dialogue with its quick exchange of short speeches shows a new lightness of touch. There is none of the stiffness which marred his first play. But the thinness of the plot gave little scope for the rich exposition of ideas at which he excelled.

V.   *THE COUNTRY-WIFE*

In *The Country-Wife* Wycherley succeeded in combining the thoughtfulness of his first play with the high spirits of his second. He had now turned to comedies by Molière for his plot material, and the example of the great French dramatist seems to have helped him to clarify his own aims. Certainly in *The Country-Wife* he has absolute control over his medium. Built partly out of incidents in *L'Ecole des Maris* (*The School for Husbands*) and *L'Ecole des Femmes* (*The School for Wives*), it is a masterpiece of dramatic design. The plot is planned as a detailed demonstration of the play's main thesis: the failure of contemporary marriage arrangements. Wycherley begins by supposing two typical arranged marriages. These are, as it were, the agreed premises necessary before any argument can take place. Pinchwife, a middle-aged rake, has deliberately picked out for his wife a naïve country girl, on the assumption that ignorance will keep a woman submissive and faithful. Sir Jaspar Fidget, an old businessman, too occupied with business affairs to spend any time on his young wife, imagines he can prevent her thinking about other men by confining her to a trivial social life among safe companions of his own choosing. Blown up into the exaggerated form usual in comedy, these two marriages represent assumptions commonly held by men at the time. Wycherley sets out to show that they contain the seeds of their own destruction, contradictions which can only lead to unhappiness and infidelity. It only needs the appearance on the scene of a determined libertine, Horner, to spark off the inevitable explosion. Having spread the rumour that an attack of venereal disease has left him impotent, Horner becomes in Sir Jaspar's eyes tame enough to join the circle of friends he allows Lady Fidget. Once the opportunity presents itself, she and other women of the town, similarly starved of love, come rushing into the welcoming arms of Horner. The hypocritical mask of prudery, demanded of women by husbands and parents, drops, while the simple country wife develops all the brilliant cunning of a sophisticated townswoman in her efforts to tear a way through to her lover. A third marriage is being arranged. Pinchwife plans to give his sister Alithea to the affected Sparkish, a fool who thinks of her only as a means of making money and as a beautiful possession to show off to his friends. Here again an agent appears, Horner's companion, Harcourt, who opens Alithea's eyes to Sparkish's real motives and himself offers the genuine respect and affection on which they can build together a sound alternative to the diseased marriages all about them.

The action illustrates perfectly Horner's maxim that 'a foolish Rival and a jealous Husband assist their Rival's Designs; for they are sure to make their Women hate them, which is the first step to their love, for another Man'. Once the catalyzing agents are introduced, the process of change sets in quite automatically; to use Wycherley's own image, the disease spreads like an epidemic. Sir Jaspar actually forces Horner on to his wife, so that he can get away to his business; just as Sparkish forces Harcourt on Alithea, so that he can run off to the playhouse. As for Pinchwife, every effort he makes to keep his wife in ignorance only helps to teach her what he wishes to conceal. The situation is rich in irony. The very simplicity of his wife, the quality for which he married her, leaves him completely helpless. Here he is explaining why he has forbidden her to go to the theatre:

> *Mr. Pin.* First, you like the Actors, and the Gallants may like you.
> *Mrs. Pin.* What, a homely Country Girl? no, Bud, no body will like me.
> *Mr. Pin.* I tell you, yes, they may.
> *Mrs. Pin.* No, no, you jest—I won't believe you, I will go.
> *Mr. Pin.* I tell you then, that one of the lewdest Fellows in Town, who saw you there, told me he was in love with you.
> *Mrs. Pin.* Indeed! who, who, pray who wast? (II.i)

Every step Pinchwife takes to protect his wife brings her closer to her lover. As his treatment grows more cruel, she grows correspondingly more cunning. The humour involves continuous use of dramatic irony. The audience has been shown the logical fallacy in Pinchwife's method and knows that his disappointment is quite unavoidable, that all his efforts are as futile as King Lear's shouts against the wind and rain. No hint of tragedy creeps in, however, since Pinchwife has only himself to blame for his suffering. The country wife does not need our pity, since she remains imperturbable even with a knife thrust in her face. Here Pinchwife is forcing her to write a rude letter to Horner:

Mrs. Pin. Indeed, and indeed, but I won't, so I won't.

Mr. Pin. Why?

Mrs. Pin. Because he's in Town, you may send for him if you will.

Mr. Pin. Very well, you wou'd have him brought to you; is it come to this? I say take the pen and write, or you'll provoke me.

Mrs. Pin. Lord, what d'ye make a fool of me for? Don't I know that Letters are never writ, but from the Countrey to *London*, and from *London* into the Countrey; now he's in Town, and I am in Town too; therefore I can't write to him you know.

Mr. Pin. So I am glad it is no worse, she is innocent enough yet. [*Aside*

Yes you may when your Husband bids you write Letters to people that are in Town.

Mrs. Pin. O may I so! Then I'm satisfied.

Mr. Pin. Come begin — Sir — [*Dictates*

Mrs. Pin. Shan't I say, Dear Sir? You know one says always something more than bare Sir.

Mr. Pin. Write as I bid you, or I will write Whore with this Penknife in your Face.

Mrs. Pin. Nay good Bud — Sir — [*She writes*

Mr. Pin. Though I suffer'd last night your nauseous, loath'd Kisses and Embraces — Write.

Mrs. Pin. Nay, why shou'd I say so, you know I told you, he had a sweet breath.

Mr. Pin. Write.

Mrs. Pin. Let me but put out, loath'd.

Mr. Pin. Write I say!

Mrs. Pin. Well then. [*Writes*

Mr. Pin. Let's see what have you writ? — [*Takes the paper and reads*] Though I suffer'd last night your kisses and embraces — Thou impudent creature, where is nauseous and loath'd?

Mrs. Pin. I can't abide to write such filthy words. (IV.ii)

But having learnt the use of the words, she is ready enough to apply them to her husband when the occasion arises.

This splendid action leads up to a forceful dramatic symbol. His wife being heavily disguised, Pinchwife unwittingly takes her by the hand and leads her into the arms of her lover.

How fresh and unforced Wycherley's wit seems in these scenes! Yet all the time he is building up connections, searching out the root causes of the folly he is satirizing. Sir Jaspar, Sparkish and Pinchwife seem, on the face of it, completely unlike one another. One is a businessman; one a dilettante; one a rake turned countryman. Pinchwife guards his wife like a jailer; Sir Jaspar and Sparkish cannot escape from their women quickly enough. Wycherley finds a common connection: a refusal to recognize that women have an intelligence equal to that of men. That 'sweet, soft, gentle, tame, noble Creature Woman, made for Man's Companion'—Sir Jaspar's phrase captures exactly that mixture of reverence and contempt which, for more than two centuries, reduced women to the position of idolized slaves. Wycherley understood that there was really nothing to choose between the praise of a Sir Jaspar and the contempt of a Pinchwife who saw women as 'dough-bak'd, senseless, indocile animals', or the scorn of a Sparkish who felt that 'virtue makes a Woman as troublesome, as a little reading or learning'. They all contained the assumption expressed so crudely in Pinchwife's description of his wife as 'my own Free-hold'; and they all led to tyranny, whether the physical imprisonment of Mrs. Pinchwife or the intellectual imprisonment of Lady Fidget.

Wycherley's satire on the affectation of Lady Fidget and her companions is a real tour de force. Words like *honour*, *innocent*, *virtue*, *reputation*, *noble* and *breeding* appear over and over again in situations which undercut their ordinary meaning, until Wycherley only has to introduce one of them to get a laugh. Watch the sly way he attacks the word *honour* in the scene where Lady Fidget discovers Horner's virility. It becomes almost obscene. Lady Fidget has, as Wycherley puts it, so much honour in her mouth, that she has none elsewhere:

Lady Fid. But, poor Gentleman, cou'd you be so generous? so truly a Man of honour, as for the sakes of us Women of honour, to cause your self to be reported no Man? No Man! and to suffer your self the greatest shame that cou'd fall upon a Man, that none might fall upon us Women by your conversation; but indeed, Sir, as perfectly, perfectly, the same Man as before your going into *France*, Sir; as perfectly, perfectly, Sir.

Hor. As perfectly, perfectly, Madam; nay, I scorn you shou'd take my word; I desire to be try'd only, Madam.

Lady Fid. Well, that's spoken again like a Man of honour, all Men of honour desire to come to the test: But indeed, generally you Men report such things of your selves, one does not know how, or whom to believe; and it is come to that pass, we dare not take your words, no more than your Taylors, without some staid Servant of yours be bound with you; but I have so strong a faith in your honour, dear, dear, noble Sir, that I'd forfeit mine for yours at any time, dear Sir.

Hor. No, Madam, you shou'd not need to forfeit it for me, I have given you security already to save you harmless, my late reputation being so well known in the World, Madam.

Lady Fid. But if upon any future falling out, or upon a suspicion of my taking the trust out of your hands, to employ some other, you your self should betray your trust, dear Sir; I mean, if you'l give me leave to speak obscenely, you might tell, dear Sir.

Hor. If I did, nobody wou'd believe me; the reputation of impotency is as hardly recover'd again in the World, as that of cowardise, dear Madam.

Lady Fid. Nay then, as one may say, you may do your worst, dear, dear, Sir.

Sir Jas. Come, is your Ladyship reconciled to him yet? have you agreed on matters? for I must be gone to *Whitehall*.   (II.i)

Although he ridicules the pretended virtue of society ladies like Lady Fidget, Wycherley looks on them quite sympathetically. He shows that their deceitfulness develops naturally as a reaction to the cruelty and indifference of men. The progress of the country wife demonstrates exactly how craft grows in response to tyranny. The women are not ultimately responsible for their behaviour, and so they are left unpunished at the end of the play. But they are not rewarded with the happiness which the true lovers, Alithea and Harcourt, arrive at. 'Love', as Alithea remarks, 'proceeds from esteem'; and esteem cannot exist side by side with hypocrisy.

Though he obviously believed passionately in what he was saying, Wycherley in this play never gives the impression that he is preaching. Mainly, of course, this is owing to his perpetual delight in the absurd; but another important reason is the remarkable fluency of his dialogue. In one sense the language is more artificial than anything he had written before. We have already seen something of his ingenious use of double meanings, and images of every kind abound. There can hardly be another comedy in English which contains so many similes. Nevertheless, the speeches seem tailored to fit the different characters. Take one of the many passages where Wycherley builds up the idea that sexual desire is spreading like a disease. Spoken by Margery Pinchwife, it involves extremely elaborate play on words associated with illness. The organization of the sentence is actually highly sophisticated. Yet, with its simple words, mostly of one syllable only, and its tiny clauses, it has the very ring of a naïve, childlike person talking to herself:

Well, 'tis e'en so, I have got the *London* disease, they call Love, I am sick of my Husband, and for my Gallant; I have heard this distemper, call'd a Feaver, but methinks 'tis liker an Ague, for when I think of my Husband, I tremble and am in a cold sweat, and have inclinations to vomit, but when I think of my Gallant, dear Mr. *Horner*, my hot fit comes, and I am all in a Feaver, indeed, & as in other Feavers my own Chamber is tedious to me, and I would fain be remov'd to his, and then methinks I shou'd be well. (IV.iv)

Compare this with the conversation between Pinchwife and Sparkish a little further on. They are carrying on with the same analogy, but Sparkish appears foolish and affected, Pinchwife grave and pompous:

Spar. Lord, how shy you are of your Wife, but let me tell you Brother, we men of wit have amongst us a saying, that Cuckolding like the small Pox comes with a fear, and you may keep your Wife as much as you will out of danger of infection, but if her constitution incline her to't, she'l have it sooner or later by the world, say they.

Pin. What a thing is a Cuckold, that every fool can make him ridiculous — [*Aside*

Well Sir — But let me advise you, now you are come to be concern'd, because you suspect the danger, not to neglect the means to prevent it, especially when the greatest share of the Malady will light upon your own head ... (IV.iv)

In *The Country-Wife* Wycherley brought to perfection his system of writing in maxims. Here a warning may be necessary. One tends to assume that any finely expressed idea in a play carries with it the author's approval. Wycherley's maxims, however, take their place in the normal course of the dialogue. Each character is given witty sentiments appropriate to his special situation and peculiar cast of thought. These may well be the exact opposite of Wycherley's own beliefs. The main advantage of the method is that it allows the dramatist to draw out the general significance of a situation without interrupting the flow of the action. Examined closely, some scenes in *The Country-Wife* seem perilously near to formal and static debate, but, in fact, they are moving the plot forward at the same time. Consider the remarkable scene where Horner worms out of Pinchwife his real reasons for marrying a country wife. On the story level Pinchwife is being teased about his marriage and his past life by the three young men, Horner, Harcourt and Dorilant. It is part of the torture he has inflicted on himself, and the audience enjoys watching him squirm. But the teasing, an ingenious analogy with gambling spread over several speeches, takes the form of a series of general maxims. These raise the particular scene to a more abstract level where Pinchwife becomes only one of thousands, and where Wycherley is able to establish a wider connection between licentiousness and jealousy:

Hor. But tell me, has Marriage cured thee of whoring, which it seldom does.

Har. 'Tis more than age can do.

Hor. No, the word is, I'll marry and live honest; but a Marriage vow is like a penitent Gamester's Oath, and entring into Bonds, and penalties to stint himself to such a particular small sum at play for the future, which makes him but the more eager, and not being able to hold out, loses his Money again, and his forfeit to boot.

Dor. Ay, ay, a Gamester will be a Gamester, whilst his Money lasts; and a Whoremaster, whilst his vigour.

Har. Nay, I have known 'em, when they are broke and can lose no more, keep a fumbling with the Box in their hands to fool with only, and hinder other Gamesters.

Dor. That had wherewithall to make lusty stakes.

Pin. Well, Gentlemen, you may laugh at me, but you shall never lye with my Wife, I know the Town.

Hor. But prithee, was not the way you were in better, is not keeping better than Marriage?

Pin. A Pox on't, the Jades wou'd jilt me, I cou'd never keep a Whore to my self.

Hor. So then you only marry'd to keep a Whore to your self; well, but let me tell you, Women, as you say, are like Souldiers made constant and loyal by good pay, rather than by Oaths and Covenants, therefore I'd advise my Friends to keep rather than marry; since too I find by your example, it does not serve one's turn, for I saw you yesterday in the eighteen penny place with a pretty Country-wench.

Pin. How the Divel, did he see my wife then? I sate there that she might not be seen; but she shall never go to a play again.   [*Aside*

Notice here how Horner's generalization slides perfectly easily into the particular information that he has seen Mrs. Pinchwife. Pinchwife's embarrassment now leads back quite naturally to a further generalization:

Hor. What dost thou blush at nine-and-forty, for having been seen with a Wench?

Dor. No Faith, I warrant 'twas his Wife, which he seated there out of sight, for he's a cunning Rogue, and understands the Town.

Har. He blushes, then 'twas his Wife; for Men are now more ashamed to be seen with them in publick, than with a Wench.   (I.i)

It is difficult to imagine a finer medium for dramatic satire. Packed with meaning, the speeches can carry as much imagery as verse; yet they have all the speed and vigour of colloquial prose.

The Country-Wife is certainly one of the great English comedies. It has gusto, abundant wit and perfect form. Moreover, its shapely structure is no mere embellishment of style; it is the instrument with which Wycherley probes social behaviour to achieve that 'studied insight into the springs of character' which Hazlitt admired so much.

VI. *THE PLAIN-DEALER*

It was *The Plain-Dealer* and not *The Country-Wife* which made the deepest impression on fellow writers and critics, however. Wycherley's last comedy had a new earnestness: that unmistakeable note of moral seriousness which critical theory insisted the best literature ought to have. It struck the literary world as the grandest, most worthy comedy of the age. But the general public does not always take the favourite of the critics to its heart. *The Plain-Dealer* did not arouse the spontaneous enthusiasm which had greeted *The Country-Wife*. The first night audience had to be prodded into applauding by its betters, and, though the play remained in the repertory for a century, it was less popular than many other Restoration comedies. The instinct of the ordinary theatre-goer in this instance proved sounder than the considered verdict of the critics. *The Plain-Dealer* is an interesting, in many ways an admirable play, but it is less than a masterpiece.

For the first time Wycherley had difficulty in adapting his source material to his own purposes. The play is based on Molière's great comedy *Le Misanthrope*, which deals with an embittered man who, shocked at the hypocrisy and corruption around him, deliberately sets out to make a martyr of himself. The French play contains some satire on affectation and injustice, but its main purpose is to plead for compromise, for a sense of proportion; and its ridicule falls mostly on the central figure of the misanthropist. Wycherley had no more of the man-hater about him than Molière, but he was here more intent on satirizing society. He decided that the figure of the misanthropist could be turned into an excellent satiric spokesman. Being a balanced and urbane man himself, however, he could not resist keeping something of Molière's ridicule of extremism. The result is confusing. Sometimes one is looking at society through the eyes of the misanthropist, Manly; sometimes one is looking at him critically from the outside.

But the failure of the play goes deeper. Wycherley was finally moving away from the analysis of a particular social problem to a more general indictment of society. This in itself deserves praise, for it is unique on the Restoration stage. Yet one is forced to ask whether Wycherley was really equipped to make a sweeping comment of this kind. Moving only in a small social circle, how could he be? He did what he could. He put more stress than ever before on treachery among friends and on the flattery of courtiers. He also brought in the one other field he knew well, the law. But he was unable to invent incidents strong enough to support the ambitious generalizations he wanted to make. He relied, instead, on the long tirades of his plain dealer, Manly:

... here you see a *Bishop* bowing low to a gaudy *Atheist;* a Judge to a Door-keeper; a great Lord, to a Fishmonger, or a Scrivener with a Jack-chain about his neck; a Lawyer, to a Serjeant at Arms; a velvet *Physician*, to a threadbare Chymist: and a supple Gentleman Usher, to a surly Beef-eater: and so tread round in a preposterous huddle of Ceremony to each other, whil'st they can hardly hold their solemn false countenances.   (I.i)

: . . here thou wilt live to be cherish'd by Fortune and the great ones; for thou may'st easily come to out-flatter a dull Poet, out-lie a Coffee-house or Gazette-writer, out-swear a Knight of the Post,[1] out-watch a Pimp, out-fawn a Rook,[2] out-promise a Lover, out-rail a Wit, and out-brag a Sea-Captain.   (I.i)

Forceful all this may be, but it cries out for a plot of great range, the kind of plot Jonson could offer, sweeping through every corner of society from the palace to the gutter. In fact *The Plain-Dealer* only tells the story of a man who is betrayed by his friend and jilted by his mistress. It is too flimsy to bear the weight of Wycherley's wholesale indictment.

This weakness helps to explain the unsatisfactory figure of Fidelia, a woman dressed in boy's clothes who follows Manly through all his dangers and distresses with dog-like devotion. Wycherley was an optimist at heart. He always included in his comedies characters who stood for the right way of doing things. In the earlier plays the true lovers who join in an intelligent equal partnership provide an effective and convincing contrast to the particular evil of mercenary marriage. Now Wycherley obviously needed a more comprehensive good alternative. Fidelia was his answer, a character representing faithfulness, whose symbolic quality is suggested by the fact that she lapses into blank verse whenever she is left on her own. As an answer to social corruption she seems totally ineffective. One feels that Wycherley is asking decent personal relationships to solve weaknesses in the structure of society. Moreover, the solemnity with which he handles Fidelia strikes an utterly false note in the comedy.

'In Works of Wit and Fancy', Wycherley wrote,'every-thing that is not perfectly excellent displeases.' Fortunately this is only a half truth, and there is much to please in *The Plain-Dealer*. On familiar ground he is as entertaining as ever. Manly's outspokenness gives rise to plenty of amusing satire. His effect on the polite world is rather like

[1] *Knight of the post:* a man hired to give false evidence in court.
[2] *Rook:* a swindler.

that of a nasty smell. This is how he receives the genteel Lord Plausible:

> *L. Plaus.* What, will you be singular then, like no Body? follow, love, and esteem no Body?
> *Man.* Rather than be general, like you; follow every Body, court and kiss every Body; though, perhaps at the same time, you hate every Body.
> *L. Plaus.* Why, seriously with your pardon, my dear Friend —
> *Man.* With your pardon, my no Friend, I will not, as you do whisper my hatred, or my scorn, call a man Fool or Knave, by signs, or mouths over his shoulder, whil'st you have him in your arms: for such as you, like common Whores and Pickpockets, are only dangerous to those you embrace.
> *L. Plaus.* Such as I! Heavens defend me! — upon my Honour —
> *Man.* Upon your Title, my Lord, if you'd have me believe you. (I.i)

When the marriage of Vernish and Olivia, Manly's false friend and mistress, falls apart, the results are riotously funny, with both husband and wife chasing lustfully after the epicene Fidelia. 'Did you not hear my Husband say, he found me with a Woman in Man's clothes?' asks Olivia, 'And d'ye think he does not know a Man from a Woman.' 'Not so well, I'm sure, as you do', her cousin replies. When Olivia receives her lover in the dark only to discover that the man in her arms is her husband, her reaction is unforgettable: 'Ha! my Husband returned! and have I been throwing away so many kind Kisses on my Husband, and wrong'd my Lover already?'

The play also succeeds in capturing something of the robust spirit of earlier English comedy. With its sailors and lawyers and bailiffs, it shows a wider, rougher world than his other plays. Towering above the rest stands the forbidding figure of the Widow Blackacre, a woman eaten up by a passion for legal brawling, a mother who has crushed all the independence out of her miserable son, Jerry:

Go, save thy breath for the Cause; talk at the Bar, Mr. *Quaint:* You are so copiously fluent, you can weary any one's ears, sooner than your own tongue. Go, weary our Adversaries Counsel, and the Court: Go, thou art a fine-spoken person: Adad, I shall make thy wife jealous of me: if you can but court the Court into a Decree for us. Go, get you gone, and remember — [*Whispers*]   [*Exit* Quaint]

Come, Mr. *Blunder*, pray bawl soundly for me, at the *Kings-Bench;* bluster, sputter, question, cavil; but be sure your Argument be intricate enough, to confound the Court; And then you do my business Talk what you will, but be sure your tongue never stand still; for your own noise will secure your Sense from Censure: 'tis like coughing or heming when one has got the Belly-ake, which stifles the unmannerly noise. Go, dear Rogue, and succeed; and I'll invite thee, ere it be long, to more souz'd Venison.   (III.i)

The Widow Blackacre has all that vigorous abusive speech the Elizabethans delighted in, a gift for the absurdly mundane image. She is derived from characters like Ursula, the pig woman, in Jonson's *Bartholomew Fair*, and she looks forward to Congreve's Lady Wishfort. She is essentially English, with a coarseness French audiences would not have tolerated, but full of life. This is her reply to an old fellow who proposes marriage:

Wid. Thou sensless, impertinent, quibling, driveling, feeble, paralytic, impotent, fumbling, frigid Nincompoop!

Jerr. Hey, brave Mother, for calling of names, ifac!

Wid. Wou'dst thou make a Caudlemaker,[1] a Nurse of me? Can't you be Bed-rid without a Bed-fellow? Won't your Swan-skins, Furs, Flannels, and the scorch'd Trencher[2] keep you warm there? Wou'd you have me your Scotch warming-Pan,[3] with a Pox to you? Me! — (II.i)

If the liveliness of *The Plain-Dealer* needs any further testimony, what more impressive than the enthusiasm of the great French satirist, Voltaire, who declared that he did not know a single comedy, ancient or modern, which contained so much wit.

---

[1] *Caudle:* gruel mixed with wine and spices.
[2] *Scorched trencher:* a wooden dish heated to warm a bed.
[3] *Scotch warming pan:* a slang phrase for a prostitute.

VII. POEMS AND MAXIMS

Some twenty years later Wycherley began to turn out verse in enormous quantities. His debts had forced him to pocket his pride, and he was now making a business of writing. He was no poet, and he knew it. In the errata list to the collection published during his lifetime, 'that Damnd Miscellany of Madrigals of mine' as he called it, he disarmingly included 'the Whole BOOK'. The wits, who had long looked forward to a new work by their leader, had to agree. Wycherley had relied on his good sense and his genius for paradox to carry him through. But his readers demanded a certain minimum of grace and elegance. This Wycherley could not provide. His satires were rambling and shapeless, and even his songs could not be scanned. Senile decay must have been partly responsible, as he had once been able to write competent lyrics for his plays.

The satires shed further light on his beliefs, but there is little that cannot be deduced from the comedies. Once again he attacks misers, poor wits, fortune hunters and flatterers. One poem proves that priests are worse than pimps, because marriage is more mercenary than prostitution; another that business is really idleness because the results of its activity are futile. Some of the light-hearted, risqué love songs might amuse the casual reader, though the titles are often as witty as the poems themselves, and sometimes almost as long: 'To a *Fine Singer*, who had gotten a *Cold;* and, whose *Lover* endeavour'd to stop Her *Tongue* in Her *Mouth* with His, to save her *Honour* (as He call'd it.)'; 'To a fine Young *Woman*, who being ask'd by her Lover, *Why she kept so filthy a thing as a Snake in her Bosom;* answer'd, *'Twas to keep a filthier thing out of it, his Hand;* and, *that her Snake was to play with, and cool her in hot Weather;* which was his Aversion.' One or two of the drinking songs come near to the gracious ease one expects from a good Restoration lyric:

Reason our Foe, let us destroy,
  Which still disturbs us, when we drink;
Which lets us not our selves enjoy,
  But puts us to the pains to think.

But even here the clumsiness of the third line intrudes.

When looking over the poems Pope kept making the sensible suggestion that Wycherley should turn some of the wittier paradoxes into prose maxims after the manner of La Rochefoucauld and other French writers. Wycherley evidently took the proposal to heart, for the papers published after his death include a collection of over three hundred such maxims. With these he was far more at home:

MAY we not fairly say Marriage makes more Sinners than free Love, since it forces most of its Disciples, first or last, to Repentance?

Anyone who has enjoyed the maxims George Bernard Shaw published with *Man and Superman* would appreciate Wycherley's collection. Not all are original, however. He kept a volume of maxims by various French writers in front of him, and half way through he began translating, carefully taking one from each author in turn so that no one would notice the extent of his borrowing. One feels almost ashamed that modern scholarship should have caught him out. But he had an excellent defence, for, as he insisted in the Preface to his *Miscellany Poems*, necessity 'is always an Excuse for all Thefts'.

Wycherley would not have wanted to be remembered for his dotages, for works created in need. He had been the great dramatist of the seventies, writing then for pleasure, not for business. He had seen his plays direct the course of English drama for thirty years. The best of the younger dramatists had all followed in his footsteps. Congreve had refined upon his wit, Vanbrugh had inherited something of his seriousness. But neither had launched out in strikingly new directions. Until the arrival of sentimental comedy at the turn of the century, his own *Plain-Dealer* had remained the most significant attempt to move away from the pattern set by *The Country-Wife*.

He can hardly affect us now as deeply as he did his contemporaries. The social problems in which he was most interested have lost their urgency, in England at least; though there are many countries where his satire on arranged marriage would still seem relevant and challenging. But he has survived remarkably well the hazards which befall any writer who concentrates on the social scene. We do not have to learn outdated jargon to understand him. There are few of those topical details which make performance of Ben Jonson's comedies so difficult. If we have to rebuild in our imagination the conditions in which he lived, little effort is needed to understand his beliefs. Even in the Victorian era some critics, like Charles Cowden Clarke, could see that 'Wycherley had by nature a generous and an honourable heart, and his real nature shone through his writings'. Today, the deep-rooted faith in the intellectual equality of women which runs through all his work and the importance he attached to sound personal relationships in a world crippled by self-interest compel our sympathy. Despite the cries that he is obscene, or morbid, or trivial, on his rare appearances in the theatre he is still able to set audiences laughing in the same critical spirit that he intended.

WILLIAM WYCHERLEY

A Select Bibliography

(Place of publication London unless stated otherwise)

Collected Works:

MISCELLANY POEMS (1704)
—a folio, with a fine mezzotint portrait-frontispiece.

THE WORKS (1713)
—contains the four comedies. Reprinted in 1720; 1731; 1733, Dublin; 1735; and subsequently.

THE POSTHUMOUS WORKS, ed. L. Theobald (1728)
—contains poems, a collection of maxims, and a memoir by R. Pack.

THE POSTHUMOUS WORKS . . . Vol. II, ed. A. Pope (1729)
—not a continuation of the previous work, but an attempt to prove Theobald's unreliability as an editor. It contains different texts of some poems and the Wycherley-Pope correspondence.

THE DRAMATIC WORKS OF WYCHERLEY, CONGREVE, VANBRUGH, AND FARQUHAR, ed. L. Hunt (1840).

PLAYS, ed. W. C. Ward (1888)
—in the original Mermaid Series.

THE COMPLETE WORKS, ed. M. Summers. 4 vols. (1924)
—the limited Nonesuch Press edition. Amply annotated but textually unreliable.

Separate Works:

HERO AND LEANDER, IN BURLESQUE (1669). *Verse*
—published anonymously.

LOVE IN A WOOD, OR, ST JAMES'S PARK (1672). *Drama*

THE GENTLEMAN DANCING-MASTER (1673). *Drama*

THE COUNTRY-WIFE (1675). *Drama*
—edited with *The Plain Dealer* by G. B. Churchill, *The Belles-Lettres Series*, Boston, 1924. Adaptations by J. Lee, 1765; by D. Garrick (as *The Country Girl*), 1766; by B. C. d'Arien (as *Das Landmaedchen oder Weiberlist geht über Alles*), Schwerin and Weimar, 1794.

41

THE PLAIN-DEALER (1677). *Drama*
—edited by A. Beljame and H. S. Symmes in *Representative English Comedies*, Vol. IV, New York, 1936. Adaptations by F. M. A. de Voltaire (as *La Prude ou la Gardeuse de Cassette*) in *Œuvres de M. de Voltaire*, Vol. VIII, Dresden, 1748; by I. Bickerstaffe, 1766 (further revised in 1796 by J. P. Kemble).

EPISTLES TO THE KING AND DUKE (1682). *Verse*
—published anonymously.

THE FOLLY OF INDUSTRY (1704). *Verse*
—reissued in 1705 as *The Idleness of Business: A Satyr*.

ON HIS GRACE THE DUKE OF MARLBOROUGH (1707). *Verse*
—published anonymously.

Note:

Three short poems were first published in miscellaneous collections of verse by various authors: 'The Answer' to 'A Letter from Mr. *Shadwell*, to Mr. *Wicherly*' in *Poems on Affairs of State. Part III*, 1698; 'To my Friend, Mr. *Pope*, on his Pastorals' in *Poetical Miscellanies: The Sixth Part*, 1709; 'An Epistle to Mr. *Dryden*, from Mr. *Wycherley*. Occasion'd by his Proposal to write a Comedy together' in *Poems on Several Occasions*, 1717.

Correspondence:

LETTERS UPON SEVERAL OCCASIONS, by J. Dennis, Wycherley and others (1696).

THE CORRESPONDENCE OF ALEXANDER POPE, ed. G. Sherburn. 5 vols. Oxford (1956)
—vol. I contains the Pope-Wycherley correspondence.

Some Biographical and Critical Studies:

LETTERS OF WIT, POLITICKS AND MORALITY, ed. A. Boyer (1701)
—includes a memoir by G. Granville, Lord Lansdowne.

THE TATLER, No. 3, by Sir R. Steele (1709).

MEMOIRS OF THE LIFE OF WILLIAM WYCHERLEY, ESQ., by C. Gildon (1718)
—published anonymously. It includes Lansdowne's memoir.

'Letters on Milton and Wycherley', by J. Dennis (1722)
—reprinted with other works containing critical and biographical remarks on Wycherley in *The Critical Works of John Dennis*, 2 vols., edited by E. N. Hooker, Baltimore, 1939-1943.

LETTERS CONCERNING THE ENGLISH NATION, by F. M. A. de Voltaire (1733).

'On Wycherley, Congreve, Vanbrugh, and Farquhar', by W. Hazlitt. In *Lectures on the English Comic Writers*, 1819.

ANECDOTES, OBSERVATIONS, AND CHARACTERS, OF BOOKS AND MEN, by J. Spence (1820)
—contains Pope's reported comments on Wycherley.

'On the Artificial Comedy of the Last Century', by C. Lamb. In *Elia*, 1823.

'The Dramatic Works of Wycherley, Congreve, Vanbrugh, and Farquhar', a review of Hunt's edition by T. B. Macaulay in *The Edinburgh Review*, xxii, 1841.

'Wycherley and Congreve', by C. Cowden Clarke. In *The Gentleman's Magazine*, vii, 1871.

THE COMEDY OF MANNERS, by J. Palmer (1913).

ENGLISH DRAMA OF THE RESTORATION AND EIGHTEENTH CENTURY, by G. H. Nettleton. New York (1914).

WILLIAM WYCHERLEY. SA VIE—SON OEUVRE, par C. Perromat. Paris (1921).

A HISTORY OF RESTORATION DRAMA, 1660-1700, by A. Nicoll. Cambridge (1923)
—revised edition as *A History of English Drama 1660-1900*, vol. i, Cambridge, 1952.

RESTORATION COMEDY, by B. Dobrée. Oxford (1924).

COMEDY AND CONSCIENCE AFTER THE RESTORATION, by J. W. Krutch. New York (1924).

THE COMIC SPIRIT IN RESTORATION DRAMA, by H. T. E. Perry. New York (1925).

THE SOCIAL MODE OF RESTORATION COMEDY, by K. M. Lynch. New York (1926).

THE OLD DRAMA AND THE NEW, by W. Archer (1929).

BRAWNY WYCHERLEY: FIRST MASTER IN ENGLISH MODERN COMEDY, by W. Connely (1930).

'Wycherley and Dryden', by H. Granville-Barker. In *On Dramatic Method*, 1931.

THE EARLY CAREER OF ALEXANDER POPE, by G. Sherburn. Oxford (1934) —this gives the best account of Wycherley's relations with Pope.

THE RELATION OF MOLIÈRE TO RESTORATION COMEDY, by J. Wilcox. New York (1938).

'Restoration Comedy: the Reality and the Myth', by L. C. Knights. In *Explorations*, 1946.

THE GAY COUPLE IN RESTORATION COMEDY, by J. H. Smith. Cambridge, Mass. (1948).

THE COURT WITS OF THE RESTORATION, by J. H. Wilson. Princeton (1948).

THE THREAD OF LAUGHTER, by L. Kronenberger. New York (1952).

THE RESTORATION COMEDY OF WIT, by T. H. Fujimura. Princeton (1952).

THE FIRST MODERN COMEDIES, by N. N. Holland. Cambridge, Mass. (1959).

Bibliographical Series
of Supplements to 'British Book News'
on Writers and Their Work

★

GENERAL EDITOR
Geoffrey Bullough

GEORGE MOORE

Detail from a pastel drawing by HENRY TONKS *in the*
National Portrait Gallery

GEORGE MOORE

by

A. NORMAN JEFFARES

Humour, irony, indignation, anecdote passed
from him. We were his guests; he exhausted
himself to entertain and hold us, having then—as
always except when Amico Moorini showed his
head—an ancient and elaborate courtesy.

Charles Morgan

PUBLISHED FOR
THE BRITISH COUNCIL
AND THE NATIONAL BOOK LEAGUE
BY LONGMANS, GREEN & CO.

LONGMANS, GREEN & CO. LTD.
48 Grosvenor Street, London W.1

*Associated companies, branches and
representatives throughout the world*

First published 1965
©A. Norman Jeffares, 1965

*Printed in Great Britain by
F. Mildner & Sons, London, E.C.1*

CONTENTS

Acknowledgement: Our grateful thanks are due to Messrs. Macmillan & Co. Ltd. for permission to quote from *An Epitaph on George Moore* by Charles Morgan; and to J. C. and R. G. Medley, owners of the copyright in George Moore's literary works, for permission to quote from the works and letters of George Moore.

¶ GEORGE AUGUSTUS MOORE was born on 24 February 1852 at Moore Hall, Muckloon, Lough Carra, Co. Mayo, Ireland. He died on 18 January 1933 in London, and his ashes were buried on Castle Island, Lough Carra.

GEORGE MOORE

I

THE LIFE

GEORGE AUGUSTUS MOORE was born on 24 February, 1852 at Moore Hall, a Georgian house overlooking Lough Carra, in Co. Mayo in the west of Ireland. Another George Moore, his great-grandfather, had built the house out of the large fortune with which he had returned to Ireland from Alicante, after a successful period as a merchant in Spain. While there he had drawn up a pedigree which traced the family back to Sir Thomas More; the document was certainly accurate as far back as the author's own great-grandfather, Captain George Moore, the Vice-Admiral of Connaught, and the connection with Sir Thomas More may well have been genuine. The family was originally Protestant; the first marriage into a Catholic family occurred early in the eighteenth century. George Moore the merchant was a son of this marriage and passed as a Catholic in Spain. His third son was an author, who wrote a Whiggish *History of the British Revolution* and a liberal and rational treatise attacking Kant. His son George Henry returned from Cambridge and subsequent travels in the East to occupy himself with racing and hunting. But at the time of the Irish famine of 1846-48 he sold his stable and turned to politics, heading the poll as an Independent in 1847, a seat he retained for ten years. In 1859, however, he returned to racing and won large sums of money, some of which he spent on his sons' education, sending them to Oscott, the Catholic college where he had himself been educated in England.

His eldest son, George, went to Oscott in the winter of 1861. An attack of bronchitis in 1863 gave him a happy spell at home, fishing on the lake with his brother Maurice, shooting, and joining in the life of his father's racing stables. Both he and Maurice, who joined him at Oscott in 1865, did

7

badly at the school, and the headmaster wrote many letters to their father about George's lack of progress. Eventually he left the school, where a younger brother, Augustus, joined Maurice; he spent a year at home, and then moved to London when his father abandoned racing for a second time and was re-elected to the House of Commons in 1868.

In London George Moore was influenced by the artist Jim Browne and began to attempt to paint; he was, however, sent by his father to work with an army crammer. When his father died he inherited an income of three to four thousand pounds a year from the property in Ireland, but only an income of about five hundred pounds of this was left after the payment of mortgages. He still wanted to become a painter and study in Paris, but, not being of age and as his guardians disagreed with his plans, he had to spend three years in London. He had financial scrapes, he lived a gay life, he made friends, but as soon as he was twenty-one he went to Paris.

In Paris he tried at first to obtain private tuition, but became a pupil in Jullian's Academy. Lewis Weldon Hawkins—the Lewis Ponsonby Marshall of the *Confessions* and *Hail and Farewell*—became his friend. There was a brief return to London where he painted, and lived beyond his income, but, back in Paris in 1875, he made the difficult decision to give up painting. He thought of marrying for money, also of becoming a writer, and he collaborated with Bernard Lopez in *Luther*, a verse drama which he had printed in 1878, a year after his poems, *Flowers of Passion*, were printed, reviewed savagely and later withdrawn. His friendship with Lewis diminished and Hawkins left the luxurious rooms in the Rue de la Tour des Dames, so richly described in the *Confessions*:

... our salon was a pretty resort—English cretonne of a very happy design —vine leaves, dark green and golden, broken up by many fluttering jays. The walls were stretched with this colourful cloth, and the arm-chairs and the couches were to match. The drawing-room was in cardinal red, hung from the middle of the ceiling and looped up to give the appearance of a tent; a faun, in terra-cotta, laughed in the red gloom, and there were Turkish couches and lamps. In another room you faced an altar, a Buddhist temple, a statue of Apollo, and a bust of Shelley. The bedrooms were made unconventional with cushioned seats and rich canopies; and in picturesque corners there were censers, great church candlesticks, and palms; then think of the smell of burning wax and you will have imagined the sentiment of our apartement in Rue de la Tour des Dames. I bought a Persian cat, and a python that made a monthly meal off guinea-pigs; Marshall, who did not care for pets, filled his room with flowers—he used to sleep beneath a tree of gardenias in full bloom.

Moore was moving in French society now, and the period from 1877 to 1880 was also the time of his 'café education', when he got to know Manet and Degas and their circle of friends, whom he met frequently in the Nouvelles Athènes in Montmartre. Yeats described him as 'sitting among art students, young writers about to become famous, in some café; a man carved out of a turnip, looking out of astonished eyes'. His appearance was indeed unusual. He had a receding chin, a long neck, a full if straggling moustache and sloping shoulders; his hair was pale yellow, his prominent eyes a pale grey-green, his complexion delicately pink; in Yeats's phrase again, his body was 'insinuating, upflowing, circulative, curvicular, pop-eyed'.

In 1880 Moore had to face the effects of the Land War in Ireland. His tenants refused to pay their rents, agricultural prices were down, and his uncle, Joe Blake, honest but chaotic, handed over the agency, to be replaced by Tom Ruttledge, young, untried but efficient. After a winter in Ireland, Moore settled down in London to write, living a very frugal and thrifty life, undertaking journalism—he wrote on the naturalistic novel, striving to bring Zola's work before British readers.

Moore's first novel, *A Modern Lover*, was published in 1883, to reappear in rewritten form as *Lewis Seymour and Some Women* in 1917. This was a study of an artist who is

helped throughout his life by women. Shaw remembered
Moore at this time as

always telling stories about himself and women. In every story there was
a room full of mirrors and chandeliers and the story usually ended with
some woman throwing a lamp at George and driving him out of the
house. Everybody used to laugh at George and no one believed him, but
he had an imperturbable good humour and if you said: 'But, George,
don't talk such nonsense, you are making it all up', he was not in the
least put out or angry but just said: 'Don't interrupt me', and went on as
before.

Moore realized later that his ability to write prose was
questionable (as much so as were his earlier attempts to paint
and to become a poet) but the story, he said, enthralled him.
His novel received favourable notice, but the circulating
libraries thought it unsuitable for their readers, so his next
venture was a one-volume novel published cheaply by
Vizetelly. This was *A Mummer's Wife*, a study of a touring
company, which he wrote in Ireland in the winter of 1883-
84, first at Moore Hall and later in Dublin, where he went to
observe and take part in the season at the Viceregal Court,
the Levee, the State Ball, and other social events, thus laying
the foundations of *A Drama in Muslin*.

He moved to chambers in London and there completed *A
Mummer's Wife*, his active answer to the sentimental school,
a novel in which he deepened his portrayal of character and
successfully applied the method of the French naturalistic
writers to English life. The winter of 1884-5 he spent in
Ireland where he finished *A Drama in Muslin*. He launched
an attack on the Viceregal Court in nationalist newspapers,
as he had not been invited, despite his requests, to a State
dinner party. He read Pater with great delight, then trans-
ferred himself to London and made a telling attack on the
circulating libraries. He made friends with the English
artists Sickert and Steer; a neighbouring landlord from
Galway, Edward Martyn, recently down from Oxford,

became another close friend. Martyn was portrayed in *A Mere Accident*, a novel written in and about Sussex, which marks the end of Zola's influence on Moore. (This reached its zenith in *Parnell and his Island*, but its waning is perhaps best captured in his 1894 account of a visit to Medan in 1888.) The effect of Huysmans and Flaubert on his writings now became apparent.

Moore had come to Sussex as the guest of old friends, the Bridgers, and in 1887 he joined with Collyer Bridger in a rabbit-farming venture there. He enjoyed what he called the Protestantism of Sussex, and *Spring Days* records this liking, captured in a Balzacian way. Dujardin's writings had a noticeable effect upon Moore, as is shown by his *Confessions of a Young Man* (1888); this rich and full account of his life in Paris led to his alienation from Degas and Zola. Though his next novel *Mike Fletcher* proved a failure, he was already engaged upon *Esther Waters* in 1890; he laid it aside, however, to write *Impressions and Opinions*, a successful collection of essays. *Vain Fortune* was a serial for the *Lady's Pictorial*, but did not do well. The winter of 1891-92 he spent writing *Esther Waters*.

Moore's criticism flourished, and his articles in *The Speaker* were collected as *Modern Painting* (1893). He had extended his friendships among the artists, and now knew William Rothenstein, Henry Tonks and D. S. MacColl, who was currently art critic of the *Spectator* and an equally enthusiastic supporter of the French Impressionists.

During the 'nineties Moore enjoyed a wider social life in London and even joined Boodles, the exclusive Tory club. Though he talked much about his love affairs, sentimental or promiscuous, and though he had set his mind against marriage, he seems to have fallen deeply in love with Mrs. Craigie, an American heiress, who wrote novels under the *nom de plume* John Oliver Hobbes. He collaborated with her in several plays. But she dismissed him savagely, probably because she had hopes of marrying Lord Curzon.

Esther Waters (1894) proved a popular success, and Moore

followed it with the short stories of *Celibate Lives* (1895), in which Mrs. Craigie appears as 'Mildred Lawson'—she is also depicted in 'Lui et Elles' in *Memoirs of my Dead Life* (1921), and in 'Henrietta Marr' in *In Single Strictness* (1922). Hone relates in his biography the story of the third quarrel with Mrs. Craigie which took place in 1904 after Moore and she had agreed to collaborate again in writing a play. Moore told his friend Dujardin what had happened:

'I was walking in the Green Park', he said, 'and I saw her in front of me. I was blind with rage and I ran up behind her and kicked her.' At first he related this story with some embarrassment, but when he grew accustomed to his invention, with relish. The scene in the Green Park was afterwards used in the sketch 'Lui et Elles' . . . where a heartless woman on whose face he detected a mocking smile, receives the assault 'nearly in the centre of the backside, a little to the right', and seems highly gratified to find that she has aroused such a display of feeling. 'It was inevitable, I said, part of the world's history, and I lost sight of all things but the track of my boot on the black crêpe de Chine.'

Mildred Lawson was incapable of love, her sensibility warped by her revulsion from sexuality; she turned to religion, but this was as unsatifactory as the independent life she had sought earlier in her pursuit of art. *Evelyn Innes* (1898) also owed something to Mrs. Craigie's life, though Moore had to learn a lot about music and convents to write it, a thing he did with 'pure joy'. The novel seemed at the time to be very successful indeed, but its sequel, *Sister Teresa* (1901), was less so. Yeats remarked that Moore was jealous of his own creation, Sir Owen Asher, a man about town and materialist; adding that Moore was all self and yet had so little self that he would destroy his reputation, or that of some friend, to make his audience believe that the story running in his head at the moment had happened, and only just happened. He was indeed a master of indiscretion.

By the time *Sister Teresa* was published Moore had left London for Dublin. He was deeply disturbed by the Boer

War, by Kiplingesque Imperialism, and found life in England distasteful. But there were also positive reasons for his move. The formation of the Gaelic League in 1893 had stirred his imagination. As a child he had grown up in a Gaelic-speaking area. He admired Yeats; Edward Martyn was his friend; and so he sympathized with their plans for an Irish literary theatre. He loathed the conventional English theatre; he despised the state of English dramatic criticism; he disliked the power of the great actors and actor-managers; and, as the third Director of the Irish Literary Theatre, he joined eagerly in the early work of getting Martyn's *Heather Field* and Yeats's *The Countess Cathleen* on to the stage in Dublin in 1899. Indeed Yeats wrote that the Irish theatre could not have been founded without his help and his knowledge of the stage. He felt that great art could coincide with national revival and he brought to Dublin his own cosmopolitan concept of art, literature and music.

He hurled himself into the movement to create a culture for Ireland. He spoke at meetings; he wrote art criticism; he wrote *The Bending of the Bough*, a patriotic play begun by Martyn which he took over, and this was produced in Dublin in February 1900. With Yeats he collaborated in the writing of *Diarmuid and Grania;* it was performed in Dublin in 1901. He developed a strong if short-lived enthusiasm for Irish. He settled in a house in Ely Place and, though he lived a laborious life, became part of the Dublin scene. He did not lack company, for a woman friend of his, the 'Stella' of *Hail and Farewell*, came to live in Rathfarnham, near Dublin, and he formed a friendship with AE (George Russell) and with John Eglinton (W. K. Magee, a librarian in the National Library).

The Irish Literary Theatre was replaced by the Irish National Dramatic Company in 1902; this year marked Moore's quarrel with Yeats over further collaboration and, in Yeats's phrase, he 'dropped out of the movement'. Then he wrote *The Untilled Field* (1903), a collection of stories which developed an earlier anti-clericalism and were also brilliant Turgenev-like pieces of observation. He demonstrated his anti-catholicism in a letter to the *Irish Times*, declaring his conversion to the Church of Ireland, an action which led, ultimately, to his estrangement from his brother Maurice, whom he had invited to live in Moore Hall with his family from 1905 onwards. But though he became disillusioned with Irish life, with what he saw there as an eternal conflict between literature and dogma, his return to the Irish scene gave him fresh material. *The Lake* (1905) seemed to him a triumph over the difficulty of preserving unity of scene. It also represented a new phase in his art, a continuous weaving of memories, of highly imaginative reverie, which reached its peak in the mischievous, malicious and yet deeply appreciative vignettes of his friends and acquaintances in *Hail and Farewell* (1911, 1912, 1914) for which *Memoirs of my Dead Life* (1906) with its memories of various love affairs had been a lively rehearsal. His biographer, Joseph Hone, remarked that in later life Moore when mentioning an episode with a woman would usually say that he was now coming home 'to write an account of it for his new book'. His brother, Colonel Maurice Moore, said his adventures were 'half imagination, half reality'.

With the first volume of *Hail and Farewell* about to be published it was time to leave Dublin for London. Moore sold his estate to the Land Commission, and, after repaying mortgages, received between twenty-five and thirty thousand pounds; he retained Moore Hall and about five hundred acres around it. He had in the 'nineties broken the original settlement of the property upon his brother Maurice, the second son, though they were then on good terms. But their estrangement had increased steadily until, in 1911, Colonel Maurice Moore and his family left Moore Hall. (The house was never again occupied. It was burnt down in 'the Troubles' in 1923, and Moore eventually received £7,000 in compensation.) A house in Belgravia, 121 Ebury Street, seemed suitable, and Moore lived here from 1911 until his death in 1933. He made a few trips to Ireland, and a visit to France was virtually an annual event, with Dujardin often acting as his host. He also visited the Holy Land in 1913. Having written *The Apostle* (1911), a melodramatic play about St. Paul's finding Jesus still alive, he wanted to deal again with the biblical past, and to get the background right. He spent fourteen months writing *The Brook Kerith*, concentrating now on the character of Jesus rather than that of Paul, keeping the stream of his ideas and narrative flowing continuously and melodiously.

This style of his animates *A Storyteller's Holiday* (1918), but in these somewhat contrived tales Moore had to rely upon James Stephens's help with the dialogue. This was the first of his works to be issued in the limited and expensive editions in which the rest of his writings continued to be published in the first instance, before going into cheaper editions. By this means of publication he generally earned at least two thousand pounds on each book.

In 1918 he began to think up *Héloïse and Abélard* (1921), spending three years on it, travelling in France to absorb atmosphere, consulting many friends on points of detail, and developing for the first time his method of dictating about 1,500 or 2,000 words a day, then later revising the whole book. This was a laborious method of writing which, as a letter to a friend put it, made his life pass 'in loneliness and composition'. He saw his friends by appointment only, but he enjoyed regular meetings at Tonks's house, and at Sir Edmund Gosse's. Nancy Cunard, Charles Morgan, David Garnett, Mrs. Belloc Lowndes were added to his friends; there were his older friends, John Eglinton, Richard Best, Oliver Gogarty, Mr. and Mrs. St. John Hutchinson, whom he saw from time to time. There were houses he visited; he had many correspondents; the routine of his own house was watched over by his housekeeper, Clara Warville. It was an agreeable life, darkened only by kidney and prostate troubles from 1927 onwards. He was not strong enough for a major operation, and his friends often found him difficult. Sir John Thomson-Walker, the surgeon, helped him a great deal, became a close friend, and Moore's last completed book, *Aphrodite in Aulis* (1930), was dedicated to him.

The last years of Moore's life were filled with work. He revised his writings constantly, always polishing, removing obstacles and obscurities that might hinder the progress of the tale. He told Geraint Goodwin that if he had a tombstone he would like this written on it: 'Here lies George Moore, who looked upon corrections as the one morality.' He followed *Héloïse and Abélard* with *Ulick and Soracha* (1926), a story of thirteenth-century Ireland. He made a delightful translation of *Daphnis and Chloë* (1924) which gave scope to his skill in story-telling; he wrote more essays, the *Conversations in Ebury Street* (1924) and *A Communication to My Friends* (1933), as well as plays and short stories. At eighty he was an impressive figure in the world of letters. Though he himself sometimes thought his merits had been overlooked by that world of letters, of scholarship, and of politics, he was praised generously in a message in *The Times*, signed by many distinguished writers, which recognized his single-mindedness, his toiling in the perfection of his craft, his effect upon the users of the language and his revival of the art of narrative.

He died, regretting the fact that he seemed unable to accomplish *A Communication to My Friends*, 'telling the story of how writing was forced upon me and the persecution I have undergone for forty years and which is just ended, leaving me a wreck'. He was fundamentally a serious artist, a conscious writer, who through his forty years of work managed to create his own style and to make it the flexible expression of his own personality. He wrote in his *Confessions* that he came into the world

apparently with a nature like a smooth sheet of wax, bearing no impress, but capable of receiving any; of being moulded into all shapes. Nor am I exaggerating when I say I think that I might equally have been a Pharaoh, an ostler, a pimp, an archbishop, and that in the fulfilment of the duties of each a certain measure of success would have been mine.

The result of his experience of life was to make him a mixture of naivety and shrewdness, of mischievousness and an acute awareness of his own limitations. He became a personality filled with apprehensions of beauty and ecstasy, as well as of the absurd, a writer always sharply and persistently aware of the mystery and terrifying speed and shortness of human life.

II

THE NOVELS AND STORIES

Moore has his secure place in the history of the English novel. Most readers, for instance, will have read or know of *Esther Waters*, with the new dimension of naturalism it brought into English writing; they will also know how he developed after 1903 a new kind of prose, a blend of the written and spoken word peculiarly his own achievement. But how many realize how much more there is to Moore, the novelist, than the achievement of his best-known novel or to Moore the raconteur than the apparently artless gossip of *Hail and Farewell*? Of the early works, for example, there is the unusual felicity of *A Drama in Muslin*, foreshadowing the limpidity and brilliance of *The Lake*. The maturity of *The Brook Kerith* and the virtuosity of *Héloïse and Abélard* round off a quintet of novels extremely varied in subject-matter, imaginatively rich and supremely readable. These are his outstanding novels: but there is much to be enjoyed in the others, and this survey will mention them briefly as well as concentrating on Moore's major work.

When Moore looked back at his first novel *A Modern Lover* (1883) in 1917, he thought it the book of a young man who 'in a moment of inspiration, hit upon an excellent anecdote, and being without literary skill to unfold it, devised an uncouth text out of his memories of Balzac, Zola and Goncourt'. He summarized the book neatly:

Three women undertake to work for a young man's welfare: a work-girl, a rich woman, and a lady of high degree. All contribute something, and the young man is put on a high pedestal. One worshipper retains her faith, one loses hers partially, and one altogether.

Filled with revulsion as he re-read the book he finally decided that a new book could be moulded around it, and the Preface to the new version, *Lewis Seymour and Some Women* (1917), tells us engagingly how joyously he dictated and completed the work in three months.

His early desire was to observe and record accurately: the wish to tell a story was, perhaps, a later rationalization. This novel broke new ground in its first version and allowed Moore to portray his knowledge of art and a somewhat flashy view of fashionable life. He was writing an often clumsy English, not to be compared with that of the later version, which has some urbane satire on the relations of the sexes and is more efficiently told as a story: neither version, however, is fully satisfactory.

A Mummer's Wife (1885) was begun with the hope of being, as he wrote to the French novelist, 'Zola's ricochet in England'. He was applying the French Naturalistic method to English material, to the lives of actors in a provincial setting: he spent several weeks with a touring company, and he listened to many stories of the lives of actors and actresses. Out of this came a much more lively interplay of characters than he had achieved in his first novel. Kate Ede, who is seduced by Dick Lennox, is drawn with great sensitivity as well as realism, for Moore had developed and deepened his understanding of personality, of the effect of one sex upon the other, of the human heart; and the treatment of the scenery and the action, despite the mediocre, plain prose style, was sharper than before, more effective and indeed much more frank than anything Moore's contemporaries dared give the public. His desire to escape the bondage of the libraries (evinced in *Literature at Nurse, or Circulating Morals*) had no doubt sharpened his powers of shocking their particular audience. The realism of the early part of the book gives credence to the developing hysteria and violence of the heroine, who is always measured against the stolid matter-of-factness of Dick Lennox.

With *A Drama in Muslin* (1886), however, Moore developed a much more complex theme and treatment of it, and this novel is still most rewarding to read. In it he describes the two Irelands, of gentry and peasantry, during the tensions of the period of the Land League which was set up in 1879. The peasants, exasperated by evictions and bad agricultural seasons, were using weapons of boycott, and their 'No-Rent' campaign was very effective. There were shootings of landlords and their agents until the 1881 Act at last gave the tenants a right in the land without destroying the right of the landlord; it also reduced rents by twenty per cent. Further Land Acts of 1887, 1891 and 1903 were to make Ireland a country of peasant proprietors, and Moore had read the writing on the wall. He was a humane man, who, though he liked the social standing of being a landlord, realized instinctively that the era of the ascendancy was virtually over. The novel, therefore, draws a contrast between the social glitter and tinsel of the Viceregal Court in Dublin and the uneasiness, even boredom, of life in the big houses and lesser Georgian mansions, whose occupants were perpetually conscious of 'the disturbed state of the country'. Chapter Thirteen, for instance, is one of the scenes dissimilar yet interdependent, which are still technically interesting; it is a piece of *montage* which gives an alternating account of the arguments taking place in front of the house between peasants and their landlord and his agent, and of those occurring inside the house between the landlord's wife and an army captain, an unsuccessful suitor for her daughter. The human relationship of the girl and her lover is affected by the general situation:

From the drawing-room window Mrs. Barton watched the conflict. On one side she saw her daughter's beautiful white face becoming the prize of a penniless officer; on the other she saw the pretty furniture, the luxurious idleness, the very silk dress on her back being torn from them, and distributed among a crowd of Irish-speaking, pig-keeping peasants.

The girl, Olive Barton, is one of several well-born (and some not quite so well-born) girls who have grown up together in Galway, and who are presented and dine and dance during the Dublin season. Moore hated this marriage market: he was, like Ibsen, convinced that woman was more than a domestic animal. He had read *A Doll's House* when half-way through his own story, but remarked, so he says in the Preface to the 1915 edition of *A Drama in Muslin*, that he was himself writing of a puritan heroine, 'but not a sexless puritan, and if women cannot win their freedom without leaving their sex behind they had better remain slaves, for a slave with his sex is better than a free eunuch'. He thought that Olive's sister, Alice Barton, was a more objective portrayal than Ibsen's Nora, and this girl is drawn with dignity. She thinks for herself; she begins to write professionally because she does not regard the capture of a husband as the prime aim of her life. She is no prig, however, and supports the harum-scarum May, who has an illegitimate child; eventually she marries a dispensary doctor. To realize herself she has to resist the activities of her mother, who is drawn ruthlessly in all her vulgarity and energy.

The novel has some unevenness in style. It matches the richness, the bustle and crowding, the hectic excitements and the ensuing enervations of its social scenes with a voluptuous prose. Here is a portion of the famous description of the dressmaker's shop:

Lengths of white silk clear as the notes of violins playing in a minor key; white poplin falling into folds statuesque as the bass of a fugue by Bach; yards of ruby velvet, rich as an air from Verdi played on the piano; tender green velvet, pastoral as hautboys heard beneath trees in a fair Arcadian vale; blue turquoise faille francaise fanciful as the twinkling of a guitar twanged by a Watteau shepherd; gold brocade, sumptuous as

organ tones swelling through the jewelled twilight of a nave; scarves and
trains of midnight blue profound as the harmonic snoring of a bassoon.

The Misses Robinson, whom he used to visit, read him out a
passage which they had added in the margin of their copy:
'Everything was represented there, from the light clarinette
of the embroidered lace handkerchief to the profound
trombone of the red flannel pantaloons.' How could he
write such a thing, they asked, and he fell into their trap and
defended the phrase he had never used. He later saw himself
like 'a hound yelping at every trace of scent' in this book.
He records the serious conversations and the gossip with
skill; he catches the crippled Cecilia's religious attacks on
sensuous life in suitably matching tortuous prose. He contrasts the life of wretched cabin and glittering salon effectively; he describes the scenery with economical sensitivity;
he analyzes the situation of women. And the story holds us
with its mixture of satire, objectivity, and insight. It is an
unreasonably neglected novel, and it is also a piece of highly
significant social history.

When did the author of *A Drama in Muslin* change,
Moore asked himself in 1915, and answered himself with
1888, the year of the *Confessions* and *Spring Days*. He wrote
four novels which he did not include in his collected works.
In *A Mere Accident* (1887) he had attempted to capture both
the monastic spirit and its opposite, the 'sleepy smug
material' of Sussex. The model for the hero of the novel was
Edward Martyn, and Moore drew in him a somewhat
paradoxical aesthetic ascetic who ran his estates efficiently,
collected Monets and Renoirs, read mediaeval Latin authors
as well as Pater and Schopenhauer, and liked Wagner and
Palestrina. His mother tried to get him to marry and
eventually he fell in love with a young girl, who was,
however, assaulted by a tramp and died melodramatically
after a fall from a window. The novel shows Moore's
ability to make use of his friends' characters and to get his
material in order, for he drew heavily upon his friends'

knowledge, in this case of mediaeval Latin and music. The story appeared again as 'John Norton' in *Celibates* (1895), and a comparison of the two versions shows the great speed with which Moore's technique was advancing.

Spring Days (1888) was intended as a prelude to a trilogy, which would give a large sweeping survey of human nature. It told the story of three English girls in Sussex who fail to marry, but the narrative wandered a little and the hero, Frank Escott, heir to an Irish peerage, is not an interesting enough dreamer. The trilogy was to deal, first with young men in London, next with a servant's view of servants and finally with the attitudes of old people to their children. *Mike Fletcher* (1889) mainly describes an Irish journalist, a second-rate cad about town, and a complete failure; the other characters were Frank Escott and John Norton. The idea of a serious novel about servants occurred to him shortly after *A Drama in Muslin* was published; it promised to be more human than *Mike Fletcher*. (Mention of this novel irritated him intensely in later life, so much had he come to dislike its lack of order and development.) He told Madame Lanza that he intended to bathe himself in 'the simplest and most naïve emotions, the daily bread of humanity'. But before completing this story of servants he spent the winter of 1890-91 writing *Vain Fortune* (1892) for the *Lady's Pictorial*, where it was published serially under a *nom de plume* and illustrated by Maurice Greiffenhagen. This novel, not as bad as has sometimes been alleged, nor yet, as Moore wrote in a letter, a pot-boiler, has a plot dealing with the frustrations of an unsuccessful author and the girl whom he disinherits. She falls in love with him and commits suicide when he marries her companion.

By 1893 he had completed *Esther Waters:* his plan he announced to Madame Lanza in a letter:

. . it is all about servants—servants devoured by betting. It begins in a house in the country where there are race horses. Towards the end of the book—past the middle—the servants set up a public house. They cannot

get custom unless they have betting. Then come the various tragedies of
the bar—the hairdresser who cuts his throat—the servant who loses
thirty years' character for six shillings—the woman who pledges the
plate to give her lover money to bet with. The human drama is the story
of the servant girl with an illegitimate child, how she saves the child from
the baby farmers, her endless temptations to get rid of it and to steal for
it. She succeeds in bringing up her boy, and the last scene is when she is
living with her first mistress in the old place, ruined and deserted. The
race horses have ruined masters as well as the servants.

The book was very well received; it sold well, and the
circulating libraries gave way, Mudie at first, but Smith's
after an argument in which Moore proved that they had
lost £1,500 by not taking *Esther Waters*. The novel was his
tribute to England, 'Pecksniff done seriously, and if the feat
does not seem impossible, with love'.

Esther Waters contains Moore's knowledge of horse racing
and of betting, and their effects upon human life. There are
the great kaleidoscopic scenes of Derby day, the boom of the
'great mob', the cockney crowd; there is Mr. Leopold in his
pantry, a picture of the butler of Moore Hall; there are the
scenes, too, of the lying-in hospital, and there is the baby-
farmer. Balzac inspired this work, and in it Moore achieves
a story of commonplace heroism. He begins with the
description of the receding train as it appeared to the girl of
twenty, and Chapter 44 begins in exactly similar words;
but the train is seen now by a woman of seven or eight and
thirty; and we realize now with a jolt how much has
happened to her in the eighteen years since she first arrived
to be a kitchenmaid. His picture of how Esther is deserted
and how she wrestles with life to bring up her son is realistic,
but it is also written with an innate if unobtrusive compassion.
It is a humane book, matching its acute observation with
sensitive understanding.

In *Evelyn Innes* (1898) Moore described the battle within
an opera singer's heart between her religious feelings and her
delight in the pleasures of the world. She is torn between

love for Sir Owen Asher (probably modelled on a mixture of Arthur Symons's intellectualism and Sir William Eden's aristocratic sophistication), and for Ulick the Celtic musician (modelled in the first edition upon Yeats, and later upon AE). The novel reflects Moore's own development: he drew upon Arnold Dolmetsch for the character of Evelyn's father, the musician; he attended some of the informal concerts held in the Dolmetschs' house in Dulwich where he set part of the novel, and he learned much from Dolmetsch and from Arthur Symons about Renaissance and baroque music. This novel is one of the first to make use of music as a background. It reflects, as well as Moore's own interest in Wagner, a good deal of fashionable aestheticism. Factual information gives solidity to the story, which is also based upon Moore's own progress in the fashionable world and his financial success. The furniture and the Aubusson carpet in this novel are described with the loving attention that his own similar possessions were receiving in his new flat in Victoria Street, into which he had moved from the Temple.

Evelyn Innes is one of the novels in which he was conducting his education publicly but the sequel, *Sister Teresa*, has less of this interest, for in it Moore, possibly stimulated by Mrs. Craigie's conversion to Roman Catholicism, was writing an account of life in a convent which allowed him to explore the religious impulse more fully, but with less certainty of touch, as though he were himself affected by Evelyn's hesitation between life in the convent or outside it. Finally, however, the novel ends with her at peace, but with the reader probably sharing the view of the priest quoted by Yeats, who remarked of the novel, 'everything is there of the convent, except the religious life'. In this novel Moore was echoing the current interest in the opposition of art and reality, spirit and flesh; and the heroine withdraws to the convent's ritual, disappointed by her bid for individual artistic freedom.

A reversal of this progress takes place in *The Lake* (1905), the first of Moore's fully symbolist novels. Some of the hints for it exist in *A Drama in Muslin*, where the influence of Huysmans was clear. In that novel Moore had explored the complications of character, and had shown signs of matching it with a less drab style. Now he was to explore the complexities of style also and, in so doing, to create his own contribution to English prose, the melodic line. The story of *The Lake* is relatively simple. A priest drives a pregnant but unmarried schoolteacher from his parish; he later corresponds with her, and falls in love with her, without ever seeing her again. His desire for the world increases, his belief diminishes, until finally he leaves his clothes beside the lake and swims across it, to leave his parish and Ireland, and begin another life. Father Oliver Gogarty (the name was chosen in mockery of that unpriest-like figure Oliver St. John Gogarty, who appears as Buck Mulligan in Joyce's *Ulysses*) walks by the lakeside, and the story slowly unfolds itself with a convincing, compellingly persuasive development. The technical achievement is superb; the movement from *Esther Waters* to *The Lake* is parallel to that of Joyce from *Dubliners* to *A Portrait of the Artist* (and *Hail and Farewell* captures another aspect—Moore's life in Ely Place—of that Dublin which is also so brilliantly immortalised in Joyce's Eccles Street in *Ulysses*). The change was brought about after he had completed the stories of *The Untilled Field*, in which he had examined some of the sterility and sadness he saw in Irish life, where he attributed poverty and emigration to the work of a puritanical, priestly church. These earlier stories, especially 'The Wedding Gown', 'The Widow' and 'So on he fares' are masterly pieces of story-telling, spare, economical but highly emotive.

The Lake opens with a passage that shows us the kind of association Moore is to evoke throughout the novel between scene and mood; he was writing about the place in which he himself grew up and he wrote with deep feeling:

It was one of those enticing days at the beginning of May when white clouds are drawn about the earth like curtains. The lake lay like a mirror that someone had breathed upon, the brown islands showing through the mist faintly, with gray shadows falling into the water, blurred at the edges. The ducks were talking softly in the reeds, the reeds themselves were talking; and the water lapped softly about the smooth limestone shores. But there was an impulse in the gentle day, and, turning from the sandy spit, Father Oliver walked to and fro along the disused cart-track about the edge of the wood, asking himself if he were going home, knowing quite well that he could not bring himself to interview his parishioners that morning. On a sudden resolve to escape from anyone that might be seeking him, he went into the wood and lay down on the warm grass, and admired the thickly-tasselled branches of the tall larches swinging above him.

After the priest has reached his decision to leave his parish, the lake is still there, its serenity matching the excitement with which he contemplates the oneness of Nature. 'Every man', he says, 'has a lake in his heart', and Moore carries the symbolism forward through the novel, building up his suggestions with subtlety through the apparent simplicity of the famous melodic line:

He walked along the shore feeling like an instrument that had been tuned. His perception seemed to have been indefinitely increased, and it seemed to him as if he were in communion with the stones in the earth and the clouds in heaven; it seemed to him as if the past and the future had become one.

The moment was one of extraordinary sweetness, never might such a moment happen in his life again. The earth and sky were enfolding in one tender harmony of rose and blue, the blue shading down to grey, and the lake floated amid vague shores, vaguely as a dream floats through sleep. The swallows were flying high, quivering overhead in the blue air. There was a sense of security and persuasion and loveliness in the evening.

The Brook Kerith (1916) is often described as a prose epic and fully deserves the name. It is constructed with skill, and its conversational style has a directness, freshness and spontaneity which gives it warmth and colour. In it Moore retells the story of the New Testament with the difference that in the account which he puts in the mouth of Joseph of

Arimathea, Jesus has not died on the cross, but has been rescued by Joseph. He is later discovered by Paul, who seeks refuge among the community of Essenes among whom Jesus has lived as a shepherd in the wilderness for twenty years. Paul at first believes that Jesus is a madman, then fears he may return to Jerusalem to destroy his own work. But Jesus tells him that we must learn to live for ourselves and to suffer our fellows to do likewise; all learning, he says, 'comes out of ourselves, and no one may communicate his thought; for his thought was given to him for himself alone'. The Biblical imagery and rhythms add to the epic quality of the story: it is simple and the narrative unfolds effectively, action, description, thought and speech blending in a pattern which provides variation and tension as well as information and reflection. It is easy to read, and it reads aloud superbly; it is spacious, dignified and captivating, an example of the supreme flexibility of the art of a great story-teller whose essential seriousness of artistic purpose is enlivened by the subtle humour and by the inconsequential trivia which give to the novel its feeling of concrete detail:

Hast slept well, Paul, and hath sleep refreshed thee and given thee strength to pursue thy journey? Paul answered that he was very weary, but however weary must struggle on to Caesarea. Thy strength will not suffer thee to get farther than Bethennabrio, and thy sandals will need mending even to reach the village. And seating himself on a smooth stone Paul watched Jesus's hand tying new thongs, wondering if the madman's mind was still set on Jerusalem and if he would go thither as soon as he (Paul) was safely out of the ways of the Jews. Each shut himself within the circle of his own mind, and the silence was not broken till Paul began to fear that Jesus was plotting against him; and to distract Jesus's mind from his plots, if he were weaving any, he began to compare the country they were passing through with Galilee, and forthright Jesus began to talk to Paul of Peter and John and James, sons of Zebedee, mentioning their appearances, voices, manner of speech, telling of their boats, their fishing tackle, the fish-salting factory of Magdala, Dan, and Joseph his son. He spoke a winning story of the fishing life round the lake, without mention of miracles, for it was not to his purpose to convince Paul of any spiritual power he might have enjoyed, but rather of his own simple humanity. And Paul listened, still believing his guide to be a madman. If thou hadst not run away crying: He is mad! he is mad! thou wouldst have heard how my crucifixion was brought about; how my eyes opened in the tomb and—Interrupting Jesus, Paul hastened to assure him that if he cried out: He is mad! he is mad! he had spoken unwittingly, the words being put into his mouth by the sickness in which Jesus had discovered him. And the sickness, he admitted, might have been brought about by the shock of hearing thee speak of thyself as the Messiah. But, Paul, I did not speak of myself as the Messiah, but as an Essene who during some frenzied months believed himself to be the Messiah. But shepherd, Paul answered, the Messiah promised to the Jews was Jesus of Nazareth, who was raised by his Father from the dead, and thou sayest that thou art the same. If thou didst once believe thyself to be the Messiah thou hast repented thy blasphemy. In the desert these twenty years, Jesus answered. But not till now did I know my folly had borne fruit, and that Joseph knew a story had been set going; or it may be that the story was not set going till after his death. Now it seems too late to go into the field thou hast sown with tares instead of corn. To which Paul answered: It is my knowledge of thy life among rocks that prompts me to listen to thee. The field I have sown like every other field has some tares in it, but it is full of corn ripening fast which will be ready for the reaping when it shall please the Lord to descend with his own son, Jesus of Nazareth, from the skies. As soon as the words: Jesus of Nazareth, had left his lips Paul regretted them, and upon a sudden resolve not to utter another word that might offend the madman's beliefs, he began to tell that he had brought hope to the beggar, to the outcast, to the slave; though this world was but a den of misery to them, another world was coming to which they might look forward in full surety. And many, he said, that led vile lives are now God-fearing men and women who, when the daily work is done, go forth in the evening to beseech the multitude to give some time to God. In every field there are tares, but there are fewer in my field than in any other, and that I hold to be the truth; and seeing that Jesus was listening to his story he began to relate his theology, perplexing Jesus with his doctrines, but interesting him with the glad tidings that the burden of the law had been lifted from all. If he had stopped there all would have been well, so it seemed to Jesus, whose mind was not able to grasp why a miracle should be necessary to prove to men that the love of God was in the heart rather than in observances, and the miracle that Paul continued to relate with much unction seemed to him crude; yet he once believed that God was pleased to send his only begotten son to redeem the world by his death on a cross. A strange conception truly. And while he was thinking these things Paul felling to tell his dogma concerning predestination, and he was anxious that Jesus should digest his reply to Mathias, who had said that predestination conflicted with the doctrine of salvation for all. But Jesus, who was of Mathias's opinion, refrained from expressing himself definitely on the point, preferring to forget Paul, so that he might better consider if he would be able to make plain to Paul that miracles bring no real knowledge of God to man, and that our conscience is the source of our knowledge of God and that perhaps a providence flourishes beyond the world. (ch. XLI)

Héloïse and Abélard (1921) has a rich content: in this philosophical romance Moore mixes thought and tragedy, description and story. Tension begins in Canon Fulbert's house overlooking the Seine; the lovers, the Canon's niece and the brilliant academic, travel through the forests to Britanny with a background of spring sights and sounds; there is always a background unobtrusive yet atmospheric; there is both movement and contemplation:

But to reach Chécy before nightfall they would have to hasten, and the innkeeper told them that the road through the forest looped so that the village of Lorris might be taken into the circuit; but there was no need for him to follow this winding, he would find a by-path across certain low hills which he could not miss. Abélard did not feel sure that the by-path might not be missed, but to hear the road explained out again would be merely a waste of time, and so they hastened towards the forest in a sort of half-knowledge of the way, allowing the horses to trot a little, thinking that they might draw rein when they passed through the fringe of birch-trees that encircled with their pallor the great district of pines that showed in black masses over against Etampes. Now we are well within the forest, Abélard said, as much in the forest as if we were in the middle of it; and he asked Héloïse to peep over the undergrowth that lined the rutted path down which they were riding, so that she might see the pines rising up naked and bare some fifty or sixty feet, some straight, some leaning, in endless aisles. Like the spears, Héloïse said, of Crusaders going into battle; and how penetrating is the smell of the resin. But the pines were in patches only, and the forest passed quickly into rocky hillsides overgrown with oak and beech; and so faint was the path they followed that Abélard often asked Héloïse and Madelon to draw rein while he went forward in search of the path. For if we all went forward together, he said, we should not be able to go back to where the path ends: a tree is no sure landmark; one forgets which tree, and wanders in a circle. I've got it, he cried to them, and they came forward, the forest getting lonelier as they proceeded into it.

All bird cries have ceased, and we hear only the sighing of the boughs, Héloïse said, and the smell of the forest is different from all other smells; a more mysterious smell is about, a smell of earth and moss. There is also a warm smell, said Madelon, that reminds me of our Brittany forests, the great forest about Clisson, where we shall be—Héloïse, myself and my boy—before the month's end, should we catch a fast-sailing barge from Orléans. Did he not say that a little over three leagues from Etampes we should find the by-path that would save us several leagues' journey? Abélard asked, and some hundreds of feet after he told them to rein in while he went on ahead in search of the path. Here it is, he cried, from a clearing; we have but to follow the path that leads through the hollows younder up to the rising ground that the innkeeper spoke of. He spoke to me of oak-trees, and here they are. And they rode beneath the boughs not yet in full leaf, following the path as it wound through hollows, losing it and finding it amid rocks, pushing their way through thickets that seemed impenetrable at a distance but did not prove so hard to force through as they had appeared. There is a rutted way under the brambles, Abélard said; cattle and horses have been through here; and stooping low in their saddles, they broke through somehow, losing bits of clothing in the passage. Soon after the path led them up hills, through thorn and hazel mingled with inter-spaces, till it brought them to a heath, and Abélard said: those pines standing so solitary at the end of the lake embedded in rocks are the trees the inn-keeper told me I was to look out for. We have not missed the way, he continued; look back and see the forest that we have come through. And he pointed to a dark ragged line of pines flowing down the northern sky. But is our way to the right or to the left? Madelon asked. To the left, he answered; we have to ride southward, keeping the setting sun on our right. (ch. XVI)

Abélard's arrogant ambition, Héloïse's agonized love, their joint readiness to lie in pursuance and defence of love, are part of the whole life of the book. Moore's sensualism, and his occasional mischievousness underlie the simplicity of the story; his attitude is consistent. The peasant driving his cart, and Madelon, the Canon's servingwoman, are two examples of an earthy contrast opposed to the intellectualism of the lovers. The romance gains in depth because the conversations and thoughts of Héloïse and Abélard are sharply focussed against a very crowded background of cities and convents, of trouvéres, of classical culture, even of the contentions between nominalists and realists. Moore took immense trouble to get his picture of eleventh century life right. Its complexity is gained through digressions and repetitions in the talk and the learning; the liveliness comes from its picture of the ceaseless sifting of the human mind on earth; the resolution rests upon a human will to believe in heaven and immortal happiness.

Ulick and Soracha (1926) deals with mediaeval Ireland, but it lacks the sheer beauty of *Héloïse and Abélard;* and *Aphrodite in Aulis* (1930) runs the risk of appearing disjointed, for its author's habit of digression and complication is not under the fine architectonic control he had earlier displayed.

It is perhaps fitting to conclude a brief account of Moore's fiction with some comment on the five stories—'a single narrative divided into five chapters'—of *Celibate Lives* (1927) which were based on earlier work in *Celibates* (1895), *A Story-Teller's Holiday* (1918) and *In Single Strictness* (1922). They show Moore's developed artistry in illustrating, in smooth narrative, with calm detachment, the finer points of character, indeed his never ceasing fascination with human motive and behaviour. That the stories were about women reminds us that he had remarked in the *Confessions* that he was enthralled by 'the mystery of petticoats' and confessed in the *Memoirs* that his thoughts ran upon women as the legitimate object of men's thoughts. His own thoughts he translated into an objective portrayal of women's role in a society within which they were moving to greater freedom; his apparently detached portraits were drawn not only with skill but with deep sympathy.

III

THE PLAYS

In all Moore wrote eleven plays, the first two of which, *Worldliness* (1874) and *Martin Luther* (1879), were not performed. Several managers, including Hare and Beerbohm Tree, refused his next play, *The Strike at Arlingford* (1893), but after a few years Moore turned its five acts into three, and it was performed in February 1893. He was greatly attracted by the Ibsen-like qualities of Martyn's *The Heather Field*, and when Martyn's next play, *The Tale of a Town*, was disappointing, he took it over and it was produced, under Moore's name, as *The Bending of the Bough* (1900). He explained the situation thus:

> I am afraid Martyn suffered a good deal. He says I spoil[ed] his play but that is an illusion. I recast the play, but not enough. I should have written a new play on the subject . . . Then Edward said he could not sign it, and he refused to let it be played anonymously, so I had to sign it.

The play revolves around nationalist and unionist attitudes. The potential leader gives up the struggle because of his love for a girl, and his backsliding is received with philosophical serenity by the nationalist *eminence grise*. It is a dull play, but in the politically charged atmosphere of the Dublin of that time it was well received.

Moore's next collaboration was with Yeats, and their work on *Diarmuid and Grania* led to much disagreement between them. The play was put on in Dublin in 1901, but the critics there regarded the treatment of the heroic legend as unsatisfactory. The susceptibilities of nationalists could be easily upset. Moore wrote to his brother that 'they first of all enjoyed the play, and having enjoyed it they repented in sackcloth and ashes, and I really believe that the repentance was much greater than their enjoyment of the play'.

His next adventure into drama was *The Apostle* (1911)

which dealt with a meeting between Jesus and Paul after the crucifixion: it was hastily published, but contains his fascinating *Prefatory Letter on Reading the Bible for the First Time*. In 1906 Moore had begun work on a dramatic version of *Esther Waters* and Lennox Robinson was called in to help with the dialogue—Moore's old weakness—in the second act. The play was performed twice, but unsuccessfully, at the Apollo Theatre. Moore, however, was not put off by its reception, and resumed work on *Elizabeth Cooper* (1913), which was produced by the Stage Society in 1913. Moore had enlisted the aid of Mrs. Craigie in this play in 1904, and five years later was helped by Dujardin (who produced the French version, *Clara Florise*, at the Comedie Royale). Moore's correspondence with a foreign lady of title, begun some ten years earlier, formed the basis of the plot. In the play the foreign countess mistakes the young secretary of the author for his employer and, in one version, marries him. Another rewriting appeared as *The Coming of Gabrielle* (1921) which was rehearsed in 1921 but finally abandoned. It was a near-miss.

The Brook Kerith led to a second play entitled *The Apostle* (1923); this added a scene to the novel, but was also lacking in good dialogue. Moore followed it with *The Making of an Immortal* (1928), an amusing Shakespearean conceit, with clever character sketches; this was well received after its production at the Arts Theatre in 1928.

The Passing of the Essenes (1930) was yet another handling of the theme of *The Brook Kerith*, and the relationship of Jesus and Paul. This time the reception was warm, the play's run extended, and Moore even went to see it himself. He came back as critical of actors as ever, since the

poor play did not come out as it should have come out, and what pleasure is it to me that other people liked it? I wanted to like it and I didn't. The uninspired actors were between me and it all the time.

Moore was his own best actor, and his best writing self-dramatization. His weakness was inability to write good dialogue; his strength was in duologue, provided he was inventing both parts of the conversation.

IV

AUTOBIOGRAPHIES AND ESSAYS

Moore's *Confessions of a Young Man* (1888) were written when he was thirty-six; they describe his life in Paris; they record his impressions of Manet, Degas, and Renoir, of Zola, and of Verlaine and Mallarmé. The book gives us an excellent impression of aestheticism, and of Moore's youthful desire to shock and astonish people. It was certainly original, and the self-portrait is one of Moore as he seemed to Theodore Dorret, 'a golden-haired fop, an aesthete before the days of Wilde . . . his manners were amusing and his French very funny'. Always, Dorret remarked, he remained a gentleman and would never associate with those he thought to be below his rank as an Irish landlord. As a result he describes his early life with satiric detachment. The *Memoirs of my Dead Life* (1906) contained more material likely to astonish, if taken seriously, rather than to shock. 'The Lovers of Orelay' became famous as an account of an elderly man's adventure with a young woman in France, told with comic relish, as well as some naivety, as in the account of the purchase of the silk nightshirt. The volume contained memories of Mayo, London, Paris and Sussex (a moving account of Mrs. Bridger's death). The love stories reflected his comment that his thoughts ran on women: 'On what would you have them run? On coppermines? Woman is the legitimate subject of all men's thoughts.' When he wrote the *Memoirs* he was fifty-four; his energies were increasingly occupied by his writing and rewriting, and this gave him a reputation for cold detachment. It is true that he used his friends as material for his writing, but he used himself even more. During his stay in Ireland at the beginning of the century his style had developed from the flowing narrative of the stories of *The Untilled Field* into the complexities, the repetitions, linkages and cadences of *The Lake*. There he became the raconteur, there he changed from his livelier youth into a search for and a discovery of himself. The *Memoirs* show his flair for maintaining the fluidity of his tales, his mixture of speech and reflection, his blending of past and present thought.

Throughout the superb comedy of *Hail and Farewell*, which is his masterpiece, there runs the ground swell of his preoccupation with Protestantism as he imagined it, with the issues of life as he experienced them, emotionally and instinctively, often wilfully and impatiently. He was not concerned with the reputation of Moore the man; he cared deeply for the reputation of Moore the writer. And so *Hail and Farewell* is a devastating book: ironic, witty, provocative, even at times profound in its accounts of the men and women he observed around him in Dublin. His brilliant evocation of Edward Martyn, his delicate appreciation of AE, his caustic commentary on Yeats, contribute to our sense of human comedy.

The forthrightness of Moore's comments stemmed from his belief that once the veracity of a biographer (or autobiographer) is impugned the book becomes discredited and its value depreciated. And so he gives us magnificent scenes —the dinner in the Shelbourne Hotel, the bicycling around Tara, New Grange and Dowth with AE, as well as the account (which disturbed so many of his contemporaries) of the end of his affair with Stella. This is the artist at work— with the disciple he called Amico Moorini emerging at intervals to nudge his comic work into the risk of seeming farce—for flippancy and wilfulness have never appealed greatly to critics, however much they were an almost inevitable minor part of such an unusual talent as Moore's, committed to both the artistic and the ruthless rendering of a situation, a nuance, an anecdote, which would convey his own attitude of curiosity, of almost innocent interest, to the reader. He recreates yet again but with entirely new memories his days in the Temple, in Paris, in Mayo, in Sussex. With Whelan he avoids mass when staying with Edward Martyn, with whom he visits Bayreuth for *The Ring*. The flow of his mind is strong; he observes Lady Gregory and Yeats in the west of Ireland; he gives us vignettes of Dublin as he walks by the Liffey or the Dodder; he recounts conversations, and retells Dublin gossip: of how, for instance, Sir Thornley Stoker the surgeon collected his antiques:

... on the trail of a Sheraton sideboard and Naylor has been asked to keep it till an appendix should turn up. The Chinese Chippendale mirror over the drawing-room chimney-piece originated in an unsuccessful operation for cancer; the Aubusson carpet in the back drawing-room represents a hernia; the Renaissance bronze on the landing a set of gall-stones; the King Cloisonnee a floating kidney; the Buhl cabinet his opinion on an enlarged liver; and Lady Stoker's jewels a series of small operations performed over a term of years.

All of this is recounted with limpidity; the transitions from speech to thought, to memory, to speech again invite us to tour with him through reveries of rich reminiscence and ideas which are lively, stamped always with a zest and appreciation of living, with shrewdness and naivety.

These qualities permeate his critical prose also. *Avowals* (1919), for instance, contains opinions on literary works 'discovered' by Moore over the years. These are delivered with some panache, for, as Moore reminds us in Chapter XVI, his only affectation was complete naturalness, and on the subject of writing he held strong views. The English eighteenth-century novelists, Jane Austen and Pater, Tolstoi and Turgenev are discussed with vigour and delight. Moore did not read a great deal, but he had listened and discussed; he had formed his opinions and he gave them a curiously personal flavour:

In the fifties was the Word and it was with Flaubert, I said, and began to trace the origin of his reputation to a reaction against Byron, his going to Greece to die for an idea, to Chateaubriand's tomb, to pirates and brigands who had become so intolerable in literature that everybody welcomed the idea that a writer need not dine in a baronial hall among retainers, nor keep for pets pythons, eagles, wolves or jaguars, and of all it was pleasant to hear that Monsieur Flaubert spent much time at his window watching the Seine flowing by, thinking of the inevitable Word, which he never found till late in the evening. Everybody was delighted; fellow-feeling makes wondrous bed-fellows, and when it became known for certain that *Madame Bovary* was written in a dressing-gown, the reaction against romanticism carried the book along with it, and if this explanation prove inacceptable, we shall have to fall back on the depressing belief, for which, indeed, much can be said, that the masterpiece is but our mood, and that as soon as the mood passes—all moods except the Bible, Shakespeare and Sterne pass—the inspired and the uninspired are live as twins.

Conversations in Ebury Street (1924) ranges widely. Balzac, George Eliot and Hardy are discussed with zest. Then the artists Tonks, Steer, and Sickert are given life, and there follow further literary comments and speculations, among them enlightened praise of Anne Brontë's work. There is not, however, so much concentration as in the essays of *Avowals* which represented the flowering of Moore's literary views in the mid-summer of his career, with *Esther Waters*, *The Lake*, *The Brook Kerith*, *Héloïse and Abélard* and *Hail and Farewell* already achieved.

V

THE ACHIEVEMENT

Moore's achievement needs reconsideration. His works have been allowed to drop out of print—one hopes only temporarily—but his merits should not be ignored. For he is a writer of great skill, a serious writer who can give much pleasure to his readers. He affected the course of English fiction and the style of English prose; he developed his own literary personality; he was a man in whom imagination and narrative skill, capacity for industrious work and artistic conscience so fused that he produced fiction and fictionalized autobiography which has the timeless quality of all great art. He carries us on when we read him, and that is perhaps the secret of the enjoyment he can give: it is the art of the story-teller he develops and he appeals to our common delight in and enjoyment of a story well told.

GEORGE MOORE

A Select Bibliography

(Place of publication London, unless stated otherwise)

Bibliography:

BIBLIOGRAPHIES OF MODERN AUTHORS: NO. 3, GEORGE MOORE, by
I. A. Williams (1921).

'George Moore: A Bibliography, 1878-1921', by H. Danielson, in
J. Freeman, *A Portrait of George Moore* (1922).

'George Moore: An Annotated Bibliography of Writings About Him',
by H. E. Gerber, in *English Fiction in Transition (1880-1920)*, vol. ii,
no. 2 (parts i and ii), 1959, and Supplements; vol. III, no. ii, 1960;
vol. iv, no. 2, 1961

—the fullest and most accurate bibliography of Moore yet published.
The information (and sensible comments) are essential for any serious
study of Moore's work.

Collected Works:

THE WORKS OF GEORGE MOORE. 20 vols. (1933)
—the uniform edition.

THE WORKS OF GEORGE MOORE. 20 vols. (1937)
—the Ebury edition.

Separate Works:

WORLDLINESS. A COMEDY IN THREE ACTS (c. 1874)
—'The author believes, and hopes, that no copy of this, his first
published work, now exists.'—I. A. Williams.

FLOWERS OF PASSION (1878). *Verse*

MARTIN LUTHER. A TRAGEDY IN FIVE ACTS (1879). *Verse Drama*
—in collaboration with Bernard Lopez.

PAGAN POEMS (1881).

A MODERN LOVER. 3 vols. (1883). *Novel*
—re-written as *Lewis Seymour and Some Women*, 1917.

A MUMMER'S WIFE (1885). *Novel*
—French translation, Paris, 1888.

LITERATURE AT NURSE, OR CIRCULATING MORALS (1885). *Polemic*
—pamphlet on the selection of books at Mudie's Library.

A DRAMA IN MUSLIN. A REALISTIC NOVEL (1886)
—largely re-written as *Muslin*, 1915.
A MERE ACCIDENT (1887). *Novel*
—'John Norton' in *Celibates*, 1895, is a re-writing of this.
PARNELL AND HIS ISLAND (1887). *Sketches*
CONFESSIONS OF A YOUNG MAN (1888). *Autobiography*
—edited and annotated by Moore, 1904, 1917; revised edition, 1926; in Uniform edition, 1933.
SPRING DAYS. A REALISTIC NOVEL. A PRELUDE TO 'DON JUAN' (1888)
—with preface, 1912.
MIKE FLETCHER (1889). *Novel*
IMPRESSIONS AND OPINIONS (1891). *Criticism*
VAIN FORTUNE (1891). *Novel*
—revised 1895.
MODERN PAINTING (1893). *Criticism*
—enlarged, 1898.
THE STRIKE AT ARLINGFORD. A PLAY IN THREE ACTS (1893).
ESTHER WATERS (1894). *Novel*
—revised and privately printed, 1920; in Uniform edition, 1932; dramatic version, 1913.
CELIBATES (1895). *Stories*
—contains three tales: 'Mildred Lawson', 'John Norton', and 'Agnes Lahens'.
THE ROYAL ACADEMY, 1895 (1895). *Criticism*
—New Budget Extra, No. 1.
EVELYN INNES (1898). *Novel*
THE BENDING OF THE BOUGH. A COMEDY IN FIVE ACTS (1900).
'Literature and the Irish Language' (1901). *Criticism*
—in *Ideals in Ireland*, edited by Lady Gregory.
SISTER TERESA (1901). *Novel*
—continuation of *Evelyn Innes;* entirely re-written, 1928.
THE UNTILLED FIELD (1903). *Short Stories*
—part of the book was first published in Gaelic, Dublin, 1902; revised edition, 1926; in Uniform edition, 1932.
THE LAKE (1905). *Novel*
—revised edition, 1921; in Uniform edition, 1932.
MEMOIRS OF MY DEAD LIFE (1906). *Fictional autobiography*
—revised and enlarged 'Moore Hall' edition, 1921; revised for Uniform edition, 1928.
REMINISCENCES OF THE IMPRESSIONIST PAINTERS. Dublin (1906). *Memoirs.*

HAIL AND FAREWELL: A TRILOGY. 3 vols. (1911-14). *Autobiography*
—*Ave* 1911; *Salve* 1912; *Vale* 1914. Limited edition in two volumes, 1925; in Uniform edition, three volumes, 1933.

THE APOSTLE. A DRAMA IN THREE ACTS. Dublin (1911)
—revised, limited edition, 1923.

ELIZABETH COOPER. A COMEDY IN THREE ACTS. Dublin (1913).

MUSLIN (1915). *Novel*
—revision of *A Drama in Muslin;* in Uniform edition, 1932.

THE BROOK KERITH: A SYRIAN STORY (1916). *Novella*
—5th edition revised, 1921; revised for Uniform edition, 1927; limited edition with engravings by Stephen Gooden, 1929.

LEWIS SEYMOUR AND SOME WOMEN (1917). *Novel*
—revision of *A Modern Lover.*

A STORY-TELLER'S HOLIDAY (1918, limited edition). *Short Stories*
—revised edition in two volumes, including *Ulick and Soracha,* Uniform edition, 1928.

AVOWALS (1919, limited edition). *Criticism*
—in Uniform edition, 1924.

THE COMING OF GABRIELLE. A COMEDY IN THREE ACTS (1920, limited edition).

HÉLOISE AND ABÉLARD. 2 vols. (1921, limited edition). *Historical Romance*
—in Uniform edition, 1925.

FRAGMENTS FROM HÉLOISE AND ABÉLARD: ADDITIONS AND CORRECTIONS (1921).

IN SINGLE STRICTNESS (1922, limited edition). *Short Stories*
—revised as *Celibate Lives* for Uniform edition, 1927.

CONVERSATIONS IN EBURY STREET (1924, limited edition). *Criticism*
—revised for Uniform edition, 1930.

THE PASTORAL LOVES OF DAPHNIS AND CHLOË. DONE INTO ENGLISH (1924, limited edition). *Translation*
—from Longus. In Uniform edition with *Peronnik the Fool,* 1933.

PERONNIK THE FOOL. New York (1924). *Short Story*
—new limited edition, New York, 1926; revised limited edition, Eure, France, 1928; with engravings by Stephen Gooden, London, 1933; in Uniform edition with *The Pastoral Loves of Daphnis and Chloë,* 1933.

PURE POETRY. AN ANTHOLOGY (1924, limited edition). *Anthology*

ULICK AND SORACHA (1926, limited edition). *Novel*
—included in revised edition of *A Story-Teller's Holiday*, Uniform
edition, 1928.

THE MAKING OF AN IMMORTAL. A COMEDY IN ONE ACT. New York (1927).

A FLOOD. New York (1930). *Short Story*

APHRODITE IN AULIS (1930, limited edition). *Novel*
—revised for Uniform edition, 1931.

THE PASSING OF THE ESSENES. A DRAMA IN THREE ACTS (1930)
—limited edition of a further revision of *The Apostle*.

A COMMUNICATION TO MY FRIENDS (1933, limited edition). *Autobiography*
—in Uniform edition with *A Mummer's Wife*, 1933.

DIARMUID AND GRANIA. A PLAY IN THREE ACTS BY GEORGE MOORE AND
W. B. YEATS. In the *Dublin Magazine*, xxvi (April-June 1951)
—with an introductory note by William Becker.

Note: Moore also wrote introductions to Zola's *Piping Hot!* (1885),
Dostoevsky's *Poor Folk* (1894), and several other books.

Letters:

LETTERS FROM GEORGE MOORE TO EDOUARD DUJARDIN 1886-1922. New
York (1929)
—translated by 'John Eglinton' (William Magee).

LETTERS OF GEORGE MOORE. Bournemouth (1942)
—with an introduction by 'John Eglinton'. A frank and convincing
picture of Moore as a man.

GEORGE MOORE'S LETTERS TO LADY CUNARD, ed. R. Hart-Davis (1957)
—a record of the great sentimental friendship of Moore's life. Well-
edited.

Some Biographical and Critical Studies:

A PORTRAIT OF GEORGE MOORE IN A STUDY OF HIS WORK, by J. Freeman
(1922)
—the first full-scale study of Moore's works.

EDWARD MARTYN AND THE IRISH REVIVAL, by D. R. Gwynn (1930)
—appraises Moore's work for the Irish literary revival.

GEORGE MOORE, by H. Wolfe (1931)
—enthusiastic but dated.

EPITAPH ON GEORGE MOORE, by C. Morgan (1935)
—extremely good brief interpretation of Moore as man and writer.

THE LIFE OF GEORGE MOORE, by J. Hone (1936)
—the most important book written on Moore; detached, accurate, and well written; an admirable biography.

AS I WAS GOING DOWN SACKVILLE STREET, by O. St. John Gogarty (1937)
—a picturesque view of Moore and Yeats.

THE MOORES OF MOORE HALL, by J. Hone (1939)
—describes the life of Moore's brother, Colonel Maurice Moore, as well as that of the novelist.

'George Moore's Revisions of *The Lake*, *The Wild Goose*, and *Esther Waters*', by R. A. Gettman, in PMLA, lxix, June 1944
—points out that Moore's habit of revising his work was not confined to his old age.

GEORGE MOORE: A RECONSIDERATION, by M. Brown. Seattle (1955)
—useful and appreciative.

G. M.: MEMORIES OF GEORGE MOORE, by N. Cunard (1956)
—personal memories, and a friend's appreciation.

THE IRISH WRITERS, 1880–1940, by H. Howarth. New York (1959)
—excellent and informative.

EDWARDIANS AND LATE VICTORIANS, by G. Hough (1960)
—'George Moore and the Nineties', pp. 1–27, is a good survey, setting Moore in his period.

FROM GAUTIER TO ELIOT, by E. Starkie (1960)
—a good account of French influence on Moore.

'George Moore and literary Wagnerism', by W. F. Blissett, in *Comparative Literature*, xiii, Winter 1961
—deals with Moore's use of Wagnerism and his originality.

'A newly discovered drawing by Degas of George Moore', by R. Pickvance, in the *Burlington Magazine*, June 1963
—useful on Moore's art criticism.